Understanding
ISLAMIC
Fundamentalism

Understanding ISLAMIC Fundamentalism

The Theological and Ideological Basis of al-Qa'ida's Political Tactics

Sayed Khatab

The American University in Cairo Press
Cairo New York

First published in 2011 by
The American University in Cairo Press
113 Sharia Kasr el Aini, Cairo, Egypt
420 Fifth Avenue, New York, NY 10018
www.aucpress.com

Dar el Kutub No. 24792/11
ISBN 978 977 416 499 6

Dar el Kutub Cataloging-in-Publication Data

Khatab, Sayed
        Islamic Fundamentalism: The Theological and Ideological Basis of al-Qa'ida's Political
    Tactics/ Sayed Khatab. —Cairo: The American University in Cairo Press, 2011
        p. cm.
        ISBN 978 977 416 499 6
        1. Islamic Sects—Afghanistan
        297.8

1 2 3 4 5 6   14 13 12 11

Designed by Adam el-Sehemy
Printed in Egypt

Contents

Introduction

Islamic fundamentalism has risen to world prominence since the 1970s. It began locally, but reached its moment of climax in 2001 with the tragic events of September 11. Al-Qaʻida's terrorist attacks on the United States (U.S.) on September 11, 2001, constitute a real turning point, not only in the world order, but also in international relations. If September 11 occurred because of the presence of the U.S. in the Middle East, as extremists say, it is notable that the current level of the United States' involvement in the Middle East is the greatest it has been for the past sixty years. These terrorist events have changed the manner in which terrorism is perceived. Contemporary terrorist groups are characterized by features that differ to a great extent from those of previous decades, in terms of their organizational structure, weaponry, methodology, and, more importantly, their ideas and objectives. The shift in the theological and ideological narratives of Islamic fundamentalism constitutes a new and more serious threat to national and international human security. Indeed, the change in theological narrative has had a profound influence on extremist ideology and has transformed the attitude of fundamentalists toward violence and terrorism. Currently, terrorism is a global phenomenon with an ideological dimension that propounds ideas more lethal than the network itself. The Global Islamic Front for the Jihad against the Crusaders and the Jews (al-Qaʻida) cannot live without its theocentric ideology, which has polluted our politics, our economy, our social relations, and our world. As to the identity of the polluter, the agent of this change, who has wrought a new level of complexity and controversy in international relations, al-Qaʻida is the primary focus. A great deal has been written about al-Qaʻida, much of it focused on the terrorists' personality traits, and much, too, that may be categorized as journalism. With a few exceptions, no systematic in-depth study has so far been conducted on al-Qaʻida's theological narratives and their origins in medieval Islamic thought and movements. This, then, is the main objective of this book.

The processes set into motion by fundamentalism, extremism, and radicalization are still contentious issues within political arenas and the sociopolitical sciences. In seeking to understand fundamentalism, terrorism, and the process of radicalization, and how individuals and groups become indoctrinated and attracted to carrying out acts of terrorism, past studies have focused on sociopolitical, economic, and religious factors, as well as individual motivations, interpersonal relations, leadership behavior, and influencing attitudes.

While most of the existing research on the emergence of al-Qaʻida and its networks and terrorist acts correctly draws attention to the importance of theology and ideology, it has tended to focus on those individuals who went to Afghanistan and fought against the Soviets, established a global jihadist network, and maintained its growth and terrorist activity. These studies outline how al-Qaʻida emerged as a result of the influence of certain individuals who rose to prominence during a particular period and planned terrorist activities.[1] Other studies have correctly referred to cultural factors that have been a driving force behind this terrorist movement, yet have focused largely on the links between individuals and how their interpersonal relationships facilitated the movement's growth.[2] While possessed of many merits, previous studies have paid little attention to what other forces may have contributed to al-Qaʻida's growth and activity. Notably, al-Qaʻida, together with its associated movements, has used selected theological, political, and intellectual narratives with the intention of developing the movement and generating ties among multiple cross-border networks.[3] These theological and intellectual narratives are thus shared by these networks.[4] It is appropriate, therefore, to consider that despite previous studies' demonstrable virtues and merits, a focus on personality traits downplays the distinct importance of the theo-political and intellectual ideas that indoctrinate youth and attract many of them to violent acts of terrorism.

Recent studies have confirmed that radicalism sustains terrorism at its very roots.[5] They also have confirmed the organizational and tactical growth of radicalism.[6] This growth is invariably coupled with selective religious narratives and radical interpretations. Terrorism cannot survive without its theological narratives: had it been dependent on interpersonal relations or military power alone, it would never have gained any real foothold in global politics. Hence, winning the war against radicalism requires a better understanding of its underlying narratives.

Generating a counterargument to extremism and radicalization requires a more in-depth understanding of the narratives that al-Qaʻida uses to attract followers and to connect terrorist networks across borders. In investigating these issues, it is important to point out that many of these radical narratives have not come out of a vacuum and are not owned by al-Qaʻida, as such, but are borrowed from movements that emerged before al-Qaʻida. These key ideas and their related issues constitute the main focus and argument of this book.

This book contends that the theological and ideological discourse of Islamic movements of the modern age is largely the result of deliberate attempts to establish an Islamic order, and to confirm the theoretical relevance of Islam to the modern world. These movements were not established in isolation from the social and political circumstances surrounding them, which became dominant in the Muslim world and the Middle East, particularly during the second half of the twentieth century.

Al-Qaʻida as a title is new, but not as an ideology. An ideology is simply a set of ideas in which individuals and/or groups believe, and, based on it, take certain actions. Al-Qaʻida's theocentric ideology is not an offshoot of the present age, as it has come to be understood by a number of scholars, particularly since the tragic events of September 11, 2001 and their consequent conflicts. Al-Qaʻida's ideology is also not born of: the Islamic Revolution in Iran; the Soviet war in Afghanistan; the existence of the Taliban; the establishment of the Shiʻi Amal and Hizbullah movements in Lebanon; the revival of Sufi movements in Eastern Europe and the Balkans; the formation of separatist movements in China, India, and the Philippines; or the rise of violence and terrorism in Egypt, Algeria, and North Africa.

Al-Qaʻida's ideology has historical roots, an intellectual heritage, and a blueprint for political activity, and it must also be understood in terms of its relation to surrounding psychological and sociopolitical circumstances, similar to those which emerged repeatedly over the centuries and which have continued until the present period. The meeting of ideology and circumstance is evident, for example, in the Islamic Liberation Party's attempt to overthrow the Egyptian government in April 1974; the assassination of Egypt's Azhari minister Sheikh al-Dhahabi in 1977; the assassination of Egyptian President Sadat in 1981; the assassination of certain writers and activists such as Farag Fouda, in 1992; and the many attempts on the life of Egypt's former president Mubarak.

Much of al-Qa'ida's theology and ideology is the offshoot of the theo-ideological discourses of Islamic movements that have emerged throughout the history of Islam. Among them are the Kharijis, 'Ibadis, Hanbalis, and Wahhabis, which are examined and presented in this book as examples of movements whose ideologies substantiate the links between medieval movements and movements of the modern era.

All of them call for rule by shari'a, but with different approaches. In pursuing their goals, movements may differ among themselves, not only in time and space, or in terms of their infrastructure, character, and function, but also in respect of their theological, ideological, and intellectual themes and frameworks. Their differences will also spring from the political, economic, social, intellectual, and moral environments of the societies within which they exist and function.

In al-Qa'ida's writings, the ideas of medieval movements have been used repeatedly as theological and sociopolitical tools with which to criticize their opponents, as well as acting as a source and basis for the movement's beliefs and practice. For example, al-Qa'ida accuses its opponents of being Kharijis, but al-Qa'ida has itself adopted many Khariji ideas, including those of loyalty, charging others with unbelief *(takfir)*, and the change of government by force. Conversely, al-Qa'ida accuses its opponents of not being true Wahhabis, while describing itself as a true Wahhabi movement. So one might ask, what is Wahhabism? Al-Qa'ida occasionally borrows from the Hanbali school of thought, mentioning scholars and thinkers such as Ibn Hanbal, Ibn Taymiya, or Ibn al-Qayyim as points of reference. However, many of the ideas used by al-Qa'ida, with reference to these and other, similar Islamic scholars and theologians, have been paraphrased or used out of context in order to deceive its audiences. Examples of this are numerous, as outlined throughout this book, but for now the following example is sufficient to illustrate the point. The idea of *al-tatarrus* (to shield) is one of the lethal ideas upon which al-Qa'ida has based almost all of its operations, including September 11 and other terrorist activities, which have harmed civilians and destroyed buildings and property. Al-Qa'ida paraphrased this idea, took it out of context, and thereby warped its real meaning in order to suit its purposes. This idea is outlined in greater detail in Chapter 6. Many of al-Qaʿidaʾs followers are incapable of examining and understanding the details of the movement's ideology. Thus, as previously outlined, ideology plays a significant role not only in maintaining al-Qaʿidaʾs growth by means of deception, but also in generating the ties that bind its various networks across borders.

Therefore, the purpose of this book is to investigate, in the context of al-Qaʿidaʾs theological and ideological bases, certain medieval movements, to identify the similarities and differences between them and al-Qaʿida, and to distinguish the truth from al-Qaʿidaʾs deceptions, which circulate in the literature.

Chapter 1 examines the concept of Islamic fundamentalism in relation to both Islamic and western connotations of the term. It posits the idea that fundamentalism, seen through an Islamic lens, is not such a bad thing. Islam advises its followers to adhere to the fundamentals of their faith. Fundamentalism in Islam is also limited to a framework of rules and regulations. A movement away from this framework gives rise to a belief system that is something other than fundamentalist. Chapter 1 outlines the different interpretations of fundamentalism, and proceeds to focus on the nature of the challenge posed by Islamic fundamentalism and its contours and implications for human security. It appears that the present challenge is no longer between east and west, but rather between North and South, and past and future. However, the worldwide use of the term fundamentalism with reference to Islam makes it difficult in the current climate for writers and researchers to avoid applying the term to Islam.

Chapter 2 examines four medieval movements, to which al-Qaʿida networks are the legatees. In its four sections, this chapter focuses on Kharijism, ʿIbadism, Hanbalism, and Wahhabism, all of which, as indicated above, have been referenced in al-Qaʿidaʾs writings. Kharijism is the ideology of the Kharijis (al-Khawarij), the first rebel group to take the law into its own hands and change the government by force in the early decades of Islam. The Kharijis subsequently split into many groups, a number of which have been investigated by researchers, and their ideologies have been examined with a particular focus on the similarities and differences between them and al-Qaʿida. ʿIbadism (al-ʿIbadiya) is the ideology of a Khariji offshoot, which survives to this day. Hanbalism, on the other hand, refers to the Islamic school of law that was named after its founder, Ahmad ibn Hanbal, and represents another trend within Sunni Islam. Studies have tended to focus on Ibn Hanbal and his legacy. However, after his death, Ibn Hanbal's legacy was left to the pens of his followers. Scholarly investigations focused, therefore, on the School of Ibn Hanbal after his death, and surveyed what happened to it. Here, the chapter focuses on al-Barbahari and his followers, and the later Ibn Taymiya. It looks at how Ibn Taymiya returned Ibn Hanbal's legacy to the truth, and cleansed his ideas of the distortions that had attached to it through generations of politically motivated writings. The period between Ibn Hanbal's time and the beginning of Ibn Taymiya's is a critical one that researchers should consider. It is in this period that al-Qaʻida finds its interest and sources of inspiration. Similarly, whatever al-Qaʻida has said about jihad and other relevant ideas (that is, who declares jihad, who is the enemy, the killing of civilians, suicide bombings, *al-tatarrus*, and so on) with reference to Ibn Hanbal or Ibn Taymiya should be examined carefully and within the historical context. The last section of this chapter focuses on the ideology of Muhammad ibn ʻAbd al-Wahhab, from whose name the term 'Wahhabism' derives. It investigates this ideology within the Ottoman-Turkish and Arab-Islamic contexts. The link between Wahhabism and both earlier and later movements, including al-Qaʻida, is also outlined. Overall, the four sections of this chapter link medieval to modern movements, including al-Qaʻida, and highlight the similarities and differences between them.

Chapter 3 explores the connections between medieval and modern movements in greater detail. It investigates the transformation from medieval fundamentalism to the recent neo-jihadist ideology adopted by al-Qaʻida and similar jihadist networks. Apart from defining the concept of neo-jihadism, and its source in the literature of al-Qaʻida, the analysis focuses on the process of transition from fundamentalism to neo-jihadism, including the factors involved, the roots of al-Qaʻida in these processes, and these networks' main theological and intellectual inspirations, and their scholarly sources of information.

Chapter 4 investigates the war in Afghanistan, the establishment of al-Qaʻida, the transformation of Usama bin Laden from an exclusively Afghan-based jihadist to an al-Qaʻida neo-jihadist, the role of the U.S. within the Arab-Muslim countries therein, and the Bin Laden–Taliban relationship.

Chapter 5 investigates al-Qaʻida's neo-jihadist ideology and compares it with the notion of jihad and the qualifications to it in the Muslim consensus. It also investigates the question of who declares jihad, and argues that al-Qa'ida's neo-jihadist dogma is outdated.

Chapter 6 investigates al-Qa'ida's political tactics before and after September 11, al-Qa'ida's plan of action, the principles underpinning al-Qa'ida's military actions, and al-Qa'ida's political games, and compares al-Qa'ida's concept of *al-tatarrus* with the views of Islamic jurists.

Chapter 7 investigates the ongoing ideological war within al-Qa'ida. It focuses on the theo-political and ideological disputes between the main ideologues of global jihad. It looks, among other examples, at the dispute between Dr. Fadl and Ayman al-Zawahiri, which did not become known until late 2007. It was a war of ideas that caused a number of key jihadists, individuals, and groups to abandon al-Qa'ida and renounce violence and terrorism. This chapter is intended to bring the ideas of these two jihadist rivals face to face in an attempt to address the following questions: When, how, and why was the Jihad organization established in Egypt? When and how did it come into contact with al-Qa'ida? When and why did Jihad leave Egypt for Afghanistan? What were they doing there? What was their relationship with 'Abdullah 'Azzam, Bin Laden, and al-Qa'ida? What was their role in the establishment of al-Qa'ida's tactics and theological narratives? How do they see al-Qa'ida's theology, ideology, and tactics now? What is their view on al-Qa'ida's leadership and the relationship between Bin Laden and his associates now? Seeking to address these issues, this chapter focuses on the criticisms of al-Qa'ida's theology and ideology from various camps, the role of Egypt's Jihad group in al-Qa'ida's theology, the theological basis for certain jihadist individuals' and groups' abandonment of al-Qa'ida, and finally the Islamic verdict against al-Qa'ida ideas and leadership. These questions and related issues are dealt with based on the works of these two rival groups.

The primary sources used in this study are mainly al-Qa'ida's Arabic writings. These consist of works, interviews, and speeches by Bin Laden, Dr. Fadl, Ayman al-Zawahiri, 'Abdullah 'Azzam, al-Mas'ari, Abu Bakr Naji, al-Maqdisi, and many of al-Qa'ida's other ideologues. Among these works are: *Risalat al-'umda fi i'dad al'udda fi sabil Allah* (The Master Message in the Preparation for Jihad; Dr. Fadl, 1988); *al-Jami' fi talab al-'ilm al-sharif* (The Compendium for the Search of Noble Knowledge; Dr. Fadl, 1993); *al-Murshid ila tariq Allah* (The Guide to the Way of God; 2006); *Wathiqat tarshid all-jihad fi Misr wa-l-'alam* (Rationalization of the Jihad in Egypt and the World; Dr. Fadl, 2007); *al-Tabri'a: risala fi tabri'at ummat al-qalam wa-l-sayf min manqusat tuhmat al-khawr wa-l-da'f* (Exoneration: A Treatise Exonerating the Nation of the Pen and the Sword from the Blemish of the Accusation of Weakness and Feebleness; al-Zawahiri, 2008); *al-Hasad al-murr* (The Bitter Harvest; al-Zawahiri, n.d.); *Tahdi'at al-ghadab fi qulub al-Muslimin* (Allaying the Anger in the Believers' Hearts; al-Zawahiri, n.d.); *Tharthara fawq saqf al-'alam* (Meditation over the Roof of the World; al-Zawahiri, n.d.); *Firsan taht rayat al-Rasul* (Knights under the Banner of the Prophet; al-Zawahiri, n.d.); *al-Muslim wa-l-kafir* (The Muslim and the Kafir; al-Amin, n.d.); *Muqaddima fi-l-hijra wa-l-i'dad* (Introduction to the Hijra and Preparations; 'Abdullah 'Azzam, n.d.); *Durus wa ara' fi-l-'asr al-hadir* (Lessons and Views in the Present Age; 'Abdullah 'Azzam, n.d.); *Idarat al-tawahhush* (Management of Barbarism; Abu Bakr Naji, n.d.); *Qatl al-madaniyyin* (The Killing of Civilians; al-Mas'ari, 2002); *Muntada al-tajdid al-islam* (The Organization of Islamic Reform; al-Mas'ari, n.d.); *Qital al-tawa'if al-mumtani'a* (The Fight against the Rejectionists; al-Mas'ari, 2003); *Ahamiyyat al-jihad* (The Importance of Jihad; al-Alyani, n.d.); *al-Amn wa-l-istikhbarat* (Security and Intelligence; Sayf al-Adl, 2004); and *Markaz al-tijara al-'alami* (The World Trade Center; al-Mas'ari, 2002). These represent merely a sample of the important works that are, to a large extent, in the hearts and the minds of al-Qa'ida networks.

1

Islamic Fundamentalism

Fundamentalism is a word, like many words in both Arabic and European languages, that has a range of meanings across cultures. This is relevant to the task at hand. In the science of politics, for example, the concept of 'the Left' in western literature traditionally refers to workers, laborers, the lower classes, and needy and unfortunate people.[1] However, in Arab-Islamic literature, 'the Left' refers to the aristocrats, to wealthy people who lead a comfortable life. Likewise, the concept of 'the Right' in western literature refers to aristocrats, the owners and controllers of capital, the upper classes, and those who do not desire change but seek to influence government through their connections as an elite, and so the term also tends to refer to rigid and reactionary people. In Arab-Islamic literature, however, 'the Right' refers to the righteous who do good deeds.[2] Therefore, Muslims might seek membership of 'the Left' in this world, but may wish to be among 'the Right' in the next.[3]

Modernization is another example of a word that gives rise to potentially misleading interpretations, because it can be mistakenly equated with westernization. However, the latter means no more than the adoption of certain alien (western) social and cultural habits that may not be inherently superior or more advanced, although this is often implied. For example, the Ottoman Sultan Mahmud II (who ruled from 1808 to 1839) considered modernity to be the imitation of the west in terms of lifestyle and even fashions. He replaced the turban with the Roman fez[4] and issued a decree that declared European dress as the official dress of the State's workforce, whether military or civil. The Ottomans underwent many forms of borrowing from western cultures, but none of this saved the caliphate, and Turkey was not, in any notable way, more advanced than a country like Egypt, whose revolution took place more than a century later, whose development was arrested by not inconsiderable colonial rule and numerous wars, and who did not have to deny her own culture as Turkey did.

Secularism is another western notion, and secularization has very much been a part of modernization in the western context. Its history is rooted in the domination of the Church over the State through the Church's control of 'learning' and 'capital,' and the clergy's interference in scientific, sociopolitical, and economic matters. Secularism, however, has no parallel in the history of Islam, because Islam has no Church and no clergy in the sense of an elaborate ecclesiastical hierarchy.

Likewise, the term fundamentalism in western society has been widely used since the 1960s to characterize those Muslim individuals and groups who have been involved in Islamic revivalism in Egypt and other Muslim countries. This period has also been filled with many events that have been attributed to Islamic revivalism. These include: the Arab–Israeli wars of 1967 and 1973, and the subsequent tragic conflicts between Sadat and the Islamists in Egypt; the civil war in Lebanon, which broke out in 1975; the Sudanese Islamic Republican Brotherhood's relationship with President Numayri reaching an intolerable impasse; Ayatullah Khomeini's Islamic Revolution in 1979, which brought Islamic clerics to power in Iran; the hostage crisis at the U.S. Embassy in Tehran in 1979–80; the coming to power of Saddam Hussein in Iraq in 1979, and the start of his attacks on Iraqi Kurds; the Iraq–Iran war; Saddam's opposition to President Sadat's peace process between Egypt and Israel in 1979 under the banner of the 'Rejectionist Front'; the assassination of Sadat in 1981, which brought Islamists to the verge of revolution in Egypt; and, more generally, the threat of Islamic terrorism to western interests. All these events have become a source of increasing and ever-present concern.

It is within this complex historico-political context that the term fundamentalism has been applied to Muslims. Thus, the term 'Islamic fundamentalism' is seen by many people in the west through the prism of the above-cited and similar crises that took place in the Middle East. The application of the term fundamentalism to Muslims, as James Barr has emphasized, is, however, far from precise.[5] The term assumed, through this use, a wider spectrum of meaning, as almost all Islamic revivalist movements were tagged with fundamentalist labels connoting extremism, radicalism, and other, similar terms that carry the force and intent of violence and terrorism. Such application, however, should not be taken at face value or as a rigid and mutually exclusive classification of cultures and thought. Fundamentalism does not necessarily equate to or engender extremism, radicalism, or terrorism. From an Islamic perspective, terrorism is terrorism, and fundamentalism is fundamentalism. The impact of the term is obvious, as its application can carry a certain weight.

Before the term fundamentalism was used to brand Muslims, it was and still is being used by certain Christian denominations. Some of them, in the view of many scholars, are radicals and take pride in being called fundamentalists. A great number of individuals and groups around the world, ranging from Protestant and Catholic churches to governments, have also being tagged with the fundamentalist label.[6]

Historically, the term was used to denote the literal, yet creative, interpretation of the Bible. Indeed, a history of Christian fundamentalism was written in 1931 by Stewart Grant Cole, and another account published in 1954 by Norman Furniss. Many authorities date fundamentalism from the time of the Holy Book Conference, which convened in the U.S. in 1902.[7] This conference led to the publication of a series of radical Protestant booklets, entitled "The Fundamentals," in the U.S. between 1910 and 1915. It was on the basis of this title and the contents of these booklets that the term fundamentalism was derived to characterize those "doing battle royal for the Fundamentals."[8]

Consequently, fundamentalism has been defined as a U.S. Protestant movement, guided by the doctrine of complete faith in the fundamentals of the inerrancy of the Bible; the virgin birth and divinity of Jesus Christ; the vicarious and atoning character of his death; his bodily resurrection; and his second coming. These fundamentals, in the Protestant view, constitute the irreducible minimum of authentic Christianity. This minimum is rooted in what is known as the fourteen-point creed of the Niagara Bible Conference of 1878 and later in the five-point statement of the Presbyterian General Assembly of 1910.[9]

During the period spanning the 1970s through to the 1990s, fundamentalism resurfaced to again become an influential force in the U.S. Promoted by popular television evangelists and represented by such groups as the Moral Majority, the new politically oriented 'religious right' opposed the influence of liberalism and secularism on U.S. life. This movement has adopted the term 'fundamentalism' as originally used to refer to a specific Christian experience in the U.S. in the early years of the twentieth century.[10]

Further, the assumption underpinning the use of the term fundamentalism in the western context is that modernism and fundamentalism are inherently opposed. Some others consider fundamentalism a negative tendency that counters the processes of modernization and rationalism.[11] Thus, the application of the term fundamentalism carries the implication of a dramatic conflict between fundamentalists and modernization, the former seeking to divorce themselves from modern life, rejecting new scientific discoveries, and refraining from interacting with the reality of the modern epoch. In this sense, the term fundamentalism has no Arabic source or Islamic reference.[12]

In other words, the term fundamentalism, born of unique historical circumstances, does not exist in Arabic and Islamic literature. For this reason, Joachim Wach emphasized that many observers, Muslims and non-Muslims alike, have stipulated that the term fundamentalism should not be applied to Islamic movements.[13] Muslims, especially those of the Islamic resurgence for example, reject the use of the term fundamentalism to characterize Islamism, which takes the teaching of the Qur'an and faith seriously; and if that were the criteria, then all Muslims would indeed be 'fundamentalists,' but the term would cease to be of any use.[14]

Etymologically, the term fundamentalism in Arabic translates to *usuliya*. This is an abstract noun of quality derived from the Arabic root (*a-s-l*), the substantive *asl* (root, origin, foundation, or basis of a thing) being the basic word from which the trilateral verb *asula* is derived. The present participle or the *nomen agentis* is *usuli* (fundamentalist, singular) and the plural is *usuliyyun* and *usuliyyin* (fundamentalists). Thus, the singular substantive *asl* or the plural *usul* means root(s), origin(s), foundation(s), fundamental(s) or principle(s) of a human being or of anything else, in general, including ideology(s), idea(s), or concept(s).[15]

The Qur'an uses the term 'fundamental(s)' as in the following: *Whatsoever palm-trees ye cut down or left standing on their roots* [usul], *it was by God's leave* (Qur'an 59:5); *Lo! it is a tree that springs out of the base* [asl] *of hell* (Qur'an 37:64); and *Have you not considered how God sets forth a parable of a good word (being) like a good tree, whose root* [asl] *is firm and whose branches are in heaven?* (Qur'an 14:24). Thus, the word 'fundamentalism' as known in western literature is not found in Arabic.

Further, all of the contemporary major political or social systems have their own fundamentals (*usul*: origins, foundations, or bases) upon which they have been established and which distinguishes them from each other. In other words, capitalism, socialism, communism, democracy, and Islam are each based on their own distinct fundamentals. Thus, neither the capitalist nor democratic systems can be called communist systems.[16] Likewise, the Islamic system cannot be called a communist system or even democratic in western terms. This does not, however, mean that the Islamic system is theocratic or autocratic, or anything but Islamic. Islam is a broader sociopolitical system than democracy, and accommodates the substance and values of democracy within it. The phrase 'democracy in Islam'[17] means that Islam is bigger than democracy, and when Islam incorporates contemporary democracy within it, there still remains more space within which to encompass more permutations of democracy with no change to the inherent Islamic identity of the system.

Although the existence of democracy *in* Islam is clearly evident, those who are called fundamentalists do not appreciate any view that erases the name of Islam in favor of a label of democracy. They argue that Islam is adequately equipped and that its system has the characteristics and qualities necessary to give that system all the rights to retain its name 'Islam.' In their view, Islam will gain nothing by being called democracy. In other words, democracy is democracy, socialism is socialism, and Islam is Islam.[18] Each of these systems, in the fundamentalist view, has its own historically based origins, principles, and fundamentals, which define the nature of the system and distinguish one system from the other. Thus, 'Islamic fundamentalism' or 'fundamentalism in Islam' signifies searching for the fundamentals and Islamic authority, rather than referring to a specific political or religious movement.[19]

Searching for the fundamentals of Islam and its authority is the meaning preserved in Arabic literature, as in the sciences of the fundamentals (*'ulum al-usul*). For example, among the academic institutions of al-Azhar University in Cairo, there is the Faculty of the Fundamentals of Religion. The title indicates the subject core and the objectives of the teachings in this faculty. Further, among the Arabic and Islamic disciplines are the science of the fundamentals of religion (*'ilm usul al-din*), the science of the fundamentals of Islamic jurisprudence (*'ilm usul al-fiqh*), the science of the fundamentals of Arabic language (*'ilm usul al-lugha*), and the science of the fundamentals of Hadith (*'ilm usul al-Hadith*). Nothing within these disciplines has any parallel to the western concept of fundamentalism.[20]

Historically, Muslim scholars who specialized in any of the sciences of the fundamentals were honored with the title 'fundamentalists' *(usuliyyun)*. Among the celebrated fundamentalist scholars in the medieval epoch were, for example, Imam Ahmad Ibn Hanbal (780–855), Imam Ibn Taymiya (1263–1327), Imam 'Abd al-Jabbar Ibn Ahmad (946–1036), and Imam Abu al-Hasan al-Bisri (d. 436/1057), the author of *Sharh al-'umad* (The Natural Hearing), a commentary on Aristotle's book of physics.[21] Hence, the title 'fundamentalist' in Islamic terms denotes the force and intent of the concepts of honor, fame, and celebrity.

Fundamentalism is also explained alongside the concept of Salafism (traditional or ancestral). In an oft-quoted statement, Hasan al-Banna (d. 1949) defined his Muslim Brotherhood organization, founded in 1928, as an 'Islamic society' on a 'Salafi' mission that follows the Qur'an, the Sunna (tradition of the Prophet), and the conduct of the Muslim ancestors *(salaf)*.[22]

The term *salaf*, as a noun, refers to the venerable Muslim ancestors, while the term *khalaf* refers to the succeeding generations.[23] Muslims are overwhelmingly agreed that the *salaf* are better in their application of Islam than are the *khalaf*. This also applies to all Abrahamic religions, as mentioned in the Qur'an. The Qur'an refers to God's messengers (that is, Abraham, Isaac, Jacob, Moses, Aaron, Isma'il, Idris, Jesus, Zakariya, and John), their immediate followers *(salaf)*, and the succeeding generations *(khalaf)* with an emphasis on their application of faith as follows:

> *These are they unto whom God showed favor from among the Prophets, of the seed of Adam and of those whom We carried (in the ship) with Noah, and of the seed of Abraham and Israel [Jacob], and among those whom We guided and chose. When the revelations of the Beneficent were recited unto them, they* [salaf] *fell down, adoring and weeping. Now there hath succeeded them a later generation* [khalaf] *who have ruined worship and have followed lust. But they will meet deception. Save him who shall repent and believe and do right. Such will enter the Garden, and they will not be wronged in aught.* (Qur'an 19:57–59).[24]

The words and language indicate that the immediate followers *(salaf)* of the messengers were more successful in their application of their faith than were the succeeding generations *(khalaf)*. This passage also suggests that after the immediate generation of the messengers, selfishness and godlessness at times gained the upper hand among some of the succeeding generations *(khalaf)*. Hence, there are always those who see the failures in the applications of the faith and try to correct them and adhere to the fundamental principles of the religion. In this sense, the Qur'anic text cited above highlights that the Muslims of the succeeding generations *(khalaf)* are always seeking to be like their ancestors *(salaf)*. Their intentions are noble but not always their actions.[25]

Consequently, the ultimate goal of Muslim fundamentalist movements is to establish more Islamically oriented states and societies, based on Islamic principles and values. In this context, scholars consider Islamic fundamentalism to be a combination of Islamic devotion and political activism, and conscious attempts to confirm or restate the theoretical relevance of Islam to the modern epoch.[26]

Islam is based mainly on shari'a (law), which regulates an individual's relationship to God *('ibadat)*, as well as to other individuals, the community (Muslim and non-Muslim), and the state (Muslim and non-Muslim). Many Muslims believe in Islam as a way of life and not simply a religion or state. This fusion of matters of belief with matters of conduct in Islam makes it difficult to separate religion from politics. In this regard, there is a big question mark in many Muslim circles as to whether separation of church and state would be either desirable or appropriate. Islam is believed to be comprehensive and all-pervasive.

In addition, Islamic law is based on complete submission *('ubudiya)* to the will of God. This is also a fundamental tenet of the Islamic religion. Since Islamic law is based on the Islamic religion, it proceeds on the same fundamental assumptions. As a way of life, Islamic law applies to all aspects of a person's existence and behavior. No realm of human experience is given precedence over another in this regard, and there is a great coordination and coherence, a blending and balance between the material, the rational, and the spiritual elements of humanity's journey. The will of God embraces all aspects of the universe, life, and humanity, and the law covers all of them. The law is a path, or a way, that guides Muslims, and the revealed law governing all of these aspects is known as shari'a. It is a comprehensive concept expounded by fundamentalists including Sayyid Qutb (d. 1966), who stated:

> The shari'a is everything prescribed by God to order human life. This takes the form of the fundamentals of belief, the fundamentals

of government *(hukm)*, the fundamentals of behavior, and the fundamentals of knowledge. It takes the form of the creed and the conception and all the components of this conception. It takes the form of legislative decisions and it takes the form of principles of ethics and behavior. It takes the form of the values and standards that rule society and evaluate people, things and events. Then it takes the form of knowledge in all its aspects and of all the fundamental principles of intellectual and artistic activity.[27]

According to Weeramantry, Chief Judge at the International Court in Swaziland, "the shari'a is not, strictly speaking, a legal system, for it reaches much deeper into thought, life, and conduct than a purely legal system can aspire to do."[28] The shari'a places the individual in his or her relationship to society, to the universe, and to the Creator. In addition to its legal system, the shari'a defines an individual's religious duty. The textual sources for Islamic law are the Qur'an and the Sunna of the Prophet of Islam. These textual sources are also the main stimulus to learning. In this regard, the first revealed verse of the Qur'an was *Read: In the name of thy Lord Who createth man from a leech-like clot. Read: And thy Lord is the most Bounteous, Who teacheth by the pen, Teacheth man that which he knew not* (Qur'an 96:1–5). The Prophet Muhammad reportedly said, "The ink of the scholar is holier than the blood of the martyr."[29] According to Ma'adh ibn Jabal,

> Acquiring the knowledge is worship, knowing the knowledge is reverence, searching for the knowledge is jihad, teaching the knowledge is charity, examining the knowledge is glorification of God. With knowledge, you know God and how to worship Him; and with knowledge you glorify God and unify Him *(tawhid)*. With knowledge God raises people, making them leaders and guiding imams.[30]

The Prophet enjoined his followers to seek learning wherever they could find it: "Go ye in search of learning even if you have to go to China for it."[31] His followers did just that—traveled to China, and learned the art of papermaking. The new type of paper they obtained enabled scholars to multiply the number of books printed in a manner that had been impossible with papyrus sheepskin. Thus, Islam made acquiring knowledge a jihad, and jihad requires patience *(sabr)*. In this regard, Ibn

Taymiya pointed out that "God mentioned the word patience more than ninety times and linked it with Prayer in His saying, *Seek* [God's] *help with patient perseverance* [sabr] *and Prayer. It is indeed hard, except to those who are humble* (Qur'an 2:45). God established that leadership (*imama*: imamate) in religion was hereditary out of patient perseverance and steadfastness, in his saying: *And We appointed, from among them, leaders, giving guidance under Our command, so long as they persevered with patience and continued to have faith in Our Signs* (Qur'an 32:24).

Thus, the textual sources of Islam did not solely encourage learning but also discussion and analysis. In this regard, the Prophet is reputed to have said, "If there is difference of opinion within my community that is a sign of the bounty of God."[32] In other words, if there is a difference of opinion that requires scholars to pit their intellects against each other, this is a stimulus to intellectual advancement, for it is out of the clash of intellects that fresh knowledge is born. In this way, Islamic intellect came to grapple with every known intellectual problem over the centuries. Hence, fundamentalists are of the view that Islam is not rigid or suited only to the intellect of a specific epoch or generation, but rather is flexible and has something to offer all periods and generations.

Consequently, conceptions such as fundamentalism and terrorism must be distinguished from each other. Richard Nixon considered fundamentalists to be people who have a strong hatred for the west, and are determined to bring the Islamic civilization to dominance, through a revival of the past. He also believed that fundamentalists refer to Islam as a religion and state in one, and look to the past to guide the future. Thus, on this view fundamentalists are not conservatives but revolutionaries.[33]

Fundamentalism involves a search for authority or the following of the ordinance of the faith. In this context, following the ordinance of the faith has never equated with extremism or similar notions that suggest violence and terrorism. Fundamentalism is one thing, and extremism is another. The fundamentals of human rights are well known worldwide, but views about these rights differ from one state to another, from one community to another, and from one individual to another—and these differences can be extreme. The lawmaker gives each individual his or her rights within a framework with clearly defined limits. Each person then must observe his or her rights within this framework. Imposing the rights of one person over the rights of another person is a violation of the law, whether that law is a natural, civil, or religious law. It is because of this potential for conflicting rights that problems and wars of all forms, including cold and hot wars, take place. Such conflict led to the two world wars, and more recently to the wars in Afghanistan, Iraq, Kosovo, Chechnya, Darfur, and Georgia, among others. Examples of other types of racial conflict or discrimination resulting from a clash of rights are innumerable. The offensive cartoons against Islam and its Prophet Muhammad published in 2006 in Denmark and other European states; the cartoons published in Sweden in 2007; the Dutch politician Geert Wilders's film *Fitna* in 2007; and the comments made by Pope Benedict XVI about Islam and the Prophet in Germany on 12 September 2006 all illustrate this point.

Although the cartoons and the Pope's comments offended Muslims deeply, Denmark and other European states defended both on the grounds of 'freedom of speech.' Yet freedom of speech was never intended to allow people to insult others. Indeed, the freedom to insult others is an act of terrorism. Terrorism is any act that terrorizes people's lives, rights, and property. This includes any act that terrorizes the freedom of their conscience, terrorizes the freedom of their souls, terrorizes their freedom to believe, terrorizes their freedom to admire their culture, and terrorizes their freedom to maintain their own civilization.

Lawmakers give each person the rights to freedom; however, the freedom given to any citizen is never absolute, as societies must weigh up competing freedoms for the overall greater good. We as citizens give up some freedoms in return for certain forms of protection. In all of its shapes and forms, 'freedom' is not absolute, because absolutism is not in the nature of things. Absolutism does not fit with the nature of human society, which must by its very nature balance or compromise between differences and conflict. The freedom of person A must have a limit to allow for the freedom of person B. Overlapping the freedoms of these two persons will certainly adulterate the concept of individuality, the cornerstone of democracy, as emphasized by John Locke, the so-called Prince of Individualism![34]

Accordingly, each person has the right to adhere to the fundamentals of his or her culture and faith; however, this freedom is limited. Understanding the text and how to practice the ordinances of one's faith within the limits of freedom afforded by society is also critical and, at times, people may move beyond such limits. Such transgression can lead to violence and terrorism. In other words, fundamentalism in the Islamic conceptualization remains fundamentalism so long as it is working within its borders. Violating those borders by attacking others physically, intellectually, or morally constitutes an act of violence and terrorism, regardless of the religion, race, or nationality of the perpetrators.

Islamic fundamentalism is not necessarily radical or reactionary, and in no way does it inherently lead to violence and terrorism. While some of those who have been called fundamentalist groups have turned violent, the majority of fundamentalists are not violent, but rather work within the system and live by the accepted norms of mainstream society. When Egypt's militant groups turned violent, the Egyptian press misappropriated the term fundamentalism to carry such labels as extremism, activism, fanaticism, and terrorism.[35] In the worldwide media the term fundamentalism continued to be used as the principal term to denote violence and terrorism. Thus, Frederick Denny made the point that "probably the worldwide media use of the term fundamentalism and fundamentalists with reference to Islam makes it impossible to avoid applying the term to Islam."[36]

The Nature of the Challenge

There is no doubt that Islamic fundamentalism has increasingly become a global phenomenon and has occupied the international press as well as the corridors of world politics. There are also various interpretations of fundamentalism, each with its own characteristics, which can be understood as relevant to the environment in which it exists and operates. In the Middle East, Islamic fundamentalist movements have increasingly come to pose a threat to the sociopolitical order in the region. In Asia in general, and in the Indian subcontinent in particular, Islamic fundamentalism has surfaced in the chronic national and ethnic conflicts that have marred this region. In Central Asia, the resurgence of Islamic fundamentalism has created anxiety and stress for the regimes in Moscow and Beijing. While China is struggling to deal with the version of fundamentalism there, certain issues[37] and trends have recently emerged among Muslims who have actively integrated Islam into the nationalist discourse of the various ethnic groups of the Russian Federation. In addition to Iran and Saudi Arabia, Afghanistan and Pakistan are at the center of this emergence of different forms of fundamentalism. In Indonesia, the Philippines, Malaysia, and other Islamic states of the Far East, Islamic fundamentalism has asserted itself over the political arena in the context of a decaying social order.

According to some, Islamic fundamentalism is a direct response not only to the break-up of the Ottoman Empire in the aftermath of the First World War, but also to the powers that rose to dominance in the post-Second World War era. The world was divided between such dominant powers, with Britain, France, and the U.S. on one side of the divide, and the former Soviet Union (USSR) on the other. These powers, in the view of fundamentalists, constitute totalitarian colonialist regimes that occupied most of the Muslim world and considered themselves to represent the only political and social model that the Muslim world should emulate. However, the ideology of Islamic fundamentalism rejects all systems other than the Islamic system.

In the context of this theme, medieval fundamentalism from the time of Ibn Hanbal (781–855) until the time of Ibn Taymiya (1263–1328) and his disciple Ibn al-Qayyim (d. 1350)[38] became, in the eighteenth century, part of a public movement preceded or rather, accompanied, by the call for 'Pan Islamism,' which appeared in the movement of Muhammad ibn 'Abd al-Wahhab (1704–87) in Arabia,[39] and Muhammad ibn Ali al-Shawkani (1760–1834) in Yemen.[40]

In the nineteenth century, the fundamentalist movement re-emerged as a public movement at the hands of al-Sunusi (d. 1859) in Libya, 'Abd al-Qadir al-Jaza'iri (d. 1883) in Algeria, and al-Mahdi (d. 1885) in Sudan.[41]

In the twentieth century, the fundamentalist movement reappeared once more to favor and support Pan Islamism as a response to western military and commercial expansionism. This theme occupied the thought of the pioneers of modern reform, some of who were steeped in the colonial movement.[42] These pioneers can be represented by figures such as al-Tahtawi (d. 1873), al-Afghani (d. 1897), Ahmad Khan (d. 1898), Khayr al-Din al-Tunisi (d. 1899), 'Abd al-Rahman al-Kawakibi (d. 1903), Muhammad 'Abduh (d. 1905), Rashid Rida (d. 1935), Muhammad Iqbal (d. 1938), Hasan al-Banna (d. 1949), Ahmad Amin (d. 1954), Ahmad Lutfi al-Sayyid (d. 1963), and Sayyid Qutb (d. 1966).

In terms of their ideas, they are the pioneers of Islamic reform and revivalism. They were rational thinkers who renewed interest in Islam as an endogenous ideology. They called for liberty, social justice, equality, cooperation, and solidarity, and for humankind to master modernity, economy, and technology.[43] They were, as asserted by Robert Lee, both modernists and fundamentalists,[44] who believed in the Qur'an and the Sunna as primary sources of Islam, and did not reject human reason or rationality but called for *ijtihad* (legal reasoning). Hence, the present Islamic fundamentalist movement can be seen as a link in a long chain of events and movements, rooted in Islamic history. Contrary to the western experience of fundamentalism, the term fundamentalism in Islamic culture does not equate with opposing modernity or rejecting the role of the intellect, but rather encourages development in all aspects of human life, including the political, social, and economic realms.[45]

Islamic preachers in general, and fundamentalists in particular, claim that all types of regimes, including capitalist and socialist ones, have been tried in Muslim countries but have not cured their problem of weakness and backwardness. Conversely, the Muslim modernizing elites usually claim credit for managing the transition to these systems with reasonable efficiency, while fundamentalists blame them for the failure and backwardness of the Muslim community. Many Muslims criticize western political and economic models for creating these problems. As a result, fundamentalism has been a reaction against not only local corruption but also against European countries' political and commercial expansion into Muslim countries.

Since the 1940s, Islamic fundamentalists have been in conflict with their opponents. In the Arab world, the most important underlying causes that have moved fundamentalists toward violence have been foreign occupation and humiliation, and repression at the hands of foreign regimes. This treatment of Muslims has proved to be a failure and demonstrated misunderstanding of the nature of their aspirations and grievances. The conflict between Islamic fundamentalists and their opponents is essentially ideological, and relates to the power of sovereignty (*hakimiya*),[46] which is the highest governmental and legal authority over humanity. This notion of the power of sovereignty is popular among fundamentalists and young people. It determines that Muslims should govern themselves according to Islamic law, and validates condemnation of leaders who do not facilitate the application of Islamic law.[47] The conflict between Muslims and the west is therefore ideological and concerned with the nature of sovereignty and its implications for the relationship between the state and its citizens.

Fundamentalists argue that in the medieval period there appeared to be no significant ideological challenge to Islam. Liberal democracy as an ideology or even as an idea had not yet emerged in either pre-Napoleonic France or colonial America. Communism did not yet exist—Karl Marx was not born until the nineteenth century, and Lenin did not set foot on the world stage until the early decades of the twentieth century. Thus, there was no ideology to challenge Islam until the rise of the western military-industrial complex. Western military expansionism has dramatically transformed the world order. With its weaponry and military technicalism, the west was able to create a state of affairs in which the major global actor was no longer Islam but the colonial west. The greater challenge then became not the conflict between Islamic and western ideologies, but that western ideology was to be served by armaments. The shift, from the Muslim perspective, was cataclysmic: "Islam had lost leadership on the world plan."[48] Europe emerged as an empire between 1550 and 1850, to be succeeded by capitalism from 1850 to the present. As Muslim countries fell into the hands of European colonialism, the leadership of Islam fell in its territories, and Muslims went weak and backward. The processes of European colonialism aggressively victimized Muslims, including their rulers, territories, laws, and economies.[49]

Subsequently, the dispute between fundamentalists and their opponents was the natural result of political developments in the twentieth century. One of the most significant characteristics of the twentieth century was the emergence of what was called a bipolar world order, which can be seen clearly in the divide between communism and capitalism. It has also led to conflict between east and west, which began as an ideological struggle but ended with a military confrontation between the Eastern and Western blocs.[50]

Consequently, the ideological conflict between east and west increasingly became a worldwide class struggle between the bourgeoisie and the proletarian class.[51] Such a struggle was reshaped to include, in addition to class struggle, military conflict. Here, the destiny of this ideological conflict between communism in the east and capitalism in the west had come to be decided not by ideology alone, but also by armaments.

Consequently, the bipolar world order of the 1960s and 1970s came to an end when former U.S. President Ronald Reagan shifted conceptualization of the armaments race from Earth to heaven, when he gave it the name 'Star Wars.' It was at this point that the Eastern bloc lost its last breath in the race. When President Reagan unveiled his Star Wars plan in the 1987 summit in Washington, Mikhail Gorbachev, then leader of the Soviet Union, addressed him with words more of sorrow than of anger:

> Mr President, you do what you think you have to do . . . . And if in the end you think that you have a system that you want to deploy, go ahead and deploy it. Who am I to tell you what to do? I think you are wasting money. I do not think it will work. But if it is what you want to do, go ahead. [52]

Gorbachev was at that time striving to maintain some sort of balance between east and west by maintaining the bipolar world order without further acceleration of the armaments race. However, Gorbachev's failed attempts in this regard took down with them the Soviet communist camp and a politically balanced world. The failure of communism confirmed that western capitalism could not establish itself on the world stage without armaments. Thus, the fate of the conflict between east and west was decided, not by the ideology itself, but also by the heavenly missiles of Star Wars. Islamic organizations in Egypt, Pakistan, and elsewhere are therefore now of the view that no ideology can take hold in the global political arena without equipping itself with sufficient armaments proportionate to those of their rivals. This view is self-evident to Islamic militant groups, as history reveals how ideas and ideologies have come to predominance on the world stage—through military might.

The fall of the communist system created a single world order, in which the opposition had all but vanished. President Richard Nixon claimed there was no candidate other than Islam to fill this void.[53] The west had to some extent employed Islamic radicals for this role. As Islamic ideology, especially that which was often labeled as 'fundamentalism,' came to prominence, Islam increasingly became the focal point of world politics. In this way, the nature of global conflict has completely altered: the new challenge is no longer about east versus west, but rather North versus South. The challenge is no longer between *classes*, but between past and present, between people who trust in their present to create a better future and people who trust in their past to gain a prosperous future. It is between people who see their future through the prism of their present, and others who see their future through the prism of their past. While the former group of people in the global North (the wealthy developed countries, such as those of the west) have placed their trust in their present and see a promising future, the latter in the global South (the poorer developing countries which make up much of the Muslim world), see little that is good in their present and their future is not secure, promising nothing more than misery, unemployment, humiliation, and identity crises. The latter do not place their trust in their present because they have no present; hence they can only see a route to the future through the past. In the fundamentalist view, the future of Muslims is only to be realized in a return to their faith, to their Islamic identity, to adherence to the fundamentals of Islamic law, and to presenting themselves to the world as Muslims. Hence, the present challenge is no longer between east and west, but between the North and South, and between past and future.

The nature of this challenge is critical, as the psychological character of some fundamentalist movements has shifted over time. Since the 1970s, the Islam that was integrated into the various nationalist ideologies has increasingly been replaced by a trans-nationalistic Jihadism. In the process, the theme and framework of their ideology, as well as the geographical contours of their activity, have also changed. This shift from debate to violence has, without a doubt, grave implications. This violence has ranged from fighting, suicide bombing, kidnapping, killing, and hijacking to other forms of terrorism well known to the world media and security agencies. All of this has been committed in the name of Islam. Further, in the name of Islam, al-Qa'ida has come to be known as the chief of terrorism. Al-Qa'ida hijacked Islam in order to make the challenge somehow ideological and linked to some specifics of religion that apparently resist eradication by a purely security- and military-based agenda. In other words, terrorism is a transnational phenomenon of ideological dimensions and therefore must be challenged using the same—that is, ideological—weapons and at the same scales, that is both local and global.

Accordingly, much of the debate over al-Qa'ida and the War on Terror, and much of the work on al-Qa'ida published in both Arabic and European languages, has been dominated by a focus on three major areas: personality traits; certain conceptual binary oppositions, such as resurgence as opposed to decline, tradition as opposed to modernity, decadence as opposed to renewal; and themes of collective division, such as here and there, us and them, or our civilization and their civilization. This theoretical approach becomes even more complex as terms such as secularization, westernization, and globalization have come into play and been used to taint the debate as one about superiority and inferiority. Thus, identifying the theological and ideological bases of al-Qa'ida's political tactics, therefore, might go far beyond developing an effective strategy to combat terrorism. Subsequently, the ongoing discussion about the War on Terror has shifted, as less attention has been paid to the religio-political forces and the root causes that have motivated Islamic fundamentalists to adopt methods of violence and terror on both the national and later the international levels. As Burke argues:

> The debate over the prosecution of the ongoing 'war on terror' has been skewed. Instead of there being a reasoned and honest look at the root causes of resurgent Islamic radicalism, the discussion of strategies in the war against terror had been almost entirely dominated by the 'counter-terrorist experts' with their language of high-tech weaponry, militarism, and eradication. The latter may be useful to treat the symptom but does not, and will never, treat the disease . . . . Bin Laden and al-Qaeda are the radical, extremist fringe of the broad movement that is modern Islamic militancy. Their grievances are political but articulated in religious terms . . . . The movement is rooted in social, economic, and political contingencies. The smoke and the vapour trails over Tora Bora may have signalled the end of Afghanistan as a favoured destination for aspirant terrorists but it did nothing to eradicate the reasons for the volunteers wanting to go there.[54]

Thus, the challenge is ideological and involves some specific contingencies and qualifications that are difficult to deal with purely militarily or using high-tech weaponry, as we have seen in Afghanistan and Iraq. Seven years have passed since the War on Terror began, yet both al-Qa'ida and the Taliban are still at work. Accordingly, the time and energy that have been used in depicting the aforementioned binary oppositions should be applied instead to analyzing and defining a global counter-terrorism strategy. Those binary opposites should not be taken at face value, or understood as a rigid and mutually exclusive classification of cultures and thoughts. It is wrong to consider that Islamic radicalism was established and developed in isolation from the political, economic, and cultural circumstances in the Muslim world from which it emerged. In the words of Bouma, "Resorting to terror is a symptom of unacceptable and unchanging social dislocation."[55]

Islamic fundamentalism is not a recently established movement. It has existed since early Islam and continued to develop in step with political and cultural developments within the Muslim community, and thus includes a range of movements and thinkers up to and including al-Qaʿida. The Islamic fundamentalist movements' thinking and activity was previously limited to the national arena and an interest in reforming their own nations. In the words of Burke:

> There was room in their programme for gradualism and compromise. There was room in their movement for a huge multiplicity of different strands of political thought. There was room for the parochial, radical, and conservative movements of rural areas and for the clever, educated, and aware ideologues of the cities. There was even room for those extremists who were committed to violence and who saw the world as a battlefield between the forces of good and evil, of belief and unbelief.[56]

Al-Qaʿida and its terrorist conspirators have drawn from previous manifestations of Islamic fundamentalism, yet transformed much of their theological and ideological discourses into something different, with different geographic contours. The terrorist attacks on September 11, 2001, in the name of Islam or jihad, illustrate this point. Hence, in its theological and ideological framework, al-Qaʿida might borrow some Islamic conceptions from the earlier fundamentalists, but appropriates and distorts these conceptions in an environment that is very different in time and place from that of the past, with the aim of serving al-Qaʿida's goals and objectives. Therefore, al-Qaʿida's repeated attempts to present itself as an Islamic 'reformist movement' should not surprise us. In its books, al-Qaʿida uses such titles and intentionally refers to prominent scholars in order to deceive its audience and to hide its terrorism behind the respect and authority implied by such titles and names. This is despite the fact that al-Qaʿida calls its opponents in the Muslim world Kharijis, Murjiʾis, or Haroris, or similar groups that appeared in the early history of Islam. Al-Qaʿida also charges Muslims who condemn al-Qaʿida's terrorism with apostasy, or of 'not [being] true Wahhabis.' This indicates the importance of undertaking a careful reading of the literature of the early Islamic movements, including Kharijism and its splinter groups, such as Murjiʾism and ʿIbadism, and later Wahhabism, from which al-Qaʿida claims authority. This is the task of the following chapter.

2

The Origins of Fundamentalism

The aims of Islamic movements of the modern epoch are to establish an Islamic order and to confirm the theoretical relevance of Islam to the modern world. The theological and ideological discourse of contemporary Islamic movements also has its roots in Islamic history and has developed in step with social and political contexts through the centuries. Numerous movements have emerged throughout the history of Islam. Among them are the Kharijis, 'Ibadis, Hanbalis, and Wahhabis, which are presented here as examples that substantiate the link between medieval and modern movements including al-Qa'ida. All of these movements call for rule by shari'a, but they have different approaches to achieving their goals. Islamic movements differ from each other, not only in time and space, or in their infrastructure, character, and function, but also in terms of the themes and framework of their theological and intellectual discourses. These differences are based on the political, social, intellectual, and moral contexts in which they exist and function.

Kharijism

Kharijism, as both a term and an ideology, has been used by al-Qa'ida and its opponents as a diacritical mark with which to label the other. While al-Qa'ida calls its Muslim opponents Kharijis, it considers itself a "jihadist reformist movement" and what it does as jihad on behalf of all Muslims: "We consider our jihad in this stage to be the jihad of an *umma* (nation). Therefore, any individuals or groups that enter the jihad and exchange loyalty with us on the basis of 'blood for blood and destruction for destruction'; they are part of the jihadist movement."[1] Here the link between al-Qa'ida and the Kharijis begins. Al-Qa'ida borrowed the idea of loyalty from the Kharijis and made loyalty to al-Qa'ida a 'special loyalty,' embodied in a covenant, the most important of which is 'blood for blood and destruction for destruction.'

The word Kharijism refers to the ideological views of the Kharijis, the first radical group in Islam, who rebelled against 'Uthman ibn 'Affan, the third caliph (ruled 644–56). He was one of those early Muslims whom the Prophet Muhammad admired. 'Uthman perfected his interpretation of Islam under the guidance of Muhammad, married Muhammad's daughter, worked as his secretary and ambassador, and was later elected to the office of the caliphate as the third of the Four Rightly Guided Caliphs. Under his leadership, the caliphate expanded from Arabia to the rest of Persia, North Africa, the Caucasus, and Cyprus. In this vast state, Muslim centers of learning began to emerge in different territories that naturally varied in their cultural ethnicity and linguistic backgrounds. These centers began to develop their own dialectic traditions of reading and studying the Qur'an. This alarmed 'Uthman, who feared that religious controversy might result if Muslims sought to develop and adhere to their own dialectical styles. He appointed a committee to compile the text into one volume and to make copies for all the cities and centers in the caliphate. This is the Qur'an as it is known today. However, in 656, after twelve years in office, 'Uthman was besieged in his house for twelve days and was finally murdered by Muslim radicals. Their motives have been detailed in the literature, as part of the great upheaval, or Fitna. In short, the radicals accused the caliph of nepotism and misrule. The Egyptian literary critic Taha Hussein (1889–1973) stated that

> When 'Uthman became caliph, he not only lifted the ban placed by 'Umar [second caliph] upon the companions to go to the other territories, but also gave them rich presents from the public treasury. He gave al-Zubayr ibn al-'Awwam 600,000 dirhams in one day, and gave Talha 100,000 dirhams in one day, enabling them to buy lands, property, and slaves in other territories.[2]

Whatever the reasons might have been, Caliph 'Uthman was murdered by this Islamic radical group, which later came to be called the Kharijis. The Kharijis have influenced the history of Islam ever since, and have served as a spiritual parent to many medieval and modern radical groups, including al-Qa'ida. For example, al-Qa'ida has borrowed several ideas from the Kharijis, among which is their notion of disloyalty to the government. The Kharijis were the first to rebel against the legitimate government and ultimately assassinated their ruler, who was a prominent friend of the Prophet of Islam. In the present day, Ayman al-Zawahiri, now the head of al-Qa'ida, has incorporated the Khariji idea of rebellion against the government and the state, which has led to acts such as the planned assassination, alongside other jihadist groups, of Egypt's President Sadat in 1981.

Etymologically, the word *khariji*s (pl. *khawarij*) is an abstract noun that refers to those who 'go out' of the legitimate authority of the state. Whoever rebels against legitimate authority is called a *khariji*.[3] In this sense, al-Qa'ida's leadership, namely, al-Zawahiri and his affiliates, are Kharijis, who have rebelled not only against their own states, but also against religious authority. They have killed political and religious figures, and innocent civilians, both Muslim and non-Muslim, of countries with whom Muslim countries have treaties and mutual relationships.

Following the controversial murder of 'Uthman, 'Ali ibn Abi Talib was elected to office, but Mu'awiya ibn Abi Sufyan ('Uthman's nephew) rejected him. Mu'awiya had been appointed by 'Uthman as governor of Damascus, after which he sought to reach the highest office. As a result, a struggle for succession ensued between the two men. They fought each other in two big battles. 'Ali won the first, but the conflict persisted, leading to a second battle. The two men mobilized their forces and met each other at Siffin, a town that now forms part of Syria, close to the border with Iraq. Camping there, 'Ali tried to resolve the dispute by means of arbitration, but the situation continued and Mu'awiya demanded that the murderers be brought to justice while the upheaval was still at its peak, and the house of the caliphate still disorganized from within. Mu'awiya publicly displayed the bloodied clothes of 'Uthman in the mosque in Damascus to foster ill feeling against 'Ali. The failure of 'Ali's attempts to resolve the dispute peacefully led the two rivals to once again engage in armed hostilities at Siffin. After several skirmishes, the fighting became fierce. Both 'Ali and Mu'awiya were unhappy about the heavy losses on both sides, but Mu'awiya was particularly dejected, and hoped that the battle would decide their fates. However, the battle did not go in favor of Mu'awiya's wishes. In danger of defeat, Mu'awiya took the advice of his general 'Amr ibn al-'As and ordered a special army unit to stick Qur'ans onto the ends of their lances.[4] Neither Mu'awiya nor his advisory general necessarily believed that 'Ali's army would accept arbitration at this point, especially after 'Ali's previous attempt to resolve the matter by peaceful means had failed, and with his army now advancing to victory. Mu'awiya and his general, however, were certain that some of 'Ali's forces would favor arbitration, and so at the very least it would cause dissension in 'Ali's army, which is precisely what happened. Some of 'Ali's soldiers, who had rebelled against 'Uthman, refused to continue fighting against Mu'awiya's men when they saw the Qur'an stuck on the end of their lances. They believed that because the Qur'an had come between the two sides, the *hukm* [rule and judgment] *rests with God alone* (Qur'an 12:40). This meant that the two sides should settle their differences through arbitration under Islamic law. 'Ali urged these soldiers to keep fighting, saying that Mu'awiya was trying to trick them and was on the brink of defeat, but they did not listen. While 'Ali was arguing against those soldiers that "I know better about what is in the Book of God," his general, al-Ashter, pursued Mu'awiya's retreating army and was advancing to victory. However, the rebellious soldiers within 'Ali's camp threatened to attack General al-Ashter from the rear if he did not withdraw. They even 'threatened 'Ali that they would do with him as they had done with 'Uthman if he did not order al-Ashter to stop fighting.' Having no choice, 'Ali ordered al-Ashter to "stop fighting and accept the arbitration."[5]

The next stage in this conflict was arbitration. Both sides agreed upon the principle that one person should represent each side as a judge. They also agreed that both arbiters should base their judgment on the Qur'an, and both sides should accept and implement that judgment. Mu'awiya selected his top general and main supporter, 'Amr ibn al-'As, to represent his side. "Amr was a shrewd general and 'an able negotiator loyal to his cause.'"[6] As for 'Ali's side, the rebel soldiers made their choice: Sheikh Abu Musa al-Ash'ari. They insisted on Abu Musa, although 'Ali protested against the choice. 'Ali's concern was over Sheikh Abu Musa's absolute neutrality, especially as he was to negotiate the matter with General 'Amr, Mu'awiya's main supporter. A treaty was drawn up and agreed to, one which ordered both parties to lay down their arms and accept the judgment of the arbiters. The nobles of the two armies added their signatures, but the radicals from 'Ali's army did not. On their way back from the battlefield toward Kufa, the radicals quarrelled with 'Ali and used theological arguments to justify their political stance against him. The radicals had wanted 'Ali to stop fighting and accept arbitration, but when he did so the group changed its view and rejected arbitration on the pretext of *No rule but God's* (Qur'an 12:40). They now blamed him on the grounds of this theological view, namely that his acceptance of human judgment would make the future of any judgments dependent on human opinion rather than on divine judgment. This group detached itself from legal authority (that is, 'Ali's caliphate), for which they became known as Kharijis (that is, those who 'went out').[7]

Subsequently, the Kharijis made an attempt on 'Ali's life. As he was entering Kufa with the rest of his army, they wounded him. The traitors rejoiced and marched to camp in Harura, a small town in the Kufa province. However, 'Ali sent his envoys to settle the dispute with the rebels, some of whom then renounced their radical views and returned to 'Ali's camp. Those who refused regarded 'Ali as not a true Muslim. According to Ibn Khaldun:

> They demanded from 'Ali to repent, and break the Treaty and go back with them to fight Mu'awiya . . . . 'Ali said, "We have a treaty and a covenant with them" . . . . Harqous [a Kharijite] said to 'Ali "this is your sin for which you should repent" . . . . 'Ali replied, "It is not a sin but let's say a weak opinion" . . . . Zar'ah [a Kharijite] said, "If you do not condemn this human judgment and renounce it we will fight you."[8]

Al-Tabari pointed out that 'Ali himself went to them in a final attempt to resolve the dispute, but that they

> argued and asked him: "Do you think human judgment is just? Why have you considered human judgment?" . . . 'Ali reminded them of the role that they played in the whole course and said, "You have decided on the matter of the entire case; you have decided for the arbitration and selected Abu Musa; and that the judgment was also based on the Qur'an . . . . The Qur'an is but words printed on paper and cannot speak without humans . . . . Those human arbiters made the Qur'an speak and they spoke of the Qur'an" . . . . Some of them accepted 'Ali's view and returned to his camp.[9]

The remaining Kharijis withdrew to the east of the Tigris River toward al-Nahrawan (southeast of Baghdad). On their way, the Kharijis encountered people and became increasingly fanatical and condemned all those who disagreed with them, including 'Uthman, 'Ali, Mu'awiya and the arbiters, as well as those who accepted the arbitration. They branded them all as *kuffar* (infidels; sing. *kafir*)[10] and worthy of execution. This was their early stock of theology, which 'went out' *(kharaja)* with them to the east of the Tigris province, and on their way they dealt harshly with those who did not share their views. According to al-Shahrastani (1086–1153), "the people feared for their life and property at the hands of the Kharijis."[11] The terror they inflicted during their travels forced 'Ali to take action. His army engaged with them and defeated them at al-Nahrawan in 658, but some survived and ultimately assassinated 'Ali in 661. They also organized simultaneous attempts against the lives of both Mu'awiya and 'Amr for being 'infidels.'[12]

In terms of their theology, Julius Wellhausen has described the Kharijis as "people of deep conviction, much nobler than the Jewish Zealots and no worse than Christian heretics and saints, because they were men of action who found martyrdom not upon the scaffold but upon the battlefield."[13] Their movement was initially religious, but it gradually developed into an aggressive and uncompromising force, accepting no authority except that of "a caliph whom they themselves select and whom they could, and frequently did, at any time reject."[14] Their uncompromising character and their theological discussions also created the foundations upon which they would later split into "twenty groups,"[15] eight of which were large and subdivided into ten other smaller groups, such as those referred to by al-Shahrastani as the 'early' Muhakkima, al-Azariqa, al-Najadat, al-'Adhiriya, al-Bayhasiya, and al-'Ibadiya.[16] Their radicalism took various shapes and forms, from theology to weapons, debates to skirmishes, and cold to hot wars. In their debates, each party supported its position with texts from the Qur'an and Hadith (sayings of the Prophet). It was out of this great upheaval, from the divisions and subdivisions of the Kharijis, that radical Islamic groups were born, spread, and had a significant impact on the Muslim world.[17]

The Kharijis inspired other extremist groups that were not necessarily Kharijis. For example, the Early Muhakkimis (Muhakkima) called themselves the Jama'at al-Muslimin ('Community of Muslims') on the pretext that people outside their group were infidels. It was based on this group that a number of modern radical groups selected their names. For example, one of the jihadist groups in Egypt calls itself the 'Community of Muslims' (Jama'at al-Muslimin) to signify that they are the only Muslims and that all others are infidels. This belief is also shared by the Indonesian Jama'at Islamiya and by al-Qa'ida. The Muhakkimis inspired the Murji'i groups (al-Murji'a), who held distinctive views about religion and its practices, but agreed with other Kharijis on some points, including issues of governorship.[18] Today, members of al-Qa'ida think of themselves as the only true Muslims and consider their opponents, whether Muslim or non-Muslim, to be infidels. The organization attaches the label of 'apostasy' to Muslim governments and calls the public and Islamic groups who oppose al-Qa'ida's violence and terrorism 'Murji'is,' after one of the Khariji groups. On this subject, the al-Qa'ida theorist al-Maqdisi wrote a book entitled *Imta' al-nazar fi kashf shubuhat Murji'at al-'asr* (Pleasing the Sight by Unveiling the Suspicion of the Murji'is of the Epoch). He argues that "the Murji'is in our era are many, some of them are but ordinary people and some others are linked to the religion."[19] This book is based on a Wahhabi book, attributed to Ibn 'Abd al-Wahhab, with a similar title: *Kashf al-shubuhat* (Unveiling the Suspicion).

Similar to the Murji'is, the Wa'idis (al-Wa'idiya) were another extremist group that was part of the Khariji network. It condemned and branded as infidels any Muslims who did not follow them. Similarly, the Azariqis (al-Azariqa) were one of the largest and most extreme of the Khariji groups. They moved from Basra, conquered al-Ahwaz (in Iran), and killed all of its governors appointed by Ibn al-Zubayr, who ruled in Medina from 682 to 692. The Azariqis did so because they did not consider his rule legitimate.[20] This group also influenced al-Qa'ida's theology and ideology. The Azariqis called their Muslim opponents "polytheists, unbelievers, or infidels [who] should be killed." They also called those who "did not join them polytheists, even if they agreed with them," and stated that "any one [who] came to join the Azariqis was subject to investigations and examinations, even if he claimed to be one of them"; further, "they permitted the killing of civilians, the wives and children of their opponents."[21] According to the Egyptian historian Shawqi Dayf:

> The Azariqis think of themselves as the only true Muslims in the world, and people other than them, as infidels that are forbidden to eat their food or to have a link with them through marriage or inheritance but their men and women must be killed with their children . . . . Any territory other than the territory of the Azariqis, is but the territory of infidels (*kufr*).[22]

The ideas and the language expressed in this quote comprise the theme and framework of the ideology of al-Qaʻida and similar groups. One should bear in mind that the differences between the radical groups of our modern times are the same as the differences that existed between the medieval radical groups. Thus, the theological differences among these radical groups should not obscure their affinity. Irrespective of their differences in religious dogma, the radical groups are very much alike in their approach to religious reality and the way they carry out their affairs in general. Their differences lie in their political tactics, which depend on the circumstances of their leadership and military strength, and their particular historical and geographic context. Their theology, described by Wellhausen as a form of active fundamentalism, reflects their uncompromising observance of the Qur'an. To these groups, anyone who opposes their views should be ostracized or killed.[23]

Hence, the Khariji groups were numerous, but were all rooted in the tradition of the Early Muhakkimis. Another common feature of the Kharijis and present-day radical groups is that they believe in change from the top down and the spread of their views by violent means. Perceiving themselves to be the only Muslims, they consider their terror as righteous jihad and *the* holy means to spread their views. Hence, all radical groups, including al-Qaʻida and the Khariji groups, have come to be known to the majority of Muslims as assassins and bandits.[24]

The Kharijis' radicalism continued to grow, and reached its zenith in the period between 690 and 730. Their radical activities contributed to the fall of the Umayyads at the hands of the Abbasids in 750.[25] Throughout these conflicts the groups' aims became confused and twisted as the ends came to justify the means. This idea underlies one of the important tactics of al-Qaʻida today. The group justifies its terrorist acts including suicide bombings and killing civilians as a means to achieve its aims.

The Abbasids saw their war against Kharijism as a war of ideas. This vision is worthy of consideration when looking at the 'War on Terror' today. It is becoming increasingly evident that the War on Terror should not be confined to a purely military agenda. Indeed, terrorism cannot survive without its radical ideas. The Abbasids increased the number and quality of their learning centers. As the processes of writing and inter-pretation of authoritative texts, and the schools of law and philosophy, flourished, the Kharijis' radical ideas were refuted. Some views could not stand up to questioning and thus were eliminated; others found their way to moderation; and others took their discourse to the far extreme. It is in the latter—the radical Khariji literature—that al-Qa'ida has found its area of interest and conviction.

'Ibadism

Anyone who is familiar with the literature of the Khariji and al-Qa'ida groups knows that among the links between them is the perception that the Qur'an may only be read literally. In addition, the 'Ibadis' idea of *takfir*, which charges others with unbelief, is one of the most motivational ideas in al-Qa'ida's doctrine. *Takfir*, as emphasized in al-Qa'ida's writings, leaves the gate wide open for all forms of violence and terrorism. Al-Qa'ida's ideologues, such as al-Zawahiri and Abu Bakr Naji, consider all opponents of al-Qa'ida as *kuffar*, who must be fought and killed.[26] This and other lethal ideas are rooted in the Khariji splinter groups, such as the 'Ibadis, who developed their own ideology, 'Ibadism *(al-'Ibadiya)*, out of Kharijism and later split into subgroups—in a manner similar to that seen among radical groups in the Muslim world today.

Thus, the 'Ibadis are the heirs and legatees of the Kharijis. Kharijism has survived into our age, in the form of more than one group, among which is the 'Ibadi group and its ideology. 'Ibadism was named after its founder Abu 'Abdullah ibn 'Ibad (d. 715). He was a member of the Kharijis' Early Muhakkimi group and spent a considerable amount of time in Yemen and Iraq. Ibn 'Ibad was the political mentor of the group, but its spiritual leader and imam was Jabir ibn Zayd. His followers founded communities in parts of southern Arabia, North Africa, Iran, Iraq, and Yemen as well as on the coastal territories of the Arabian Gulf. From the ninth to the eleventh centuries, the 'Ibadis conducted a series of sporadic radical actions and confirmed the presence of the Kharijis in theological, ideological, and political arenas.

Following the line of the Kharijis, the 'Ibadis legitimized regime change from the top down. It is in this literature that al-Zawahiri found the authority to kill Egypt's President Sadat in 1981, and to kill civilians, Muslims and non-Muslims alike. They charged both caliphs 'Uthman and 'Ali as being *kufr*. If those caliphs were charged as *kufr*, it was easier for al-Qa'ida to charge the current Muslims and non-Muslims (rulers and ruled) as *kufr*.[27]

The 'Ibadis radical stance against the government made it difficult for them to live in eighth-century Basra. Most of them moved to Arabia's remote areas such as Oman and Hadramawt, but some also went to North Africa and even to Zanzibar in East Africa, and Khurasan in Asia.

The original 'Ibadi movement split into three groups, each of which had its own theology and ideology, which governed a group's radical activism. The Yazidis (al-Yazidiya), the Hafisis (al-Hafisiya), and the Harithis (al-Harithiya) reacted violently against what they considered to be *kafir*. The latter two groups, in particular, had a few theocentric ideas that were inherited by al-Qa'ida. Among these ideas are: "their opponents should choose either to follow them or to be fought and be killed"; "all the territories of their opponents are territories of Islam"; "the courts of the elites are places of *kufr* that should be fought"; "the ability to act is a state that comes before the action itself"; and "there is no end for jihad."[28]

Thus, al-Qa'ida mimics the 'Ibadis and uses religion for purely political gain. As emphasized by Ibn Khaldun, the spirit of fanaticism lives on in the souls of the 'Ibadis and communicates itself through them; they radically opposed their own government and revolted against it.[29] The 'Ibadi groups consider government, namely the imamate, to be a matter of the achievement of heroes. Heroism is always in great demand among Khariji groups. As Wilkinson put it: "The imamate becomes a highly competitive position; various tribal factions try to seize it, each claiming to champion the cause of the qualified imam."[30]

From the time of the first Kharijis until the time of Bin Laden, the need for hero imams has continued to predominate among all radical groups, which has led to the loss of innocent lives. The 'Ibadis believed that their leadership must be vested in an imam who combines religious and political authority. Thus, the imamate is the cornerstone of the 'Ibadis' life and creed. Due to their focus on establishing the imamate, the 'Ibadis were more interested in war than intellectual debate or the production of scholarly works. They also considered their imams to be more 'war heroes' than scholars or 'ulama.[31]

This trend can also be seen in modern Islamic groups, including al-Qa'ida. Indeed, al-Qa'ida is focused on war and its scholarly works are aimed at justifying war. Al-Qa'ida followers understand their actions and methods as legitimate jihad, and that the jihad will continue until the end of this world. 'Abdullah 'Azzam, one of al-Qa'ida's ideologues, wished not only to win the war against the Soviets and establish an Islamic imamate (state) in Afghanistan, but also to open another war front somewhere else to continue their jihad and extend their state.[32] Likewise, al-Zawahiri, formerly al-Qa'ida's second-in-command, admitted that the jihad will never stop, but will continue to the end of this world.[33] In addition, al-Qa'ida's imams are, like those of the 'Ibadis, closer to war heroes than to 'ulama. The publications of al-Qa'ida are raw materials, selectively extracted to fit their ideological and political tactics. Like the 'Ibadis, al-Qa'ida has raised its leaders to the status of war heroes and imams; even Bin Laden became the crowned sheikh and leader of heroism and the imam of all imams. Bin Laden and his general, al-Zawahiri, thought of their group as the only 'Muslims,' and the rest as infidels. In this regard, the difference between the radical groups of old and those of the modern era can be reduced to one of political tactics.[34]

The 'Ibadis say that any Muslim who opposes *them* is an unbeliever (*kafir*), as in the following:

> All those who pray in the direction of the *Ka'ba* in Mecca but oppose us are unbelievers. It is lawful to take as booty such things as their weapons and horses but nothing else. It is unlawful, however, to kill them or take them captives by a surprise attack unless the war has been declared and their unbelief has been established.[35]

These words mirror the theme and framework of al-Qa'ida's theology today. Establishing an Islamic state is, for al-Qa'ida, an obligatory duty for all true Muslims. To the 'Ibadis, the imamate is also obligatory as an ordinance of God to command and interdict: to enact justice and to fight the enemy. Therefore, the concept of sovereignty is very closely linked to the Islamic state that al-Qa'ida seeks to establish, and to the imamate in the case of the 'Ibadis. In either case, the situation of the state and the imamate is seen as similar, and described by the 'Ibadis as following these four stages: (a) rise (*zuhur*); (b) defense (*difa*); (c) spread (*intishar*); and (d) concealment (*kitman*).[36]

The first stage (rise) occurs when an imam is in office and is visible in both the religious and political spheres. This means that there must be a *visible* imam, not a *hidden* imam. During this stage, the imamate is established, the 'Ibadi laws rule the sovereign, and the community is in full control of its own affairs, free from foreign (non-'Ibadi) control. For them, non-'Ibadis are foreigners (whether Muslim or not) and ultimately unbelievers. The second stage of defense takes place when the 'Ibadi community falls under foreign (non-'Ibadi) rule. Here their imam must mobilize the 'Ibadis against the foreigners. This is not only his religious duty, but also the duty of his office. The third stage (spread) occurs if the imam fails to mobilize the 'Ibadis, in which case the 'Ibadis are free to organize themselves into groups to fight the foreigners by any means, without an imam leading them. The fourth and final stage (concealment) eventuates if the previous three stages have failed to establish the imamate. During this stage, the 'Ibadis refer to their imamate as in the 'concealment' stage.[37] It is important to note that the concealment of the imamate in the 'Ibadis' view is completely different from the understanding of concealment held by the Shi'is.

To 'Ibadis, their imamate signifies the existence of their imam and their sovereignty. Thus, their concept of sovereignty expresses the existence of their imamate under their imam and symbolizes the Ibadis' collective religio-political consciousness. The indissoluble link between the existence of the imamate and sovereignty requires the imam to act as a 'hero' and a 'liberator,' rather than merely a scholar. This means that the imamate is 'a personal achievement, not a divine appointment' as in the Shi'i view. The 'Ibadis hold the belief that the imam is a 'builder' of 'cities and states' rather than a successful manifestation of 'divine justice,' as the Shi'is perceive him to be.[38]

Toward Moderation
The 'Ibadis were originally Kharijis, but over time became moderate. They were relatively few in number and lived in largely remote areas. Today, the 'Ibadis live in the territories of the coastal Gulf, principally Oman, the Naffusa mountains and Zuwara provinces in Libya, the Island of Jerba in Tunisia, the Mzab valley in Algeria, and Zanzibar province on the east coast of Africa. In these areas, the 'Ibadis' religious, legal, and political traditions can be traced back directly to their earliest days in Basra. Today's largest 'Ibadi community is in the Sultanate of Oman in southeast Arabia, where the 'Ibadis form the majority of the population and 'Ibadism is the state religion.[39]

Wherever they dwell, the 'Ibadis have always been willing to sacrifice their lives in order to establish their imamate and express their religio-political consciousness. Therefore, they consider the Omani town of Nizwa 'the core of their Islam,' because Nizwa was always at the center of their rebellious activities and was the site where the 'Ibadi imamate was finally established in 793. This imamate maintained power without any major resistance until the first half of the eighteenth century, when a struggle for the imamate erupted and dragged the region into a series of violent clashes that continued until the early decades of the twentieth century. These conflicts were not religiously motivated, but rather driven by political and economic factors. The economic resources that Oman had secured from its invasion of the East African coast and later from oil excavations were central to the conflict.[40]

These wars weakened the 'Ibadi factions. The Persians were watching them closely and ultimately captured Muscat in 1743. However, Ahmad bin Sa'id was able to liberate the 'Ibadi imamate and become its imam in 1749. He united the northern imamate with that of the south under his leadership. Sa'id then began to develop the imamate's economy from a localized pasture-grazing and agricultural model to one based on international trade. The discovery of the Cape Sea route shifted trade from the Red Sea and the Arabian Gulf to the Indian Ocean. A new, more influential 'Ibadi merchant class began to emerge, which played a significant role in the imamate's politics and economy. The merchants were the political force that supported Imam Ahmad in his bid to expand the trade between his Omani imamate and India. A number of seaports on the East African coast and on the Indian coast began to grow with the obvious domination of the 'Ibadis.[41]

Imam Ahmad established the Bu-Sa'id dynasty, which has continued to rule over the imamate in Oman, Zanzibar, Pemba, and Kilwa in East Africa, in one form or another, to the present day. From the time of Imam Ahmad Bu-Sa'id (father of Sa'id) to the present reign of Sultan Qaboos bin Sa'id, wars between 'Ibadi factions have taken place from time to time. The political authority in Muscat and the religious authority in Rustaq have been unified at times, and separated at other times. Zanzibar was also one of those areas that was dominated and ruled by the 'Ibadis until 1960 when it was finally annexed by Tanganyika, known today as Tanzania.[42]

The present Sultan Qaboos Bin Sa'id assumed power on 24 July 1970. As soon as he gained power, he was confronted by an insurgency but finally defeated the rebels in 1975. One of his first measures was to expand the armed forces and upgrade the military's equipment, to abolish many of the previous regimes' harsh restrictions, to offer amnesty to all opponents of the previous regimes, and to launch a major program to modernize religious perceptions.

Sultan Qaboos, although an 'Ibadi, is not the imam and is not considered the religious head of 'Ibadism. However, since his accession to power in Oman, he has launched a sustained program for the publication of major 'Ibadi works, so that it at last became possible to understand the 'Ibadis through their own traditional texts. He also began to modernize Oman's infrastructure, social programs, and government bureaucracy. The sultanate adopted a foreign policy that encouraged foreign investment, maintained ties with British and U.S. interests, and aligned itself with the moderate Arab powers.

Currently, the imamate has disappeared into the sultanate. The 'Ibadi Sheikh Ahmad bin Hamad al-Khalili is the top religious authority and Supreme Mufti of present-day Oman, and vice-president of the International Union of Muslim Scholars (INUMS). In 2004, the mufti represented his country in the Sixteenth Convention of the Supreme Council for Islamic Affairs, which convened in Cairo during 28 April–1 May 2004. During this period, the widely read Egyptian daily *al-Ahram* interviewed the mufti and asked him about many of the pressing issues of the day, including jihad, the War on Terror, the war in Iraq, and Islam and Muslim affairs in general.

In terms of jihad, the mufti outlined that jihad as referred to in the Qur'an should only be understood within the framework of "the defense against aggression. God says: *And fight in the way of God against those who fight against you but be not aggressive, Surely God loves not the aggressors*" (Qur'an 2:190).

Focusing on whether or not the resistance in Iraq is jihad, the mufti stated that "Muslims are Mujahidin as long as they are defending themselves, their country, their wealth, their property, their honour, and their dignity."

As to the issue of liberty in Islam, the mufti emphasized that freedom is not absolute but "limited to the frameworks of morals," and that "Islam permits no one to walk undressed in the street, or to be a thief who transgresses the rights of others." He continued: "Islam permits no one to transgress the sacredness of others. The freedom which transgresses the rights and the sacredness of others does not exist in Islam."

In terms of women's liberty, which has spread all over the Arab world, the mufti pointed out that humankind, whether men or women, must adhere and limit themselves to the framework of morals and virtues.

However, "liberty, which liberates man and woman from the framework of the morals and virtues, is not liberty but profligacy and this is not healthy for either man or woman."[43]

The mufti's words reflect the views of modern 'Ibadis. This interview took place on 19 June 2004. At that time, the women's movement in Oman was going from strength to strength, and by appointing female ministers, Oman became the only Arab country, apart from Egypt, in which a number of women occupied positions of high office.

Hanbalism

Hanbalism refers to Ibn Hanbal's school and theory of law. He was a theologian, a major collector and critic of Hadith, a jurist, and the founder of the fourth Sunni school of law, which is today the official school of law in some countries, including Saudi Arabia and Qatar.[44]

When examining al-Qa'ida's ideas, scholars usually mention the writings of Ibn Hanbal (780–855) and Ibn Taymiya (1263–1328) as well as the writings of Ibn 'Abd al-Wahhab (1703–92). Some of their works are regarded as being among the main early sources of the theological and intellectual discourse of the Islamic radicalism of the present era.

However, while Ibn Hanbal and Ibn Taymiya made original contributions toward formulating new jurisprudential ideas accepted by the vast majority of Muslims, Ibn 'Abd al-Wahhab offered a philosophical dogma accepted by only a small minority of Muslims and advocated that those who did not follow his dogma should be known as polytheists (mushirkun) and deserving of jihad against them. In either case, these scholars are the products of different generations, different sociopolitical contexts, and different approaches to the issues of concern. While Ibn Hanbal was alive during the time of the Abbasids, Ibn Taymiya dealt with the remnants of the Seventh Crusade, and witnessed the Eighth Crusade and the Mongol aggression. Ibn 'Abd al-Wahhab, however, was around during the time of the Ottoman Empire and the early stages of western military expansionism in the Middle East.

Ibn Hanbal was a scholar with a taste for the concrete and the specifics of faith, and a dislike for the theoretical and abstract. He lived at a time when all of the elements of Abbasid rule (750–1258) had reached their zenith and borne fruit, whether sweet or sour. When the Abbasid caliphs came to power in Baghdad, Islam was entering its golden age. The sciences of the Qur'an and Hadith, in addition to Arabic language,

Islamic philosophy, history, physics, and other disciplines, were very well established.

Subsequently centers of learning became an intellectual marketplace for many new ideas, religious and otherwise.[45] This led to the emergence of groups with different views, ranging from Manichaeists to Shu'ubis, Jabaris, and others. Some of these groups had views similar to that of the radical groups of our time. For example, the Jabaris (al-Jabariya) share similarities with al-Qa'ida in interpreting the Qur'an literally, and in the view that humankind did not have free will in anything it did, and that humans, like a feather blowing in the wind, have no control over their motion—thus the human mind is seen as merely a receiver.[46]

It was in opposition to such 'heretics' that a movement, led by the jurist Imam Ahmad Ibn Hanbal, emerged that encouraged Muslims to return to the Qur'an and Hadith. Ibn Hanbal devoted himself to studying these sources and the rulings based on them. However, his time and sociopolitical context did not allow his views to remain immune from distortion. Nevertheless, they continued to possess outstanding merits that paved the way for the fame he later acquired. In the words of Abu Thawr (764–854):

> If anyone were to say that Ahmad Ibn Hanbal was one of the people of Paradise, he would not be rebuked for that. This is because if you went to Khurasan, you would hear the people there saying, "Ahmad Ibn Hanbal is a righteous man." The same is true if you went to Syria and Iraq. That is the consensus, so if he was to be rebuked for his opinion it would be like saying that the consensus was invalid.[47]

Similarly, 'Abd al-Raziq al-Sana'ani (who was from Yemen and died in 826, some twenty-four years before the death of Ibn Hanbal) stated that

> I have never seen a more erudite and God-fearing person than Ahmad Ibn Hanbal. . . . Among the leading scholars of Hadith who came to Yemen from Iraq were four men. Al-Shahadhakuni (d. 849, six years before the death of Ibn Hanbal) was the best in the memorization of Hadith; Ibn al-Madini (d. 849) was the most versed in Hadith differences; Yahya ibn Ma'in (d. 847) was the most conversant on the *rijal* (the narrators of Hadith); and Ahmad ibn Hanbal was the best of them in all these disciplines.[48]

Ahmad ibn Hanbal was born in 780 (thirty years after the establishment of the Abbasid dynasty). He devoted himself to studying the Sunna and jurisprudence *(fiqh)*. His faithful adherence to the primary sources of Islamic jurisprudence in his exegesis of the Qur'an and Hadith cleansed Islam of the heretical ideas that were attached to it at the time. He replaced what gave him doubt with what gave him certainty. His school of Islamic law became one of the four main canonical schools of Sunni Islam.

Ibn Hanbal's birth, education, and early teachings until he reached intellectual maturity all coincided with the reign of Harun al-Rashid (763–809), when the Abbasid empire reached its peak in many spheres of human endeavor, including the military, commerce, agriculture, philosophy, literature, the arts, and the sciences. The name of Harun al-Rashid was a dominant one in the global politics of the day as a symbol of higher culture and a more advanced civilization. His capital city and power base, Baghdad, had flourished into the most splendid city in the world. With its glorious centers of learning, arts, and philosophy, Baghdad surpassed Constantinople as the city without peer on earth. Schools and universities thrived, hospitals were built, and goods from every corner of the world filled its bazaars. Harun al-Rashid, who himself was a scholar, poet, and outstanding soldier, routinely rewarded artists, poets, writers, scientists, and philosophers for their talents. The people prospered along with the caliph and his court, and affluence and sophistication were in evidence everywhere.

Harun al-Rashid died in 809, taking his legacy with him. He was succeeded by his elder son al-Amin (ruled 809–813), but quarreled with his younger brother, al-Ma'mun, who wanted the top job. The tension between them worsened until there was a bloody struggle for the throne. Later, al-Amin was assassinated and replaced by al-Ma'mun.[49]

In 809, when al-Rashid died, Ibn Hanbal was in his thirtieth year and was widely regarded as an authority on Islamic jurisprudence. During the civil war, he collaborated closely with other scholars to protect the Islamic faith and culture from the influence of rival factions' ideas. Conversely, al-Ma'mun founded the House of Wisdom (Bayt al-Hikma), a celebrated university where Greek philosophy was translated by the empire's best minds, Muslims, Christians, and Jews. The use of philosophy to present the articles of Islamic faith gave way to the emergence of a new theology that in turn gave rise to new factions. Among the debated issues were the reality of faith; God's will and determination *(al-qada' wa-l-qadar)* in relation to humankind's will and action; human reason and revelation; governmental authority and legitimacy; and the concept of jihad and related issues.

Other controversial issues included the 'createdness' of the Qur'an, the caliphate, the previous caliphs, and the differences between the views of scholars and those of the Prophet's Companions as well as among the Companions themselves.

Subsequently, various factors moved Ibn Hanbal to make certain statements, especially when al-Ma'mun himself attempted to compel the imams of jurisprudence and Hadith to accept his opinion, willingly or unwillingly. In 827, in the face of those hugely influential scholars, the Caliph al-Ma'mun proclaimed the doctrine that the Qur'an was created, not eternal. In 833, al-Ma'mun went a step further and issued a decree that imposed his will on the Muslim community to accept his doctrine that: (i) the Qur'an was created; (ii) after the Prophet, 'Ali ibn Abi Talib is better than the first three caliphs before him;[50] (iii) government employment must only be granted to those who accept this doctrine; (iv) the position of judge must only be granted to those who accept this doctrine; (v) testimony in courts is accepted only from those who believe in this doctrine; and (vi) scholars must be interrogated about their opinions concerning this doctrine, and punishment will be inflicted upon anyone who rejects it.[51]

When al-Ma'mun issued the order to all provinces that all scholars be questioned to ensure they subscribed to his doctrine, Ibn Hanbal refused to accede to the caliph's demand. As a man of faith, Ibn Hanbal instead issued certain statements regarding Islam, which are as true to the position of the *Salaf* (referring to the early generations of Muslims, the so-called 'Pious Predecessors') as is his jurisprudence. Al-Ma'mun persecuted Ibn Hanbal and jailed him several times.[52] Riots then broke out and remained until al-Ma'mun left the office to his son al-Wathiq (r. 842–47). He followed his father's directives, and left Ibn Hanbal in detention. With this in mind, the leading jurists of Baghdad visited Ibn Hanbal in detention and asked him about the legitimacy of the caliph's authority and whether they should reject his authority. Ibn Hanbal advised that they were obliged only to renounce him in their hearts but not disobey or cause civil unrest and conflict in the community.[53]

This position is directly opposed to al-Qa'ida's ideas and tactics, as advocated by its leaders Bin Laden and al-Zawahiri. Al-Qa'ida does mention Ibn Hanbal in its writings in order to deceive al-Qa'ida's affiliates or followers; and not all of them are keen to search for the details of historical fact. Ibn Hanbal promotes the view that one should not overthrow the government from the top down. His legal opinion is that the jurists should keep the Muslim community united behind the government they hate most. Despite his imprisonment, Ibn Hanbal believed that neither the rulers nor anyone in their circle should be killed, and changing the regime by force was not an element of Ibn Hanbal's legacy.

When the caliph al-Wathiq learned about the jurists' meeting with Ibn Hanbal, he issued a declaration prohibiting Ibn Hanbal from seeing anyone. Yet riots did not cease and the public did not abandon Ibn Hanbal. The size of the angry crowd grew daily, as did opposition to the caliph. Judges even refused to take their seats at the bench. This situation alarmed the caliph, as all his measures failed to quell public anger. The caliph put a number of people, including jurist rioters, to their deaths, and their heads were displayed in different cities. Fearing the unrest and the possibility of popular rebellion, al-Wathiq decided to free Ibn Hanbal and send him away from Baghdad. The caliph's message was that "you should go to live wherever you like, but not in the city where the caliph lives."[54]

Ibn Hanbal left at once, but a few months later al-Mutawakkil came to power, in 847. The caliph al-Mutawakkil dismantled al-Ma'mun's doctrine, removed all restrictions imposed on Ibn Hanbal, and sent out for his return. Ibn Hanbal returned to Baghdad and resumed his lectures. He was also invited to the palace to teach the royal family, including the caliph's son al-Mu'tazz, the future caliph. Ibn Hanbal enjoyed the rest of his life as a celebrity in the highest echelons of government and was guaranteed independence of thought.

In the context of al-Qa'ida's theology, Ibn Hanbal's views on faith and law are critical. His political view is based in his understanding of faith, as he says:

Faith is word and deed. It increases when you do good and decreases when you do evil. A man [ruler or ruled] can leave the faith but remain within the fold of Islam. He is only removed from Islam if he associates partners with God or rejects one of His ordinances. If he abandoned them through ignorance or laziness, in either case, he is subjected to God's will that He may punish or may pardon him.[55]

This view is directly opposed to that of al-Qa'ida and similar groups of the modern era. It reflects Ibn Hanbal's adherence to the notion of freedom of belief. While this view is seen as traditionalist by some, it can also be seen as pragmatic by others. If one considers Ibn Hanbal's position through the prism of the Companions, Ibn Hanbal is then a traditionalist or a fundamentalist. Yet this fundamentalism is not opposed to human reason and is not outside the scope of rationality. If one considers his view from the perspective of the freedom to practice one's faith, he appears pragmatic, and there are illustrations of this on many pressing and sensitive issues including the issue of *takfir* (unbelief) in the quotation above.

Ibn Hanbal's pragmatism is also evident in his political views on the caliph and caliphate, and how the caliph should be chosen. Regarding these matters, Ibn Hanbal avoided sedition and civil disobedience. He did not approve of treason or the change of government by force. Ibn Hanbal strove for the unity of the community and preferred to obey the ruler, even if the ruler was unjust. To Ibn Hanbal, rebellion against the ruler is a rebellion against the community.[56] His view on all of these sensitive issues is in direct opposition to that of al-Qa'ida's ideologues, including Bin Laden and al-Zawahiri, as will be detailed in subsequent chapters.

By the middle of the ninth century (855), Ibn Hanbal had died but his legacy had spread across Arabia, Damascus, Khurasan, Egypt, and other Islamic centers and territories. It is, however, important to note that the original legacy and the heritage of Ibn Hanbal, which played a significant role in the history of Baghdad, came to "acquire notoriety as a troublemaker through the exploits of Barbahari (d. 329/941)."[57]

After Ibn Hanbal

Ibn Hanbal left his legacy to the pens of scholars of varying interests and political inclinations located within a range of political environments, from Iraq to Arabia, Egypt, Damascus, and Khurasan. As Ignaz Goldziher emphasizes, the school of Ibn Hanbal went on "an evolution from an *ecclesia pressa* to an *ecclesia militans*, with a penchant for 'fanatical terrorism.'"[58] Examples of this are numerous, including that of al-Barbahari, which well illustrates the point. Al-Barbahari became a powerful Hanbali scholar with a number of followers in Baghdad. The followers' response to al-Barbahari, as Ibn Abi Ya'la (d. 1131) says, "drew the attention of the Caliph." Portraying al-Barbahari's influence on his followers, Ibn Abi Ya'la noted the sad contrast between this Hanbali generation of al-Barbahari and Ibn Hanbal, "the faithful master who never liked to be followed by anyone, even on the street."[59]

Al-Barbahari took Ibn Hanbal's thought to the extreme. For example, al-Barbahari asserted that on the day of resurrection God would place the Prophet Muhammad beside Him on the Throne,[60] a dogma that had not been mentioned by Ibn Hanbal, nor had he elevated the Prophet to the status of divine Throne. The eminent historian al-Tabari (838–922) took issue with these new Hanbalis on this matter. When al-Tabari died, his burial had to take place at night to avoid the Hanbalis, led by al-Barbahari, disturbing his funeral, for they accused him of being a rejectionist (rafidi)[61]—a charge that is used by al-Qa'ida today against its Muslim opponents (both rulers and ruled). In this regard, al-Qa'ida's idea of rejectionism is not taken from Ibn Hanbal but from al-Barbahari, who himself borrowed the idea from the Khariji rejectionist group, al-Rafida.

Al-Barbahari and his followers zealously took the law into their own hands and persecuted those who rejected their views. The accounts of their radical activity are innumerable.[62] They harassed and assaulted their opponents, raided shops and homes in search of liquor and musical instruments, and surveilled men and women seen walking together in public. The activity of these militants alarmed the authorities, and it appears that the police also made a good number of arrests. The caliph warned al-Barbahari that they would be faced with "fire and sword" if they did not put an end to their fanaticism. They were also prohibited from holding meetings—not even two followers were allowed to meet together in one place at any one time.[63]

This new Hanbali generation imposed on Ibn Hanbal's legacy rules that he had not created, and of which he had never approved. While his school, for instance, was on good terms with the caliphate and its authority, some of the later Hanbalis came close to crossing the line into outright conflict with caliphal authority. Ibn Hanbal's teachings stood for unhesitating obedience to the ruler, except in disobedience to God. He was neither an active opponent of the caliphs nor a loyalist pledged to their support, and he never instigated social disobedience. The later Hanbalis' exploitation and violence occasionally "erode[d] the foundations of Ibn Hanbal's political politics."[64]

The Hanbalis' fanatical activism continued until the fall of the Abbasid caliphate at the hands of the invading Mongols (Tartars) in 1258, who destroyed Baghdad.[65] Thereafter, the Hanbali influence shifted to Damascus. Their number was small and the state ensured that their thought remained insignificant. It was not until the Ayyubid state (1171–1250) that the Hanbalis' influence increased and gradually they began to win positions in the offices of state.

The Hanbali influence extended with the advent of the Mamluks who took over the Ayyubid state. The Mamluk state (1250–1517) adopted a tolerant policy toward the Hanbalis and appointed their judge, for the first time, in Damascus. Generally, salaried appointments in institutions of learning became a popular role for Hanbali scholars.[66]

Subsequently, the Hanbalis became increasingly visible. 'Abd al-Ghani al-Maqdisi (d. 1203) was a prominent Hanbali scholar who would not hesitate to take the law into his own hands. He clashed with al-Malik al-'Adil (who ruled Egypt from 1200 to 1218), and stood against practices that he regarded as evil.

Thus, the Hanbali influence was always of a piece with the level of their involvement in society. One of the Hanbali scholars who fitted well into the political arena was Ahmad Ibn 'Abd al-Halim ibn Taymiya (1263–1328).

Ibn Taymiya and the Concept of Jihad

Ibn Taymiya was a celebrated scholar and a legendary figure who gained considerable prominence, much like Ibn Hanbal. If we consider his stand against outside invaders, his stand against the Mamluk kings, his enduring popularity, and his contribution to the military activity of his time, one finds that all are indicative of an eminent scholar of outstanding character whose fame also earned him jealous enemies.[67]

Ibn Taymiya was born in Haran, a city in northern Syria, which had a strategic location and a great history. It was located at a central point along the highways between Damascus, Edessa, and Raqqa in northern Syria, awarding it strategic value from an early date. The Bible tells us that Haran was named after Abraham's paternal uncle, Haran. The Bible also indicates that Haran was the city to which Abraham (Ibrahim) migrated with his wife Sarah, his father Terah (Tarih), and his nephew Lot. It was also the city where Abraham's father Terah died and was buried.[68] In Hebrews 11:8 and in Genesis 12:1, Haran was the city where Abraham received the revelation. Thus, Haran had a special significance for travelers, a significance underscored by the fact that Haran bore a unique relationship to the city of Ur, the birthplace of Abraham in

Babylon (in Iraq). Haran was also among the territories of the purely Arab tribes of Mudar, and later hosted the seat of the caliphate and its centers for education, translation, and intercultural dialogue. Haran retained its importance during the periods of the Umayyads, the Abbasids, the Ayyubids, the Crusaders, and finally the Mongols.

It was in Haran that Ibn Taymiya was born to a Hanbali scholarly family in 1263, five years after the fall of the Abbasid caliphate in Baghdad at the hands of the Mongols in 1258. In 1260, three years before his birth, Sultan Qutuz defeated the Mongols at 'Ayn Jalut.[69] However, the invaders, whether Crusaders or Mongols, kept coming back, despite being defeated several times. Ibn Taymiya saw the glory of the Abbasid caliphate crumbling under the Crusades and the Mongol aggression. The Muslims had had no caliph since the fall of Baghdad. Aleppo, Hama, and Homs (the burial place of General Khalid ibn al-Walid, who never lost a battle) were under attack. In 1269, wars destroyed the city of Haran. Ibn Taymiya's family took their six-year-old son and left to settle in Damascus. They abandoned their property but managed to take some of their books.[70]

The fall of Baghdad at the hands of the Mongols in 1258 was also the time when the Mamluks came to power in Egypt and began to consolidate their rule over Damascus and Arabia. In the midst of this political and social upheaval, religious movements spread ideas and practices not condoned by Islam. It was in this context that Ibn Taymiya formulated his views on the causes of the weakness of the Muslims and on the need to return to the Qur'an and the Sunna as the only means of revival.[71]

He structured his ideology on the basis of scholarly combinations of legitimate schools of thought, including the Maliki, the Hanafi, the Shafi'i, and the Hanbali schools of jurisprudence.[72] This comparative approach enabled Ibn Taymiya to cultivate and accommodate certain tendencies within the thought of his predecessors and to develop their ideas further. He produced a large number of works that strongly confirmed his mastery over the sciences of Arabic lexicology, logic, rhetoric, criticism, philosophy, theology, Hadith, and jurisprudence.[73]

Ibn Taymiya found himself assuming the role of a sociopolitical reformer, working in several spheres. He analyzed and exposed the reasons behind the weakness and instability of Muslim society. He developed a political and ideological legacy by locating the roots of Islamic revivalism in contemporary political processes and associated events. He provided a systematically focused and balanced explanation of theological, political, and social issues related to a variety of complex events associated with the Crusades and the Mongol invasions and their brutal influence on the caliphate and Muslim society.[74]

The violence of the Crusades and Mongols urged Ibn Taymiya to call upon his contemporary rulers to help rebuild a strong and enlightened nation, and to reform various sectors of society and the polity, including prevailing cultural and intellectual institutions. He considered the defects in the governmental, educational, cultural, and moral spheres as causes for the weakness of the Muslim community at the time.[75]

The Mongols referred to themselves as Muslims during this period, as a tactical maneuver to strengthen their rule—but this tactic did not convince people like Ibn Taymiya. He proved that the Mongols were invaders who used religion only as a means to divide and conquer. The Mongols did not implement the shari'a, but implemented their Manichaean law called *Yasa*, or in Arabic *al-Yasiq*. This law was a compound of the Mongols' various tribal beliefs and philosophies, and based on it, they not only destroyed all Islamic books found in Baghdad, but also burned Baghdad, Damascus, Aleppo, and Haran to the ground, and did not differentiate between soldiers and civilians, women, children, and elderly people. Ibn Taymiya viewed this behavior as that of invaders, and therefore declared that jihad against them was legitimate.

Religion is often used tactically for political gain. When Napoleon came to Egypt, he adopted the Mongols' tactics and identified himself as a Muslim; he even dressed as a Muslim, appeared in public squares, and visited al-Azhar Mosque in Cairo with a large Taliban-style turban on his head. After his visit, the 'Grand Imam Napoleon,' as he was referred to in Egypt's *Rose al-Youssef* magazine, permitted his horses to enter al-Azhar Mosque, and ordered his artilleries to destroy al-Azhar in Cairo. Like his Mongol pioneers in Iraq and Syria, Napoleon came to Egypt with both public and private motives. In public, Napoleon, in the words of Rodenbeck, came "as a servant of Allah and of the Ottoman Sultan. His mission was to punish the wicked Mamluks and secure Egypt from their grasp. In private of course, there were other more practical reasons: the economic potential of Egypt and the weakness of its Ottoman masters, Napoleon's megalomania and his romantic visions of the East, and his wish to threaten Britain's hold in India."[76] Thus, the 'Grand Imam Napoleon' used religion for political gain.[77]

Muslims from the extreme right to the extreme left viewed the Mongols' faith as corrupt. It was through the prism of this consensus that Ibn Taymiya saw the potential of the Muslim community and believed that victory does not come from debating theological matters. Victory comes from the community's return to the Qur'an and the Sunna, to unify its forces and to stand firm in jihad to liberate the country from invaders. It was to this idea and its underlying framework that Ibn Taymiya dedicated himself and he campaigned tirelessly to put his theories into practice in society.

On the issue of defense and security, he provided sharp and focused ideas. He did not vacillate about adopting jihad and fighting against the invaders, and urged his fellow Muslims to sacrifice their lives in order to liberate and protect their country.[78] Consequently, Ibn Taymiya's concept of jihad was a reflection of his time. It was not only Ibn Taymiya who focused on jihad in Damascus: when the Abbasid caliph Ahmad ibn al-Imam al-Zahir moved the seat of the caliphate to Cairo, his first speech also focused on jihad. He emphasized the aggression of the invaders, their brutal activities, and their destruction of the cities and of peoples' livelihoods. The caliph urged the people to use jihad to defend themselves, their property, and their country. Conversely, he urged scholars to embark on *ijtihad* (legal reasoning) and to do their best to promote and revive the jihad as a Muslim duty, an obligation of every able Muslim to liberate the country. In this context, the caliph said:

> O people, you should know that the jihad is necessary in human life, and that the knowledge about jihad cannot certainly stand without the consensus of the people. Gross violations were committed against every sacred and inviolable truth in our land. If you have seen the enemy when they entered our land; when they deemed lawful, human blood and properties; when they killed our elders and babies; when they captured the boys with the girls and killed the parents with their progeny; when they violated the honor of women and the honor of the caliphate in the lands and the seas; when the fearful cries raised to the high skies from the pains of suffering and blaze. O, slaves of God, tuck up to the hand of *ijtihad* and revive the duty of jihad.[79]

The caliph's words reflect the theme and framework of Ibn Taymiya's concept of jihad and even his own active involvement in the jihad against the Mongols.

As for the issue of jihad, I have explored this notion and its qualifications in some detail in previous publications,[80] and further discussion on jihad is presented in later chapters of this book. In this section, however, the focus is on jihad as observed by Ibn Taymiya. The difference between his view and that of al-Qa'ida will also be outlined.

Based on the Qur'an and the Sunna, Ibn Taymiya called upon his community for jihad against aggression. To him, every Muslim can carry out jihad to liberate his/her country. Hence, he authorized everyone in society with the sword of jihad, so that farming was the sword of the farmer, medicine was the sword of physicians, production was the sword of factory workers, and knowledge was the sword of school and university teachers. This indicates that Ibn Taymiya considered jihad the defensive duty of every able Muslim, and that it could take varying shapes and forms. It could take the form of warring, spying, educating, writing, advising, transmitting, security, farming, medicine, food production, transporting, embargoing, interpreting, and other non-physical conflict. It could take the form of a cold war, a war of words, or psychological warfare, and it could take the form of persuasion.[81]

Thus, Ibn Taymiya's concept of jihad was clearly different from that of al-Qa'ida, which considers jihad to refer only to physical hostilities, characterized mainly by suicide bombing, killing civilians, destroying property, kidnapping civilians for ransom, and stealing money and personal property to finance jihad. These are crimes and not the jihad approved by Ibn Taymiya.

Ibn Taymiya divided the penalties decreed in Islamic law into two categories: penalties to be executed on person(s) completely subjugated to the ruler; and penalties to be executed on those rebellious individuals or groups who cannot be subjugated except through fighting or force. He classified jihad as part of the latter category. To him, if the country is attacked, jihad becomes an urgent duty for Muslims to defend themselves, their honor, their property, and their country. Based on the Qur'an, which declared, *Fight in the cause of God those who fight you, but do not transgress limits* (2:190), *[a]nd fight them until there is no more tumult or oppression* (Qur'an 8:39), Ibn Taymiya considered jihad a defensive duty against aggression.[82]

With reference to the destruction of Baghdad and Damascus, Ibn Taymiya emphasized that any able Muslims summoned to defend their country, who refused to do so, should be regarded as rebels, to be fought against until there was no more civil discord. He stressed that if the people do not defend their life and property, there will be no one to defend them. Since jihad was lawful warfare against aggression, then anyone who refused jihad would be considered a rebel against their country, their government, and their army, and should be fought—a view that is agreed upon by all Muslims. At any rate, those who do not defend their property and country are those who will suffer the negative consequences of their apathy and infidelity. He supported his view with reference to the following Hadith: "If the guilt was kept secret, it would be injurious only to its author; but when it is made public—and no one combats it—then it would be injurious to the community at large."[83]

Who is the Enemy?
As for those who should be fought, Ibn Taymiya distinguished between the People of the Book and others who do not have a revealed book or scriptures. He defined the People of the Book as the Jews and Christians, but named those who have received no scriptures "unbelievers." In either case, he emphasized that Muslims should only fight aggressors, and that jihad is not decreed in order to be used against everyone, but only against aggression. He stated:

> We should fight those who fight us. *God said: And fight in the way of God against those who fight against you but be not aggressive, Surely God loves not the aggressors* (Qur'an 2:190). The Prophet also said: "Kill neither a *dhuriya* (women, children, and the handicapped) nor an *'asif* (hireling)."[84]

As for 'the People of the Book,' Ibn Taymiya further states: "They should be fought only for the violation of the terms of the treaties concluded with them, not because they are non-Muslims, until they embrace Islam or until they pay the tribute."[85]

This is the core of the concept of jihad in Ibn Taymiya's thought. From where, then, does al-Qa'ida's concept of jihad against the Jews and Crusaders originate? Its lack of origins in the Qur'an confirms that al-Qa'ida is seeking to deceive its audiences and followers, especially when using Ibn Taymiya or Ibn Hanbal as a point of reference. Al-Qa'ida has paraphrased the views of Ibn Taymiya and Ibn Hanbal to suit its own political ends. Both Ibn Taymiya and Ibn Hanbal excluded non-combatants from intentional harm,[86] but al-Qa'ida has included them (women, children, men of religion, the elderly, the permanently disabled, and those who are not able to hold defensive or offensive power).

There is strong juridical support for the argument that the practices of the Prophet and his policy on war were based on the basic attitude of defense, and not offense. According to a number of classical works, the precedents of the Prophet do not support wars of aggression.[87] The Prophet and his followers were persecuted severely for many years, while there was no order to fight back. His followers asked for his permission to fight, but he rejected their calls because there was as yet no higher order. It was not until the higher order permitted them to defend themselves that the Battle of Badr in 624 occurred. Thus, jihad of aggression is supported by neither the Qur'an nor the Prophet.

It is well known that the Prophet did not fight foreign wars, except on two occasions: once when he was compelled to do so because of the assassination of his envoy to the court of Busra; and the second when he invaded Tabuk as a defensive measure to counter an overwhelming and immediate danger of attack by the Byzantine emperor.[88]

History is also on Ibn Taymiya's side in confirming that jihad is solely a defensive duty. For example, he referred to the defense of Medina against the blockade made by Quraysh to take over the city, stating that "God permitted none to abandon the jihad to defend Medina, although he did permit them not to pursue the enemy after the siege was raised."[89]

Defending Medina was jihad, or as Ibn Taymiya put it, "jihad to defend the country, the religion, the family, and the lives of community." This "defense type" is what "duty permitted to do" and "this is obligatory. However, to hunt or pursue the enemy after their siege around Medina has been left was not permitted."[90] Thus, Ibn Taymiya's concept of jihad is clearly different from that of al-Qaʻida, which involves attacking civilians and destroying property beyond the oasis and seas. Hence, references to Ibn Taymiya in al-Qaʻida's literature should be evaluated carefully and within the appropriate context.

Turning to the caliphate's internal affairs during the wars against the invaders, Ibn Taymiya focused on the rebellions and pointed out the jurists' variant views on the matter. He noted that the rebels were those Muslims who did not follow or submit to the rule of law and its establishments and institutions. At that time, the rule was the rule of the shariʻa law. Ibn Taymiya here refers to the fundamentals, which are both explicit and general and include prayer, *zakat* (tax), fasting, and others. Ibn Taymiya described how the jurists agreed that he or she who neglects the fundamentals should be brought to justice and dealt with according to the law. If he or she agrees to abide by these duties and prohibitions, charges against him or her should be dropped. If a rebel initiates a fight or attack (like al-Qa'ida and similar groups), fighting him becomes an urgent duty. Ibn Taymiya considers the Kharijis and similar warring factions to be lawbreakers who should be fought unless they submit to the law and its institutions.[91]

Ibn Taymiya's influence on al-Qa'ida's ideologues should also be considered within the appropriate context. Ibn Taymiya has influenced scholars in various disciplines, both of his own and of later generations. According to Chamberlain, during his time Ibn Taymiya's influence illustrated his versatility and capacity to work in any environment.[92] He was the man of the people and the mind of the state. He developed a strong relationship with King al-Nasir Muhammad ibn Qalawun (d. 1341), who came to power three times. A group of his students, including al-Amir Zayn al-Din Katabagha al-'Adili (d. 1321), Sayf al-Din Buraq (d. 1356), and Salih al-Din al-Takriti (d. 1341), were from the ruling elite and were devoted to his teachings. Other supporters, such as Fakhr al-Din al-Sa'igh (d. 1341), were judges.[93] The eminent scholars al-Dhahabi (d. 1348) and Ibn Kathir (d. 1372) were Shafi'i scholars who were influenced by Ibn Taymiya. In addition to their mastery of the Arabic language and literature, they were prominent imams, head of Hadith masters, perspicacious critics and expert examiners of Hadith, encyclopedic historians and biographers, and foremost authorities on the canonical readings of the Qur'an. If these were Shafi'i scholars, others like Imam Ibn al-Qayyim (d. 1350) and Ibn Muflih, the judge of Damascus and its ambassador to Tamerlane in 1400, were Hanbali scholars.[94] Al-Zar'i was an eminent Asha'irite scholar, while al-Tufi (1361) claimed to be Shi'i, but both studied under Ibn Taymiya.[95] Despite the differences in their interests and backgrounds, these scholars were all influenced by Ibn Taymiya's creed and the clarity of his approach and thought.

The influence of Ibn Taymiya was widely felt among members of his own generation and those that followed, including ours. The following examples of those who have shared his influence involve a number of the leading Hanbali scholars of their times. They were selected from different generations only to illustrate the unbroken chain of transmission: al-Mizzi (d. 1341), al-Dhahabi (1347), Ibn al-Qaiyyim (d. 1350), Ibn Kathir (d. 1373), Ibn Abi al-'Izz (d. 1390), al-Jura'i (d. 1478), Ibn Muflih (d. 1479), al-Mardawi (d. 1480), al-Hajjawi (d. 1561), al-Futuhi (d. 1564), al-Karmi (d. 1624), al-Buhuti (d. 1641), and Ibn 'Abd al-Wahhab (d. 1792).

Ibn 'Abd al-Wahhab revised his Wahhabist tract, which influenced later scholars, including the Saudi scholars al-Sa'di (d. 1956) and Ibn 'Uthaymin (1928–2000). Later, al-Qa'ida scholars and ideologues such as 'Abdullah 'Azzam, Dr. Fadl, Ayman al-Zawahiri, Muhammad ibn 'Abdullah al-Mas'ari, al-Maqdisi, and Abu Bakr Naji consulted those earlier scholars, reappropriated views and rulings, and applied them to different environments and different contexts, as will be detailed in the subsequent chapters.

It is imperative to note that the extent of Ibn Taymiya's influence differs from one scholar to another. Indeed, citation of Ibn Taymiya's opinions by scholars does not necessarily mean they were influenced by or agree with them. For example, some Hanbali scholars like Ibn al-Qayyim, who was inseparable from Ibn Taymiya, and later, al-Sa'di, do not cite a great deal from the writings of their master Ibn Taymiya, but they were clearly influenced by him. Other scholars such as Ibn Muflih and al-Mardawi cite a great deal of Ibn Taymiya's opinions without evidence of much impact on their own jurisprudential opinions. Some scholars, therefore, were more profoundly influenced than others by his overall methodology. In this regard, the influence of Ibn Taymiya on Ibn 'Abd al-Wahhab is significant, but this does not necessarily indicate that Ibn 'Abd al-Wahhab followed Ibn Taymiya or Ibn Hanbal. We know that Ibn Taymiya rejected many rulings attributed to Ibn Hanbal as false. Conversely, there are many accounts indicating that Ibn 'Abd al-Wahhab subscribed to certain opinions with which Ibn Taymiya disagreed.

Wahhabism

Wahhabism has achieved great momentum in contemporary Islam, particularly in terms of its connotations of violence and terrorism. However, the Saudis claim that the core of Wahhabism is purification, while some critics of Wahhabism have argued that religious purification is used as a prescription for the present Islamic radicalism. The former Saudi ambassador in London emphasized that "from our view in the Saudi kingdom, there is nothing called Wahhabism."[96]

In the aftermath of September 11, the U.S. authorities outlawed a number of Saudi charity associations and criticized some segments of the curricula taught in Saudi schools. In this regard, the Saudi authorities said that they have revised the list of books taught in their schools. This, however, did not convince their education official, Hasan al-Maliki, who rejected their claim and said "they teach to the students that whoever differs from the Wahhabi interpretation is either a *kafir* or a deviated person who must repent or be killed."[97]

The Saudi kingdom cooperated with the U.S. in financing the war or jihad against the Soviets in Afghanistan and trained the jihadists there. Afghanistan then became the pot into which jihadist groups of varying colors melted together to produce a new movement called al-Qa'ida. Al-Qa'ida is a transnational network whose ideological framework is formulated by ideologues from varying cultural backgrounds, with Wahhabism as the indisputably leading ideology. Hence, "the genie had emerged from the bottle and those who are concerned could not put it back in."[98]

Wahhabism refers to the ideology and the movement founded by the Saudi scholar Muhammad ibn 'Abd al-Wahhab (1703–92). His scholarship is widely considered as an important root of fundamentalism in the modern age. During his time, most of the Arab territories formed parts of the Ottoman Empire (1300–1924). The Ottomans were Muslims and stood for Islam, not as the *salaf* (ancestors) were supposed to have conceived it, but as it had developed over those centuries of disputed ideas.[99] Accordingly, the Wahhabi movement, launched in central Arabia, aimed to bring purity to religion. The legacy of Ibn 'Abd al-Wahhab has since been encapsulated in the term 'Wahhabism.' The followers of Ibn 'Abd al-Wahhab consider Wahhabism to be a term coined by their enemies to connote their deviation from mainstream Islam.

The teachings of Ibn 'Abd al-Wahhab came under the spotlight after the terrorist events of September 11, 2001. Ibn 'Abd al-Wahhab's teaching is new to some, but for others it is not. In addition, there are some who can see a similarity between the pattern of action of the Wahhabis and that of modern radical groups such as al-Qa'ida. As the majority of the perpetrators of September 11 were Saudi nationals, who were born and educated in Saudi Arabia, Wahhabism became one of the pressing issues of concern. Bin Laden, the former leader of al-Qa'ida, was himself a wealthy Saudi national who was born and educated in Saudi Arabia. These facts led some to consider the influence of Ibn 'Abd al-Wahhab's teachings on Bin Laden, while others considered Ibn 'Abd al-Wahhab to be the godfather of Bin Laden.

Hence, Wahhabism has been criticized by its opponents as the intolerant and puritanical ideology that influenced Bin Laden and his conspirators and provided some Muslims with the ideological and intellectual tools to express their anger and hatred. Conversely, Wahhabism is considered by its adherents (Wahhabis) to be one of the main Islamic schools of thought, and they view Ibn 'Abd al-Wahhab as one of the most prominent Muslim reformers of his time. Wahhabis have always referred to their master, Ibn 'Abd al-Wahhab, with titles such as 'imam' (political and religious leader), 'Sheikh al-Islam' (religious authority), and *'mujaddid'* (renewer or restorer). In the words of a Wahhabi, Ibn 'Abd al-Wahhab is "Sheikh al-Islam [and] a renowned religious scholar and a great reformer of his time."[100] It is in the context of these connotations that Ibn 'Abd al-Wahhab's grandson sees Wahhabism as the only "true Islam," and the non-Wahhabi others as not true Muslims.[101]

Wahhabism, like 'Ibadism, is among those unique Islamic movements that incorporated some specific elements of the Khariji and Hanbali ideas, embodied in the thought of Ibn Taymiya, into modern Islamic movements, including al-Qa'ida networks. It is difficult to believe that modern Islamic movements were born out of a vacuum. In other words, modern Islamic movements constitute a rebirth and thus an extension of historical Islamic ideologies, which were embodied in such Islamic movements as those of the Kharijis, the 'Ibadis, the Hanbalis, and the Wahhabis. The Wahhabi movement is an inseparable link in the chain of Islamic movements that connect medieval to modern Islamic thought.

Muhammad ibn 'Abd al-Wahhab was born in al-'Uyayna, a town located at al-Yamama in the province of Najd, seventy kilometers northwest of Riyadh, the capital city of today's Saudi Arabia. His brother was a Hanbali scholar and his father was a Hanbali judge, who exercised his rulings based on the Hanbali school of jurisprudence. The School of Ibn Hanbal (780–855), previously discussed, was prominent in the Najd area during the time of Ibn 'Abd al-Wahhab. He studied first with his father and then moved to the centers of learning in the surrounding territories. He visited Mecca, Zubayr, Ahsa, and Medina, spending four years in each. He then traveled to the centers of Basra, Kufa, and Baghdad (all in modern-day Iraq). Whether or not 'Abd al-Wahhab visited Damascus is still in dispute, but Wahhabi opinion dictates that he proceeded from Damascus to study philosophy in Hamadan, Qum, and Isfahan (in Iran).[102]

While in Basra, the young Ibn 'Abd al-Wahhab fell under the influence of an undercover British spy nicknamed 'Humphrey' who was one of many spies (such as George Belcoud and Henry Fanse) sent by London to the Arab countries to destabilize the Ottoman Empire. Humphrey is referred to by numerous authors as the man who inspired Ibn 'Abd al-Wahhab and shaped his extreme tenets of Wahhabism.[103] In its colonies, Britain usually followed the strategy of divide and conquer—that is, the fostering of diverse groups or sects and encouraging them to stand against each other, so that colonial Britain might exploit such divisions to dominate colonized peoples. Humphrey learned to speak Turkish and some Arabic while in London. Before receiving the order for the Basra assignment, he was sent to Istanbul and, as he said, "pretended to be [a] Muslim" named "Muhammad," and came "to work in Turkey and to live in the shadow of the caliphate, the representative of the Prophet Muhammad. Indeed, this was the pretext I used to stay in Istanbul."[104]

During his two-year stay in Istanbul, Humphrey worked as a carpenter and learned Arabic, and studied the Qur'an and Hadith under the tutelage of a scholar called Ahmad Effendi. Humphrey related:

One day I said to Ahmad Effendi, my parents are dead. I do not have any brothers or sisters, and I have not inherited any property. I came to the centre of Islam to work for a living and to learn the Holy Qur'an and the Sunna, that is, to earn both my worldly needs and my life in the Hereafter. He was delighted with the words of mine, and said: "You deserve to be respected for these three reasons."[105]

Humphrey stated that he used to send his "reports" of "observation monthly to the Ministry of Colonies" in London. After returning to London, Humphrey was once again assigned to serve his country, this time from Basra. Among the aims of Humphrey's mission in Basra, as he later revealed, was "to discover the Muslims' weak points and the points through which we can enter their bodies and disjoin their limbs. Indeed this is the way to beat the enemy."[106] With these colonial tactics, the British hoped to pit the Arabs against the Turks. The British knew, as explained by Humphrey, that religion is useful and that Ibn 'Abd al-Wahhab was an easy target. In his memoir, Humphrey stated:

One day, in the Ministry of Colonies, I made a conference to the difference between the Sunnis and the Shiites, saying, if Muslims knew something about life, they would resolve this Shiite–Sunni difference among themselves and come together. Someone interrupted me and remonstrated, "Your duty is to provoke this difference, not to think of how to bring Muslims together."[107]

In Basra, Humphrey used all the information he had already collected about Istanbul, the names of his teachers, the name of the mosque where he used to pray, and the name of the mosque's imam. Deploying his skills as a spy, his ability to speak both Turkish and Arabic, his knowledge of the Qur'an and Hadith, and of some Islamic and Arabic traditions, Humphrey, as he said, "managed to survive" when he was "subjected" to a "shower of questions." In Basra, he had to show the Basrans that he was a Muslim from Istanbul who prayed in that mosque behind that imam, and show them that he had knowledge of the Qur'an and Hadith. He then began to go to the mosque and pray with them. The Basrans believed him, although he had no passport or any other form of identification. He then worked as an "assistant to a carpenter" and lived in a room rented from a Mr. Murshid Effendi, before moving to live at his workplace, which was owned by a "Mr Abd-ur-Rida, a Shiite from Khorassan, Iran." Humphrey took advantage of his "company" with Abd-ur-Rida, and began to "learn Persian." The workplace, owned by Abd-ur-Rida, was the place where "the Shiites would meet and talk on various subjects from politics to economy."[108] It was at Abd-ur-Rida's place that Humphrey met the young Muhammad ibn 'Abd al-Wahhab and a relationship between them began. In this regard, Humphrey says:

> From time to time a young man would call at our carpenter's shop. His attirement was that of a student doing scientific research, and he understood Arabic, Persian, and Turkish. His name was Muhammad bin 'Abd al-Wahhab al-Najdi [from the Najd area]. This youngster was an extremely rude and very nervous person. While abusing the Ottoman government very much, he would never speak ill of the Iranian government. The common ground that made him and the shop-owner Abd-ur-Rida so friendly was that both were inimical toward the caliphate in Istanbul. But how was it possible that this

young man, who was a Sunni, understood Persian and was friends with Abd-ur-Rida, who was a Shiite? In this city Sunnis pretended to be friendly and even brotherly with Shiites. Most of the city's inhabitants understood both Arabic and Persian. And most people understood Turkish as well.[109]

Humphrey found in Ibn 'Abd al-Wahhab the qualities of the person that he was looking for. In the words of Humphrey: "Muhammad of Najd was the sort I had been looking for. For his scorn for the time's scholars, his slighting even the (earliest) four Caliphs, his having an independent view in understanding the Qur'an and the Sunna were his most vulnerable points to hunt and obtain him."[110]

Humphrey then "established a very intimate friendship with Ibn 'Abd al-Wahhab" and they became "brothers." In connection to this, Humphrey once said to Ibn 'Abd al-Wahhab:

> I have heard that the Prophet made his companions *(ashab)* brothers to one another. Upon his positive reply, I wanted to know if this Islamic rule is temporary or permanent. He explained, "It is permanent." Then I offered him to be my brother. So, we were brothers. From that day on, I never left him alone. We were together even in his travels—I was sending monthly reports to the Ministry of Colonies in London. The answers I received were very encouraging and reassuring. Muhammad of Najd was following the path I had drawn for him.[111]

During their travels, Humphrey showered Ibn 'Abd al-Wahhab with money and other pleasant and luxurious gifts. He found Ibn 'Abd al-Wahhab to be "a Sunni outwardly" who was also of the view that "there was no reason for Sunnis to adapt themselves to one of the four *madhhabs* (schools of thought). Allah's Book does not contain any evidence pertaining to these *madhhabs*."[112] Acting as a good, practicing Muslim, Humphrey claimed that he was able to convince Ibn 'Abd al-Wahhab that he was the only one who understood Islam correctly, as the Prophet Muhammad had understood it. He also convinced Ibn 'Abd al-Wahhab that the Prophet loved him. Humphrey said that he told Ibn 'Abd al-Wahhab about his dream. In Humphrey's own words (translated from the Turkish):

One day I fabricated the following dream: Last night I dreamed of our Prophet. I addressed him with the attributes I had learned. He was seated on a dais and around him were scholars that I did not know. You [pointing at Ibn ʻAbd al-Wahhab] entered. Your face was as bright as halos; you walked toward the Prophet, and when you were close enough, the Prophet stood up and kissed you between your both eyes. He [the Prophet] said, "You [Ibn ʻAbd al-Wahhab] are my namesake, the heir to my knowledge, my deputy in worldly and religious matters." You said, "O Messenger of Allah! I am afraid to explain my knowledge to people." "You are the greatest. Don't be afraid," replied the Prophet. Ibn ʻAbd al-Wahhab was wild with joy when he heard the dream—He was sure I had told him the truth. I think, from then on, he was resolved to publicize the ideas I had imbued him with and to establish a new sect.[113]

Subsequently, Humphrey attempted to explain his dream by viewing it in the context of the idea that Muslims are ignorantly on the "wrong side" of the teaching of the Prophet. Therefore, on this account, Muslims are weak and currently on the "decline" while Christians are "gaining ascendancy." Muslims have gone "astray" and must come "back" or be "fought" and "killed" because they are no longer Muslims.[114]

The question of Britain's interaction with the Ottoman Empire in general, and with Wahhabism in particular, can be gleaned from today's Internet technology. One need only type in a few key words or phrases, such as 'British and Wahhabism,' on any search engine to find an answer. Many websites point to the British influence on the rise of Ibn ʻAbd al-Wahhab and Wahhabism, similar to the question of who created Bin Laden and introduced him and his jihadism onto the world stage, and to the question of who 'made' Khomeini and Saddam Hussein. One might also ask who encouraged certain religious factions to oppose each other, as is the case in many scenarios involving conflict currently taking place in Iraqi towns and cities, from Basra to Anbar and from Samurra to Baghdad. If Ibn ʻAbd al-Wahhab took the bait once, Saddam took it twice: first to go after Iran and second to go after Kuwait, until finally he himself was caught like a wild rat. In either case, neither the responsibilities of Saddam nor those of Ibn ʻAbd al-Wahhab can be laid at the doorstep of others. Ibn ʻAbd al-Wahhab's ideology cannot be placed on the shoulders of either the British or Humphrey. In other words,

Ibn 'Abd al-Wahhab must be seen as wholly responsible for creating the ideological movement that is Wahhabism.

The British role in creating and supporting Ibn 'Abd al-Wahhab is outlined in a number of documents, among which is "Memoirs of Mr. Humphrey."[115] These were serialized in *Der Spiegel*, and later in a prominent French newspaper, and translated into Arabic by a Lebanese intellectual, as well as into many other languages. Humphrey was one of the British colonial office intelligence operatives and was mentioned in the book *Mir'at al-Haramayn* (The Mirror of the Two Holy Mosques), written by Ayyub Sabri Basha in 1888.

Ibn 'Abd al-Wahhab's travel sketches are also interesting. He traveled to Medina to find it still an important center of Islamic knowledge and intellectual exchange, one which attracted scholars and students from every corner in the Muslim world. In Medina, he studied under the tutelage of 'Abdullah ibn Ibrahim ibn Sayf from al-Majmaa oasis in Sadair. Ibn 'Abd al-Wahhab was later to say about his teacher: "The sheikh once asked me, "Do you want to see the weapon I have prepared for al-Majmaa?" "Yes," I replied. He brought me to a house where many books were stored and said, "This is the weapon I have prepared. "[116]

These books, as implied by Ibn 'Abd al-Wahhab, were the ideological weapons that his teacher had prepared to combat what he saw as innovations and which had come to be seen as the essential beliefs and religious habits of his compatriots. It is useful here to note that among the scholars who also studied with Ibn 'Abd al-Wahhab under 'Abdullah ibn Ibrahim ibn Sayf was Muhammad Hayat al-Sindi (a well-known scholar from Sind in India), and Shah Waliyyuallah al-Delhawi (from Delhi in India, who, like Ibn 'Abd al-Wahhab, was born in 1703).[117] This may indicate how certain ideas that are similar to what has come to be called Wahhabism traveled to India. After Medina, Ibn 'Abd al-Wahhab traveled to Baghdad, where he married a wealthy woman and settled down for five years, before he moved to Iran to undertake further studies and met Humphrey before returning to his home town al-'Uyayna in the Najd region.[118]

In the beginning, Ibn 'Abd al-Wahhab's teachings were not new, but had been preached by others. Through his scholarly family and through his travels and studies in Arabia, as well as in Ottoman Iraq and Syria, he had felt the influence of the school of Ibn Hanbal, which was embodied in the thought of Ibn Taymiya. When Ibn 'Abd al-Wahhab started to teach, as Humphrey explained, he denounced Ottoman rule, Ottoman Islam, and the Ottoman Empire all at the same time. According to Albert Hourani (d. 1993), Ibn 'Abd al-Wahhab drew his inspiration from the Hanbali school as handed down to him and proclaimed that Islam does not take the form of mere words or imitation of what others have said, stating that on Judgment Day, it will not be enough to plead "I heard people saying something, and I said it too."[119] In his opinion, Muslims must discover the true nature of Islam. Islam overall is a rejection of all gods except God, a refusal to allow others, be they "king or Prophet, or saint, or tree or tomb," to share in the worship. To worship pious men is as bad as worshiping idols, and it is not simply words and thoughts that constitute *shirk* (associating partners with God), but also the will and the actions that imply it—"a man's will to do the acts of this [material] world is a form of *shirk*."[120]

Ibn 'Abd al-Wahhab saw that his exegesis and the call for a return to the authoritative texts (the Qur'an and Hadith) had become highly influential. Hence, true Islam is the Islam of the first generation, the pious forerunners *(al-salaf al-salih)* and the companions of the Prophet. In their name, Ibn 'Abd al-Wahhab protested against all those who encouraged innovations that were not prevalent in seventh-century Arabia. Those innovations, in Ibn 'Abd al-Wahhab's view, brought other gods into Islam. Against such innovations, Ibn 'Abd al-Wahhab interpreted Islam with a firm exclusiveness that was alien to his masters, both Ibn Hanbal and Ibn Taymiya. He was strictly literalist and uncompromising, and applied his ideas with an aggressive and intolerant approach that went far beyond the canon for which his pioneers and his contemporaries, including his brother and his father, as well as later scholars, stood.[121]

Ibn 'Abd al-Wahhab's focus on Ibn Taymiya did not mean that he absorbed the latter's views or that their beliefs were identical.[122] Teachers cannot be in any way held responsible for whatever notions their students may subsequently develop, and neither can the essential constituents of Ibn 'Abd al-Wahhab's teachings be retrospectively imposed onto his pioneers or on Ibn Taymiya's teachings. There is no doubt that Ibn Taymiya was a far more rigorous and careful thinker and an infinitely more prolific scholar than was Ibn 'Abd al-Wahhab. Among the key differences between the two men is that the medieval thought of Ibn Taymiya is important to the modern reformist movement led by Jamal al-Din al-Afghani (d. 1897) and Muhammad 'Abduh (d. 1905).[123] In addition, the form of Ibn Taymiya's opposition to Sufism is different, for it was not a total rejection, but rather an objection to certain aspects of Sufism that he regarded as immoral or incompatible with Islam. Ibn 'Abd al-Wahhab's rejection of Sufism was broader, however, and not merely a rejection of certain aspects of Sufi behavior. It should not surprise us that Ibn Taymiya was himself an initiator of the Qadiriya order,[124] and was buried in the graveyard of the Sufis with his brother Sharaf al-Din 'Abdullah.[125]

Further, anyone familiar with their works knows that Ibn 'Abd al-Wahhab abridged some of Ibn Taymiya's writings, among which was *Minhaj al-sunna* (The Way of the Sunna). He also abridged some of the works of Ibn Taymiya's students, especially those of Ibn al-Qayyim. For example, Ibn 'Abd al-Wahhab's book *Mabhath al-ijtihad wa-l-ikhtilaf* (Research in Legal Reasoning and Difference) is an abridged version of Ibn al-Qayyim's book *I'lam al-muwaqqi'in* (Informing the Signatories). He also abridged the book *al-Insaf fi ma'rifat al-rajih min al-khilaf* (The Equity in the Knowledge of the Preferred from the Controversial), written by Ibn Taymiya's student 'Ala al-Din al-Mardawi, with the aim of accurately identifying Ibn Hanbal's opinions. Ibn 'Abd al-Wahhab was selective in his choice of what works to abridge, and attempted to draw on the thought of his predecessors to develop his own political position.

Ibn 'Abd al-Wahhab's books comprise a general collection of raw materials without any commentary, mostly drawn from the Qur'an and Hadith. His most important book, *Kitab al-tawhid* (The Book of Monotheism), for example, is described by its translator Isma'il al-Faruqi (d. 1986) as having "the appearance of a student's notes."[126] As this and others of Ibn 'Abd al-Wahhab's books are available to me, I can confirm that al-Faruqi's description can be applied to other writings of Ibn 'Abd al-Wahhab. Overall, Ibn 'Abd al-Wahhab did not, out of the raw materials, create as many works as one might think. He was occupied more by the affairs of the newly established Wahhabi state (the Wahhabi state was not officially adopted in Saudi Arabia until 1932).[127] Therefore, his authorship of jurisprudence is composed merely of various raw materials, the majority of which are from the Qur'an and Hadith, compiled into two small volumes with large Arabic font, and published in Saudi Arabia by the University of the Imam. Seeking to reform his society, Ibn 'Abd al-Wahhab revealed that his methodological approach was not focused on writing or on educating people, but rather was grounded in the social and physical worlds, in a way that has widely been described as radical. Indeed, he implemented his opinions by force.[128]

Accordingly, when Ibn 'Abd al-Wahhab returned to Najd he joined his father in the town of al-'Uyayna and began to voice his criticism of innovation *(bid'a)* and what he considered to be *shirk*. In this regard, his father, 'Abd al-Wahhab, apparently did not share his son's views and rejected his method of imposing them on people. Ibn 'Abd al-Wahhab's brother Sulayman also did not accept all of his brother's teachings, and led the opposition movement against him for a long time. Thus, Ibn 'Abd al-Wahhab's teachings were, in some respects, contrary to the teachings of his father and brother, both leading Islamic scholars of their time. According to 'Uthman ibn 'Abdullah ibn Bishr, a Saudi historian who wrote a standard Saudi chronicle, the father discussed these matters with his son and "words were exchanged between them" *(waqa'a baynahu wa bayna ibnihi kalam)*.[129] Here, the son's methodological approach to reform created a rift between him and both his brother and father, as well as some of the inhabitants of al-'Uyayna. Muhammad ibn 'Abd al-Wahhab's most credited and learned grandson, Sheikh 'Abd al-Rahman ibn Hasan ibn Muhammad ibn 'Abd al-Wahhab, similarly claimed that "exchange *(niza'*, or 'dispute') of words and arguments *(jidal)* between him [Ibn 'Abd al-Wahhab] and the people, including his learned father ['Abd al-Wahhab] took place."[130]

Ibn 'Abd al-Wahhab's radicalism, according to the Saudi chronicler Ibn Bishr, resulted in the removal of his father from the judgeship *(al-qada')* in al-'Uyayna. In another version of the story, Ibn 'Abd al-Wahhab's father had been removed from his judgeship in al-'Uyayna by the ruler of the time, Muhammad ibn Mu'ammar, for reasons that remain unclear. Whatever happened, the father "changed residence" from al-'Uyayna to the nearby town of Huraymila in 1726.[131] Ibn 'Abd al-Wahhab followed his father to Huraymila, but restrained his political activity by remaining "low key" until his father died in 1740.[132]

The death of his father released Ibn 'Abd al-Wahhab from all constraints on standing for what he believed was right. Now the son saw himself as *the* sheikh who could take his father's position of the judgeship and annihilate all that he considered to be *"shirk* and innovation." This status in religious and political circles has persisted, and in contemporary Saudi Arabia, Ibn 'Abd al-Wahhab's view of himself has spread into society's consciousness. He *is* seen as *the* sheikh, and his progeny bear the title 'Al al-Sheikh' (family of the Sheikh). With his great ambition to destroy *shirk*, Ibn 'Abd al-Wahhab decided to achieve his objective by any means, even if this required the use of force. In this regard, the anonymous author who introduced Ibn 'Abd al-Wahhab's most important book *Kitab al-tawhid*, which was published in Riyadh by Dar al-Salam (1996), wrote:

> The Sheikh was resolved to make every effort to *fight* against the circumstances to the extent of jihad. He urged the 'ulama (scholars) to strictly follow the Qur'an and the Sunna and derive the issues directly from them. He forcibly contradicted the blind following of any scholar of the *umma* in preference to the Qur'an and Hadith.[133]

The language used here confirms that Ibn 'Abd al-Wahhab's pattern of reform consisted of using force and jihad against all people including the 'ulama. It is important to note that the above quotation is taken from the introduction, written by an author who preferred to conceal his or her identity. This unknown author believed that it was sufficient to mention the name of Ibn 'Abd al-Wahhab rather than his/her own name. The introduction was entitled "Sheikh al-Islam Muhammad ibn 'Abd al-Wahhab—a Renowned Reviver and Great Reformer." Under this title, this mystery author devoted eight pages (9–16) to Ibn 'Abd al-Wahhab's introduction and his *Kitab al-tawhid* (Book of Monotheism) to readers of English. There is no indication that the publisher wrote this section. Indeed, the publisher only provided two pages (7–8) of his own notes, signing off with his name, 'Abd al-Malik Mujahid, and identifying his position as "General Manager, Dar-us-Salam Publications."

Thus, the anonymous author wrote the introduction as though Ibn 'Abd al-Wahhab himself were introducing the book to its readers. However, one must ask why the author of the introduction felt it necessary to conceal his/her name. Such concealment of an author's identity, even for a short piece of writing, is unacceptable, and raises questions about the authenticity of the book and its author. However, identifying complete data (that is, author, publisher, and year and place of publication) is problematic for some Arabic sources, including Ibn 'Abd al-Wahhab's literature (that is, books written by Ibn 'Abd al-Wahhab or attributed to him).[134]

Whether or not the introducer of Ibn 'Abd al-Wahhab's *Kitab al-tawhid* is him/herself a Wahhabi is not known, but their use of certain key words and phrases in the introduction, such as 'fight,' 'jihad,' 'forcibly,' and 'urged the 'ulama',' is revealing. The force and intent of these words in the context of the preferred title, "Sheikh al-Islam Muhammad ibn 'Abd al-Wahhab—a Renowned Reviver and Great Reformer," clearly emphasizes the radical methodology of Ibn 'Abd al-Wahhab's pattern of reform. It also points to the causes of the rift that he created between himself and his father, the 'ulama, and the inhabitants of al-'Uyayna and Huraymila.

Due to his radical understanding of reform (that is, through the way of "jihad, fighting, and force"), Ibn 'Abd al-Wahhab was politically ordered to leave Huraymila. He gathered some followers and was able to secure a return to al-'Uyayna under conditions that he found far more favorable than the conditions he faced when he had been compelled to leave the same town fifteen years earlier. At that time, al-'Uyayna's ruler was 'Uthman ibn Mu'ammar, who found it of value to extend his protection to Ibn 'Abd al-Wahhab. The alliance was strengthened also by Ibn 'Abd al-Wahhab's marriage to Jawhara, "the aunt of the ruler 'Uthman ibn Mu'ammar."[135]

Protected by the ruler, Ibn 'Abd al-Wahhab gradually embarked on preaching his understanding of *tawhid*. In this regard, the Saudi mufti and government scholar Shaykh 'Abdul 'Aziz ibn 'Abdullah ibn Baz (d. 1999) has emphasized that when Ibn 'Abd al-Wahhab aligned with this ruler, the state protected him and provided him with the power he needed to achieve his objectives. Ibn 'Abd al-Wahhab's pattern of reform is described by Ibn Baz in the following words:

> He [Ibn 'Abd al-Wahhab] knew that nothing could be achieved without jihad. When he noticed that his call to Islam had no affect on some, one day, the Sheikh said to the governor, "Let us demolish the dome at the grave of Zaid ibn al-Khattab (Zaid was the brother of 'Umar ibn al-Khattab [the second caliph] and a martyr who died in the fighting against Musaylima al-Khadhdhab [Musaylima the Fallen Prophet] in AH 12)." The Prince agreed and mobilized an army of six hundred soldiers headed by the Sheikh [Ibn 'Abd al-Wahhab] and marched toward the grave. As soon as they approached the dome, the people came forward to defend it but when they saw the Prince with his army, they changed their decision. Then, the Sheikh took the action of demolishing and removing the dome. God removed it by his hands, thanks to God; none of its traces remains now. Similarly, there

were other domes, caves, trees, and so on that were also destroyed and removed. The Sheikh, thus, continued his mission by words and action for which he became very famous. In addition, one day a woman came to him and confessed that she had committed adultery. After realizing that she was sane, married, and had confessed her sin without external compulsion, he gave the order, according to the Sunna, that she should be stoned to death as a punishment.[136]

Thus, Ibn 'Abd al-Wahhab's pattern of reform involved the use of force and jihad. Whatever he said must be implemented or would be forcibly implemented. Hence, the rationality that was highlighted by the Qur'an was rejected, and human reasoning became irrelevant. To him, human reason had no right to say anything about any situation that a person might encounter. He left his writing on jihad wide open to interpretation, unlimited by the rules and conditions of Islamic shari'a. His *fatwa* (legal opinion) emphasized that the Muslims should engage in jihad against the *kuffar* (unbelievers) and *munafiqun* (hypocrites); again, this is rather a broad declaration without limitation or qualification. Ibn 'Abd al-Wahhab's notion of pragmatism was revealed in his saying that if his teachings were not followed in practice, the declaration of jihad would be necessary.[137]

Consequently, scholars and the established religious and political authorities in Najd, Mecca, and Medina came to disagree with him. They reproached his mission and rejected both his arguments and his approach. The ruler could not protect him or his marriage any longer, and expelled Ibn 'Abd al-Wahhab from the region of al-'Uyayna once again.[138]

This lack of protection in al-'Uyayna was the first step on Ibn 'Abd al-Wahhab's path to success. He left al-'Uyayna for Dir'iya, which was under the governorship of Muhammad ibn Saud (d. 1765). After his arrival, Ibn 'Abd al-Wahhab stopped preaching until he had cemented a new alliance with Muhammad ibn Saud in 1745, and sealed it with another marriage and a formal oath-taking ceremony between the two parties. Muhammad ibn Saud's son, 'Abd al-'Aziz, then married the daughter of Ibn 'Abd al-Wahhab.[139]

By marrying his daughter into the tribe of Ibn Saud, Ibn 'Abd al-Wahhab secured the alliance and initiated a process that led to the unification of a number of disparate tribes under one leadership. This pact proved permanent and established a political entity that gave rise to the first Saudi state. The alliance with Ibn Saud also ensured that Wahhabism became the religious ideology of the unification between the prevailing political entities in Arabia at the time. Everyone who joined the alliance was required to take an oath, to follow the teachings of the imam Ibn 'Abd al-Wahhab, and pay *zakat* (tax) at the rate prescribed by him.

Subsequently, Ibn 'Abd al-Wahhab created his own law enforcement body to guard public moral behavior in almost every aspect of human life, including the requirements to dress modestly and close shops to attend prayers. This law enforcement body was described as "constables for the punctuality—with an enormous staff in their hands, [who] were ordered to shout, to scold and to drag people by the shoulders to force them to take part in public prayers, five times a day."[140] This system of religious policing has continued to the present, and is currently in effect in Saudi Arabia under the title of 'Hay'at al-Amr bi-l-Ma'ruf wa-l-Nahi 'an al-Munkar' (The Organization of Commanding of Good and the Forbidding of Evil).[141]

Ibn Saud's alliance was to legitimize his military activities undertaken for the sake of state expansionism. State expansion requires additional resources such as taxation. But the people might resist the increased taxation and, therefore, might affiliate themselves with other political rivals in the region. Ibn 'Abd al-Wahhab sought to prevent Ibn Saud from levying his customary tax on the people. After some deliberation, Ibn Saud concurred with Ibn 'Abd al-Wahhab's assurance that the forthcoming jihad would yield income far in excess of any money gained through taxes. On this matter, the Saudi chronicler Ibn Bishr reported that Ibn 'Abd al-Wahhab said to Ibn Saud, "Perhaps God has in store for us, conquests and booty better than the share of the harvest."[142]

Therefore, Ibn Saud pledged that he would conduct jihad against all who did not follow Ibn 'Abd al-Wahhab's teachings. In this way, the ideological plan was sealed and the arena for jihad prepared. Therefore, when Ibn Saud began to expand his territory and conquer the people and their passions, Ibn 'Abd al-Wahhab and his followers supported him. Ibn 'Abd al-Wahhab promoted this conquest on the grounds that after Ibn Saud had completed his conquests he would focus on religious matters.[143] The Saudi forces embarked on their battle in the name of jihad and returned laden with such abundant plunder that it drew the attention of Ibn 'Abd al-Wahhab and urged him to inform his allied partner that "this is more than you get from the people of your town."[144]

Ibn 'Abd al-Wahhab considered all Muslims of his time who did not wish to share his teachings to be far worse polytheists than the people of the pre-Islamic era of *jahiliya* (ignorance). This tenet of his doctrine shocked his brother Sulayman, who highlighted 'intolerance' as a main feature of his brother's teachings. According to the Arabian historian and Mufti of Mecca, Ahmad ibn al-Zayni Dahlan (1816–86):

> Sulayman once asked his brother Muhammad, "How many are the Pillars of Islam?" "Five," he answered. Sulayman replied, "No, you have added a sixth one: He who does not follow you is not a Muslim. This, to you, is the sixth pillar of Islam."[145]

The historian and author 'Uthman ibn Sanad, who lived in Basra in the 1780s, also noted this tone of extremism:

> When Tuais, a black slave, killed Thuwayni [a sheikh from the Muntafiq tribes in the lower region of Euphrates], Saudi's adherents did not condemn the murder but praised it not only because they were convinced of Thuwayni's infidelity, but they were also convinced of the infidelity of all people on earth who did not share their views.[146]

The coalition of Ibn 'Abd al-Wahhab's theo-ideology and Ibn Saud's political ideology gave rise to a theo-political Wahhabi state that later adopted the name Saudi Arabia in 1932. The use of religion as a basis for legitimacy differentiated the House of Saud from neighboring tribes and built a base of support that helped to establish the House of Saud in the Arabian Peninsula. It is remarkable, then, to find that the twentieth-century Saudi state came to acquire a second raison d'être as a privileged instrument of foreign—first British and then U.S.—interests in the Middle East.[147]

The Saudi state's abhorrence of non-Wahhabi Muslims has manifested itself on many occasions. Emphasizing his allegiance to western powers during the twentieth century, 'Abd al-'Aziz ibn Saud, who ruled from 1902 to 1953, once told St. John ('Abdullah') Philby, his go-between with the British Foreign Office, that he preferred Christians to non-Wahhabi Muslims. Christians, Ibn Saud stated, "were of a kindred faith because they were 'people of the Book'; being believers according to their lights, they were less abhorrent to him than lax Muslims—*Mushrikin.*" Ibn Saud further explained that Christians act according to their religion, whereas Muslims who do not follow the Wahhabi understanding of *tawhid* are guilty of *shirk* (polytheism).[148]

Ibn 'Abd al-Wahhab's experience of his previous expulsions and resistance to his ideas led him to appreciate that the regime of godliness could only be established with the backing of temporal forces. Hence, if uncompromising monotheism was to be enforced, polytheism would have to be eliminated, jihad waged, 'good' ordered, evil forbidden, and the support of men of the sword would be necessary.

With the establishment of the alliance in 1745, jihad was declared, and by 1765 most of the Najd and 'Asir regions and even parts of Yemen had been conquered and subjugated under Wahhabi rule. The response of Ibn 'Abd al-Wahhab to opposition to his teachings was usually swift and uncompromising; the consequences were painful for those who stood against him. Those who opposed the Wahhabis were considered "apostate," deserving of "chastisement." For example, when Wahhabi forces set out for Jalajil in Sudayr, they ambushed the inhabitants, demolished their houses, and cut down some of their palm trees.[149]

In 1766, Muhammad ibn Saud was assassinated and succeeded by his son, 'Abd al-'Aziz. In this new era, the alliance between Ibn 'Abd al-Wahhab and the state strengthened. 'Abd al-'Aziz was married to the daughter of Ibn 'Abd al-Wahhab. 'Abd al-'Aziz renewed the alliance with his father-in-law and both men reaffirmed their declaration of jihad in the name of Wahhabism and its expansion.[150]

Embarking on jihad, Ibn 'Abd al-Wahhab and his son-in-law 'Abd al-'Aziz expanded their power and wealth. The Wahhabis considered their wealth and power to be God's reward for their faithful adherence to Islam. People other than Wahhabis were seen as disbelievers who should be overcome and whose possessions should be confiscated. With this in mind, the jihad that the Wahhabis embarked on made their state a famous center, not only for Wahhabism but also for dominant political rule over most of Arabia. Wealth, luxury, and power were among the features of the lifestyles of the powerful elite. This was evidenced, as Ibn Bishr points out, by the "possession of money, property, luxuries, herds of varying types, including rare horses and dromedaries, even arms and weapons [which] were decorated with gold and silver."[151]

This wealth and power were further augmented when Riyadh and its surroundings fell into Wahhabi possession: in 1773, the Wahhabis conquered Riyadh and made it their capital. Yet Riyadh did not mark the limits of their ambition, as their sights were set on the rest of Arabia, as well as Iraq and Syria; yet this would require more preparation and commitment.[152]

By 1773, Ibn 'Abd al-Wahhab had reached his seventies and deemed it appropriate for him to start planning for the future of religious and political authorities. Allen and Delong-Bas claim that Ibn 'Abd al-Wahhab resigned from the office of imam in 1773.[153] However, resignation had not previously existed in the lexicon of behavior in Arabic authorities and institutions. Religious and political authorities usually remain in their positions until their death, whether natural or by other means. Ibn 'Abd al-Wahhab did not therefore resign, but remained imam until his death in 1792.

Before his death, Ibn 'Abd al-Wahhab witnessed his son-in-law 'Abd al-'Aziz, the young Wahhabi, ruling over the greater part of Arabia from the center of Riyadh. The Saudi chronicler Ibn Bishr argues that Ibn 'Abd al-Wahhab, further strengthening his legacy, awarded the title of imam to his son-in-law, and entrusted him with the command over the religious, military, and economic affairs of the state.[154]

Awarding the title of imam to 'Abd al-'Aziz did not mean that Ibn 'Abd al-Wahhab had resigned. He remained the Grand Imam and the supreme authority to the extent that not a stone could be turned without his approval. In the words of Ibn Bishr, "No camels were mounted and no opinions were voiced without the approval of Ibn 'Abd al-Wahhab."[155]

'Abd al-'Aziz then became both the amir and imam of the Wahhabi state. His title of imam enhanced his leadership as Ibn 'Abd al-Wahhab's general, and distinguished him from others in Arabia. He was the top general of a wealthy and powerful state, and men of the sword were ready to execute his orders. Fearing the power of the Wahhabis and seeking their security, smaller entities joined the Wahhabis. Any individuals or groups who joined the Wahhabis were required to take an oath of loyalty and allegiance, and to observe their religion according to the Wahhabi tenets. Tribes were fully aware that the Wahhabis would conquer them, eventually:

> At the moment when they were least expected, the Wahhabis would arrive to confront the tribe they wished to subject, and a messenger would appear bearing a Qur'an in one hand and a sword in the other.

His [Ibn 'Abd al-Wahhab's] message was stark and simple: "to the Arabs of the tribe of—hail! Your duty is to believe in the book I send you. Do not be like the idolatrous Turks, who give God a human intermediary. If you are true believers, you shall be saved; otherwise, I shall wage war upon you until death."[156]

Ibn 'Abd al-Wahhab died in 1792, but his death did not temper the Wahhabi offensive in Arabia and did not diminish the Wahhabi creed or desire for conquest and wealth. In 1802, 'Abd al-'Aziz appointed his son Saud to lead a raiding cavalry and ordered them to attack Karbala, in southern Iraq, one of the holiest places for Shi'i Muslims. It contains the burial site of Imam al-Husayn ibn 'Ali, the paternal cousin of the Prophet. The attack was planned to take place on 12 May 1802 (the anniversary of 10 Muharram 1217) the day on which Shi'is gather to commemorate the martyrdom of Imam al-Husayn. This timing was aimed at inflicting maximum insult and pain upon the Shi'is. Recounting the event the Saudi chronicler Ibn Bishr said:

> Saud [son of 'Abd al-'Aziz and grandson of Ibn 'Abd al-Wahhab] set out with the divinely supported army. He made for Karbala and began hostilities against the people of the city of al-Husayn. The *Muslims* [the Wahhabis] scaled the walls, entered the city by force, and killed the majority of its people in the markets and in their homes. Then they destroyed the dome placed over the grave of al-Husayn. They took whatever they found inside the dome and its surroundings. They took the grille, which was encrusted with emeralds, rubies, and other jewels. They took everything they found in the town: different types of property, weapons, clothing, carpets, gold, silver, precious copies of the Qur'an as well as much else—more than can be enumerated. They stayed in Karbala during the morning, leaving around midday with all the property they had gathered and having killed about two thousand people. Then, Saud departed by way of al-Ma'al-Abyad. He had the booty assembled in front of him. He deducted one-fifth for himself and then distributed the rest among the *Muslims* [the Wahhabis], giving a single share to each foot soldier and a double share to each equestrian.[157]

Ibn Bishr emphasized the word 'Muslim' in the above quote to signify the Wahhabis, because Wahhabis call themselves Muslims to the exclusion of others. In addition, the language used in this account indicates the Wahhabis' pattern of what they called jihad and illustrates their approach to reform and their belief in *tawhid*. Since that time, Saud has come to be known as the 'butcher of Karbala.'[158]

Repeating this pattern of oppression, the Wahhabis dominated peoples throughout Arabia. They conquered Ta'if in February 1803, and Mecca and Medina in 1805, and annihilated those who did not wish to accept the Wahhabi creed. They committed massacres and burnt any books found other than the Qur'an and books of the Hadith. Describing their attacks against Ta'if, Ibn Bishr relates: "Their forces entered the city and took it by force but without fighting [*sic*], and killed some two hundred of its people, in the market places and in their homes. They took much property, valuable items such as coins, weapons, cloth, and jewelry, beyond all measure and computation."[159]

The Wahhabis' radicalism, and the fall of Mecca and Medina to them, was felt by the 'ulama and the public in all corners of the Ottoman Empire. The Wahhabis consolidated their power in the regions of Mecca and Medina, and shut down the pilgrimage route to Mecca. The pilgrimage caravans from Ottoman Syria and Egypt were deemed to be bearers of *shirk* and were therefore denied access to the Holy Sites. The Wahhabis were sending the message that "the Islam that the Sultan protected was not the true Islam, and that the Sultan was not the true leader of the *ummah*."[160]

Wahhabism alarmed both the Ottomans and the British. Both forces were working against each other tactically and strategically in the region. The British and the Ottomans viewed Wahhabism from different perspectives and out of different motives. The British believed that their plan to destabilize the Ottoman Empire was working well, and saw Wahhabism as another energetic factor they could exploit to ensure the success of their plan. They kept watch and left things to develop of their own accord. The Ottomans observed the Wahhabis' domination of most of Arabia as they increasingly became a threat to the political order of the Ottoman Empire in regions including Iraq and Syria along the main route to Istanbul, the center of the Empire.

In addition to their threats against the Ottoman Empire, the Wahhabis demolished the Ottoman sultan's claim that he was the Guardian of the Holy Sites of Islam. The closure of the pilgrimage routes by the Wahhabis had also removed an important source of revenue in the form of taxes for the Ottomans. At that time, the Ottoman Empire was in turmoil, as it was confronted in the east by the Wahhabi conquest, and by the Napoleonic invasion of Egypt. In the west, the Ottomans were also forced to deal with recurrent hostilities, including those from Russia and Austria.

Focusing on the Wahhabis, the Ottomans assigned Egypt's Muhammad 'Ali to the task of liberating the holy cities and reopening the pilgrimage routes to all Muslims. In 1812, Muhammad 'Ali landed at the port of Yanbu' on the Red Sea coast, and recaptured Medina. Three months later he recaptured Mecca and Riyadh, and expelled the Wahhabis from Hijaz, sending them back to the Najd region. He then followed them to Najd and captured their new capital city, al-Dir'iya, in 1818. 'Ali called the Wahhabi scholars to the Mosque of Dir'iya, where he presided over a theological debate in order to convince them of their errors. The debate lasted for four long days after which a number of the scholars were finally convinced. However, others led by Ibn 'Abd al-Wahhab's sons were not. After deliberation and the issuance of a *fatwa*, 'Ali executed two of the grandsons of Muhammad ibn 'Abd al-Wahhab. 'Abdullah ibn Saud was arrested and sent to Cairo and from there to Istanbul where he, too, was executed, based on a *fatwa* issued by Mustafa Asim Efendi, Sheikh al-Islam of the Ottoman Empire.[161]

3

From Fundamentalism
to Neo-jihadism

The transformation from fundamentalism to neo-jihadism is one of the remarkable processes of recent Islamic history. It is unrealistic to assume that Islamic extremism, which has recently grown into the most energetic force in the Middle East, emerged out of a vacuum. Contemporary Islamic extremism, rather, is the product of previous movements and has been reshaped over time in step with the shifting political climate of the Middle East. Currently, Islamic extremist movements have their own jurisprudential view and continue to push their operatives and their narratives deeper into the region and beyond. Al-Qaʻida and similar networks are distinguished by their lethal ideology, which permits the killing of civilians, Muslims and non-Muslims alike, in the name of jihad. This, however, must be seen as a neo-jihad, which Islam does not condone, but forbids both in general and specific terms. However, al-Qaʻida's ideologue and the leader of Jihad in Egypt and Afghanistan, Dr. Fadl, has outlined the "motive," the "aim" and the "importance of jihad." He labeled these items the "milestones of jihad," and stated that "We can call these milestones the "Creed of Jihadism [al-ʻaqida al-jihadiya]."[1]

In relation to this, Peter Lentini coined the term neo-jihadism to specifically denote the ideology of al-Qaʻida and similar trends, which consider their violence and terrorism as jihad and the only means to achieve their political goals. Lentini defines neo-jihadism as follows:

> Neo-jihadism is a diverse, syncretic form of global organization and interaction that emerged from within Islam, that is unique to the late twentieth and . . . early twenty-first centuries, and through its advocacy

77

and execution of violence and selectively literal interpretations of sacred texts, radically differentiates itself from the faith's mainstream and constitutes a distinct body of thought and actions. Neo-jihadism is simultaneously a religious, political, paramilitary, and terrorist global movement, a subculture, a counterculture, and an ideology that seeks to establish states governed by laws according to the dictates of selectively literal interpretations of the Qur'an and the traditions of the Prophet Muhammad . . . through enacting violence.[2]

On this account, examples of the movements cited above include, among others, the networks that operate at the global level, such as al-Qa'ida, and regional actors like al-Jama'a al-Islamiya (JI) or those with distinct separatist orientations within established nation-states, such as those in the North Caucasus.

Further, the progression from fundamentalism to neo-jihadism can be seen as a transformative process characterized by theological and ideological challenges, as well as by cultural and even countercultural narratives and interpretations.

Medieval Islamic fundamentalist movements conducted a purely internal dialogue, centered on their understanding of Islamic principles and their prescriptions of early Islam. In engaging in this dialogue, fundamentalists did not have to consider an ideology or a system of thought, either to be compared with Islam or for the formulation of new elements. There was no examination of religious or political systems other than the Islamic system. This deficiency was not identified or felt by medieval fundamentalism perhaps because Islam was dominant and there was no rival sociopolitical system to challenge it in the Muslim territories. However, this deficiency has been acutely felt, and began to be addressed, by the fundamentalists of the modern epoch, since sociopolitical systems beyond Islam have been adopted to govern some Muslim societies.

In the modern era, the Islamic sociopolitical system had to face the rise of European powers and their influence on Muslim society. Since the eighteenth century Muslims have increasingly encountered European powers through military, as well as commercial and colonial, expansionism. The impact of European occupation on the Muslim community led to political, economic, social, intellectual, and moral conditions that resulted in the imposition of secular ideas and regimes upon Muslim culture. Thus, the shock of European colonialism played a significant role in reshaping the character of Islamic fundamentalism and compelled fundamentalists to initiate a dialogue, for comparative purposes, with respect to Islamic and European ideas and systems, political and otherwise. Thus, modern fundamentalism has participated in a dialogue, which, unlike that of its medieval ancestors, is not purely internal, but contemplates the differences and similarities between Islam and cultural others with a view to reform. Through this dialogue, modern fundamentalism has attempted to compare Islam, as a way of life, with European systems, and to articulate Islamic laws regarding freedom, equality, and social justice, and to facilitate the application of shari'a to political and other spheres of human society.[3]

Modern Islamic preachers in general, and fundamentalists in particular, repeatedly claim that all types of regimes, including capitalist and socialist regimes, have already been tried in Muslim countries but have failed to cure social ills or create harmonious and productive societies. Conversely, Muslim modernizing elites usually claim credit for managing the transition to these systems with reasonable efficiency, while fundamentalists blame them for the failure and backwardness of Muslim society. As a result, fundamentalism emerged as a reaction not only to local corruption, but also to Europe's political and commercial expansion into Muslim countries.

Accordingly, medieval fundamentalism, which was handed down through the generations to Ibn Taymiya and Ibn al-Qayyim in the fourteenth century, was reshaped and became, in later centuries, national movements that called for Islamic solidarity against western colonialism and influence. In this way, the character and thought of medieval fundamentalism was reformed in the nineteenth and twentieth centuries under the leadership of a great number of thinkers, including al-Shawkani (d. 1834),[4] al-Sanusi (d. 1859), al-Mahdi (d. 1885), al-Alusi (d. 1923), al-Banna (d. 1949), Sayyid Qutb (d. 1966), and Mawdudi (d. 1979).[5]

These are just some of the many figures involved in Islamic revivalism, who renewed interest in Islam as an endogenous ideology. They also called for liberty, social justice, equality, cooperation, tolerance, and solidarity, and encouraged humankind to master the economy, technology, and the earth.[6] They were, as asserted by Robert Lee, both modernists and fundamentalists, who believed in the Qur'an and Hadith as fundamental sources of Islamic culture and did not reject human reason but called for *ijtihad*.[7]

Thus, Islamic fundamentalism does not necessarily oppose modernity, or reject the role of reason in human affairs. According to the Egyptian thinker and fundamentalist Sayyid Qutb, who was executed on the gallows during Nasser's regime in 1966, the fundamentals of Islam do not resist the achievements of humanity, but encourage Muslims to learn about their own and other cultures, and to develop all aspects of human experience, including the political, economic, and cultural domains. Muslims are permitted to take from western culture those elements that they believe are right, so long as they do not conflict with Islamic culture.[8]

In this regard, fundamentalists differ among themselves, and their theology differs not only from one country to another, but also from one group to another within a country. These groupings range from self-avowed modernists searching for new ways to reconcile Islam and modern society, to the most intransigent militants opting for a complete break with modern society, to radical retreat and armed jihadist groups. They also range from Islamic charitable and self-help associations to Islamic banks, hospitals, investment, trade, and commercial companies, and from Islamic groups active among students and artisans to intellectuals, lawyers, writers, scholars, politicians, judges, army and security officers, thinkers and other professions.[9] Islamic fundamentalism, then, was defined as an attempt to articulate authoritative Islamic laws on freedom, equality, and social justice, and to facilitate the application of shari'a in all spheres of human society and defend its application regardless of the systems already established.[10]

All this indicates that fundamentalism and neo-jihadism are not really identical, even though the latter is, somehow, an offshoot of the former. Indeed, they spring from the same culture, but each has its own character and ideas developed in line with the development of their understanding of political, economic, and social contexts in different times and places. In other words, the present Islamic fundamentalist movement is just one link in a long chain rooted in Islamic history.[11] According to Hanafi, who is himself currently leading a school of thought called the Islamic Left, Islamic fundamentalism is not the product of the present age as it has come to be seen by numerous intellectuals since the Islamic Revolution in Iran, the war in Afghanistan, or the establishment of the Shi'i Amal and Hizbullah in Lebanon. Islamic fundamentalism is also not the offshoot of the revival of the Sufi movements in Eastern Europe or in some Baltic and Caucasian states. Further, Islamic fundamentalism is not the offshoot of the involvement of Islamic political parties in the political arena in Indonesia, Malaysia, or the Philippines.[12]

The origins of contemporary Islamic fundamentalist movements are, however, to be found in Muslim history. These roots are not only in Islamic intellectual heritage and political activity, but also in the psychological and social circumstances that prevailed at various times over the centuries. This history has led to events such as the violence in Egypt in the 1970s instigated by young Islamic groups, which attempted to overthrow the ruling order in Egypt first by taking control of the Military Technical Academy in April 1974. This attempt failed but they remained determined, and assassinated the then Egyptian president Sadat in October 1981, in another attempt to overthrow the dominant order and establish their Islamic caliphate, which also failed. After the assassination of President Sadat, the Egyptian press called these Islamic groups extremists, terrorists, activists, and fanatics because they resorted to violence.[13]

These groups were initially considered to be a part of modern fundamentalist movements, but after they resorted to violence they were referred to by different labels, such as extremist and terrorist. In this regard, the term neo-jihadism as outlined above encapsulates these labels. In other words, fundamentalism gave rise to neo-jihadism, and there were a number of factors involved in this transformation.

One of the main features that distinguishes a number of contemporary Islamic movements from their predecessors is the perception that religion is politics. Regardless of their varying labels and ideologies, the current Islamic-orientated movements are a manifestation of social dislocation and the existence of a disillusioned popular mass in many countries of the Middle East. In addition to corruption, the determined policy of restriction and repression of Islamic movements in many Middle Eastern countries has resulted in radical trends that advocate violence as the means to achieve what moderate and mainstream Islamic organizations have failed to accomplish through the ballot box. In Egypt, for instance, the policy of restriction, humiliation, and repression of Islamic organizations in the 1950s and 1960s led to violence in the decades that followed.

In the Arab world of the 1950s and 1960s, Arabs pinned their hopes mainly on pan-Arabism. Many of the Islamic movements considered Arab nationalism as a step on the way to the unity of all Muslims. After the Arabs' defeat in the Six Day War with Israel, there was a strong revival of Islam among Muslims, which this time assumed a fairly right-wing orientation. Those revivalists also argued that Israel could not succeed without the strong support of western democracies. This recognition of Israel's alliance with the west led these new fundamentalist groups to consider who their enemies were and to classify each as either a close (Arab and Muslim regimes and Israel) or a far enemy (Israel's supporters such as the United States and other countries), as well as the best methods for dealing with each.

The conditions in many Middle Eastern countries during the 1950s and 1960s facilitated a move to the extreme right among right-wing groups and movements. With the assumption in the United States of a right-wing political leadership, the terrorist attacks of September 11, 2001 took place. Before this event, these more right-wing Islamic groups had only been operating locally in the Middle East, but later went to Afghanistan where they planned for their biggest-ever terrorist operation, September 11. Among such groups are jihadist groups of varying titles and geopolitical and language backgrounds, who believe in jihad as the only means to overthrow the government and establish their caliphate. This was an aim that began to take shape in Egypt where al-Qa'ida's Ayman al-Zawahiri and many of al-Qa'ida's operatives were ideologically and militarily trained.[14]

In terms of theological and ideological orientations, the main intellectual inspiration for most contemporary Islamic movements has come from the Islamic thinker Ibn Taymiya. Horrified by the atrocities of the self-avowed Muslim Mongol invaders and disgusted by the compromises of the contemporary rulers to appease the Mongols and the Crusader settlers, he incorporated into his tracts certain justifications for disobeying corrupt rulers, which are considered by many to be highly influential. The teachings of Ibn Taymiya have always been regarded as having had an impact on those militant movements that express Islam in a way that is more orientated toward the past. Ibn Taymiya's disciples are innumerable, and include Ibn 'Abd al-Wahhab (d. 1792) in Arabia, al-Shawkani (d. 1834) in Yemen, and Muhammad al-Sanusi (d. 1859) in Libya among those who have preserved his philosophy.[15]

Further, among the twentieth-century Islamic thinkers who have influenced many Islamic militant groups are Sayyid Qutb (d. 1966), Abu al-A'la Mawdudi (d. 1979), and Ayatollah Ruhollah al-Khomeini (d. 1989). These thinkers have provided authoritative guidelines that delineate the philosophical discourse of Islam and politics. With regard to al-Khomeini, his success raised the hopes of the neo-jihadists that they might also come to power soon. The heart of Qutb's ideas revolves around the concept of sovereignty and stipulates the shari'a as *the* highest governmental and legal authority (*hakimiya* or sovereignty), and a belief that anything other than rule by *hakimiya* is the rule of ignorance (*jahiliya*). Qutb postulated a qualitative comparison of the philosophies of Islamic and western cultures. He emphasized Islam as a complete way of life, but did not reject the achievements of humanity. He also marked the differences between the doctrinal foundations of Islam and modern Islamic philosophical currents.[16]

Following the execution of Qutb in 1966, in Egypt, demonstrations swelled across the Muslim world. Islamic fundamentalists then regrouped, and reviewed their infrastructure and ideas. From their experience with the regime in Egypt, these Islamist revival groups had learned that their security and strength were not based in one large pyramid structure like that of the Brotherhood. They lost confidence in the leadership of the Brotherhood.[17] Subsequently, the Islamists founded jihadist Islamic groups, small in size and based on their own strategies and means. These groups were, and still are, likely the largest and most heterogeneous movement in the Arab world. They believed that the Brotherhood's educational program had proved futile; it had led to the death of Qutb and other leaders, and it had failed to establish an Islamic state. Therefore, the right course was to overthrow the regime and proceed to the task of applying the shari'a. It was here that violence and terrorism began to take shape on the local level, mainly in Egypt. Whenever the government moved against Islamists, those who escaped arrest found their way to other countries in the Middle East, or to Europe and the U.S. In addition to these countries, Afghanistan, during both the counter-Soviet war and later under the Taliban regime, became a safe haven for many. Some governments, western, Arab, and Muslim, helped them to travel to Afghanistan. It is here that the roots of al-Qa'ida are located and where its ideology of neo-jihadism emerged.

Ayman al-Zawahiri, who is currently al-Qa'ida's leader, was a member of these groups in Egypt and contributed to their blueprint, promoted their jihad, and substantiated their claim that the Muslim Brotherhood had strayed from the path of guidance. Al-Qa'ida's ideology, theology, and tactics are largely the product of those Egyptian affiliates. Dr. Fadl, together with al-Zawahiri and his associates Abu al-Yazid and those who carried out the September 11 terrorist attack, are just a few examples of prominent Islamic fundamentalists who emerged from this Afghani context. Al-Qa'ida's ideology, theology, and tactics are outlined in the following chapters.[18]

4

Al-Qaʻida

During the twentieth century, there was a widespread assumption that the role of religion would gradually diminish across all cultures as modernity and secularity came to reign supreme. In the early 1990s, the Egyptian Muhammad Ahmad Khalafallah suggested that the future would not favor an Islamic resurgence.[1] Similarly, in 1992 the French scholar Olivier Roy published his book, *The Failure of Political Islam*, a title that indicates the book's theme and contents.[2] Adopting a similar theme, the French scholar Antoine Basbous published his book *L'Islamisme une révolution avortée* in 2000.[3] This is the same premise that the French scholar Gilles Kepel sought to substantiate in his own book, *The Trail of Political Islam*. Kepel published this book in France in 2000, but the U.S. edition has a preface written after September 11, 2001, which concludes that Islamic movements are in decline.[4]

The last two decades of the twentieth century witnessed the opposite trend, however. There has been a global revival of religion in all of the major centers of civilization, including the Muslim world.[5] With the turn of the twenty-first century, the tragedy of September 11, 2001 and the developments that followed have not supported the thesis shared by these writers.[6]

Radicalism is on the rise, from Afghanistan to Iraq, from Arabia to the Caucasus, and from cartoons to suicide bombings. The War on Terror is also raging without any clear end in sight. Al-Qaʻida and similar networks of global terrorism and militancy still actively at work dominate the international media and influence domestic and international relations. In February 2010, Saudi Arabia identified 200 terrorist plots and arrested 113 al-Qaʻida suspects who were plotting to attack the oil facilities in the kingdom.[7] The recent terrorist attacks on Moscow's Lubyanka and Park Kultury metro stations (29 March 2010), which killed at least 39 people, also illustrate the point.[8] The death of Bin Laden was a big blow to al-Qa'ida but the ideology remains. Many of al-Qa'ida's leaders in Iraq, Afghanistan, Yemen, and elsewhere have been killed and arrested and subsequently replaced by other leaders. Bin Laden was replaced by al-Zawahiri, al-Qa'ida's second in command. Al-Zawahiri remains free and able to produce audio and videotapes as he pleases, to inspire Muslim youth and teach them radical ideology. Al-Zawahiri released statements about the 25 January 2011 Egyptian revolution, encouraging Arabs in one of them to follow the Egyptians and overthrow their own dictators. This reality, as outlined above, is substantiated by government officials, security intelligence organizations, scholars, policymakers, diplomats, and think-tank experts. Speaking of this reality at the Munich Conference on Security Policy held in February 2008, U.S. Secretary of Defense Robert Gates stated that:

> The threat posed by Islamic extremism in Afghanistan, the Middle East, Europe, and globally remains a steep challenge. As opinion leaders and government officials, we are the ones who must make the case publicly and persistently. So now I would like to add my voice to those of many allied leaders and speak directly to the people of Europe: The threat posed by violent Islamic extremism is real and it is not going away.[9]

It is true that al-Qa'ida has been hit hard and may have subsided or declined due to counter-terrorism activities and crushing security strikes.[10] However, they always enter a period of hibernation, be it brief or extended depending on the circumstances, and then return revived and strengthened with the same ideas and actions, as though nothing had happened. Currently, they are still capable of recruiting and mobilizing followers to challenge the authorities through varying forms of symbolic rhetoric and real actions ranging from Internet websites and the circulation of inimical leaflets to the perpetration of acts of extreme violence. Their blueprints have increased dramatically, and the number of their websites is continually on the rise and has recently risen to the hundreds, each dedicated to radicalization, and to recruiting and mobilizing followers for jihad against the west and countries deemed anti-Islamic.[11]

If Bin Laden had presented himself as relevant or postured himself as the leader of al-Qaʻida and defender of Islam, one should note that the 'phenomenon' of Bin Laden had come to the world stage and developed in step within the sociopolitical context of Arab Afghans, who are themselves the product of a particular confluence of local and world events. Al-Zawahiri, and Bin Laden before him, is therefore influenced by a particular set of events and an understanding of them, the Jihad in Afghanistan being one of the most significant and worrying examples of that worldview.[12]

In the aftermath of the Soviet invasion of Afghanistan in December 1979, an extraordinary meeting of foreign ministers from the world's Islamic states convened in Islamabad on 27 January 1980. The delegates strongly condemned "the Soviet aggression" and called for the "immediate and unconditional withdrawal" of all Soviet troops from Afghanistan.[13]

During this critical period of the Cold War, the invasion was an excellent opportunity for the U.S. and its allies to hammer the last nail into the coffin of the Soviet Union. Propagandizing on issues such as Arab identity, prosperity, and, most importantly, oil, the U.S. continued to pressure Arab governments to assume a more active role in the crisis in Afghanistan. On the other side, the USSR was also warning the Arab world against the U.S.'s interest in Arab oil. Here, the world powers' political and economic interests spilled out onto the battlefield—not in the U.S. or the USSR, but in Afghanistan. In this political game, Pakistan's interest was twofold: first, to secure its eastern frontiers and exterminate the separatist movements in the Blushistan region; and, second, to open and secure the trade route through Afghanistan to new markets in the Muslim republics in southern Russia. As for Iran, its interest was no less than to maintain its link with the Shiʻi minority in Afghanistan and to secure their share in the Afghan government. Saudi Arabia's particular circumstances, including its relations with the U.S., its fear of communism, which stretched to its doorstep in Yemen, and its concern to confirm its role as Protector of the Sacred Mosques and Defender of Islam, made it difficult for the kingdom to keep away from the Afghan issue. Each camp devised its own propaganda campaign to make it appear as a genuine supporter of an Islamic Afghanistan.

As a result, Prince Turki al-Faisal, the head of Saudi security and intelligence, stated, "At this moment we do not expect an invasion, but we do expect the Soviets to use their powers to maneuver themselves into a position to make arrangements for a guaranteed oil supply."[14] Similarly, the Egyptian president Anwar Sadat agreed to help the Afghan resistance and publicly claimed to provide military assistance. He was not on good terms with the Soviets for a number of reasons, including their failure to comply with the arms deal they had made with Gamal Abdel Nasser and provide Egypt with military hardware in 1971, while war with Israel loomed on the horizon. In response, Sadat expelled all Soviet military advisors, at once, in 1972. After the war of 1973, Sadat consolidated Egypt's relations with the United States. Therefore, when the Soviets invaded Afghanistan in 1979, Sadat joined the United States in supporting the Afghan resistance against the Soviets.

Supported by the U.S., Egypt and the Arab countries began to call for jihad to defend Islam and liberate Afghanistan from Soviet aggression. In this regard, financial and military institutions, alongside intelligence agencies, supported the jihad against the USSR in Afghanistan. Jihad was celebrated as a sacred Islamic institution and part of the duty of all Muslims to liberate Muslim Afghanistan from the invasion of Communism. The Mujahidin became well known in the corridors and centers of world politics. They were also welcomed by world leaders and were presented in the media as celebrities. Hundreds of books and articles were written that depicted Afghanistan as a sacred land of jihad, both in the past and the present. Much of the Arabic materials portrayed Afghanistan as the land in which Alexander the Great "faced his fiercest battles and grave loss to his army physically, mentally, and financially, and ultimately died in Baluchistan."[15] It was this sacred land that fought against the Mongol aggressors; it is this sacred land for which the "angels" descended from above to fight the Communists, "the enemy of God"; it was in this land that miracles appeared to the Mujahidin and their amirs, Bin Laden and al-Zawahiri, and even Abu Qutayba miraculously destroyed ten Soviet tanks with only two bullets; while 'Abu al-Qa'qa "trapped 1000 soldiers of them 200 attractive females joined the rank of slaves in the palace of amir al-Mu'minin."[16]

The removal of the Soviet forces from Afghanistan in 1988 was considered an ideological victory in the U.S.[17] However, the U.S. and its allies lost interest in Afghanistan and did little to help rebuild the ruined country. The USSR continued to help the Afghan president Najibullah until 1992, when the Russian government refused to sell oil products to his regime. Russia's aid "through 1989 approached $300 million a month, in contrast to U.S. aid to the Mujahidin which slipped to levels of $40–50 million."[18]

The departure of the last group of Soviet soldiers from Afghanistan on 15 February 1989 left a leadership imbalance. Fighting erupted among the Mujahidin factions. The U.S. had lost interest in the conflict. The "Afghan civil war roused little enthusiasm among the [U.S.] public, and the CIA was sounding clear notes of caution."[19] However, as things began to get out of control, Pakistan tried to convince the U.S. to replace the current warlords with the new 'Taliban.' These students of shari'a were effectively products of Pakistan's Inter-Services Intelligence (ISI) who were at the time supported by the U.S.[20] Pakistan favored the Taliban precisely because they were the products of its ISI. Pakistan guaranteed to the United States that those students were but dervishes who would not overstep the shari'a or cause any problems for the state, but preferred to enjoy a humble lifestyle. On 26 September 1996, the Taliban entered Kabul, and by the year 2000 Taliban forces were in control of 95 percent of Afghanistan, while 5 percent remained in the hands of local warlord, Ahmad Shah Massoud.[21]

Three countries quickly recognized the new Islamic state of the Taliban, but later developments confirmed that Pakistan's guarantee was not as accurate as stated. Once in power, the Taliban immediately ignored the text of the shari'a and human relations. With them was the ultra-Wahhabi Bin Laden, who was seen by many of Afghanistan's credulous villagers as the new messiah of Qandahar.[22]

Bin Laden

In speaking of Bin Laden, one should note that the phenomenon surrounding him, which generated significant publicity worldwide, would certainly not have been possible without the phenomenon surrounding another party. Bruce Lawrence, the former senior CIA analyst and chief of the Bin Laden Issue Station, also known as 'Alec Station,' and the Bin Laden tracking unit at the Counterterrorism Center from 1996 to 1999 stated:

> Western media have made no consistent effort to publish Bin Laden's statements, thereby failing to give their audience the words that put his thoughts and actions in cultural and historical context . . . . Bin Laden has been precise in telling America the reasons he is waging

war on us. None of the reasons has anything to do with our freedom, liberty, and democracy but everything to do with U.S. policies and actions in the Muslim world.[23]

Indeed, Bin Laden was located and killed in his compound in Abbottabad in Pakistan on 2 May 2011. President Barack Obama declared the killing of Bin Laden the "most significant achievement to date . . . on the way of defeating al-Qaeda."[24] However, it would be inaccurate to reduce the whole issue to a judgment on his personality, as many do, or to portray Bin Laden as having been an eccentric man. In the words of Michael Mann: "Despite the religious rhetoric and the bloody means, Bin Laden is a rational man. There is a simple reason why he attacked the U.S.: American imperialism. As long as America seeks to control the Middle East, he and people like him will be its enemy."[25]

Many of the published materials, in both Arabic and English, speak of Bin Laden as a foolishly eccentric man living in a cave.[26] However, had he been really abnormal and anomalous, the War on Terror would not have continued to the present. Foolish and eccentric individuals do not generate such publicity, or respect. He has been called the man who "declared war on America," the most powerful nation on earth.[27] He was the monster who tried to manufacture nuclear and chemical weapons or at least to obtain these weapons. He was also thought to be a wealthy man whose financial resources could never be depleted. It is clear that Bin Laden employed this appearance of foolishness and eccentricity to serve his methods, which included suicide bombings. Bin Laden came to believe in these descriptions himself and he sought to turn his vision into reality. He managed to draw his perceived enemies into a long struggle that now has no clear end. Killing this man did not annihilate his ideology, which is still present in the minds of many, in books, and on the Internet. The people were also able to gain access to Bin Laden's ideas, as and when they chose, and over the heads of leaders and governments.

In March 2008, the world's anti-terrorism experts convened for a conference in Stockholm. Among the attendees were senior soldiers and police officers, intelligence professionals, diplomats, think-tank experts and journalists, including Roger Hardy, the BBC's Islamic Affairs Analyst. Hardy found that optimism was in short supply at the conference. As he put it, "what struck me most, in three days of debate, was the degree of pessimism about the task at hand." In his analysis, Hardy said, "one

British defense expert remarked, 'We are not looking for a needle in a haystack—we are looking for a piece of straw in a haystack.'" Another expert reportedly said, "Our common concern was how do you defeat an insurgency—and the phrase invoked more than once was T.E. Lawrence's dictum that it is like eating soup with a knife." Hardy concluded, "It is now widely recognized that Muslim hearts and minds matter and that military successes mean little if the battle of ideas is being lost."[28]

Speaking prior to the 7 July 2005 bombings in London, the head of London Police's Muslim Contact Unit, Janet Williams, described the greatest threat to human security as "Muslim radicalization."[29] This jihadist movement is not to be thought of only in terms of resurgence as opposed to decline, or decadence as opposed to renewal. We should not take these labels at face value, or as rigid and mutually exclusive classifications of civilization, culture, and thought. This new enemy cannot be challenged effectively by a counter-terrorist strategy confined purely to a security agenda. In this new cold war, ideological hegemony is paramount. As Tony Blair declared shortly after the London attacks, "I see this as a global threat that has to be handled at a number of different levels, including the level of ideas and ideology."[30]

Bin Laden narrated his own life story to his representative in the United Kingdom (UK). In the late 1990s, Khalid al-Fawwaz was Bin Laden's representative who managed British and foreign accounts on Bin Laden's behalf in the UK.[31] He established the first media organization to promote al-Qa'ida's ideas and speak as its representative in London under the name 'Guidance and Reform.' As head of this organization in London, al-Fawwaz also received Bin Laden's *fatwa* to attack the U.S. in Africa.[32] On 28 September 1998, al-Fawwaz was arrested by the British police for his role in the bombing of the two U.S. embassies in Kenya and Tanzania on 7 August 1998. Al-Fawwaz published Bin Laden's biography on the website 'Guidance and Reform' in the late 1990s, with the foreword indicating that the biography is as narrated by Bin Laden himself.

The exact date and place of birth of Bin Laden are in dispute. According to Bin Laden's biography, he was born in 1957, but other accounts have given his birth date as 1952, 1953, 1954, and 1957 in either Riyadh or Mecca city. However, in al-Fawwaz's document the year of Bin Laden's birth is given as AH 1377, which corresponds to the year AD 1957.[33] In his statement on 10 June 1999, Bin Laden said he was born in the "al-Malazz neighborhood in Riyadh, in AH 1377." He claimed he then moved to the "holy Medina six months after I was born. For the rest of my life I stayed in Hejaz moving between Mecca, Jeddah and Medina."[34]

Bin Laden was born to a Syrian mother from Damascus. His father had more than fifty-five children from several marriages. In terms of his age, Bin Laden ranked forty-third among his siblings, but he was the twenty-first boy. His father was originally from Hadaramout in Yemen but he migrated to Jeddah in around 1930 in search of employment. Jeddah was and remains the main and busiest Saudi commercial port.

In Jeddah, Bin Laden's father, Muhammad bin Laden, worked as a dockworker and later switched to the building industry. He established his own corporation as a small building contractor; the corporation grew. During the reign of King Saud, the corporation was involved in various types of construction, including buildings, roads, bridges, mosques, airports, and other infrastructure in the Saudi kingdom and Arab Gulf states. Through his connections, Muhammad bin Laden was able to establish a good relationship with the Saudi elite, and with both King Saud and with Faisal, who was amir at the time. When the well-known power dispute between King Saud and Faisal occurred, Muhammad stepped in and convinced the king to resign in favor of his brother Faisal. Muhammad bin Laden's favor toward King Faisal did not stop at Saud's resignation, but also extended to financial support. Muhammad helped King Faisal to balance the budget financially and "payed the employee" wages in the government for about six months after the departure of King Saud. In return, King Faisal issued a decree diverting all building contracts to Muhammad bin Laden's corporation and made him responsible for the Ministry of Constructions.[35] This extended Muhammad's business to become one of the biggest construction corporations in the Middle East.

The special status of Muhammad bin Laden's corporation was further strengthened when, in 1969, the corporation carried out the project of rebuilding the al-Aqsa Mosque in Jerusalem. In addition, the Saudi government contracted Muhammad's corporation to renovate, extend, and rebuild the two mosques in Mecca and Medina. Muhammad's family therefore became highly respected among the Saudis as the builder of the three sacred mosques. Muhammad was also conscientious about education and life and took care to provide his children with a proper education. He was strict about Islam and morality, and managed to keep his large family living together until he died in an aircraft accident in 1968.[36]

Bin Laden was aged probably somewhere between ten and thirteen when his father died, but he himself said that "My father died when I was ten years old."[37] Bin Laden completed his primary, secondary, and higher education in Jeddah. After completing his schooling, Bin Laden married a Syrian woman who was a relative of his mother. He then attended the University of King 'Abd al-'Aziz in Jeddah and graduated with a degree in economics and management.[38] Contrary to press reports published in both Arabic and European languages, Bin Laden did not travel to any country other than the Arabian states, Pakistan, Afghanistan, Syria, Yemen, Sudan, and Somalia. There is no truth in the stories of his travels to Switzerland, Sweden, London, and the Philippines. In addition, he did not study engineering, nor did he study aircraft or learn to fly over Saudi Arabia or England.[39] In addition, apart from Bin Laden himself, none of his family members ever showed an interest in politics or was involved in political or religious discussions.[40]

Focusing on Bin Laden's intellectual development, one should note that his father used to invite a number of Islamic scholars to their home during the hajj, an annual tradition in which Saudi kings and wealthy individuals or groups usually partook during the hajj season. This tradition continued after the death of Bin Laden's father. It was therefore easy for Bin Laden to benefit from the knowledge of specific individuals among these visitors. At university, Bin Laden's studies in economics and management were not purely western, as western theory was compared with Islamic economic management theories and practices. It was here that Bin Laden became aware of certain Islamic movements, leaders, and scholars of Islam. He became aware of the Muslim Brotherhood and its founder, Hasan al-Banna, he was a student of the Egyptian professor Mohammad Qutb the brother of Sayyid Qutb, the ideologue of the Muslim Brotherhood, and was exposed to the teachings of the Palestinian Dr. 'Abdullah 'Azzam. This exposure, in addition to the Palestinian question, the struggle against communism in the south of Yemen, and the political circumstances in the Arab world at the time, left a strong impression on him.

Despite his awareness of Islamic movements, Bin Laden did not affiliate himself with any of them but was influenced by their ideas. Among these were the ideas of returning to pure Islam, the call for a caliphate (*khilafa*), the call for Islamization, and the notion of *hakimiya* (sovereignty), which was enunciated by Sayyid Qutb (d. 1966).[41]

From Jihadism to Terrorism

Bin Laden's interest in jihad began immediately after the Soviet invasion of Afghanistan on 24 December 1979. He considered this invasion to be one of communist ideology. This invasion strengthened the communist ideology in Yemen, on the sacred land of Arabia's very doorstep. In the wake of the invasion, Bin Laden decided to travel to Afghanistan to see for himself and assess the situation: "When the invasion of Afghanistan started, I was enraged and went there at once—I arrived there within days, before the end of 1979."[42] In late December 1979, Bin Laden left Saudi Arabia for Pakistan where he met with members of the Pakistani Jama'a Islamiya, who accompanied him from Karachi to Peshawar. In Peshawar, Bin Laden saw jihadist leaders such as Abdu-Rab Rasool Sayyaf, Burhanuddin Rabbani, Ahmed Shah Massoud, and others, whose names were not unknown to him, as he had met them when they were visiting his father during hajj season.[43]

Ahmed Shah Massoud was the military commander of Jama'at-Islami, which was led by Sheikh Rabbani. Rabbani himself was a lecturer of shari'a at the University of Kabul. In the 1970s, Rabbani translated some of Sayyid Qutb's works into the Afghan language of Dari.[44] Sayyaf also was a mullah (a madrasa, or school, graduate) and leader of the Itehari-Islami movement. Under their leadership, these movements were among seven principal movements that led the Afghani jihad against the Soviets. They were supported militarily, logistically, and financially by "multinational coalitions organized by the CIA and comprised the U.S., UK, and some Arab and Muslim countries."[45]

Before taking any decisive action, Bin Laden kept a low profile on his first visit to Afghanistan, because he was unsure about the political stance of the Saudi government. His visit took about one month, during which time he became convinced that the Afghani issue needed special consideration.

After his return to Saudi Arabia, observing the political stance of the Saudi government and the promotion of jihad in the media and in mosques, he began to discuss his visit to Afghanistan and what he had seen there to his relatives and friends. He also began to collect charitable donations for the Mujahidin and organized another trip. This time, he carried with him what he had collected, and was accompanied by a number of Pakistanis and Afghanis who were working for the Bin Laden Corporation. He left Saudi Arabia for Pakistan, where he stayed for another month in Peshawar. He repeated these types of trips several times and during each trip he carried with him collected donations and was accompanied by a number of people from different countries who were working for the Bin Laden Corporation in Saudi Arabia.[46]

After several trips, Bin Laden established an office, which was akin to a recruitment center or guesthouse of sorts, called Bayt al-Ansar (The House of the Helpers) in Jeddah. Volunteers who attend this office are called *muhajirin* (migrants). This office, together with the Bin Laden Corporation Branch that Bin Laden and his brothers established on 19 Arab League Street in the Mohandiseen neighborhood of Cairo, functioned as recruitment centers and spearheads for fundraising. In all of these trips, Bin Laden was satisfied with stopping in Pakistan, especially in the area of the earlier, primitive training camps in Peshawar, without crossing the border or entering Afghanistan.[47]

In 1982, Bin Laden decided to cross the borders into Afghanistan and, when he saw the nature of the Afghan mountains, decided to make use of this natural environment. He sought to bring his company's construction expertise to the area to build camps, roads, tunnels, bridges, and whatever he considered necessary to resource the Mujahidin. At that time, there were only a few Egyptians and Arab Mujahidin in Afghanistan preparing for jihad against the USSR. Some of these people were recruited by Bin Laden and accompanied him to Peshawar. Among the Egyptians was al-Zawahiri's mentor, Sayyid Imam 'Abd al-'Aziz al-Sharif, better known as Dr. Fadl, a surgeon "arrived to Peshawar in 1983 to help the Mujahidin in the area of my experience of medical services; then came al-Sheikh 'Abdullah 'Azzam and established the office for the services of Mujahidin toward the end of 1984."[48]

Toward the end of 1983, Bin Laden established a Bayt al-Ansar in Peshawar as he had in Jeddah. This house was a reception center and temporary guesthouse for the Mujahidin before their distribution into training camps and then later to the front line of the jihad. This office was one of the milestones on the road to building the organizational infrastructure of what later came to be called al-Qa'ida in Afghanistan. The establishment of Bayt al-Ansar coincided with the arrival of 'Abdullah 'Azzam,[49] a Palestinian born in 1941 in the West Bank town of Nablus, where he completed his elementary and secondary education. Later, 'Azzam left Palestine to complete his education in Syria. He obtained his degree in shari'a from the University of Damascus. Following the Israeli occupation of the West Bank in 1967, 'Azzam moved with his family to Jordan. He then left Jordan for Egypt, to further his studies. He completed his doctorate in shari'a at the University of al-Azhar in Cairo. 'Azzam then left Cairo to teach at King 'Abd al-'Aziz University in Saudi Arabia. He stayed there for about six years, from 1978 to 1984, where Bin Laden was one of his students. Later, teacher and student met again, this time on the battlefield of the jihad in Afghanistan.[50]

It was in Peshawar that Bin Laden and 'Abdullah 'Azzam met without previous arrangement. The two men had similar aims and objectives at the time: to liberate Afghanistan from the Soviets. In 1984, Bin Laden and 'Azzam established another office in Peshawar to organize the affairs of the foreign Mujahidin and promote their cause among Muslims, especially Arabs, to raise funds and to receive volunteers and organize their costs and arrangements for living, training, and other affairs. The office was called Maktab al-Khadamat (The Bureau of Services). The provision of services in this office, as was the case with the other centers, was carried out by volunteers from among the Mujahidin.[51]

'Azzam traveled to various Arab countries to promote jihad, to raise funds, and to recruit Muslim Mujahidin. He visited Britain,[52] Germany, and the U.S. His lecture to the American Youth Association in Fort Worth, Texas, in 1983 influenced Essam al-Ridi, who was an American national of Egyptian origin, born in 1958. In 1979, al-Ridi left Egypt for the U.S., enrolled in an aviation course at Ed Boardman Aviation School in Texas, and graduated in 1981. He earned a commercial pilot's licence and worked there as a flight instructor.[53]

Later, al-Ridi left the U.S. for Afghanistan to participate in the jihad against the USSR. He met Bin Laden and worked as a procurement officer and as Bin Laden's personal pilot. He traveled to Britain, Germany, Italy, and the U.S. to buy weapons and military equipment. In the U.S., al-Ridi bought a small military aircraft for Bin Laden—a T-389, with a maximum range of 2,400 kilometers. He then modified it with a new set of avionics, refurnished it, and obtained Federal Aviation Administration (FAA) approval of its safety. Al-Ridi then flew the plane to Khartoum, which took about one week because of difficulties encountered along the way.[54] One of the reasons he purchased the aircraft was for personal use and for the transfer of "Stinger Missiles from Pakistan to Sudan directly."[55] Thus, if al-Ridi was influenced by 'Azzam's lecture in Texas, he was later also influenced by Bin Laden, as he became Bin Laden's pilot.[56]

From 1984 to 1986, the Mujahidin began to arrive in Afghanistan in large numbers. They came from all Muslim countries but particularly from Egypt. Due to their combat experience and other skills and expertise, the Egyptians moved quickly to leadership positions within the Mujahidin. Among them was the surgeon Dr. Fadl, the founder and principal ideologue of Egypt's jihad group, who arrived in Peshawar in 1983 and later became head of the Kuwaiti Red Crescent Hospital in Peshawar.[57] Dr. Ayman al-Zawahiri, a jihadist surgeon, had been imprisoned in Egypt for three years for his role in the assassination of President Sadat in 1981. After his release, al-Zawahiri left Cairo in 1985 to work in Peshawar Hospital. In 1987, al-Zawahiri established a special center for jihad, and later became Bin Laden's deputy after 'Azzam's death in 1989. Shawqi al-Islambulli, who became one of Bin Laden's generals, was a jihadist and brother of the military lieutenant Khalid al-Islambulli who killed President Sadat.

In 1986, the idea of preparation for jihad developed in Bin Laden's mind. He decided to establish his own training camps and other services required for jihad. Prior to this, when the volunteers recruited by Bin Laden were still only small in number, he would send them to any of the principal Afghan parties, such as those led by Rabbani, Hekmatyar, Sayyaf, or Shah Massoud. Now, the large number of Mujahidin encouraged Bin Laden to establish his own training camps. Indeed, he established six training camps and other facilities that enabled him to receive the Muslim Mujahidin, mostly Arabs, from the moment of their arrival until they had completed their training and become ready to join the cavalry of jihad on the front line, under Arab leadership. These camps have come to form the basis for the infrastructure of al-Qa'ida.

Despite his privileged background, Bin Laden's personality and humanity toward Afghans and others made him more popular than he might otherwise have been, given his background. His was a generous friend to anyone who made contact with him. As Rohan put it, "Osama's philanthropy only made him more popular in Afghanistan. Although he came from a privileged background, his commitment to the jihad, his humility and simplicity and his ability to befriend and communicate with fighters on the ground appealed to the Mujahidin." Rohan quoted one of the Mujahidin as saying, "He not only gave us his money, but he also gave himself. He came down from his palace to live with the Afghan peasants and the Arab fighters. He cooked with them, ate with them, dug trenches with them. This is Bin Laden's way."[58]

Another former associate remembered that Bin Laden preferred to eat only yogurt, vegetables, a little meat, and Afghan bread. A former fighter described him as humble, calm, and accessible, recalling, "We used to sit down with him and eat together like old friends. You would never know how rich he was unless someone told you."[59]

With this attitude, Bin Laden was able to promote his cause, recruit fighters, and generate funds. During the period from 1984 to 1986, the number of Arab fighters increased dramatically. Among them were high school and university students; others were perhaps illiterate, but there were also doctors, scholars, engineers, pharmacists, police officers, and former military commanders of high rank and with fighting experience.

In the period between 1986 and 1989, the Arab Mujahidin participated in many skirmishes and limited battles against the Soviets, but later entered into fierce battles, among which was the Battle of Jaji. This village and its surrounding hills had been the focus for several years of repeated efforts by the Soviet troops to cut the Mujahidin supply lines from Pakistan. Bin Laden, al-Zawahiri, and their fellow Arab Mujahidin fought this battle and repelled the Soviet attack. Over the next three years, Bin Laden and al-Zawahiri fought hard and often exposed themselves to extreme danger during the fighting around Khost, Jalalabad, and other areas.[60] This was the best period for Bin Laden and the Arab Mujahidin because their jihad activity was permitted and supported by governments in Saudi Arabia, Pakistan, Egypt, the U.S., and elsewhere.

Toward the Formation of al-Qaʻida

During this period of intensified fighting, Bin Laden did not spend much time in Saudi Arabia. Instead, he spent about nine months of the year in Afghanistan, supervising and visiting training camps, and participating in direct combat. Due to his communication with the Mujahidin, and his personal involvement in jihad activity, Bin Laden was aware of Arab Mujahidin affairs. Toward the end of the 1980s, and particularly in 1988, Bin Laden noticed that the influx of Arab Mujahidin had grown, but that there was no record or information about them or of who was doing what. There was no record of those who had arrived in Afghanistan, those who had left, those who were in training or those who had completed it, or those who were on the front lines under either Arab or Afghani leadership. There was no record of those who had died or were wounded. The failure to record these activities was one of the most significant problems that

Bin Laden sought to solve. He started to create a detailed record for every one of the Arab Mujahidin, and he organized these records under a separate department led by one of his associates. It was necessary that the Mujahidin be aware of this department. After consultation with his associates, Bin Laden agreed to call this department 'al-Qaʻida' on the grounds that it would be the office, department, or base from which the affairs of the Arab Mujahidin were to be managed. Al-Qaʻida was a registration and information center with facilities for both newcomers and those who were leaving. It was in this sense that the word al-Qaʻida was in use among the Mujahidin at the time. If someone was in need of anything, he was told to go to the base, 'al-Qaʻida.'

'Abdullah 'Azzam used the word al-Qaʻida to refer to the center, base, and even a camp where the new Arab recruits stayed together. Al-Qaʻida, as 'Azzam emphasized, was a place where the newcomers would be living apart, for some time at least, from the rumors and confusing propaganda usually enunciated by Afghan political parties about each other. At this base, the Arabs were able to communicate and socialize. However, if the youths stayed among the Afghans, with whom they could not communicate, they would be more likely to feel isolated and therefore might not stay long. Thus, al-Qaʻida was established to overcome many problems, including the language barriers among Mujahidin, and to reduce the impact of the harsh Afghan environment on non-Afghani fighters. 'Azzam also pointed out that when the Arabs started to arrive in Peshawar, they began to hear varying stories about the Afghan political parties, and every party promoted itself as the best of all parties for Islam. Initially, this confused and surprised some Arab youths when they first arrived in Peshawar. As 'Azzam put it:

> Some have come with only one-way tickets. Then they said we want to go back. I collected money to pay for their return tickets. Sometimes we used to wait until one from the [wealthy] Arabs comes and let him pay for the ticket. Therefore, the Arabs would not stay for long in Afghanistan, before establishing these facilities for them.[61]

Later, however, the word al-Qaʻida came to be synonymous with a terrorist network led by Bin Laden. Before 1993, there were no actions to substantiate Bin Laden's radicalism and hatred for the U.S.[62] His radicalism emerged as a reaction to the presence of U.S. troops in Arabia. Thereafter, Bin Laden's radicalism rose and tended toward violence and terrorism.

In 1989, after the withdrawal of the USSR from Afghanistan, Bin Laden returned to Saudi Arabia, thinking that he would spend some time with his family and return to Afghanistan as he had done before. This trip, however, was different from his previous ones. Bin Laden learned that he was not allowed to travel outside of the Saudi kingdom. At that time, he was familiar with jihad and had started to think of Yemen. He was considering jihad against the USSR in Afghanistan as an example that could be followed to fight against the communists in Southern Yemen. He sought to begin his jihad campaign on two fronts: one from the Saudi side, and the other from North Yemen. Speaking of this intention and thought embarrassed the Saudi government and indicated to them that their wealthy national hero had become domesticated or accustomed to jihad. The other issue that embarrassed the Saudi government was his criticism of the Iraqi regime. Bin Laden started to openly criticize Saddam Hussein and warn the Saudi government of his dangerous capabilities. Bin Laden lectured on this issue while King Fahd was visiting Iraq and Saddam, who was at the peak of his glory, was the king's strongest ally at the time. As a result, the government confined Bin Laden to his house, informed him that he was not allowed to leave the country, and warned him to stay away from politics. He did not give up, but sent an advisory letter to the Saudi government, which was received by Amir Ahmad ibn 'Abd al-'Aziz. In his letter, Bin Laden focused on some general issues, including religious reform and social justice, as well as warning against Saddam's interests in the region. Bin Laden's view of Saddam caught the attention of Amir Nayif, who discussed the matter with Bin Laden.[63]

A year later, Saddam's invasion of Kuwait in August 1990 confirmed Bin Laden's view. The possibility of Saddam invading Saudi Arabia to gain control of its oil fields was the same theme used by the engineers of U.S. foreign policy. Saddam's control of Saudi oil fields, as well as of Kuwaiti and Iraqi reserves, would have given him control of the majority of the world's oil reserves. The view that this might occur was one of the substantial motives that led the U.S. to form a coalition. This theme worked very well for U.S. secretary of state James Baker, as it did with liberating Kuwait itself. Bin Laden was unaware that his views would cultivate the Saudi government's thoughts about Saddam's intentions and later facilitate the Saudi government joining the coalition.

In the aftermath of Saddam's invasion of Kuwait, Bin Laden sought responsibility to defend Saudi Arabia. After deliberation, he wrote another letter that outlined some issues, including how to mobilize the *umma* against Saddam and the practical way to face this threat. He also offered to mobilize all of the Arab Mujahidin to defend the Saudi kingdom. He sent his letter to the Saudi government by the same method with which he had sent the previous ones, and he was assured by the authorities that his letter would be carefully considered.

Bin Laden was hopeful of being invited to participate in the defense of his country. At the time, he saw the Saudi regime as Islamic, and believed any religious irregularities in the country did not extend to driving the regime out of the fold of Islam. However, the Saudi government requested assistance from the U.S. instead of Bin Laden, which had a significant impact on him. As he put it:

> This big mistake by the Saudi regime, of inviting the American troops, revealed their deception. They have given their support to nations that have been fighting against Muslims. They helped the Yemeni Communists against the southern Yemeni Muslims and are helping [Yasser] Arafat's regime fight Hamas. After it insulted and jailed the Islamic clerics 18 months ago, the Saudi regime lost its legitimacy . . . our country has become an American colony.[64]

In his view, this was the first time, since the time of the Prophet, that foreign military forces had entered Arabia. Further, these forces had not entered Arabia by force, but by invitation from the Muslim rulers. Here, Bin Laden was seeing things through his own prism of jihad, as he understood it during his time in Afghanistan. Bin Laden considered himself as one of the Mujahidin who led the anti-Soviet campaign at a strategic level. He "firmly believed that it was the actions of the Mujahidin primarily supported by the Muslim world that led to the collapse of the Soviet Union and the ending of the Cold War."[65] Therefore, he thought that the Mujahidin could defend his own country, as they had in Afghanistan. However, one might question the capacity of Bin Laden and his Mujahidin. In addition, if his Mujahidin were victorious in Afghanistan because of "miracles" and "angels" that helped them against the "*kafir* Soviets,"[66] could they also be victorious in Saudi Arabia against Saddam? The Mujahidin, the Saudis, the

Kuwaitis, and the Iraqis are all Muslims—so which side would the angels choose to help?

While in the Saudi kingdom, Bin Laden began work on two fronts. The first was to secure a *fatwa* that declared jihad a duty for all Muslims and, in particular, the inhabitants of the Arabian peninsula, to defend the Sacred Land. The second was to establish for the 'ulama an independent organization that was to be separate from that already established by the state. He failed to achieve the latter, but was successful with the former. Sheikh Ibn 'Uthaymin issued a *fatwa* on jihad, and Bin Laden used it to encourage fighters to go to Afghanistan. A large number of Saudis and other Arabs who were either working in Saudi Arabia or working for Bin Laden's Corporation responded to him and went to Afghanistan.

At the time, the authorities were watching Bin Laden, as he was still not permitted to leave the country. In the meantime, the Gulf War began with Operation Desert Storm on 17 January 1991, while Bin Laden was still in Saudi Arabia. He decided to leave the country, but how could he do so while he was under house arrest? This was perhaps one of his most difficult decisions. Challenging the regime would be no easy task, but he saw the matter as one of life and death. He felt that he would not be true to either himself or his beliefs if he did nothing and stayed in the kingdom. How was he performing jihad against the non-believers in Afghanistan, while non-believers now came to Arabia, the most sacred of all lands?

After the war on Iraq and liberation of Kuwait, Bin Laden worked out how to leave the country. He persuaded his brother, who in turn convinced Amir Ahmad ibn 'Abd al-'Aziz, the deputy minister of interior. Bin Laden then got his passport back and left the country legally in April 1991. When he arrived in Pakistan, he wrote to his brother to apologize to him for having requested the favor. From Pakistan, Bin Laden quickly entered Afghanistan.

Bin Laden's return to Afghanistan coincided with the collapse of the USSR and the beginning of the civil war in Afghanistan. He advised the Arab Mujahidin to stay neutral and not to support any faction against another. Bin Laden adhered to this tactical position until the Taliban entered Kabul in 1996, when he decided to support them. The Saudi intelligence, supported by Pakistani intelligence, tried to arrest and even assassinate him, but these efforts failed. He felt that Afghanistan, and even Peshawar, were no longer safe places for him to stay, and he decided to leave for Sudan.

The decision to move to Sudan was not based on a plan to rebuild al-Qaʻida, or establish a new base for another project, but on Bin Laden and his associates' hearing of the news that Brigadier ʻUmar Hasan Ahmad al-Bashir had come to power through a military coup that overthrew the government of Sadiq al-Mahdi, in 1989. Al-Bashir allied himself with the National Islamic Front (NIF), led by the western-educated Islamist Dr. Hasan al-Turabi, who was one of the ideologues of global Islamic fundamentalism. Sudan became an Islamic state, where the shariʻa was implemented, particularly in the northern parts of the country. Al-Turabi was the head of the Shura Council and the speaker of the parliament. Subsequently, Sudan became a safe haven for Islamists and a number of Islamist movements, including al-Qaʻida for a few years.[67]

In 1991, Bin Laden and his closest associates left Peshawar for Sudan by a special aircraft. Others arrived later by different methods. The establishment of al-Qaʻida in Sudan did not weaken al-Qaʻida in Afghanistan, but expanded it. Training programs did not cease in Afghanistan, while new training camps, living facilities, and operational infrastructure were established in Sudan. However, al-Qaʻida's leadership and a large number of the senior, more experienced fighters moved to Sudan. At the time, Bin Laden's financial resources and companies were still under his control. He established more companies and farms, and built roads and businesses in Sudan.[68]

Bin Laden's escape from Saudi Arabia was a matter of considerable seriousness for Saudi and U.S. security forces. In 1992, the Saudi regime tried many times to bring him back home, but he rejected all pressures and intimidation, to the extent that he "threw his check book" at the mediator who was sent to convince him to return to the kingdom, with the threat that his assets would otherwise would be confiscated. Bin Laden responded by saying, "Do not deal with me in this way; take it all, I do not need anything of it."[69] When all attempts failed, the Saudi regime responded in February 1994 by canceling his Saudi citizenship and freezing his assets. Canceling his citizenship coincided with a report from the Committee of Legal Rights (established by Bin Laden) that critically highlighted some human rights irregularities and the need for reform in the kingdom. The Saudi government outlawed this organization and arrested its founders, Sheikh Salman al-ʻAwda and Sheikh Safar al-Hawli. This development encouraged Bin Laden to criticize the Saudi regime openly. In March 1994, he personally responded through the media to the government's cancellation of his citizenship, claiming that the Saudi government wanted to defame his character both within and without the kingdom.[70] His retaliation also took the form of the establishment of the Advice and Legal Rights Defence Committee to replace the organization that had been outlawed by the government. He established this committee to be based in London, unaware at the time that the previous committee would shift its operations from Arabia to London, too. When the outlawed committee reappeared in London, Bin Laden and his associates led both his Advice and Legal Rights Defence Committee and the Committee of Legal Rights. In July 1994, he changed the name of his committee to the Advice and Reformation Committee, and appointed Khalid al-Fawwaz as its head. The Advice and Reformation Committee was a media organization that promoted al-Qaʻida, spoke on behalf of Bin Laden, and issued booklets and pamphlets critical of the U.S.-backed Saudi regime. In his interview with CNN, Bin Laden explained these events as follows:

> I waited for the chance when God made it possible for me to leave Saudi Arabia. I hope He would confer upon me His favor to return one day, when God's law rules in that country. I went to the Sudan and stayed there for about five years, during which I visited Afghanistan and Pakistan to work against the Communist government in Kabul. When the Saudi government transgressed in oppressing all voices of the scholars and the voices of those who call for Islam, I found myself forced—especially after the government prevented Sheikh Salman al-Auda and Sheikh Safar al-Hawli and some other scholars from doing so—to carry out a small part of my duty of enjoining what is right and forbidding what is wrong. So, I collaborated with some brothers and established a committee for offering advice (the Advice and Reformation Committee), and we started to publish some declarations. However, the Saudi regime did not like this and started to exercise pressure on the Sudanese regime. The U.S. government, the Egyptian government, and the Yemeni government also helped in doing so. They asked the Sudanese regime to extradite me, and the pressure continued.[71]

In Sudan, Bin Laden's camps flourished and became centers that received members of Islamic movements from all corners of the world.

At the time, Bin Laden was in contact with business people, scholars, politicians, media, and intelligence personnel from everywhere, including his native land and other Arab countries.[72] He was also in contact with his old friends in Afghanistan and Pakistan, including those who had returned to their homes. As a result, al-Qaʻida expanded its network worldwide and developed a unique system of communication. In the meantime, the Mujahidin who returned to their Arab countries began to use their war expertise to overthrow regimes in their own countries and establish Islamic order. In Egypt, for example, the media referred to them as the "returnees from Afghanistan." As the threat they posed intensified, some of them were arrested by their regimes, but many others who escaped arrest, fled and joined Islamist groups in Afghanistan, Chechnya, Algeria, Albania, Tajikistan, the Philippines, Kashmir, and Sudan. This network considered Bin Ladenʼs camps in Sudan to be the main center for training and financing operations against their enemies. Bin Laden financed Ramzi Ahmad Yousef, who was involved in the attack on the World Trade Center in 1993. While Bin Laden considered this attack a natural and rational response to the unbalanced and unjust U.S. foreign policy in the Middle East, he concealed his involvement in the attack. Keeping himself under the radar in this way meant he did not draw the attention of the CIA to either himself or his organization at the time. In March 1995, after Yousef was captured in Islamabad, the Pakistani intelligence (ISI) reported that "he spent a great deal of time in recent years at a Bin Laden–funded guest house in Peshawar."[73]

Later, Yousefʼs friend Ahmad Ajaj, who accompanied Yousef from Peshawar to New York, was detained at JFK airport on visa charges but was released. During his detention, Ajaj carried with him a training manual entitled ʻal-Qaʻida,ʼ which was translated by the CIA to mean ʻBasic Rule.ʼ[74] The CIAʼs awareness of the al-Qaʻida network was described in 1998 as follows:

The suspects tried and convicted in the World Trade Center bombing and the second group of extremists who plotted to bomb other landmarks in New York City, including the UN building, did not belong to a single, cohesive organization, but rather were part of a loose grouping of politically committed Muslims living in the New York City area. They were followers of Egyptian imam Sheikh Umar Abd al-Rahman and included non-Egyptians. Of the six original

WTC suspects, only one is an Egyptian. The group includes three Palestinians, one Pakistani, and one Iraqi. The fifteen individuals indicted in the second New York City case include Egyptians, Sudanese, and a Palestinian. The transitional character of these groups is also underscored by their ability to travel and operate in a variety of countries.[75]

George Tenet, director of the CIA from 1997 to 2004, stated in his book, *At the Center of the Storm*, that, until 1996, U.S. intelligence believed that Bin Laden was a financier. As Tenet put it:

> The Agency spotted Bin Laden's tracks in the early 1990s in connection with funding other terrorist movements. They [the Agency] did not know exactly what this Saudi exile living in Sudan was up to, but they knew it was not good. As early as 1993, two years before I came to the CIA, the Agency had declared Bin Laden to be a significant financial backer of Islamic terrorist movements. We knew he was funding paramilitary training of Arab religious militants in such far-flung places as Bosnia, Egypt, Kashmir, Jordan, Tunisia, Algeria and Yemen.[76]

While in Sudan, Bin Laden's views were becoming increasingly radical, in step with, or rather in response to, U.S. foreign policy toward political developments in the Middle East, the U.S. presence in Arabia, and the Saudi government's relations with the U.S.:

> It should not be hidden from you that the people of Islam have suffered from aggression, iniquity, and injustice imposed on them by the Zionists-Crusaders' alliance and their collaborators, to the extent that the Muslims' blood became the cheapest and their wealth as loot in the hands of the enemies. Their blood was spilled in Palestine and Iraq. The horrifying pictures of the massacre of Qana, in Lebanon are still fresh in our memory.[77]

The more he focused on political developments in the Middle East and the Gulf, tinged by the anger and bitter aftertaste left by his revoked nationality and frozen assets in Saudi Arabia, the more radical he became, and then he convinced himself to turn his theoretical ideas to action. The image of a brave hero of Afghan jihad was incompatible with identity crises, bankruptcy, and humiliation. His actions were those of a humiliated man, who would do anything to regain his prestigious image of bravery and heroism. His view of the U.S. was transformed into action through planning and financing the attack on the World Trade Center in 1993. He also planned his retaliation against the Saudi regime, which had stripped him of his citizenship and frozen his assets. In his desire for retaliation, Bin Laden focused on Somalia, Yemen, and Riyadh.

As to Somalia, Bin Laden sent a group of well-trained fighters to help the warlord Muhammad Farah Aideed resist the U.S. forces. This support continued until the U.S. forces withdrew from Somalia. His experience in Somalia influenced Bin Laden's perception of the U.S., to the extent that he publicly stated that their withdrawal from Somalia demonstrated the U.S.'s weakness, and that defeating it was easier than defeating the USSR in Afghanistan. He demonstrates this idea in words:

We say that the United States is very much weaker than Russia. Based on the reports we received from our brothers who participated in jihad in Somalia, we learned that they saw the weakness . . . of U.S. troops. They fled in the heart of darkness, frustrated, after they had caused great communication about the New World Order.[78]

He also sent a group to Aden in Yemen where they attacked U.S. citizens staying in hotels. In terms of the bombings in Riyadh on 13 November 1995, there was sufficient information to confirm Bin Laden's financial and planning hand in that operation.[79]

After Bin Laden's involvement in the Somali conflict, the U.S. began to pressure the Sudanese government to expel Bin Laden. The Sudanese bore the pressure for some time, but finally gave in. Bin Laden was also aware of the pressure and sought another place to continue his activities. He planned another return to Afghanistan, which was at the time divided between warlords engaged in civil war. Muhammad Najibullah was a pro-Soviet president in Kabul supported by the Russians. Mullah 'Umar and his Taliban fighters were in the Kandahar area. Mullah Muhammad Yunus Khalis and Mullah Muhammad Jalaluddin Haqqani were in the Hadda, Khost, and Jalalabad areas. Preparing for his trip from Sudan to Afghanistan, Bin Laden contacted those warlords. After he had secured a place for himself in Jalalabad, Bin Laden along with a number of his associates left Sudan on 19 May 1996, in a private plane headed for Afghanistan, where he was welcomed by both Khalis and Haqqani. On the relationship between Khalis and Bin Laden, al-Zawahiri's latest book, *al-Tabri'a: risala fi tabri'at ummat al-qalam wa-l-sayf min manqusat tuhmat al-khawr wa-l-da'f* (Exoneration: A Treatise Exonerating the Nation of the Pen and the Sword from the Blemish of the Accusation of Weakness and Feebleness), states:

> Al-Sheikh Muhammad Yunus Khalis was one of the leaders of jihad and supporters of the Taliban. He is the one who protected Bin Laden as a guest in Jalalabad. When Bin Laden requested permission to conduct media interviews and meetings with the press, he [Khalis] effectively said to him [Bin Laden], "Why do you need permission from me? Do what you see is right." After the American invasion of Afghanistan, he [Sheikh Muhammad Yunus Khalis] issued a *fatwa* for the jihad against him [Bin Laden] despite his sickness and weakness.[80]

When he arrived to stay with Mullah Khalis in Jalalabad, Bin Laden sent a message to the other Afghan warlords confirming that he would maintain his earlier agreement not to become involved in their war and to remain neutral. He stayed in Jalalabad for about a year, shifting much of al-Qa'ida's equipment and infrastructure to Afghanistan and relocating his followers there.

Bin Laden's return to Afghanistan was "in many ways," as George Tenet argues, "the worst-case scenario for us."[81] Following his arrival in Afghanistan on 19 May 1996, events developed dramatically, from the killing of U.S. personnel in al-Khobar in Saudi Arabia, to the fall of Jalalabad to the hands of the Taliban. Finally, attempts on Bin Laden's life resulted in the "Declaration of War against the Crusaders and Jews."

On 25 June 1996, the bombings of the al-Khobar towers in Dahran killed twenty U.S. military personnel and injured many others. Bin Laden did not claim responsibility for the attacks. The Saudis placed the responsibility with a Shi'i group that may have been supported by Iran. The Saudis tried to avoid mentioning Bin Laden by name, until the attacks on U.S. embassies in Tanzania and Kenya occurred in 1998, when a Saudi official told *France Presse* that the reason the Saudis ended their relations with the Taliban was the latter's protection of the al-Khobar bombers, who had affiliated themselves with Bin Laden. This version of events was never repeated again by Saudi officials, who instead referred to Hani al-Sa'igh in connection to the incident in all their subsequent communications.

On 23 August 1996, two months after the al-Khobar bombings, Bin Laden issued a statement entitled "Declaration of Jihad against the Americans Occupying the Land of the Two Holy Sanctuaries." In this twelve-page statement, Bin Laden wrote, among many other things, that "the situation in the Land of the Two Holy Mosques has become like a huge volcano on the verge of eruption that would destroy the infidels and the corruption and its sources. The explosion at Riyadh and al-Khobar is a warning of this volcanic eruption emerging as a result of the severe oppression, suffering, excessive inequity, humiliation, and poverty."[82]

In the meantime, the Saudi ambassador to Pakistan had exhausted whatever means were available to him to strike a deal with Mullah Khalis and Mullah Haqqani for Bin Laden's arrest and extradition to Saudi Arabia. Both mullahs refused to cooperate and responded, in their precise Afghani fashion, with the statement, "If a goat or animal came to us, we will protect it; so, what do you think of a man who sold his life and property in the way of God and jihad in Afghanistan!"[83] The mullahs were in control of the Jalalabad area, which came under repeated attack from the Taliban, and finally fell into their hands. Here, Bin Laden's position comes into question. He was the guest of mullahs Haqqani and Khalis, but suddenly the area and everything in it, including Bin Laden and his mullahs, came under the control of the Taliban. The two mullahs made a deal with the Taliban and joined their faction, which removed the cloud of uncertainty regarding Bin Laden's position in Jalalabad. Mullah 'Umar then confirmed Bin Laden's safety, and sent delegates to Bin Laden to assure him of his protection, but advised him to stay away from the media. However, Bin Laden met with the British television channels, Channel Four and the BBC, during this period.

The Mullah and the Hidden Imam

While in Jalalabad, Bin Laden lived as an 'imam' and a guest under the protection of Mullah Muhammad 'Umar, the leader of the Taliban. The next development was the fall of Kabul. The Taliban took control of Kabul on the night of 26 September 1996, with almost no fighting. Based here, the Taliban then became the largest and strongest faction in Afghanistan. After the fall of Kabul, Mullah Muhammad 'Umar requested that Bin Laden move to Kandahar, where security and safety were much better than in Jalalabad. Bin Laden arranged for his departure from Jalalabad by a car and a private plane that would fly him from Kabul to Kandahar. He arrived in Kandahar in early 1997. It was in Kandahar that 'Imam' Bin Laden met 'Mullah' Muhammad 'Umar, the leader of the Taliban, in person for the first time. Although there was no previous relationship between the 'Mullah' and the 'Imam,' their first meeting successfully established a good connection between the two men. Mullah 'Umar welcomed Bin Laden, first as an Arab Muslim guest, and second as a mujahid (pl. mujahidin), who fought to liberate Afghanistan from the USSR. Mullah 'Umar emphasized that he would be "honoured to protect him, because of his role in the jihad against the Soviets."[84] During this meeting, Mullah 'Umar outlined the situation in Afghanistan and the challenges facing the Taliban on the battleground since their takeover of Kabul. He also described the reality that these forces of the Tajik leader, Ahmed Shah Massoud, and of 'Abd al-Rashid Dostum, head of a powerful Uzbek militia group that had been allied with Najibullah and the Hazara faction and had formed a coalition called the Northern Alliance, continued to obtain military assistance from Russia.[85] This reality on the ground, in addition to their protection, drew Bin Laden's attention toward the Taliban. At the time, Bin Laden was in contact with the world media, even though his first meeting with Mullah 'Umar was after Bin Laden had recently completed two television interviews, including one with CNN. Therefore, when Mullah 'Umar expressed his respect and admiration, he politely requested that Bin Laden keep a low profile and stay away from the media: "This is but a request, not a command." Bin Laden's response was positive and he agreed that he would reduce his media activity or stop it altogether.[86]

After the fall of Kabul, the Taliban began to organize their government to rule the country. Mullah 'Umar invited more than one thousand of the leading Afghani 'ulama to decide the future of the country. They formed a six-member interim Shura (Consultative) Council and a seventeen-member interim cabinet, led by Mullah Muhammad Rabbani, to govern the country. They also decided to rename the country the Islamic Emirate of Afghanistan, and Mullah Muhammad 'Umar assumed the title 'Amir al-Mu'minin' (Commander of the Faithful).[87]

Along with Pakistan and the United Arab Emirates (UAE), the Saudi government accorded the newborn 'Islamic Emirate of Afghanistan' diplomatic recognition. The relationship between the Saudi and Taliban governments developed to the extent that the Saudis invited Taliban government officials and Mullah 'Umar personally to perform the hajj as official guests. In addition, Mullah Muhammad Rabbani, the new Afghani prime minister, visited the Saudi kingdom during the hajj. However, the good relationship between the Saudi and Taliban governments did not change the Taliban's position with regard to Bin Laden. In an attempt to capture Bin Laden, the Saudi regime dispatched diplomats, intelligence and business personnel, and relatives of Bin Laden to the Taliban. However, all Saudi attempts to arrest, assassinate, or extradite Bin Laden to the kingdom failed at the hands of the Taliban.[88]

The other development that raised Bin Laden's status with the Taliban was the move away from his stance of neutrality toward the war among Afghani factions. Bin Laden decided to align himself and his al-Qa'ida forces with the Taliban, to fight against 'Abd al-Rashid Dostum and Gulbuddin Hekmatyar. When Ahmed Shah Massoud insisted on supporting Dostum and Hekmatyar against the Taliban, Bin Laden issued a *fatwa*, permitting his followers to fight Shah Massoud as a legal jihad. This enhanced Bin Laden's status and consolidated his relationship with Mullah 'Umar and the Taliban. Their opponents were supported by Russia, India, Iran, Tajikistan, Uzbekistan, and above all the U.S.[89] Assisting the Taliban in the war against Dostum, Massoud, and their allies, Bin Laden put together from among his followers a guerrilla unit called the 055 Brigade that was said to consist of between 1,500 and 2,000 well-trained and experienced Arab fighters. They operated as an organization strictly separate from the Taliban, but continued to cooperate with them during the war against Dostum and his allies. They also protected Kabul from the many attacks made by the Afghan coalition. In addition to his military support for the Taliban, Bin Laden's relationship with the group was strengthened by his financial and intellectual support. He appointed a number of his skilled men to help the Taliban in planning, management, healthcare, and other areas necessary for running the new state. Although the skills of these people were limited, they were highly educated and skilled in comparison to the Taliban. In return, the Taliban treated Bin Laden as an imam and protected him against the many attempts made on his life. In this regard, in March 1997 and December 1998 Bin Laden stated:

There were several attempts to arrest me or to assassinate me. This has been going on for more than seven years. With God's grace, none of these attempts succeeded. This is proof in itself to Muslims and to the world that the U.S. is incapable and weaker than the picture it wants to draw in people's minds.[90]

An attempt on my life took place when the Saudi regime sent a number of people, who, although they were born in the Land of the Two Holy Mosques, were deprived of citizenship. The Saudi regime exploited this weakness and offered them large sums of money in return for trying to assassinate me. By the Grace of God, Praise and glory be to Him, the Taliban were able to arrest one of them . . . . He confessed that Prince Salman bin 'Abd al-'Aziz, the brother of the current king of the Land of the Two Holy Mosques, had promised to give him citizenship and a million rials if he was able, together with two other colleagues of his, to assassinate Usama Bin Laden.[91]

In an interview, Mullah Muhammad 'Umar, leader of the Taliban and amir of the Islamic Emirate of Afghanistan, noted that he refused to expel Bin Laden or hand him over to anyone.[92] Still, Bin Laden kept a low profile and adhered to his agreement with Mullah 'Umar when the two men met in early 1997. Toward the end of 1997 and the beginning of 1998, Bin Laden decided to return to his activism against the regime in Saudi Arabia and the U.S. presence there. He began to speak to the 'ulama in Afghanistan and successfully obtained a legal opinion *(fatwa)* from about forty scholars supporting his statement to evict the "infidel forces" from Arabia. Similarly, a group of Pakistani 'ulama issued a *fatwa* that supported the Afghan *fatwa* to expel U.S. troops from Arabia. These *fatwa*s were distributed widely in Pakistan and Afghanistan and published by media worldwide, including the London-based Arabic newspaper *al-Quds al-'arabi*. Indeed, Bin Laden was preparing the ground for future activity. Referring to these and other similar *fatwa*s in *al-Tabri'a* al-Zawahiri pointed out:

> The martyred al-Sheikh Nizam-u-el-Ddin Shamzi, may God have mercy on him, was one of the prominent scholars in Pakistan and one of the strong supporters of al-Sheikh Usama Bin Laden, may God protect him and his friends, and [Shamzi] visited him [Bin Laden] repeatedly in Kandahar and signed on the message, that

was issued and introduced by Sheikh Usama Bin Laden, may God protect him, entitled "Mobilizing the Umma for Jihad to Liberate the Ka'ba [the Holy Mosque in Arabia], and the al-Aqsa Mosque [in Palestine]: A message from Scholars of Muslims and Leaders of the Islamic movement." Many Pakistani scholars have signed the message with him . . . . Al-Sheikh Usama was also in contact with the scholars of Afghanistan and Pakistan, and hundreds of them visited him. They were in complete agreement with him in his call of liberating Muslim territories.[93]

In issuing these *fatwas*, Bin Laden's aim was twofold. The first was to inspire the 'ulama in Muslim countries, and unite them against the U.S. presence in the Holy Land, and against the Saudi regime, which had invited the U.S. troops to Arabia. The second was to obtain a religious, legal cover to support him in Afghanistan, and to strengthen the reason for his departure from the earlier agreement signed with Mullah 'Umar.

Mullah 'Umar was not happy with this development and indeed did consider Bin Laden's activity as a departure from their agreement. In response, 'Umar sent his deputies to meet with Bin Laden for further discussion. Bin Laden explained that the circumstances under which he was to keep a low profile from the media were over, and that there was therefore no reason to remain silent. To support his view, Bin Laden used the earlier two *fatwas* of the Afghani and Pakistani 'ulama as legal reasoning. He also said that he was willing to accept the ruling (*tahkim*, judgment) of the 'ulama. Culturally, the Taliban respect the 'ulama and do not break their word. For the Taliban, the 'ulama hold the ultimate authority. Nevertheless, Mullah 'Umar rejected Bin Laden's idea of *tahkim*, not because he did not respect the 'ulama, but because he did not want to establish this idea as a precedent of justification for any rebelliousness in the future. Mullah 'Umar had the ability to arrest and expel Bin Laden, or at least prevent him from gaining media attention or engaging in any other activity for that matter. Although Mullah 'Umar was disappointed, he preferred diplomacy when dealing with Bin Laden, but this tactic had been used for a long time, and was now no longer effective. It was at this point that the relationship between the two men turned sour, and Bin Laden did not express any good will toward Mullah 'Umar from that point forth.

Bin Laden insisted on his position and even invited a small number of journalists to a press conference. This conference took place in May

1998 in Khost, an area close to the border of Pakistan. A few days before the conference, Bin Laden released a statement focusing, among other things, on Indo-Pakistani relations. He did this from a jihadist perspective and within the context of global politics, to serve his own purposes. At the time, India had just carried out a series of underground nuclear tests in Pokhran in the northern desert of Rajasthan, about sixty-three kilometers from the border with Pakistan. The Pakistani government of Nawas Sharif was under global pressure to neither follow India nor respond to it. Thus, Bin Laden's statement attempted to draw attention to India's activity. He noted that his country had been trying to draw the world's attention to India's nuclear program for years, but that there had been no response.[94]

Not surprisingly, Bin Laden could not fail to exploit such a sensitive issue to promote his message. He also noted that Pakistan should not yield to world pressure and that Muslims should strive to develop nuclear weapons to defend themselves. He stated that he saw India's nuclear program as a threat to the millions of Muslims in India and Pakistan. The hostility of Delhi toward Islamabad had become difficult to ignore. Bin Laden's statement was circulated widely in Pakistan and Afghanistan. In the meantime the Pakistani people, including Islamists, were growing furious. The Pakistani prime minister, Nawaz Sharif, publicly assured his people that "as a sovereign and independent nation . . . Pakistan will make its own decision on the steps to be taken toward its sovereignty and defense."[95]

The style of Bin Laden's involvement in this sensitive issue disappointed Mullah 'Umar, because Pakistan was also pressuring him to arrest Bin Laden for trial in Saudi Arabia. Mullah 'Umar's diplomacy did not work well with Bin Laden, as the latter's contact with the media continued. A few days before his press conference in May 1998, Bin Laden gave a long interview with the American ABC channel. In both the press conference and the interview, Bin Laden continued to criticize the U.S. presence in Arabia, and indicated the possibility of attacks against U.S. citizens in the near future:

> The U.S. government has committed acts that are extremely unjust, hideous, and criminal, whether directly or through its support of the Israeli occupation . . . . We believe the U.S. is directly responsible for those killed in Palestine, Lebanon, and Iraq. The mention of the U.S. reminds us before everything else of those innocent children

who were dismembered, their heads and arms chopped off in the recent explosion that took place in Qana [where Israeli forces killed 102 civilian refugees and wounded more than 320 at Qana village in Lebanon, on 18 April 1996] . . . .

This U.S. government abandoned even humanitarian feelings by committing these hideous crimes. It transgressed all bounds and behaved in a way not witnessed before by any power or any imperialist power in the world. They should have been sensitive to the fact that the *qibla* [the *Ka'ba*, in Saudi Arabia, to which Muslims turn in prayers] of the Muslims raises the emotion of the entire Muslim world. Due to its subordination to the Jews, the arrogance and haughtiness of the U.S. regime has reached such an extent that it occupied the *qibla* of the Muslims . . . . Saudi Arabia is a country that has in our religion a significance of its own over the other Muslim countries. In our religion, it is not permissible for any non-Muslim [army] to stay in our country. Therefore, even though American civilians are not targeted, they must leave. We do not guarantee their safety, because we are in a society of more than a billion Muslims. A reaction might take place as a result of the U.S. government's targeting of Muslim civilians and executing more than 600,000 Muslim children in Iraq by preventing food and medicine from reaching them. Thus, the U.S. is responsible for any reaction, because it extended its war against troops to civilians. This is what we say.[96]

After the Gulf War against Iraq in 1991, not all of the U.S. troops returned home. Some twenty thousand fully equipped troops remained in Saudi Arabia. It was not until 1995, as reported by the *Guardian*, did U.S. officials acknowledge the presence of their troops in Saudi Arabia, and there was no official explanation as to why they had remained.[97] The explanation postulated by the U.S. was that the troops remained to defend the Saudi regime from a possible coup. The Saudi kingdom had a remarkable collection of high-tech weaponry and there were fears of conflicting loyalties within the army. However, the presence of U.S. troops in Saudi Arabia, as emphasized by Middle East analyst Roger Hardy, "is a strategic shift of great political as well as military significance."[98] In either case, "the U.S. troops have become a potent symbol of Washington's role in the region, and many Saudis see them as proof of the country's subservience to America."[99]

In early 1998, a number of Islamic groups from Egypt, Pakistan, Tajikistan, and other countries formed with Bin Laden a coalition for jihad. They established the al-Jabha al-Islamiya al-'Alamiya li-Jihad al-Yahud wa-l-Salibiyyin (World Islamic Front for Jihad against the Jews and the Crusaders). This so-called front or organization materialized into what later came to be known as al-Qa'ida. The creation of this organization was announced by Bin Laden in the presence of a number of his closest associates, including his second-in-command Ayman al-Zawahiri. The London-based Arabic daily, *al-Quds al-'arabi*, published the full statement or declaration in Arabic on 23 February 1998. The statement was signed first by Bin Laden and then by Ayman al-Zawahiri (listed as leader of an Egyptian Jihad group), Abu Yasir Rifa'i Ahmad Taha (representative of Egypt's al-Jama'a al-Islamiya), Sheikh Mir Hamza (listed as secretary of the Pakistani Jam'iyyat al-'Ulama), and Fazlur Rahman (identified as leader of the Jihad Movement in Bangladesh).[100]

The statement was written in an eloquent style, using poetic Arabic prose. It reflects the grievances of Bin Laden and his movement within the context of history, with which most westerners are likely unfamiliar. The issues related to peace and sovereignty in Arabia, Iraq, and Jerusalem were listed in the document as the ultimate basis for Bin Laden's statement. It begins with praise to God and his Prophet, Muhammad, followed by a quotation from the Qur'an and another from the sayings (Hadith) of the Prophet. The statement is available in both Arabic and English.[101]

The statement emphasized the need to understand the nature of the current situation in the Middle East and the Muslim world. It summarized three main factors as being the cause of the current situation. Its purpose was to "remind whoever wants to remember," so that "those who die might die after a clear sign, and those who live might live after a clear sign." Here, one might detect a warning, and that the statement was preparing the ground for the future violence to come. In other words, certain factors were selected to serve as legal reasoning for what might facilitate and justify future violence. The three factors can be summarized as follows: The first was the view that the presence of U.S. troops in Arabia must be seen as occupation of the Holy Land. The second focused on the war in Iraq and issues such as those related to sanctions, as well as highlighting the "humiliation and destruction inflicted on the Iraqi people" as "war crimes punishable by death." The third view took the first two and reworked them to consider their purpose as "not only religious and economic," but as an attempt to strengthen "the petty state of the Jews" in Palestine.

The substance of these three factors was emphasized as "fact," and a "declaration of war against Muslims." Based on their analysis of these factors, Bin Laden and his associates had decided to rectify these 'facts' through jihad. Hence, they saw jihad as obligatory for every Muslim to defend the Muslim community. Consequently, killing U.S. nationals and their allies, both military and civilians, became legal and a duty of every able Muslim in any country in the world, until such time as the three 'facts' were rectified. Bin Laden and his associates devised this declaration in order to convince their audiences that the jihad that they called for was defensive, rather than offensive. They emphasized that this jihad against the U.S. and its allies would continue "until al-Aqsa Mosque [in Jerusalem] and al-Haram Mosque [in Mecca] were freed from their grip and until their armies depart from all the lands of Islam." The statement was thus a turning point in the theology, ideology, and tactics of Bin Laden and his associates, as outlined in the following:

1. The declaration indicated a global project instead of focusing on the issue of the presence of U.S. troops in the Saudi kingdom.
2. The declaration also indicated Bin Laden's departure from the rules that he established for himself and his movement. He permitted the killing of even civilians and non-combatants and insisted on extending this permission outside Arabia.
3. By this declaration, Bin Laden confirmed his affiliation in a coalition with the jihadist groups, many of which had committed acts of terrorism. Before that, he was working with his own group and had always refused alliances, despite his agreement to help other groups and to cooperate with them only underground.
4. Bin Laden did not discuss the *fatwa* with his protector, Mullah 'Umar, the Taliban leader and head of the newly established Islamic Emirate of Afghanistan. It was a shock for Mullah 'Umar to hear about the *fatwa* through a report on the BBC Pashto-language services.[102]

Bin Laden formed this organization and issued its declaration of war in February 1998 while in Afghanistan under the protection of Mullah

'Umar, the leader of the country. In April 1998, the U.S. administration sent a delegation to the Taliban. Although the U.S. did not recognize the Taliban government, the visit of the U.S. officials to Kabul was the highest point in the relationship between the U.S. and the Islamic Emirate of Afghanistan. Mullah 'Umar wanted his emirate to be recognized by the UN, but the issue of Bin Laden stood in the way as the main obstacle. Mullah 'Umar agreed to hand Bin Laden over to the U.S., but asked the U.S. to assist in the process. Throughout the negotiations, "the United States never recognized the Taliban's need for *aabroh*, the Pashtu word for face-saving formula."[103] This would become apparent later, but in relation to this the head of the Saudi intelligence stated also that Mullah 'Umar "twice agreed to hand over Osama Bin Laden to the [Saudi] kingdom."[104]

Two months later, in June 1998, Mullah 'Umar received Prince Turki al-Faisal, the head of Saudi intelligence. The prince was able to strike a secret deal with Mullah 'Umar to hand over Bin Laden to the Saudi kingdom.[105] The only condition proposed by Mullah 'Umar was that a committee of Afghan and Saudi scholars be established to articulate a correct legal justification for the extradition.[106] In July, Mullah 'Umar sent a delegation to the Saudis to reconfirm the deal, but the Saudis did not agree with Mullah 'Umar's idea concerning the committee.[107]

In the meantime, Bin Laden and his associates were planning to bring the *fatwa* against the Crusaders and the Jews into practice. Between 23 February and 7 August 1998, Bin Laden gave a few statements that warned of attacks against U.S. interests. While U.S. security was focusing on Saudi Arabia, Bin Laden was planning to attack U.S. interests in East Africa. As the head of the CIA explained:

> The Egyptian service told us that a senior operative from Jamaah Islamiya, a Southeast Asian terrorist organization allied with al-Qa'ida, was planning an attack on U.S. and Israeli interests in order to help win the release of the Blind Sheikh. Four trucks filled with C-4 explosives had been brought to Kampala, in Uganda, and operatives there had begun casing the American embassy. We immediately contacted the Ugandans and also brought in Tanzanians and Kenyans. Al-Qa'ida had already proved how effective it could be at striking U.S. interests in Africa.[108]

On 7 August 1998, the eighth anniversary of the arrival of U.S. troops in Saudi Arabia, and four and half months after the *fatwa*, simultaneous attacks on U.S. embassies in Nairobi (Kenya) and Dar el-Salam (Tanzania) took place, resulting in the death of 291 people and the injury of 5,000.[109] The CIA stated that "there were 240 people killed and some 4,000 wounded in the two attacks."[110] The CIA pointed the finger at Bin Laden and his associates, as he had recently called for the killing of U.S. citizens: "It quickly became clear that the embassy bombings were the work of al-Qa'ida."[111] However, Bin Laden did not claim responsibility. The attacks generated comprehensive discussion in both East and West at all levels, including among government officials, policymakers, researchers, political commentators, and the media. Focusing on these discussions, which were published in both Arabic and English, one might conclude the following:

1. Many studies focused first on fundamentalists with suspicion and placed them at the top of the list of suspects.
2. Other studies focused on Iran, Iraq, and Libya, but there was no proof to suggest their involvement and they were easily exempted.
3. A number of studies focused on Bin Laden, as well as on the Egyptian Jihad groups. They pointed out Bin Laden's threats and statements, which were circulated in the press, including his interview with the U.S. television station ABC.
4. Some studies also focused on Bin Laden's declaration of the "World Islamic Front for the Jihad against the Jews and the Crusaders" and linked al-Qa'ida and the Egyptian Jihad together with the other groups who signed the declaration.
5. The attacks on the U.S. embassies brought to the fore the attacks on U.S. citizens in Riyadh and al-Khobar. Studies linked all these episodes together and pointed to Bin Laden and his al-Qa'ida network as the perpetrators.
6. Some studies also linked these attacks to the presence of U.S. troops in the region in general, particularly in Arabia.
7. The attacks were also linked to the U.S. double standards with respect to its foreign policy in the Middle East and its support of Israel.
8. The attacks were also linked to the U.S. foreign policy toward Iraq, on the one hand, and toward the support of the oppressive Arab regimes on the other.

9. Some studies also noted that the attacks against American embassies would indicate that al-Qaʻidaʼs capacity surpassed the logistic strength of those Arab regimes. The perpetrators reminded these regimes of their shame, as they could not help their American master. As the head of the CIA put it, "Al-Qaʻida had already proved how effective it could be at striking U.S. interests in Africa."[112]

In retaliation for the attacks, on 20 August 1998 the U.S. fired thirteen cruise missiles on Sudan, and seventy-two on Afghanistan, neither of which killed any one.[113] One of these missiles landed in Pakistan and none of the al-Qaʻida operatives was killed.[114] This attack against Afghanistan and Sudan was mainly based on the conclusions arrived at by the CIA and other intelligence agencies.[115] However, the timing, target, and methodology of the retaliation were all too hastily devised, and failed to serve U.S. interests. Indeed, the retaliation helped Bin Ladenʼs propaganda, and saved his life. He was well aware of the U.S. efforts, as the head of CIA states, "to capture Bin Laden" or "to snatch him in Afghanistan" and then "bring him back to the United States if possible, to face trial."[116] He was well aware of the negotiations about handing him over to the Saudi regime and that if the Taliban handed him over to the Saudis, they would in turn hand him over to the U.S., because he was no longer a Saudi national. Aware of this danger, Bin Laden believed he must do something to anger the U.S. and force them to take action.

He attacked the U.S. embassies to provoke the U.S. to retaliate and attack Afghanistan, thereby ending all restrictions imposed on him and the threat of his repatriation. This is what really happened, as emphasized by al-Qaʻidaʼs then second-in-command Ayman al-Zawahiri in 1998:

The CIA obtained information that there will be an al-Qaʻida meeting in Khost. Also they obtained information that there were WMD [weapons of mass destruction] in Khartoum. Therefore, the Americans quickly attacked. We anticipated that the Americans will not reveal the findings of the investigation until America kills those who participated in the "World Islamic Front." We anticipated that such activity will be repeated, before any evidence is put forth and without any justification. We are well aware of that before the Nairobi and Dar el-Salam episodes. There is a continual American conspiracy for killing or assassinating us, and we welcome it. We are saying to

America that you have entered the war and the Americans involved themselves in it. They previously fought in Korea and Vietnam, but in this era with the Muslims. They will know how we fight, and how we become martyrs.[117]

Preparing for retaliation, as the head of the CIA explains, "was a tough moment. . . . This act demanded some sort of retaliation."[118] On the basis of the intelligence gathered, the U.S. decided to retaliate by attacking Afghanistan and Sudan. The head of the CIA explained that "in mid-August, as we were searching for ways to respond, we received a godsend: signal intelligence revealed that a meeting would be held by Bin Laden."[119] In connection to this "godsend: signal intelligence," the question remains as to why the attacks on Afghanistan did not kill anybody at all.[120] One answer to this is that the source of this "godsend: signal intelligence" was al-Qa'ida itself, as emphasized by al-Zawahiri in the quotation above. The decision to retaliate was made hastily and emotionally, and did not in the end serve U.S. interests, but rather saved Bin Laden and helped promote his propaganda against the U.S.

As for the timing of the retaliation, the U.S. did not announce Bin Laden's responsibility, nor did it officially charge him as responsible before the retaliatory attacks were carried out. Although U.S. officials were strongly convinced that Bin Laden was responsible, they stopped short of officially charging him or announcing his responsibility before completing their investigation.[121]

In terms of the targets in Afghanistan, the U.S. sought to destroy the infrastructure of Bin Laden's training camps. However, it appeared that al-Qa'ida members were not at these camps at the time, so no one was killed.[122] These jihadists were not an organized army that the U.S. could strike at easily, as it had done previously in Libya and Iraq. These jihadists live in caves, in tunnels, in small tents, and between trees. As the head of the CIA put it, "one of the difficulties of fighting a terrorist opponent is the paucity of targets susceptible to the application of military force."[123]

With regard to the target in Sudan, the U.S. selected the al-Shifa Pharmaceutical factory in Khartoum, which Bin Laden purportedly used to produce weapons of mass destruction (WMD). The U.S. claimed that this information was based on the results of an investigation conducted by the CIA.[124] They also stated that "Bin Laden tried to obtain uranium in Sudan to be used in some types of nuclear device."[125] However, the

Sudanese government verified that this factory did nothing other than produce pharmaceutical products. Attacking a country that is a member of the UN is against international law unless certain protocols are followed and war is declared. Such behavior on the part of the most advanced and powerful nation on earth angered many Muslims, in particular because there had been no previous indication or accusation from the U.S. in connection to the factory.

Bin Laden used the attacks against Afghanistan and Sudan to mobilize his audiences and followers against the U.S. This was very effective propaganda, particularly if we consider that many of the masses in the Arab and Muslim worlds must live with their humiliation and identity crises. Such people were looking for a hero to stand up against the U.S., a country that had humiliated them in Palestine, Iraq, Arabia, and Africa, at both the local and international levels. At the United Nations Security Council, the number of vetoes used by the United States with regard to the Palestinian issue is truly astonishing. Washington used its veto thirty-two times to shield Israel from the UN Security Council's critical draft resolutions between 1972 and 1997.

Such abuses of power have galvanized the minds of Muslim youth, raised anti-U.S. sentiment across many countries, and increased support for Bin Laden. He became the people's hero who stood up against the U.S. and its servants among the Arab rulers. His photograph became increasingly popular, appearing in public demonstrations and printed on t-shirts. Reporting on the Bin Laden issue, the press have made him into a very important phenomenon and have even printed a photograph of him riding a white horse. Articles and stories in the press and on television screens have portrayed him as a hero of the people and the awaited imam coming to them victoriously 'on a white horse.'

Consequently, the logical question here is what else could the U.S. have done? Was there another option for the U.S. at the time? The answer is definitely yes. In this regard, the head of the CIA, George Tenet, who was at the "center of the storm," pointed out several methods of retaliation, and finally selected the previously cited method to seek to destroy Bin Laden.[126] Unfortunately, it did not destroy him, but instead saved his life and brought about the War on Terror, which appears to have no end. The following proposed options require the U.S., the most powerful country on the planet, to question its methods of retaliation to Bin Laden's attacks:

1. Instead of retaliating as they did, and thereby turning Bin Laden into a hero, the U.S. could have launched a counter-campaign to besiege Bin Laden and his jihadist groups: a campaign that focused on presenting to the Muslim world the case of those innocents, Muslims and non-Muslims alike, including women and children, who were killed in cold blood in Kenya and Tanzania. It was possible to portray Bin Laden and his jihadists as ill-minded people who do not value human life and were thirsty for blood, and were willing to kill innocent Muslims and non-Muslims alike. They could have portrayed them as terrorists, who would be hated by Muslims worldwide.

2. The campaign could have been organized and conducted in cooperation with the religious institutions in Egypt, Saudi Arabia, and other countries to expose these groups as ignorant of the basics of Islam and the teachings of the Prophet. Linking this to the thousands of innocent people who have been killed would certainly have maximized the success of such a campaign. If such a strategy had been adopted at the time, Bin Laden would not have been able to find a place among Muslims and more importantly with the Taliban, his protectors.

3. The U.S. was well aware that Mullah 'Umar was going to hand Bin Laden over, at least to the Saudi regime, who would then have passed him over to the U.S. Thus, the timing of retaliation was critical here. They could have launched the counter-campaign, supported by religious authorities and religious intuitions, the media and other channels, and waited for the Saudis to complete the deal with the Taliban to hand him over. However, the U.S. used its guns and missiles in what appears to have been an emotionally motivated and overly reactive fashion. The war against terrorism is a war of ideas. As Tony Blair states, "I see this as a global threat that has to be handled at a number of different levels; including the level of ideas and ideology."[127]

Attacking Afghanistan did not destroy Bin Laden or al-Qaʻida's infrastructure; rather it destroyed any potential for an agreement with Mullah 'Umar that would have allowed him to hand over Bin Laden to the Saudi authorities. However, the Saudis did not give up hope. Three weeks after the missile strikes on Afghanistan, two Saudi jets landed in Kandahar. One carried Prince Turki al-Faisal, the head of Saudi intelligence, and the other carried Saudi special forces to take Bin Laden back. The prince claimed that he came because of Mullah 'Umar's request to expel Bin

Laden. However, Mullah 'Umar rejected this claim, questioning the prince's words. The meeting was not friendly, as usual, but moody and stormy, to the extent that Mullah 'Umar accused the prince and his Saudi government of "doing the dirty work" for the U.S., which had attacked poor Afghanistan. "If the Prince was speaking in the name of the Americans," said Mullah 'Umar, "do not blame me then if I say I am speaking in the name of Bin Laden."[128] Although Mullah 'Umar was still angry with Bin Laden because of his activity against the U.S., he replaced Bin Laden and his Arab associates with the Afghans.[129] As a result, Mullah 'Umar assured the prince that he could not return to the Saudi kingdom empty-handed, but that he must take with him, not Bin Laden, but the Saudi representative in Kabul, the implication being that his relationship with the prince had reached an end. After his return to Riyadh, the Saudi retaliated and expelled the Taliban representative in Riyadh.[130]

Thus, the missile attacks on Afghanistan, intended to destroy Bin Laden, saved him and released him from the trap in which he was caught. He even used the missile attacks on Afghanistan and Sudan to portray U.S. aggression against these vulnerable and small countries. Propagandizing about these attacks with reference to a mix of issues related, for example, to Palestine and Iraq, among others, within the context of Islam, Bin Laden was able to increase anti-U.S. sentiment among Muslims and attract more Muslim youths to his cause. After 1998, al-Qa'ida increased dramatically in size. In 2001, it was a large network that had infiltrated almost every country in the world. As the head of the CIA stated: "I told the Congress, even as our counterterrorism efforts are improving, international groups are expanding their networks, improving their skills and sophistication, and working to stage more spectacular attacks."[131]

Two weeks after the missile attacks on Afghanistan on 20 August 1998, Bin Laden launched his campaign against the U.S. in a press conference held in September. At this conference it was evident that the relationship between Bin Laden and Mullah 'Umar had sweetened once again. Mullah 'Umar, who had been profoundly aggrieved with Bin Laden, fully supported and defended him. This change in their relationship was publicly demonstrated by Bin Laden in this press conference and in the Taliban magazine *Nida-ul-momineen* (The Call of the Faithful). Referring to Bin Laden's conference, the magazine ran the headline "Bin Laden calls Mullah Muhammad 'Umar Leader of the Faithful [Amir ul-Momineen] and says that he will obey him as a religious duty." The author, Maulvi

Obaid-ur-Rahmain, repeatedly stressed Bin Laden's denial of any responsibility or link to the bombings in East Africa: "The guest Mujahid denied having any link to the East African bombings." The magazine published what it called "Osama Bin Laden's written pledge to Amir-ul-Momineen." The letter was written as follows:

Hazrat Amir-ul-Momineen, Mujahid Mullah Mohammed 'Umar (may Allah protect you and keep you safe). As Salaam-o-'Alaikum.

Hazrat Amir-ul-Momineen! Allah has blessed you with fresh glorious victories in . . . Afghanistan. This is an auspicious moment for us, to heartily congratulate you and pledge ourselves anew [to] stand by you, to render all possible assistance to you for the supremacy of Islam, for the stability of the Islamic government, for the enforcement of the law of Allah till the time that all dissension, conflicts come to an end and Allah's religion reigns supreme.

On this occasion we renew our pledge too that we consider you to be our noble Amir and that obedience, allegiance and assistance to you is as compulsory upon us as it is to an Amir appointed by Shariat. We invite all Muslims to render assistance and co-operation to you, in every possible way they can.

Wasallam-o-'Alaikum,
Your brother, Osama bin Muhammad bin Laden, 15/09/1998.[132]

Thus, the missile attacks on Afghanistan transformed the Taliban from reluctant hosts into allies and partners of Bin Laden. Another dynamic that brought the Taliban and Bin Laden even closer was world politics. The UAE, Pakistan, and Saudi Arabia were the only countries to recognize the Taliban as the legitimate government of Afghanistan. However, the Afghan seat at the UN remained in the hands of the opposition, the defeated northern allies. The issue of international recognition was one of the Taliban government's top priorities, as a newly established government in a country ruined by war for decades. Recognition of their country as a member of the international community would bring public and private international funds to the country and allow for its further development and stability. This question of recognition was frequently raised by the Taliban government following its ascent to power in Kabul in 1996. The Taliban discussed this issue on approximately twenty occasions with U.S. officials, including Malinowski and the assistant secretary of state for South Asia, Karl E. Inderfurth, who met frequently with Taliban representatives.[133] Yet the Taliban's relations with the outside world were blocked by the U.S. because of the Bin Laden issue.[134]

Mullah Muhammad Rabbani, the prime minister and head of the Taliban government's Inner Shura Council,[135] together with Mullah Muhammad 'Umar, agreed to take part in a pragmatic dialogue with the U.S. and agreed to expel Bin Laden. Officials from the U.S. and the Taliban met prior to the embassy bombings in East Africa and the missile attacks on Afghanistan. The meetings continued until just a few days before the September 11 attacks.

Efforts to capture Bin Laden were undertaken first by the Saudis after he left Saudi Arabia for Afghanistan, and later by Sudan in 1991. The U.S. became interested in his capture only in 1996 when he was in Sudan. The plan was to have him arrested in Khartoum and extradited to Saudi Arabia, which would then turn him over to the U.S. Realizing the danger he faced in Sudan, Bin Laden moved to Afghanistan in May 1996, before the Taliban seized power in Kabul. Consequently, the U.S. plan to capture him shifted focus from Sudan to Afghanistan.[136] From 1996 until 2001, the U.S. designed three methods to capture Bin Laden, involving U.S. intelligence on the ground, dialogue with the Taliban, and UN Security Council sanctions.[137]

In June 1998, two months before the attacks on the U.S. embassies in East Africa on 7 August, a court in New York indicted Bin Laden, in absentia, for terrorist acts against the U.S. The indictment would give the U.S. the authority to capture him and bring him to stand trial. However, as *The Guardian* observed, "it was not clear last night precisely what alleged crimes the indictment covered."[138]

A few days after the bombing of the U.S. embassies in East Africa in 1998, the U.S. began to pressure the Taliban to hand over Bin Laden. The U.S. planned to use the UN and threats of sanctions and inflexible dialogue with the Taliban.[139]

On 15 October 1999, the Security Council issued resolution number 1267, which froze all financial resources and demanded that the Taliban hand Bin Laden over to what the resolution referred to as the "appropriate authorities" for trial. The resolution left the gate wide open for Bin Laden to be tried anywhere, but not necessarily in the U.S. In the meantime, the Taliban and the U.S. were engaged in dialogue on the Bin Laden issue. These meetings took place in many cities, including "Tashkent, Kandahar, Islamabad, Bonn, New York, and Washington. There were surprise satellite calls, one of which led to a forty-minute chat between a mid-level State Department bureaucrat and the Taliban's supreme leader, Mohammad 'Umar. There was a surprise visit to Washington, made by a Taliban envoy."[140]

Throughout this dialogue, which lasted over three years, and before September 11, the Taliban offered three proposals. The first suggested that Bin Laden could be tried in either Afghanistan or another Muslim country. The second was to try Bin Laden before a panel of three Islamic judges, one chosen each by Afghanistan, Saudi Arabia, and the U.S. In the third proposal, the Taliban proposed that Bin Laden be tried before a panel of only one Islamic judge. When the U.S. rejected the three proposals, the Taliban finally said, "show us the evidence" against Bin Laden.[141]

The Taliban's pragmatic attempts were consistently undercut by the attitude of the U.S., both prior to and following the bombings in East Africa in 1998. Milton Bearden, a former CIA station chief who oversaw the U.S. covert operations in Afghanistan, stated, "We never heard what they were trying to say. We had no common language. Ours was, 'Give up Bin Laden.' They were saying, 'Do something to help us give him up.'"[142]

Throughout the negotiations, the U.S. was not flexible and "never recognized the Taliban need for *aabroh*, the Pashtu word for 'face-saving formula.' Officials never found a way to ease the Taliban's fear of embarrassment if it turned over a fellow Muslim to an 'infidel' western power."[143] Richard Hrair Dekmejian emphasized that "we were not serious about the whole thing, not only this administration [Bush's] but the previous one [Clinton's]. We did not engage these people creatively. There were missed opportunities."[144]

The U.S. missile attacks on Afghanistan shocked the Taliban and transformed the whole issue. One week after the attacks, Mullah 'Umar said in an interview with *The Guardian*: "We told the Americans . . . . What is left for talks now? Everything was finished after the rocket attacks. We will protect him with our life." He also called on the U.S. either to "prove" Bin Laden's terrorist activity while in "Afghanistan and Sudan" or "pay compensation and apologise for its missile attacks . . . . It would be a matter of great embarrassment and shame for the United States and its intelligence agencies if America was unable to prove internationally that Usama Bin Laden was involved in the bombings of U.S. embassies in East Africa and that the pharmaceutical factory in Sudan was making chemical weapons."[145]

Al-Qa'ida, then, was able to draw the U.S. into a devastating and bloody conflict, the end of which cannot be predicted.

5

Ideology

In seeking to understand the mindset of al-Qaʻida and its affiliated individuals and groups, one must appreciate their ideological ideas and tactics. Al-Qaʻida's main objective, in al-Zawahiri's words, is to "establish an Islamic state and to uproot the regimes who are enemy to Islam."[1] It was in the name of this ideology that the leadership of al-Qaʻida, namely Bin Laden and al-Zawahiri, considered jihad to be the only means of achieving their ideological goal. Focusing on the attitude of al-Qaʻida's thinking on jihad, one first needs to appreciate the concept of jihad as conceived by a Muslim consensus.

Jihad: Muslim Consensus

The word jihad does not necessarily refer to 'war,' and the concept of jihad cannot be reduced to mean only 'war.' The words for 'war,' as mentioned in the Qurʼan, are *al-harb* (war) and *al-qital* (fight). Qurʼanic words usually have their own connotations and relate to particular circumstances, but some writers have mistakenly used *al-harb* and *al-qital* interchangeably with the word jihad. A great deal of misunderstanding with regard to the attitude of Islamic law to international relations has come about as a result of confusion regarding the Islamic concept of jihad. Thus, in the context of al-Qaʻida's terrorist activities that are claimed to be in the name of jihad, the question of what defines both jihad and 'war' in the consensus of Islamic law is critical.

The word *harb* ('war') is occasionally referred to in the Qurʼan, while frequent reference is made to the word 'fight' (*qital* and other derivations from the root *q-t-l*). The Qurʼan more often makes reference to words such as 'struggle' or 'striving' (jihad and other derivations of the root *j-h-d*). In some passages, these words could be taken in a symbolic rather than literal sense.

Etymologically, the word jihad connotes the exertion of effort. As there is exertion, then so must there be resistance. The exertion of effort thus indicates the presence of resistance or opposition. In this sense, a person may use the word jihad to describe his or her efforts to control a gambling habit. Alternatively, a pre-Islamic poet might use the word jihad to describe his efforts to control his passion after the departure of his beloved with her tribe, leaving him alone and without any hope of reunion. In this case, his passion would be the source of resistance to his efforts to control himself and his attempts to live a normal life.[2]

The Islamic conception of jihad is balanced in implying both the exertion of effort and the presence of resistance. Exerting one's efforts does not necessarily mean armed conflict or hostilities, for one may perform jihad with words. Here also, the exertion of efforts or jihad, as emphasized by Sayyid Qutb, is limited to use only "against oppression and injustice whether inflicted upon Muslims or non-Muslims, allies or non-allies."[3] Thus, jihad is not a war and is never meant to force others to believe in Islam. Freedom of belief is promoted by the Qur'an in several verses, the most significant of which is: *There is no compulsion in religion* (2:256). Moreover, the Qur'an stresses the firm relationship between the Islamic concepts of both jihad and freedom of belief. Based on the Qur'an, Sayyid Qutb says: "Islam permits no Muslim, ruler or ruled, to fight against non-Muslims in order to force them to adopt Islam. Islam consents for war, only against oppressors in order to secure the rights to freedom of belief."[4]

Further, some verses that deal with the concept of jihad in the early stage of Islam are abrogated by verses in the later stages of the revelation. For example, those rules in verses 4:87–94 that deal with non-believers and hypocrites are abrogated by the later rules of verses 9:4–14, 29. Similarly, verse 9:73, which commands the Prophet of Islam *O Prophet! Strive hard against the non-believers and the hypocrites, and be harsh against them*, is reshaped by the commands of verses 9:5, 12, 29, 36, 123, which deal with the concept of jihad in the later stage of the revelation. Thus, war is permitted only against oppressors regardless of their religion, race, or color. The Qur'an says: *And fight against them* [oppressors] *until there is no more oppression and the entire Din* [religion] *will be for God. If they stopped, fight none except the oppressors* (8:39). Muslim exegeses do not limit the command of the latter verse as relevant to a specific period, place, or people, but view it as "general and continuous until the Day of Judgement."⁵ Moreover, the meaning of the phrase *the entire Din will be for God* in this verse is but 'freedom of belief.' The word *Din* (religion) in the verse does not mean a specific religion or specifically the 'Islamic religion.' The permission to fight the oppressors does not free Muslim combatants from the order to be tolerant and generous. They must do justice and protect the freedom of belief of all citizens, both Muslim and non-Muslims, and secure their lives against oppression: *Fight for the sake of God those who fight against you, but do not be aggressive. God does not love the aggressors* (Qur'an 2:190).

Therefore, interpreting jihad to exclusively mean 'war' is incorrect, even if that war is a war of words, given that the theory of war in Islamic international law stipulates that "peace is the rule, while war is the exception."⁶ War, on this account, is an action that should be undertaken only as a last resort. In short, it is not an overstatement to note that: (i) translating the word jihad into 'holy war' is not as accurate a translation as it should be; (ii) Islam does not encourage Muslims to go to war and fight according to their impulses, but outlines to them the circumstances under which and with whom fighting is legitimate, and points out the law governing the circumstances of war and peace; and (iii) the intent of the command of all verses dealing with the issue of jihad and war should be observed within the context of time and place, and the safeguarding of human rights and the rights to the freedom of belief, at any stage.⁷ In relation to this, Arthur Nussbaum writes:

The hostility of Islam toward infidels was termed by remarkable exceptions. The Koran, despite the paramountcy of Muhammad's teachings, embodied the Old and the New Testaments in the Islamic creed, and Christians and Jews received preferential treatment. As 'peoples of the book' *(dhimmi)*—namely, of the Bible—they were permitted to stay in Moslem countries and to live their lives according to their own religions and under their own laws . . . . Perhaps the most impressive application of the doctrine occurred after the fall of Constantinople, when the conqueror Muhammad II convoked representatives of the Greek Orthodox Church, of the Armenian Church, and of the Jews to tell them that they might stay in Constantinople under their own laws and the leadership of their religious superiors. Because the Orthodox Patriarch had died before the conquest, the Sultan caused the Greeks in Constantinople to elect a new Patriarch whom he treated with high honour.[8]

The pioneering Arab sociologist Ibn Khaldun (1332–1406) observed that humanity has experienced wars and disasters of its own making since the beginning of human society, many of them rooted in a vengeful human imperative. Examining the relationships between medieval states, Ibn Khaldun emphasized that states were not in the habit of confining themselves to a specific area or a piece of land. The rule of 'might is right' was the predominant mode of the medieval interstate settlements. Derived from their feuds, the policies of medieval states were designed to seek continual expansion, at the expense of other states, whenever possible.[9] The 'private wars' in Europe, the assault of the barbarians on the Western Roman Empire, or the wars between the Persian Empire and the Eastern Roman Empire illustrate this point.

It was also out of this policy that Rome grew to become the great Roman Empire, which conquered Europe and almost all of the eastern lands.[10] The Roman Empire was then divided by the Emperor Theodosius (d. 395). In 330, Constantinople became the capital of the Eastern Roman Empire (Byzantium), which retained control over the most fruitful lands of the Arabian Peninsula and its trade routes, except the barren regions and their small towns such as Mecca and Medina. Other than this fruitless area, the Byzantine Empire controlled vast areas from Yemen, Syria, Palestine, Asia Minor, Egypt, and other North African lands, to Constantinople and its surroundings, and further to Greece, the southern Balkans, Cyprus, the northern shores of the Black Sea, Sicily, and large parts of Italy, including Rome for about two centuries.[11]

In light of this policy of expansionism, the security of the newly established Islamic state was critical. It is within this context that the attitude of jihad should be interpreted. There are many writings on the notion of jihad, but many of these writings observe jihad in the medieval world of early Islam through the prism of today's world. Much of what has been written either applies the attitude of jihad as adopted in the medieval world to modern times, or applies the attitude of modern international law to the medieval world and its mentality. In either case, such uncontextualized interpretation will certainly lead to misunderstanding.[12] The rule of 'might is right' is no longer acceptable, but has not entirely disappeared. Much of what has been written about jihad, particularly since September 11, 2001, shows a strong tendency to suggest that the attitudes prevalent in the early days of Islam are the same attitudes that prevail today.[13]

In the medieval period, the terms *dar al-Islam* (territory of Islam), or the *pax Islamica*, was used to describe Islamic territories as well as non-Islamic territories held under Islamic sovereignty. All countries beyond these territories fell within the category of *dar al-harb* (territory of war). Using jihad in relation to the theme and framework of these terms is simply wrong and evidently misleading. First, these terms (*dar al-Islam* and *dar al-harb*) are not Qur'anic terms, but were introduced by a number of jurists as a means of classification and of organizing their jurisprudential thought concerning the territories both under and outside the rule of Islam. Therefore, we find that al-Shaybani (d. 805), the author of *Kitab al-siyar al-saghir* (A Treatise on Law of Nations) and *Kitab al-siyar al-kabir* (A Treatise on International Law), did not use these terms consistently. He used terms like *dar al-harb* (territory of war) and *ahl al-harab* (people of the territory of war) interchangeably, and sometimes used *ahl al-Islam* (people of Islam) or just one word, *al-dar* (territory), in place of *dar al-Islam* (territory of Islam).[14]

Second, despite the fact that the two terms *dar al-Islam* and *dar al-harb* are not Qur'anic, a number of jurists have used these terms to classify their world into zones—namely, Islam and non-Islam, or peace and potential war zones. This classification was not unique to the Muslim state, but also was the policy of the most powerful empires that surrounded the newly established Islamic state at the time.[15] For Muslims, the two-zone classification was not a religious idea and was not a means of aggression, oppression, or conversion by force. It was rather a policy required for national security purposes, the most pressing issue of the states of that time, and indeed of all times. There are a great many medieval accounts of what has come to be known among modern states as the 'pre-emptive strike' policy, which was also devised and practically enforced by the medieval Persian, Roman, Byzantine, and Islamic governments. Al-Waqidi (d. 207/822), in his *Kitab al-maghazi* (Expeditions), which was edited by Marsden Jones (1966), pointed out in some detail that when Muslims learned of the immediate danger of the Byzantine Empire's preparation to invade Tabuk, the Muslim deliberation, led by the Prophet himself, resulted in a pre-emptive strike to counter an overwhelming danger of an attack by such a strong Byzantine army. While Heracles left his army to march on Tabuk, and resided in Homs in Syria, the Prophet himself led the Muslim army to Tabuk in the very hot summer and encouraged Muslims to fight (jihad) to protect the state.[16] Thus, jihad should be interpreted as defensive rather than offensive, and the Qur'anic statements on jihad should be considered within the historical context, not through the prism of today. In terms of the attitudes of the policies of that time, the Persian-Byzantine policies were based simply on attacks and counterattacks. Moreover, the Byzantine Empire conquered most of Italy, including Rome itself. The Byzantine Empire's actions reflected policies of international law that do not differ greatly from the attitude underlying the phrase 'might is right.'[17]

It was because of the predominance of such attitudes that the Muslims considered the territory of war (dar al-harb) and the territory of Islam (dar al-Islam) as necessary aspects of state policy. Muslims also borrowed this two-zone policy from their surrounding empires. The Pax Romana and the Pax Persiana were also policies that divided the world into two zones of peace and war and enforced the conqueror's legal system to protect the areas under their sovereignty.[18] It was out of this tradition that the later Pax Britannica came to assert itself on the world stage as a policy of the British Empire. Hence, the medieval Pax Islamica, which prevailed over the area called the territory of Islam (dar al-Islam), can be seen in the same way as the Pax Romana, the Pax Persiana, and the Pax Britannica. To be fair, Muslims added to the two zones a third one termed dar al-sulh (territory of peace arrangement), which was also called dar al-'ahd (territory of covenant, convention or treaty). This meant that the territory of Islam (dar al-Islam) recognized territory that was not under Muslim sovereignty. However, since these states did not recognize each other, there was always the potential for hostility. Persian, Roman, and Byzantine law refused to recognize the sovereignty of the new Islamic state and its right to exist. The Islamic state regarded its surrounding territories of these superpowers as territories of potential war (dar al-harb); however, it did not exclude the possibility of a peace arrangement, treaty, or covenant with them. Their territories, then, were not exclusively considered territories of war, but also where peace arrangements and covenants were possible. Thus, other than the territory of Islam (dar al-Islam), there were: (i) the territory of peace arrangement (dar al-sulh); (ii) the territory of covenant (dar al-'ahd); and (iii) the territory of war (dar al-harb). Those who seek a peaceful agreement or covenant with their surrounding states cannot be considered invaders, and their jihad cannot be observed as aggressive or offensive, but rather as defensive. It is in this context that the attitude of jihad as well as the meaning of the expressions *dar al-Islam* and *dar al-harb* should be observed.

The concept of jihad cannot be understood outside of its historical context, and can easily be misinterpreted if approached in terms of latter-day accidental conceptions. The necessity to carefully interpret scriptural passages that deal with war is not limited to the Qur'an. For example, the Hebrew scriptures, accepted by Christians as the Old Testament, contain in the book of Deuteronomy 20:10–20 the following instructions:

> When thou comest nigh unto a city to fight against it, then proclaim peace unto it. And it shall be, if it make thee answer of peace, and open unto thee, then it shall be, that all the people that is found therein shall be tributaries unto thee, and they shall serve thee. And if it will make no peace with thee, but will make war against thee, then thou shalt besiege it: And when the Lord thy God hath delivered it into thine hands, thou shalt smite every male thereof with the edge of the sword: But the women, and the little ones, and the cattle, and all that is in the city, even all the spoil thereof, shalt thou take unto thyself; and thou shalt eat the spoil of thine enemies, which the Lord thy God hath given thee. Thus shalt thou do unto all the cities which are very far off from thee, which are not of the cities of these nations. But of the cities of these people, which the Lord thy God doth give thee for an inheritance, thou shalt save alive nothing that breatheth: But thou shalt utterly destroy them; namely, the Hittites, and the Amorites, the Canaanites, and the Perizzites, the Hivites, and the Jebusites; as the Lord thy God hath commanded thee: That they teach you not to do after all their abominations which they have done unto their gods; so should ye sin against the Lord thy God.

However, any war in Islam is entirely subject to many qualifications, the heart of which are the freedom of belief and the rights of non-Muslims in general, whether combatant or non-combatant, as outlined below.

In consonance with other conventions and agreements on laws of war, Islamic law provides proper safeguards against unnecessary damage to life, wealth, and property. Modern humanitarian law seeks to provide increasing protections for civilians, non-combatants, and prisoners of war. In European international law, there is a strong interest in outlawing all weapons of mass destruction (WMD) and those that cause harm indiscriminately to civilians and combatants. These laws should also be updated to include the new generations of weapons that are still considered conventional, but cause indiscriminate damage, similar to unconventional weapons. The idea of banning WMD has been accentuated since the Second World War and has been put into practice to some extent in the past few decades.[19] In this regard, Islamic international law already has relevant pre-existing provisions and its theory and practice already include the possibility of peaceful coexistence with non-Muslims. There is a great deal of literature on the practice of Muslims in relation to their strong support for the sanctity of treaties with non-Muslims. Many Muslim countries seek to free the world from WMD and to free humanity from ill-informed policies. Regarding the treatment of enemies in war, Islamic international law has a set of principles that broke new ground in terms of their fairness toward one's enemies. Emphasizing the attitudes of Islamic international law toward war, Arthur Nussbaum writes:

> Moslem ideas on warfare are in some respects superior to Christian conceptions of the same period. A proclamation of Caliph Abu Bakr (d. 634), Muhammad's first successor, is significant. He warns his victorious soldiers to spare women, children, and old men; he exhorts them not to destroy palms and orchards, or burn homes, or to take from the provisions of the enemy more than needed; and he demands that prisoners of war be treated with pity. Ransoming and the exchanging of prisoners were far more widely practiced in the East than in the West, and in a number of cases prisoners received their freedom on a large scale by acts of generosity. Booty had to be delivered to the authorities for distribution, the treasury keeping one-fifth of it—a rule adopted, surprisingly enough, by the *Siete Partidas* of Alfonso X of Castile.[20]

The values espoused within Islamic international law in relation to war and peace can be illustrated by the examples provided below, which are taken from the time of the Prophet, who was acting according to Qur'anic injunctions. Many of these examples, considering their historical context, are striking for being surprisingly modern and relevant to our time. One difference between these laws and the laws of our time is that the former were not violated.

Islam recognizes a diversity of nations within the world community. The Qur'an provides a number of references to the division of the world into a multiplicity of nations: *And if thy Lord had willed, He verily would have made mankind a single nation, yet they cease not differing* (11:118); and elsewhere, *Had it been God's will, He could have made them all one nation* (42:8). The natural result of a multiplicity of nations is a complex and wide variety of interests, views, and political groups with political, economic, social, and psychological differences. The relationships among these nations are the natural result of the need for coexistence. In this context, Islamic international law works to regulate the relations between nations during peace as well as during periods of war, with the aim of promoting justice and peace wherever possible. Islamic international law makes peace the rule and ultimate objective, while war is the exception, as in the following examples:

1. Islamic law of war orders Muslims to respect the rights of foreigners, whether combatants or civilians, during the course of hostilities.[21]
2. During periods of peace or truce, which are both recognized in Islamic law, recognition is accorded to the authorities of the foreign state.[22]
3. If a Muslim enters foreign territory or is domiciled therein, he or she should respect the authority of the rulers of that territory and obey its laws. If there is a conflict between those laws and his or her own laws, the Muslim's obligation is to the latter.[23]
4. Under Islamic international law, Muslim individuals have the right to grant any foreigner protection by a one-sided act known as the covenant of safe conduct *('ahd al-aman)*, by which the foreigner's life, possessions, and businesses are made safe and secure. By this act the foreigner is protected *(musta'man)*. The act is binding upon the whole community and thus any violence against the *musta'man* is illegal.[24]
5. If a foreigner enters a Muslim territory or chooses to live therein, he or she should respect the authority of the rulers of that territory and obey the laws that do not conflict with his or her own religious belief (that is, obey the civil law). The foreigner's political and religious freedom is completely secured by the law. Thus, the foreigner does not pay *zakat*, which is a religious duty, but does pay taxes and can choose to switch to *zakat* without being required to change his religious belief.[25]

6. A prisoner of war is to be accorded generous treatment and can be set free (according to articles 108–109 of the *Islamic Law of Nations*).[26] The Qur'an commands that after you have subdued and captured them *thereafter is the time to either set them free as a favor or let them ransom themselves until the war is terminated* (47:4). A prisoner *qua* cannot be killed. The Prophet carried out this injunction during his lifetime. In the Battle of Badr, which was the first war in Islam, seventy were taken prisoners, some of whom were set free as an act of favor, but the high ranks and leaders were ransomed while the war with Quraysh was still in progress. In the battles of Hunayn and al-Ta'if in which a large number, about six thousand, were taken captive, all were eventually set free. The form of ransom adopted was, in some cases, that every learned prisoner should teach ten illiterate young Muslims how to read and write; some specials paid ransom ranging from 1,000 to 4,000 dirham; while others were set free for nothing in return. Regarding ransom, al-Waqidi reported with a sequence of references that goes back to the Prophet's wife 'A'isha that "when the Meccans began to ransom their people, Zaynab, the daughter of the Prophet, also sent to ransom her husband al-'As ibn al-Rabi'; she [Zaynab] sent her souvenir necklace that was a gift of her marriage given to her by Khadijah, the Prophet's first wife. When the Prophet saw the necklace and recognized it, he prayed for Khadijah, and said: 'If you see [that it is possible] to set her husband free to her, and to return her property, do it'" They said 'yes' and they freed her husband and returned the necklace to her."[27]

7. Prisoners of war must also be fed, and fed well, according to the Qur'anic injunctions: *Feed for the love of God, the indigent, the orphan, and the captive*, saying, *We feed you for the sake of God; no reward do we seek from you nor thanks* (76:8–9). Acting according to the Qur'an, the Prophet laid down the rules by saying, "Take care of the prisoners and treat them humanely."[28] Elsewhere, the Prophet said, "They are your brothers. God put them in your hands; so whoever has his brother in his hands, give him to eat whereof he himself eats and let him give to wear what he himself wears, and do not impose on them a work they are not able to do, and if you give them such a work, then help them in the execution of it."[29] Among the prisoners, Abu al-'As ibn al-Rabi' and al-Walid ibn al-Walid ibn al-Mughira testified that "If we were having lunch or dinner they usually favoured me by giving me bread while they were short of it—even whenever one of

them found a piece [of bread] he quickly hands it to me; they walk and carry us [on their horses and camels]."[30]

8. A prisoner could be tried and punished for his or her crimes, not merely for belligerency. This was carried out by the Prophet himself. After the Battle of Badr, the Prophet tried al-Nadr ibn al-Harith, not because he was a combatant or war prisoner but because of the crimes that he had committed against his fellow humans, both Muslims and non-Muslims. Al-Nadr pleaded guilty and for this he was sentenced to death.[31] 'Amr ibn 'Abdullah al-Jumahi (Abu 'Azza) was a horseman who committed a few crimes against a number of Muslims, including the Prophet himself as a human being. He was also an influential poet who used his poetry to mobilize the masses against the Prophet. At that time, poetry was an influential and effective means of mobilization, like the mass media of our time. It happened that al-Jumahi also came and fought against the Prophet at Badr but was captured. He was treated as a prisoner of war and was set free based on his pledge that he would stop persecuting Muslims and would not return to fight against the Prophet. However, he did not end his persecution of Muslims and continued to move around and employ his poetry to mobilize the masses to fight against the Prophet, and eventually joined them at the Battle of Uhud where he was recaptured as a prisoner of war. During his trial, he said, "O Muhammad let me free, I was forced to come." Muhammad's reply was, "Where is your covenant? You cannot go to Mecca to do what you did once again." Al-Jumahi was then put to death.[32]

9. The capturing state is fully responsible for the maintenance of its prisoners and must respect their dignity.[33]

10. Relatives are entitled to visit prisoners of war. The following is an example that involved the Prophet's wife. Ummu Salama, while attending the "mourning at the house of Afra," learned that her Meccan cousins had become prisoners of war. She saw them entering Medina, but did not speak to them before asking the Prophet for approval. On her way back, she met the Prophet at the house of 'A'isha and asked him, "O Messenger of God, my cousins are seeking to come to my house, so, I do treat them as guests, kempt their hairs and bring them to neatness and tidiness shape; I did not like to do that without your order (asta'miruka)." The Prophet said, "I do not dislike anything of that! So, do of this whatever you like."[34]

11. Under Islamic law, prisoners of war are entitled to lawyers or legal representatives. This right was ensured by the Prophet and leading Muslims of the time. For example, Abu Bakr, 'Umar ibn al-Khattab, and al-Miqdad all stood as legal representatives. The following account by al-Waqidi (d. 207/822) illustrates the position of prisoners and their legal representatives, and how the Prophet was making his decisions on such matters. In the aftermath of the Battle of Badr, al-Waqidi says, the Meccans invited Abu Bakr and 'Umar, one after the other, and requested that they stand in defense of their prisoners of war. Both men first spoke to the Prophet on the matter. He was the supreme judge, and before him stood Abu Bakr in defense of the prisoners, while 'Umar stood as prosecutor. The positions of Abu Bakr and 'Umar in a sense were not different. Both men were Muslims and senior commanders, and strongly believed that the Prophet was right and that those prisoners who fought against him were wrong. Both men were supportive of the Prophet and understood that the case of the prisoners of this first war was critical to the Islamic state and its wellbeing. It was agreed that all prisoners were combatants and were related to one another through marriage, including to the Prophet himself. At the hearings, before the Prophet, and as the public looked on, Abu Bakr stood to defend the prisoners saying, "O Messenger of God, among your people [Meccan prisoners] are the parents and descendants; the uncles and brothers; the fathers and cousins; the farthest of them is nearest to you; set them free may God be pleased with you; or let them ransom themselves to save them from the hellfire and their payment will support the Muslims; may God bring their hearts to you." The judge (the Prophet) kept silent. Abu Bakr stood aside and 'Umar stood up in his place, and said, 'O Messenger of God, they [the prisoners] are the enemies of God; they gave their lie to your truth; they came and fought against you; they expelled and deprived you of your home; they are the heads of Quraysh and leaders of wrong; killing them will fail Quraysh [from coming back to fight against you], and will enhance the position of the Muslims." The Prophet still kept silent. The hearing continued for a few days more, without any change in the positions of either the defense or the prosecution. The Prophet did not speak on any side. Finally, the Prophet went to his home for an hour. When he

came back, he asked the crowd about what they had heard from Abu Bakr and 'Umar. Their view was divided between supporters of Abu Bakr's view and supporters of 'Umar's view. "The Prophet made his decision to accept ransom and explained the positions of Abu Bakr and that of 'Umar through analogical examples from the earlier scriptures as mentioned in the Qur'an."[35]

12. Prisoners of war have the right to draw up their last wills. During the life of the Prophet, the wills of prisoners were transmitted to the enemy through appropriate channels.[36]

In theory, the state of war does not always need to take the form of actual hostilities under Islamic law. Rather, it can take the form of mere non-recognition, for regimes within the *dar al-harb* (territory of war) could establish treaties with Muslim states or enter into various forms of negotiation. This position is perhaps analogous to the de facto recognition accorded in modern international law to a regime that is not fully recognized de jure but is sufficiently established for its existence to be regarded as a fact. [37]

The concept of jihad, which is seen by some as referring not only to 'war' but also to a means by which the *pax Islamica* could spread to territories of the *dar al-harb*, should be reconsidered. The jihad does not necessarily mean actual hostilities or violent activities. It could be a cold war, a war of words or psychological warfare. Therefore, the jihad could take the form of persuasion.[38]

There is strong juridical support for the argument that the Prophet's practice and policy on matters of war reflected a basic attitude of defense and not offense. A war of aggression, according to some classical writings, is not supported by the precedents set by the Prophet.[39] The Prophet and his followers were severely persecuted for many years by the Quraysh tribe and its allies while there was no order to fight back. His followers asked for his permission to retaliate, but he rejected their requests because there was as yet no higher order from God. It was not until the higher order permitted them to fight and defend themselves that the Battle of Badr in 624 took place. Thus, jihad of aggression is not supported by either the Qur'an or the Prophet. Indeed, "it is well known that he [the Prophet] never fought foreign wars except on two occasions—once when he was compelled to do so consequent on the assassination of his envoy to the court of Busra and the second when he invaded Tabuk, which was a defensive measure undertaken to counter an overwhelming and immediate danger of an attack by the Byzantine Emperor."[40]

Islamic international law recognizes non-Islamic territories and encourages Muslim states to foster relations with them. This recognition is illustrated in the point made earlier that the division of the world into *dar al-Islam* and *dar al-harb* was a matter of intellectual classification and that the jihad against *dar al-harb* did not necessarily mean armed conflict or aggression and expansionism.[41] Taking this idea a step further, the classical concepts of such labels as *pax Romana, pax Persiana, pax Islamica, dar al-Islam, dar al-harb*, jihad, and the Crusade, which convey some sort of perpetual state of war, have come to be anachronistic. In the context of the geopolitical realities of the modern world, both the Christian and the Islamic ideals of one nation have come to be impracticable. Fragmentation of the Christian and the Muslim worlds into nation states and the need for coexistence produced a new theory of international and intercultural relations, namely, a relationship of enduring peace, not a relationship of armed conflicts or hostilities. The relationships between Muslim nation-states have come to be governed by general principles of international law no different from those between Muslim and non-Muslim states. Treaties had to be established, regimes had to be recognized, de jure as well as de facto. This leads us to "the law of treaties, which forms an impressive part of Islamic doctrine."[42]

The law of treaties is not new, that is, brought about by contemporary circumstances, but has existed for some time in Islamic *corpus juris* and in practice. The existence of the law of treaties is another qualification denoting that the classical concept of jihad is not and cannot be offensive but defensive. Jihad was a temporary legal device designed to achieve peace with the *dar al-harb* (territory of war) and did not necessarily involve hostility, but instead could be a war of words. Therefore, we find Muslims were more "accustomed to a state of dormant jihad rather than to a state of open hostility. In the meantime, contacts between Muslims and non-Muslims, personal and official, were conducted by peaceful means, although a state of war continued to exist between Islam and other countries."[43] In connection with the law of treaties, the Qur'an obliges believers to keep their covenants, even toward polytheists, until the end of the term. All parties should be genuine, observe the covenant with sincerity, and should not fail each other or help anyone against the other; a fortiori, the same rule applies to relations with Christians and Jews. In addition, the Prophet's first successor, Abu Bakr (d. 634), exhorted the soldiers as follows: "Let there be no perfidy, no falsehood in your treaties with the enemy; be faithful in all things, proving yourselves upright and noble and maintaining your word and promises truly."[44] There is no dispensation from treaty obligations, on any ground, religious or otherwise, within Islamic law. The Qur'anic command is to *fulfil the covenant* and *do not break your oaths after you have sworn them* (16:91). Thus, fulfilling the treaties' obligations is the rule, and withdrawal from the treaties the exception.[45] There is an opinion that a treaty might be canceled ahead of its term if this is necessary for the interests of the Islamic state. However, this is not without regulation, as a formal denunciation is required. With regard to fulfilling the obligations of treaties, Nussbaum writes, "the record of Islam is definitely good on this score. The Crusaders, although the aggressors, proceeded on the principle that no faith need be kept with infidels. Says the noted English historian Lane Poole, with an eye to the crusaders, 'The virtues of civilization were all on the side of the Saracens [Muslims].'"[46]

Based on the Qur'an, Islamic international law promotes the coexistence of Islam and other countries through certain principles meant to enhance permanent peace, the ultimate objective of Islam, rather than the perpetuation of war. The Qur'an obliges all nations, in general, to *enter into peace* (2:208). *If the enemy is inclined to peace, make peace with them, and put your trust in God. Should they seek to deceive you, God is all-sufficient for you* (Qur'an 8:61). *If they keep away from you, and cease their hostility, and offer you peace, enter into peace with them* (Qur'an 4:90).

Islamic international law obliges Muslims to behave well wherever they go, whether away from home, in their own country, or abroad. If they travel abroad for trade or other purposes, they should show keen insight and good judgment. They should respect the ruler and the system of the country in which they choose to work or dwell. They should live according to the law of that country and not describe that law or that country with such disrespectful words (that is, country of non-believers): *When a greeting is offered to you, meet it with a greeting still more courteous, or at least of equal courtesy* (Qur'an 4:86). The Qur'an also commands: *O ye who believe, show keen insight and sound judgment when you go out in the way of God* [darabtum fi sabil Allah] *and do not say to those who offered you peace "You are not believers"* (Qur'an 4:94).

Some English translators of the Qur'an translate the phrase *darabtum fi sabil Allah* as 'when you go out to fight for the cause of God.'[47] However, one might disagree with this interpretation on the basis of the language and the position of this phrase in the Qur'an, along the following lines. The words *sabil Allah*, which they translate as 'to fight for the cause of God,' do not in fact convey the notion of 'war.' The Arabic word *sabil* also means *tariq*, which means 'right way.' None of these connotes the notion of 'war.' Thus, the translation of the words *fi sabil Allah* into 'to fight for the cause of God' is not entirely accurate, particularly considering that the language provides more accurate words like *tariq* (way) and *shir'a* (that is, *tariq*: right way), which is also used by the Qur'an. In commanding the Prophet, the Qur'an says: *We put thee on the right way, so follow it* (45:18). Consequently, interpreting the word *sabil* to mean 'cause,' and then equating the cause of God with the word 'fight,' is simply wrong. In this verse, the word 'fight' is not mentioned at all, and nothing even hints at the word 'fight.' The Qur'an does use the words *harb* (war) and *qital* (fight),[48] but not in this verse (4: 94). If God wanted people to 'go out to fight for His cause' as the translator suggests, God could have used the word *harb* (war) or *qital* (fight), but He did not. In this verse, the phrase *darabtum fi sabil Allah* is general in meaning, and has nothing to do with warring or fighting. In addition, the position of the verse after the story of war does not mean that the verse relates to the preceding section on the circumstances of war, instead of the subsequent ones. The account of war ended to begin an account of travel and emigration.[49] Moreover, in the verse under discussion, the first word, *darabtum*, in the phrase *darabtum fi sabil Allah*, according to al-Qurtubi (d. 1272), connotes all endeavors (travel, trade, tilling, cultivation, learning) in which humans usually engage, whether in their country or abroad.[50] As endeavors could involve unlawful activities, the Qur'an added the phrase *fi sabil Allah* (in the way of God) to say that the endeavors should be fulfilled faithfully. People should be faithful in all things they do, in all endeavors. Therefore, *fi sabil Allah* cannot be translated as 'war' or any word other than the word groups of 'peace, faithful, and lawful.' The way of God is not about 'war,' but peace, cooperation, caring, sharing, and coexistence. To deal with aberrations from the law, there is judgment, punishment, and reward in this world and in the other.

Among the prohibited acts in open warfare outlined in the Qur'an are: (i) cruel ways of killing; (ii) killing of non-combatants; (iii) killing of prisoners of war; (iv) mutilation of human beings and beasts; (v) destruction of crops, fruits, and harvests, and cutting trees; (vi) adultery and fornication with captives; (vii) killing of delegates or envoys even in retaliation; (viii) massacre in the vanquished territories; (ix) the use of poisonous weapons; and (x) forcing others to believe in Islam. These are only a few examples of the provisions for the humane treatment of combatants, prisoners, and civilians that existed in Islamic international law before they came to be listed in the Geneva Conventions. These principles have been collected from numerous works of authority, and from the Qur'an itself. Islamic law books contain more principles that are "not yet incorporated in modern conventions."[51]

Al-Qaʿida: Neo-jihad

In this section, the term 'neo-jihad' is used to distinguish between the concept of jihad in the Islamic consensus as previously outlined, and what al-Qaʿida calls 'jihad.' I have not invented the term neo-jihad, but derived it from the writings of al-Qaʿida's top ideologues, who have used the term as a creed of their jihadist ideology. The Egyptian Dr. Fadl first used the term 'jihadism' from as early as 1988. When he was in Peshawar, he combined the ideology with the military training manual in a two-thousand-page book in Arabic, to be used in the training camps to ideologically train the volunteer fighters and prepare them for jihad against the Soviet forces in Afghanistan. He called this book *Risalat al-ʿumda fi iʿdad al-ʿudda li-l-jihad fi sabil Allah* (The Master Message in the Preparation for Jihad on the Way of God, hereafter *The Master*). He published this book in 1988, but under the alias ʿAbd al-Qadir ibn ʿAbd al-ʿAziz. Among the many things outlined in this lengthy book were the 'motives,' 'aims,' and 'importance of jihad.' He labeled these items as the 'Milestones of Jihad,' and stated that "we might call these milestones the 'creed of jihadism' [*al-ʿaqida al-jihadiya*]."[52]

Lentini (2008) made this point when he coined the term neo-jihadism to refer to the doctrine of al-Qaʿida and similar networks of local and global terrorist groups.[53] Thus, terms like neo-jihad and its derivations, such as neo-jihadism and neo-jihadist, are rooted in the blueprints of these networks. The jihad of al-Qaʿida and similar groups is therefore just a new type of jihad that is confined to their own dogmatic rules of their neo-jihadism.

The ideologues and leadership of al-Qaʿida's affiliated individuals and groups understand well the Islamic consensus rulings and ideas, which regulate the idea of jihad outlined in the section above. Ayman al-Zawahiri, who is not only al-Qa'ida's chief but also one of its top ideologues and operational chiefs, knows very well that jihad does not necessarily mean 'war,' and that the concept of jihad cannot be reduced to only mean 'war.' On the substance of this matter, al-Zawahiri appears to be very sensitive, to the extent that he considers it an offense to use the words 'jihad' and 'war' interchangeably.

When his critics used the word 'war' instead of 'jihad,' in reference to al-Qa'ida's 'Global Islamic Front for the Jihad against the Jews and Crusaders,' al-Zawahiri appeared unhappy about the change and called upon his critics to be 'precise' about the fact that "the name of the front was 'jihad' not 'war' or 'killing.'"[54] Al-Zawahiri's sensitivity to this distinction confirms not only his awareness of the critical difference between these words, but also that his persistence on 'war' and 'killing' in the name of jihad is intentional. His intention was also confirmed in his interview with the London daily *al-Hayat* in 1996. To the question of "Why violence and killing; [and] do you think the goal can be achieved through peaceful means of the word instead of bullets?," al-Zawahiri replied, "We do violence to achieve the goal; what we are doing of jihad is but an act to achieve specific aims that might lead to general change."[55] It is in this way that al-Qa'ida limits its jihad to mean confrontation or 'war.' As for their enemy, al-Zawahiri has described his 'jihad' to be a 'war against the Jews and the Crusaders, and war against the corrupt Arab and Muslim regimes.'[56]

Consequently, the ideology of the neo-jihadists, including al-Qa'ida, is based mainly on three fundamental conceptions. First, Islam is 'universal' and was revealed for all human beings. Second, the Islamic shari'a "must rule sovereign and should not be ruled" by any law or code. Third, all human beings have been "created by God" and they should "serve Him alone."[57]

Based on these three religio-political conceptions, the neo-jihadists of al-Qa'ida and similar networks divide the world into two societies: Muslims and non-Muslims. On this account, the non-Muslims are those individuals and groups, territories and states for whom the shari'a is not implemented. To neo-jihadists, present-day Arab and Muslim countries have deviated from shari'a, and therefore are no longer Islamic. They even claim that Saudi Arabia is 'not Islamic' nor is it a true 'Wahhabi or Salafi' state.[58] In other words, the neo-jihadists of al-Qa'ida and the like consider themselves to be true Wahhabi and Salafi networks. The

Wahhabist movement has been detailed in an earlier chapter, described as a precursor to neo-jihadist dogma. Like Wahhabis, the neo-jihadists consider themselves the only true Muslims. They charge people other than themselves as rejectionists (*rafida*: Rafidis) and postponements (*murji'a*: Murji'is).[59] These groups have been discussed in earlier chapters, so here it is sufficient to note that they differ from Wahhabism on some ideas and religious beliefs.[60]

Thus, all parties, other than the neo-jihadists or al-Qa'ida and similar networks, have been labeled as non-Muslims (*kuffar*; sing. *kafir*). In this way the neo-jihadists have appointed themselves as the protectors of Islam, as they understand it. Al-Qa'ida's religious duty is thus to invite all parties or opponents in both east and west to follow what al-Qa'ida believes to be right. Those who reject al-Qa'ida's invitation are considered rejectionists (*rafida* or rafidis, one of the Khariji splinter groups) who should be fought "until all religion be to God alone."[61] Thus, al-Qa'ida considers the world to be either with them or against them. Standing against al-Qa'ida means enmity that should be punished, and delivering such punishment requires ideological and military training.

To ideologically train the neo-jihadists, al-Qa'ida's ideologues outline the varying shapes and forms that the non-Muslim's enmity might take toward Muslims. According to this narrative, Muslims are specifically and only neo-jihadists or members of al-Qa'ida and similar groups, because all others are charged with being non-Muslim. This is a tricky and confusing point in their writings, as will be illustrated in the following. When they refer to Muslims, the neo-jihadists mean, in most cases, themselves and those who follow them, as well as their sympathizers and supporters, while all others are simply seen as non-Muslims. Thus, one should be aware that the phrase 'non-Muslim' refers to the opponents (Muslims and non-Muslims) of the neo-jihadists. They even critically call them the 'Murji'is of the Epoch.' In either case, the neo-jihadists believe that their opponents' enmity toward 'Muslims' (that is, neo-jihadists) may take the shape of:

- Denial and denunciation of the Islamic faith;
- Laughing at or mocking Muslims [neo-jihadists];
- Charging Muslims [neo-jihadists] with corruption;
- Charging Muslims [neo-jihadists] with backwardness but thinking of themselves as superior;

- Disputing with vain arguments in order to weaken the truth;
- Instigating the general public against the Muslims [neo-jihadists];
- Calling Muslims [neo-jihadists] a minority that wants to impose its opinion on the majority;
- Appreciating the wrong that they follow more than the true religion [of neo-jihadists];
- Using whatever available means to drag the people away from the truth and not to follow the Muslims [neo-jihadists];
- Embargos and prohibition of food to starve the Muslims and to drag them away from their religion;
- Using whatever means to seduce Muslims [neo-jihadists] away from their religion;
- Threatening the Muslims [neo-jihadists] with imprisonment and killing;
- Torturing Muslims [neo-jihadists], killing, and fighting them.[62]

In light of the theme and framework of the above-listed items, the neo-jihadists prepare themselves to take action on many fronts, which can be summarized in the following four points. The first is the *da'wa*, or the call for Islam as they understand it. This front signifies the relationship between the neo-jihadists and their opponents (Muslim or non-Muslim).

The second is exoneration. The neo-jihadists exonerate themselves from their opponents (Muslim and non-Muslim), whether alive or deceased. In so doing, the neo-jihadists intend to manifest their 'hatred' and 'enmity' toward their opponents. As for their exoneration from their deceased opponents, the neo-jihadists advise their followers that they should not assist with the burial procedures, not bury them with 'true Muslims' (neo-jihadists), and not say 'prayers' to them. If there are marriages and family relationships, neo-jihadists should not inherit anything from the wealth of the deceased opponent, and vice versa.

The third is seclusion and emigration. Here, the neo-jihadists must seclude themselves from the society of their opponents. This seclusion can take varying forms, including seclusion by the heart, by tongue, and by action. Seclusion by one's heart is to live in the society and physically mix with its people but one's 'heart' must hate the society and its people. This type represents, to some extent, what we know today of the neo-jihadists' sleeping cells as well as home-grown neo-jihadist individuals or groups. Complete seclusion from society is to 'migrate' from this territory or state. In Egypt, the neo-jihadists migrated to the mountains and barren landscapes and established their own society called the Society of *the* Muslims. In the context of seclusion, the neo-jihadists are generally charging their opponent Muslims with *kufr* (atheism). In the words of their ideologue Dr. Fadl:

> The circumstances of those who today call themselves Muslims are such that they cannot distinguish right from the wrong. They are calling for *kafir* ideas, some are calling for socialism, others are calling for democracy, and yet some others are calling for Arab nationalism. These have not exonerated themselves from the *kafir*s or their ideas. You may also find some of them are members of this or that political party and call for these *kafir* ideas even without showing any shame or wariness.[63]

Their seclusion from society and its systems reveals their hostility to all other systems including democracy. Their opposition and even hostility to democracy is proliferating in their literature. Al-Zawahiri claims that democracy is an idolatrous idea designed especially to oppose Islam. Democracy is a form of *shirk bi Allah*, or associating partners with God. To al-Zawahiri, Islam renders sovereignty to God whereas democracy renders sovereignty to the people. The legislators in democracy are the people themselves, while the legislator in Islam is the Almighty God. Hence, democracy is a blasphemous idea that usurps the right to legislation from the Almighty God and gives it to the people. Insofar as democracy is the recognition of the sovereignty of the people, by definition it requires the denial of God's sovereignty. Therefore, the members of the parliament are 'idols,' and those who elect them commit, by doing so, the arch sin of *shirk*. Thus, participating in elections or other democratic processes at any stage is forbidden *(haram)* and those who perpetrate this sin are apostates and infidels who should be fought and killed.[64]

The fourth major form of jihadist action is the jihad in the way of God. After seclusion by one's heart, and by the tongue, comes the action or the jihad. The jihad here is generally against one's opponents or the rejectionists who reject the neo-jihadist teachings and activity, or, in the words of ideologue Dr. Fadl, "against those who reject their call for Islam" (as jihadists understand it). For example, to justify his point on jihad, Dr. Fadl emphasized that the idea of jihad began much earlier than Islam, as part of the religion of the Prophet Moses. Dr. Fadl refers to a Qur'anic account that the Prophet Moses said to his people: 'O my people! Enter the holy land which God hath assigned unto you . . . They said: *O Moses! In this land are a people of exceeding strength: Never shall we enter it until they leave it . . . . Two men of those who feared, upon both of whom God had bestowed a favor, said: Enter upon them by the gate, for when you have entered it you shall surely be victorious, and on God should you rely if you are believers. They said: O Moses! We will never enter it while they are in it. So go you and your Lord and fight! We will sit here* (Qur'an 5:21–24).[65]

The jihad, then, which is the fourth stage, itself involves four more stages. Each stage complements the others and together they are considered obligations in the preparation for jihad. These stages, as emphasized by 'Abdullah 'Azzam, are: Emigration; Preparation; Stand by; and Fight.

'Azzam describes the stage of emigration as to leave one's place or country for the area of war 'jihad,' with the intention of participating in the fight. Thus, one should "leave his work, his university, his school, his family, his friends, his neighbors, his country," and everything, and migrate with the intention of participating in jihad. If it should happen that he "died on his way," 'Azzam says, "he then will be a martyr." To 'Azzam, emigration with the intention of jihad is the road to Heaven. There is a firm bond between emigration and jihad. 'Azzam argued that jihad would not stop until the end of this world, and therefore emigration would also never stop. He advised Muslims in Arab, Muslim, and non-Muslim countries to migrate to fulfill their religious duty of servitude (*'ubudiya*) to God alone. Further, the present Arab and Muslim countries, in 'Azzam's view, are no longer Islamic.[66] He emphasizes that those who do "migrate with the intention to participate in jihad" are "the true Muslims" (that is, neo-jihadists). To 'Azzam, emigration means that one has "liberated" oneself from all the "worldly life" and "desires" for the "sake" of God. One should not be concerned about his family, children, work, school, or university, because, as 'Azzam claims, "God takes care of them." "God put all worldly desires," including "wealth, family, work, and all material things that tie the person to this world, on one side of the scale of a balance, and put jihad on the other side."[67]

In terms of the preparation stage, 'Azzam says that when the migrant arrives at his destination, he should begin his ideological and military training in preparation for jihad. To 'Azzam, this ideological and military preparation is "obligatory" for jihad as much as "purification" is for prayers. As there is no prayer without ablution, so there is no jihad without preparation.[68]

'Azzam explains the stand-by (al-rabat) stage as focused on securing the borders of the Muslim territory, requiring that one live at the border of the Islamic state. On this account, the Islamic state is the area that supposedly came under the neo-jihadists' control (that is, Taliban-ruled Afghanistan) because all other states (Muslim and non-Muslim) are charged with *kufr*. Therefore, 'Azzam asserts that if there is no Islamic state, the place for the migrant jihadists must then be close to the front lines. Their duty is to ensure border security, but they can also attack neighboring states that they consider to be an enemy. 'Azzam declares that the reward for those who take this position at the border [*rabat*] is "so much better than this material world and everything in it."[69]

Al-Qa'ida and similar neo-jihadist networks divide the stage of jihad (to fight) into two types: the offensive and the defensive jihad. These two forms of jihad are discussed below.

The Offensive Jihad

The neo-jihadists refer to the offensive jihad as 'jihad of demand' (*jihad al-talab*). This is to 'demand' the enemy in its own territory, and outside it. Thus, as there is no treaty or truce between neo-jihadists and other states, the purpose of this type of jihad is to attack the enemy and its interests in its own territory or anywhere else. The substance of this type is to *begin* the hostility and not to wait for the enemy to attack. This type of jihad is a 'collective duty' or voluntary, so that the conduct of some releases others from this duty type. However, if this type of jihad were not conducted by anyone at all, the neo-jihadists would then consider themselves to be sinners. Because there is no truce with their enemies, the neo-jihadists consider this voluntary jihad as obligatory in many circumstances, including the following:

1. To free Muslim prisoners who have been captured during war and imprisoned in the enemy's territory;
2. if the Muslim ruler or governor of a given town calls for jihad, so that the jihad then becomes a duty of the Muslims;
3. if a Muslim finds himself in an area legally considered a war zone, then jihad becomes his duty.[70]

Those who conduct this jihad must be: free, Muslim, male, mature, healthy, and without mental or physical defects. Further, Dr. Fadl criticized the opponents of neo-jihadists as follows:

Those who deny the offensive jihad and say that Islam fights only in defense to expel the enemy from Islamic land are but the deniers of truth. If the deniers tried to support their claim by the Qur'anic verse *if they incline to peace, incline thou also to it* [8:61], or by the Prophet's saying "do not wish war with the enemy," or by their own saying that there is no jihad as long as the enemy is inclined to peace. Those who make these claims are but half-way believers; believing in some of the Books and denying some others.[71]

The Defensive Jihad

This form of jihad, as the neo-jihadist ideologue Dr. Fadl states, is obligatory and a Muslim duty if the Muslim homeland is invaded and if the ruler or imam calls for jihad. The obligation here is on every free Muslim male who is mature and healthy, and without mental or physical defects. If the Muslim land were to be invaded and the ruler did not call for jihad, he would then be designated a sinner and removed from office, either voluntarily or by force.[72] If we consider the above in the context of September 11, the word imam is misleading. In the case of September 11, no ruler, imam, or state declared war against the United States and those western, Arab, and Muslim countries. This issue will be discussed later in the chapter.

Jihad against the Rejectionists

The ideology of the neo-jihadists determines that they conduct jihad against those who 'reject' the application of the shari'a. In this regard, the neo-jihadists do not distinguish between individuals or groups, where a 'group' can be of two persons or more, a local government of a territory, or a sovereign state that is fully recognized as a member of the UN. In all cases, the shari'a must be applied, or the jihad against them is legal. Egypt and Saudi Arabia are, for example, still considered by the neo-jihadists to be non-Muslim states. They see the regimes of these two countries as rejectionist of the application of shari'a while protecting themselves with military and police forces. Therefore, these regimes must be fought and destroyed. In this regard, the neo-jihadists currently consider all regimes in the Arab and Islamic world to be non-Muslim.[73]

The characteristics of rejectionists have been outlined by one of al-Qaʻidaʼs top ideologues, the Saudi national who called himself Dr. Muhammad ibn ʻAbdullah al-Masʻari. He identifies himself also as general director and official speaker of the Islamic Reform Movement, which is one of al-Qaʻidaʼs media centers. In his *Qital al-tawaʼif al-mumtaniʻa* (The Fight against the Rejectionists, 2003), al-Masʻari referred to 11 September 2001 and divided the rejectionists who must be fought into seven categories as outlined below:

1. The gangs or highway robbers and similar criminals in general.
2. Those that refuse to pay the *zakat* (tax) must also be fought until they agree to pay.
3. The factions or groups that fight each other over tribal or worldly beliefs, or ideas such as "racialism, nationalism, communism, or capitalism and the like." These groups can be Muslims who are fighting each other only because of their hatred and bigotry. These and similar groups must be invited to make peace, and then any group that rejects such peace must be fought.
4. The non-Muslim states that fight Islam or stand against Muslims and perhaps occupy Muslim land. These states include those that "participated in the war on Afghanistan or Iraq in one way or another"; those states that "supported Israelʼs occupation of Palestine"; and those states that "supported or accepted Israelʼs aggression in Palestine and accepted the expulsion of Palestinians from their homeland by armed forces." These states are considered by the neo-jihadists to be "aggressors and warring states that must be fought by whatever means." The states mentioned in connection to this category are: "The United States, Britain, Israel, Spain, Australia, France, Germany, Turkey, and Pakistan."[74] The U.S. and Britain receive special mention as "enemies" that should be "punished" for their role in the "attacks on Afghanistan and Iraq." Al-Masʻari writes:

> America and Britain must be fought in the same way that they fought the Muslims in Afghanistan and Iraq. Here, the Islamic rule is to fight only their combatants and exclude their property, women, and children. However, it is permissible to target their civilians, only on the basis of similar treatment. This is what the Mujahidin did in the blessed expedition (*ghazwa*) of New York

and Washington [September 11]. They targeted civilians because America started it first, a long time before [September 11]; America started targeting Muslim civilians by killing and annihilating them. For example, America has directly targeted civilians in Iraq and Palestine. In Palestine, America targeted civilians by supporting Israel's aggression and crimes against the civilians there. America targeted civilians first, in many other countries, of which Japan is but an example. Therefore, America deserves a just punishment for its crimes and aggression against Muslims and against humanity in general. We have detailed this with concrete evidence in our essay (The World Trade Center) that should be consulted.[75]

5. The states that have occupied Muslim land, expelled its citizens, and confiscated their wealth and property by armed forces. Israel is one of these states that should be fought in the same manner in which it fights the Palestinians. Targeting the civilians of these states is legally permissible because these civilians have "usurped the land and are living on it under the protection of armed forces. They must be expelled also by force except those who choose to leave and return to their original homes, in London or New York or Moscow. They save themselves, their family and children."[76]

6. This category focuses on the ruling elites in Arab and Muslim countries. Here, the neo-jihadists define a Muslim country as one in which both the ruling elite and the majority of citizens are Muslim. In such countries, the ruling elite might include those who reject the "complete" application of shari'a, those who "fight against Muslims under the banner of non-Muslims," or those who "stand in coalition with the non-Muslims against the Muslims." These and similar ruling elites must be fought as "apostates and as non-Muslim combatants." The elite types referred to by the neo-jihadists are outlined below:

i. The present Saudi regime is referred to as the chief of the '*kafir* regimes' that should be fought. The reasons given for this include: the "regime permitted its banks to work with interest (usury: *riba*); the regime is a member of local and international non-Muslim organizations, such as the United Nations and the Gulf Cooperation Council"; the present Saudi regime was established by a "racist rotten regime in 1932"; its "deviation from shari'a is increasingly wide in all fields, including the principal system, the laws, and the courts"; and the Saudi regime is a "racist and sectarian regime of *kufr* that hides itself deceivably behind Wahhabism and Salafism."[77]

ii. Among the other deviant regimes, the regime in Iran rates first mention. The neo-jihadists charge Iran with "racism, sectarianism, and abhorrence." They have also accused Iran of being a "non-Muslim" state, and declared that its "Shi'ism belief is wrong"; it "fights Muslims in Afghanistan under the American banner"; and "it turns the Mujahidin over to the Arab regimes in order to hand them over to America, if America wants to."[78]

iii. The other regime to which the neo-jihadists refer is the ruling regime in Sudan. They describe its leader as an "opportunist military dictator" who once "shielded himself behind Islam, the Islam of al-Turabi, the swindler opportunist."[79]

iv. Similar views have emerged regarding the "tyrants of Tunis" and the "Francophone criminals of Algeria," "the soldiers of Turkey," and "the Indo-American gangs in Pakistan."

7. This category covers any country with a Muslim majority that has been invaded and occupied by a non-Muslim country. Here, the occupier may justify the occupation by calling it:

> Protection, guardianship, mandatory and other, similar labels. In any case, the sovereignty of the country is diminished and its security is no longer in the hands of its Muslim majority but rather in the hands of the non-Muslim occupier. This type of occupation had not existed for a long time, and people even thought that it had gone forever. But the catastrophic American invasion and occupation of Iraq brought this type of occupation into existence once again. If the ruling elite does not conduct jihad and fight the occupier to liberate the country, then, the ruling elite should be fought as a combatant apostate. Anyone supporting the occupier in any form is also considered an apostate that should be killed. In addition, the occupying forces should be fought until they leave the country. Then the Islamic shari'a should be restored and whatever the occupier had established there against the shari'a should be eradicated.[80]

The above-cited seven categories in general, and the last two in particular, are more important to al-Qa'ida because of the ongoing debate about the legality of al-Qa'ida's neo-jihad, not only in the Arab and Muslim countries, but also beyond the oases and the seas. The neo-jihadists of al-Qa'ida networks are well aware of the criticisms directed against them, to the extent that they mention the names of their critics in Saudi Arabia, Egypt, Iraq, Iran and other countries. Thus, the Mufti of Saudi Arabia 'Ibn al-Sheikh' became the 'Mufti of the Saud Family,' and the Mufti of Egypt Professor 'Tantawi' became the 'Mufti of Hosni Mubarak,' and the scholars of Iraq and Iran were 'wrongly named Ayatuallah.' These and similar scholars, in the view of the neo-jihadists, are merely 'non-believers (zindiq), faithless, ignorant and disloyal,' and "whatever they say about the jihad are weak and cannot respond to the affairs in Iraq and Afghanistan, or in the Gulf and Palestine."[81]

Who Declares Jihad?

The neo-jihadists have chosen whatever they wanted to believe about their jihad. While they have considered jihad to mean only 'war,' the authority that declares this 'war' remains one of the most important questions for which al-Qa'ida must find an answer. In Islamic international law, a declaration of war is the decision of the state. The manner in which a declaration of war can be made by the state has been detailed in the books of Islamic jurisprudence, such as al-Shaybani's *Kitab al-siyar al-saghir* (Introduction to the Law of Nations) and *Kitab al-siyar al-kabir* (A Treatise on International Law). It is difficult to find in Islamic law anything that justifies individuals declaring war on a foreign state under any circumstances. However, the attacks against the U.S. on September 11, 2001 have given rise to the question: who can declare war?

Bin Laden and his associates are well aware of the substance of this question and the consequences of its answer. This question has generated a comprehensive discussion at all levels within Islam. The scholars of Islam and its international law have confirmed that the declaration of war is the responsibility of the state. Their view on this issue has been outlined in the section above. The focus here is on the views of al-Qa'ida and similar networks.

Muhammad ibn 'Abdullah al-Mas'ari is a Saudi national and one of al-Qa'ida's top ideologues, who speaks on behalf of Bin Laden and his al-Qa'ida networks. All of his books and websites are dedicated to defending al-Qaʿida's leadership and operatives and justifying their ideas and activities. In his book, *Markaz al-tijara al-ʿalami*, al-Masʿari is driven by two aims: to justify the attacks against the U.S., and to establish that the declaration of war does not only have to be a state decision, but that individuals can also declare war against a foreign state. In so doing, he put forward four assertions that are outlined below.

In his first point, al-Masʿari acknowledges the shariʿa's ruling that the "declaration of war is not the responsibility of individuals or any organization other than the state." However, he argues that the war must be declared only by the state that started it. This is the first step in his argument to justify the attacks of September 11. In his view, the U.S. had already started the war against Iraq "more than ten years ago." This war, he claims, destroyed a Muslim country and killed Muslim civilians, and has continued, unstopped, since then. In addition to Iraq, al-Masʿari cites the U.S. support of Israel in Palestine, Russia in Chechnya, and India in Kashmir, among other places. He also claims that the U.S. has "attacked Sudan with no declaration of war." In short, his argument is that the U.S. is the "the aggressor" and Muslims are the "victims." Thus, "even if we accept that Bin Laden had no authority to declare war against America, his declaration was something that was already there. It was but to draw attention to the ongoing war against the Muslims."[82]

Al-Masʿari's attempt to use the 1991 Iraq War to justify what he calls "Bin Laden's declaration of war against America" is unconvincing. His point of departure is the assumption that his imam Bin Laden is the imam of all Muslims and Arab countries. However, this is simply wrong, so his argument that follows from this is also wrong. Bin Laden is not the imam of Iraq or Afghanistan or of any other country, including his own Arabian nation state. In addition, the war of which he speaks was sanctioned by the UN. Al-Masʿari should also bear in mind that Iraq was the aggressor that invaded Kuwait, occupied its capital, and attempted to change its currency and state identity. The U.S. was not alone in liberating Kuwait but was supported by Arab and Muslim countries. Regardless, Bin Laden had no authority to 'declare war' or to conduct jihad.

In his second point, al-Masʿari emphasizes that early Muslim jurists supported the obligation of jihad if a Muslim country were to be attacked. In this case, war or jihad to defend a country is an obligation of the Muslims, in general, and of the citizens of that country, in particular. He argues that "none of the Arab regimes can declare jihad against America because they are all dominated by America." Using this theme, al-Mas'ari charged all Arabs and Muslim governments with being "non-Islamic." However, his argument fails to substantiate any legal permission for individuals to declare war against America. If neo-jihadists want to establish shari'a in their own countries, as al-Mas'ari claims, their objections should be against the regimes in these countries, rather than with the U.S.

Acknowledging this view, al-Mas'ari states, "Show us our legitimate ruler who we must obey and do not conduct war without his permission." This apologetic attempt has also nothing to do with the U.S. and does not legitimize individuals of any nationality declaring war on a state.

In his third point, al-Mas'ari focuses on Bin Laden's relationship with the Taliban government in Afghanistan. To him, the Taliban regime is Islamic: "its rule is an Islamic rule." He claims that the Taliban were the "legitimate rulers" of Afghanistan. They gave Bin Laden a "place there and protected him." It was therefore "impossible," according to al-Mas'ari, for Bin Laden to "attack the U.S. without consulting the Taliban and without their permission." He meant that "Bin Laden did not rebel against the Afghan ruler, if he was behind the attacks on New York and Washington."[83]

These arguments do not support his attempt at justification. As for whether Bin Laden was behind the attacks of September 11, this also is a matter for the U.S. national security agencies and has nothing to do with the question here. Khalid Sheikh Muhammad and his associates at Guantánamo might know the truth on this issue. However, the question here is whether Bin Laden, as an individual, had legitimate authority to declare jihad and conduct warfare against another state. Al-Mas'ari himself acknowledges that the declaration of war is a state decision. He has also said that Bin Laden consulted the Taliban ruler on these important matters. Yet this claim is doubtful, as was made evident in the previous chapter. In addition, if we view this claim that Bin Laden consulted with the Taliban about the September 11 attacks as fact, it holds then that both Bin Laden and the Taliban 'state' were responsible for this decision. Hence, al-Mas'ari and his associates should not complain about the response of the U.S. in Afghanistan or the 'War on Terror' in general. Thus, if we accept this claim, the main point remains that there is nothing in the shari'a that allows individuals to make the decision to initiate war.

In his fourth and final attempt to justify the decision of war being made by individuals or groups, al-Mas'ari adopts another paradigm. He begins by acknowledging that "in shari'a the declaration of jihad and the conduct of warfare are but state decisions. These affairs are not of the responsibility of individuals, and if they do declare jihad and conduct war, they will be law breakers and should be punished."[84] However, he then challenges this tenet. As there is nothing in the shari'a to support his conviction, al-Mas'ari tries to draw justification from the history of Islam. He cites a story of one called Abu Basir, and draws a parallel between al-Qa'ida's decision to attack the U.S. and the story of Abu Basir. He has repeated this story in his books in an attempt to bolster his case and influence his readers, particularly vulnerable Muslim youth. However, he realized that repeating this story in his books was not enough, so he decided to interweave the relevant with the irrelevant in a special book entitled *Qissat Abu Basir: ta'sil shar'i mufassal li-hudud mashru'iyyat i'lan al-afrad li-l-harb* (The Story of Abu Basir: A Detailed Analysis of the Legitimacy of the Declaration of War by Individuals). In this book, al-Mas'ari prepared his audiences for his philosophism's new discovery. He said: "Yes, the earlier Jurists have not dealt with the 'Declaration of War by Individuals,' neither in the context of the story of Abu Basir or in the context of others. This is why the 'philosophers' and the 'geniuses' have come today to claim that this is illegal for individuals. They have come nowadays to tell us this nonsense."[85]

The story of Abu Basir is very much linked to the treaty of al-Hudaybiya. This treaty was concluded between the Medinan Muslims, led by the Prophet Muhammad, and the Meccan pagans, led by Quraysh, in 629 at al-Hudaybiya, a town that lies at a distance of fourteen to forty-eight kilometers from Mecca. The treaty is well known in western literature.[86] The story tells how the Prophet and a large number of Muslims left Medina, unarmed, for Mecca, intending to perform their religious duty called the *'umra*, or 'lesser pilgrimage.' On their way, the Muslims stayed at al-Hudaybiya to rest. While resting, the Prophet sent a delegation to Mecca to let Quraysh know of his intention. After the negotiations, Quraysh claimed that Mecca was not ready for this religious duty this year, and thus that the Muslims should return to Medina and come back to Mecca the following year. A treaty was then established between the two parties. Among the articles concluded in this treaty were that if "any Meccan person becomes a Muslim and then comes to Muhammad in Medina, Muhammad shall turn him over to the Meccans. But any Muslim who may go to Mecca, the Meccans shall not be obliged to turn him over to Muhammad." These two articles are of importance to the discussion of the case of Abu Basir.

After the treaty was signed, the Muslims returned to Medina. Some time later, Abu Basir was converted to Islam in Mecca. The Meccans confiscated his wealth and property and incarcerated him. After a while, Abu Basir escaped from Mecca and made his way to Muhammad in Medina. However, envoys from his clan were following him with a letter demanding his extradition. Muhammad acknowledged the justice of the demand, and when Abu Basir protested, told him that God would provide a way out of his difficulties and would help him to confirm his religious faith. Muhammad turned Abu Basir over to the two Meccans who came to take him away, under the terms of the treaty. On their way back to Mecca, Abu Basir killed one of his guardians and the other fled the scene in fear, heading back toward Medina. He came again to Muhammad and complained that "Abu Basir killed my friend and was going to kill me too." Muhammad comforted him and offered him the chance of escorting Abu Basir back to Mecca, but surprisingly, he declined. Then Abu Basir arrived and went to Muhammad and said, "O Prophet of God, you have fulfilled your covenant and turned me over to them, but God has saved me from them." In response to Abu Basir, the Prophet said, "Woe unto the *umma* starting a war for one of them." From the Prophet's response, Abu Basir understood that the Prophet intended to send him to Mecca once again, so he decided to leave Medina. He traveled to the coast and settled in a spot near the Red Sea. Some time later, Abu Jandal ibn Suhayl ibn 'Amr also became a Muslim in Mecca and when he escaped he went to Abu Basir and they lived together. In time, others had similar experiences: that is, individuals who converted to Islam and managed to flee Mecca joined Abu Basir. Within a year, there were between fifty and seventy newly converted Muslims living in this coastal area with Abu Basir.

The caravan trade route between Mecca and Syria passed along the coastline near to Abu Basir's settlement. When they heard that the Meccan caravan from Syria was approaching, Abu Basir and his friends prepared to defend themselves. The caravan was usually guarded by anywhere between sixty and one hundred strong horsemen. As the caravan approached, a fight broke out which resulted in casualties on both sides, but Abu Basir won some materials and arrested some of the Meccans. Among them was 'Abi al-'As ibn al-Rabi', the husband of Zaynab, the daughter of the Prophet. Abi al-'As was not yet a Muslim, and Abu Basir sent him to Muhammad, who also turned him over to Mecca. The Meccans found themselves unable to use force against Abu Basir at such a distance from Mecca. In the end, they appealed to Muhammad to take Abu Basir into his community. Their envoy was sent with a message to Muhammad that if Abu Basir and his friends left their coastal location and came to live in Medina, under the authority of Muhammad, the Meccans would no longer demand their extradition to Mecca. They conceded further that anyone who came to the Prophet from Mecca could remain without restriction. The Prophet sent this news to Abu Basir, who accepted the proposal and came to Medina with his associates. Abu Basir died later in the year 639 during the reign of 'Umar ibn al-Khattab.

This is the story of Abu Basir as mentioned in the books of al-Qa'ida's ideologues, including al-Mas'ari.[87] He referenced Abu Basir's account from various sources to indicate that the story of Abu Basir took place at this particular time of Islamic history. Al-Mas'ari then tried to draw strength and support from this story in an attempt to justify al-Qa'ida's declaration of war against the U.S. and other countries. His argument can be summarized by the following points:

1. Abu Basir was a good Muslim companion of the Prophet Muhammad.
2. As an individual, Abu Basir declared war on the pagan state in Mecca and conducted warfare against it.
3. Abu Basir declared war against a state with which the Muslim state had a truce or treaty.
4. Abu Basir's activities were legal because they were accepted by the Prophet Muhammad.
5. Therefore, Bin Laden's declaration of war against the United States, with which Muslim states have treaties, is legal.
6. Therefore, it is legal for jihadist individuals and groups to declare war against a 'state' in a contemporary context.

This theme is repeatedly mentioned in al-Qa'ida's books as evidence of the legality of al-Qa'ida's warfare against Arab, Muslim, and western countries. Al-Mas'ari, as a member of al-Qa'ida, considers Abu Basir's case to be of great importance and attempts to make use of it in response to al-Qa'ida's critics.

It is difficult, however, to view Abu Basir's story as a justification for al-Qa'ida's terrorism or as evidence that legitimizes the declaration of war against a state by individuals under Islamic law. Just as we have seen the weakness of the three previous arguments proposed by al-Mas'ari with regard to the question of 'who declares jihad,' so we can see the weakness of this fourth point based on the story of Abu Basir. Neither al-Mas'ari's argument nor his repetitions of it helped him; rather, they worked against him. The points of weakness in his fourth point may be summarized as follows:

1. The Prophet turned Abu Basir over to the pagan state of Mecca but he escaped.
2. When Abu Basir returned, he did not live under the authority of the Islamic state of Medina, but rather in a no-man's-land.
3. While living out of reach of the authority of the Islamic state of Medina, Abu Basir's decisions and activities were but his own responsibility. This also was recognized by the authorities of the pagan state in Mecca.
4. The authority of the Medina state, in this case Muhammad, did not agree with Abu Basir and did not instruct him to initiate war with the pagan state of Mecca. This also has been confirmed by the story itself as follows:
   i. The Prophet turned Abu Basir over to the pagan state.
   ii. The Prophet made his intentions clear that he would turn Abu Basir over to the pagan state once again. For that, Abu Basir went to live away from the Muslim state of Medina.
   iii. The Prophet extradited his son-in-law to Mecca. He was arrested by Abu Basir during the fight with the caravan security and was sent to his father-in-law (the Prophet) to detain him in Medina. However, the Prophet did not agree with Abu Basir and instead handed his son-in-law over to the pagan state in Mecca.
   iv. The booty won by Abu Basir, in what al-Qa'ida calls "his war with the pagan state," never entered the treasury of the Islamic state in Medina, as has been acknowledged by al-Qa'ida. If al-Qa'ida's claim was true, that the "war was approved by the Prophet," then the Prophet would not have left the booty to Abu Basir, but dealt with it as mentioned in the Qur'an, just as he dealt with the booty of the Battle of Badr and later battles.
   v. Al-Qa'ida's theorist, al-Mas'ari states in his essay, "Abu Basir" that "the Prophet did not accept anything from the booty because the booty was that of betrayal and perfidy" (p. 14). In other words, Abu Basir's "war" was a war of "betrayal and

perfidy," and the Prophet did not approve of the booty because he did not approve of the war.

vi. Abu Basir conducted his warfare against the pagan state of Mecca while living away from the authority of the Islamic state of Medina.

vii. It is extremely difficult to assume that Abu Basir conducted his warfare while living in the Muslim state of Medina under the authority of the Prophet. This is simply because he could not conduct a war without approval from the Prophet, the authority of the state.

viii. If the Prophet approved of Abu Basir's 'war' this would mean that the Prophet had not kept up with his side of the 'truce.' However, the Prophet, as Montgomery Watt says, "did not break the letter of the treaty."[88] Similarly, Maxime Rodinson argues that "the Prophet had fulfilled his obligation under the treaty."[89]

ix. In al-Qa'ida's language, al-Mas'ari acknowledged that the war was not approved by the Prophet. He says, "Those who have been killed by Abu Basir were not civilians, but polytheist fighters whose life and wealth are permissible to take, if the war was Islamically approved" (p. 14). However, the Prophet did not approve of this 'war'; and this fight was Abu Basir's decision.

x. At the time of this story, Abu Basir was a young, newly converted Muslim who had no opportunity to learn about his religion from the Prophet. While living away, Abu Basir's decisions were his own responsibility, and certainly not a *sunna* (or a role model) to which later Muslims should conform.

It is thus clear that a declaration of war is a state decision. The early jurists knew Abu Basir's story well, and understood that this case does not represent a *sunna* and does not provide any ruling that permits individuals to declare jihad against a state. In summary, there is no rule of this type anywhere in the shari'a, at all. Hence, the decision to attack the United States on September 11 cannot be seen as legitimate under Islamic law.

The Neo-jihad is Outdated

Al-Qa'ida's thought is based mainly on jihad, which, as outlined previously, it divides into two types: the offensive jihad as a collective duty *(fard kifaya)*;

and the defensive jihad as an individual duty *(fard 'ayn)*.[90] As to the first, no individual or group is permitted to conduct this type of jihad other than the state of *khilafa* (the caliphate). In this sense, according to Imam al-Shafi'i (d. 204/819), there is not a governorship within the caliphate that would permit this type of jihad.[91] Thus, neither an individual, nor a province or governorate, within the caliphate is permitted to declare war on another state or country. The declaration of jihad (war) is a caliphate decision. However, the caliphate fell in 1924, and so the provisions for this type of jihad are now outdated and no longer valid for Islam. Nevertheless, this type of jihad is followed by al-Qa'ida, and was used to declare war and to attack the U.S. on September 11, 2001. Therefore, al-Qa'ida has placed itself outside of the bounds of Islamic rules and frameworks and consequently should be held responsible for its criminal acts.

The second type, the defensive jihad, is applied if a Muslim country is invaded or attacked by a non-Muslim country; then jihad becomes an 'individual duty' of the residents of this country to defend themselves and their country. This Muslim country can also call on the residents of other Muslim countries for help. Any country in the world has the right to defend itself. It is also the right of other countries to help. This is now common practice in the global political environment, witnessed by both modern and postmodern generations, while in Islamic countries the defensive jihad has remained merely a theoretical idea not put into practice since the nineteenth century. During the past century, neither a Muslim country nor a Muslim group had practiced this form of defensive jihad until 1979. When the Soviets invaded Afghanistan in 1979, the U.S. and its allies among the Arab and Muslim countries revived the defensive jihad for the first time, and encouraged Islamists in many countries to migrate to Afghanistan with the intention of enacting jihad to liberate Afghanistan from the communist USSR. It was out of these developments that al-Qa'ida adopted the defensive jihad as one of its doctrines and practised it in Kashmir, Chechnya, Iraq, and other places. They also think of jihad as an end in itself, as a duty that is never completed, so theoretically, endless. Al-Qa'ida's ideologue in Afghanistan, 'Abdullah 'Azzam, was teaching his followers "jihad as a worship duty" for life. He said: "The jihad is a worship duty for life like prayer and fasting. As it is not permissible to fast Ramadan this year and stop the next year, also it is not permissible to conduct jihad this year and stop in other years; jihad is a continual worship duty for life."[92]

Further, this neo-jihadist ideology of al-Qaʻida networks can be challenged on the basis of their own doctrinal proprieties. Their habit of modifying and interweaving ideas has strongly contributed to their doctrinal ambiguities. What they say about their jihad confirms that this interpretation is outdated. It is demonstrated in their writings that all neo-jihadists, without exception, believe that there is no jihad without 'emigration' *(hijra)*. In this regard, this 'emigration' is of a special type that is limited to "one condition": that is, "to migrate to a territory where Muslims are free to observe their religion."[93] On this point, al-Qaʻida's theorist ʻAbdullah ʻAzzam says, "There is a firm bond between jihad and emigration."[94] To him emigration is a duty that Muslims must fulfill on the way of jihad. There is no jihad without emigration, and emigration must come first. Al-Qaʻida's top ideologue, Dr. Fadl, similarly outlined the importance of emigration on the way of jihad, stating that "there is no faith for him who does not migrate."[95] He also emphasized that "because emigration is a means for the jihad obligation, then emigration is an obligation too."[96] On this account, one could argue that the individual who for any reason is unable to 'migrate' must drop this duty of jihad from among his/her required religious duties.

Further, the neo-jihadists claim that the emigration 'must' be toward a place where Muslim émigrés are safe and free to practice their religion. Hence, if there is no such 'safe haven,' then there can be no 'emigration,' and ultimately no jihad.[97] With reference to the Qurʼanic verse 4:98–99, Dr. Fadl outlined two important points. First, "emigration is dropped from the list of the duties of those who cannot migrate due to their sickness or for other reasons." Second, "emigration is not obligatory on those who can observe their religious duties in non-Muslim countries."[98] These two points individually and collectively reveal how al-Qaʻida and other groups have twisted the concept of jihad. In both points, emigration is dropped from the list of Muslim duties and thus jihad is dropped from the list of duties accordingly. This confirms not only the ambiguities inherent in the ideology of the neo-jihadists, but also that their understanding of jihad is outdated. Considering the first point, if a Muslim cannot migrate because of sickness or other reasons, there is no jihad obligation on him or her. Further, because emigration must be toward a safe place, if there is no such place, there can be no migration. If we consider the neo-jihadists' claim that 'the entire world is *kafir*,' there is logically then no safe haven to which Muslims can migrate to observe their religion freely. If emigration is impossible, as Dr. Fadl states, then there is no jihad.[99] Considering the other point, if Muslims are free to observe their religion, then their emigration for jihad is not obligatory. In this context, because Muslims in Australia, Europe, the U.S., and other western countries are free to observe their religion, their emigration for jihad is not obligatory, and thus their jihad is also not obligatory. Thus, based on their own interpretation of either situation, al-Qaʻida's jihad ideology is outdated and illogical.

6

Al-Qa'ida's Tactics

T his chapter focuses on al-Qa'ida's tactics in order to identify and understand the mentality that selects targets, plans operations against them, and prepares statements to be given after each operation.

The departure of Soviet troops from Afghanistan was considered a great victory not only for the Mujahidin Afghans, but also for the jihadists in general. These are the jihadists who carried out their jihad against those whom they called 'infidels,' in the name of their doctrine of jihad. It is in this sense that when the jihadists consider their participation in the war against the Soviets in Afghanistan they do so with great emphasis on their doctrinal capacity and their capability of doing things that might shake the world and even liquidate the world powers.

Following the withdrawal of Soviet troops from Afghanistan, al-Qa'ida took considerable measures to develop its doctrinal and political tactics and to transform itself from a group of volunteers in the war against the Soviets into a network that recruited and trained Muslim youth to become neo-jihadists and to fight in wars around the world. The group had prepared the ground and in 1998 established its 'Global Front for the Jihad Against the Jews and the Crusaders.' Under the umbrella of this 'front,' al-Qa'ida began to undertake some small- and medium-scale operations against those who were perceived as enemies, but the attacks against New York and Washington on September 11, 2001 shocked the world. The consequences that followed September 11 compelled what was left of al-Qa'ida networks to take extreme measures to improve their plans and tactics in order to survive.

Thus, the tactics of al-Qa'ida generally involve using whatever means possible to achieve its aims and to survive, and present itself on the global stage as an Islamic movement with noble goals and objectives. Al-Qa'ida began to call itself a "reformative movement."[1] This should come as no surprise, as other terrorist organizations that are known to both East and West also called themselves reformative movements at that time. In this sense, al-Qa'ida planned for its tactics to include the discussion and promotion of theological issues as well as security, ideological training, and military concerns.

Its tactics might also take the form of intellectual analysis of specific doctrinal issues with the intention of providing legal clearance and jurisprudential justifications for its activities.[2] The tactics may focus on al-Qa'ida's internal and external policies on dealing with its critics from other jihadist movements, especially those who had renounced violence and terrorism, such as Egypt's al-Jama'a al-Islamiya, Jama'at al-Jihad, or critics from outside Islamic movements. These critics could be found throughout both Islamic and non-Islamic societies.[3] In either case, al-Qa'ida, which considers itself a 'reformative movement,' does not separate its tactics from its selective religious narratives and ideological interpretations. Issues related to the planning of action and retaliation; targets that are considered important; *al-tatarrus* (shield), and what they term 'counter-political games'; media and communication; the killing of civilians; and the killing of combatant prisoners are among the subjects that come in for tactical consideration.[4]

In dealing with such issues, al-Qa'ida networks benefited significantly from globalization in the reshaping of their tactics on many levels, including doctrinal thought, planning, training, and recruitment. In this regard, al-Qa'ida has also greatly benefited from advanced communication technologies, which have been used in the execution of terrorist activities. The media and Internet technology and other communication methods have been used by al-Qa'ida to promote its ideology and mobilize Muslim youth around the world, encouraging them to conduct terrorist acts in the areas in which they live. Al-Qa'ida considers the use of the Internet and media as tactics that are as important as the messages being transmitted. It is through these devices that Bin Laden and his deputy Ayman al-Zawahiri communicated with their followers in Iraq, North Africa, and other places around the world.[5]

Al-Qa'ida and similar networks have also mastered the art of intelligence and have continued to develop themselves in line with their circumstances and technology. The organization was able to thwart the plans and efforts of the CIA to arrest or kill Bin Laden in Afghanistan. As the chief director of the CIA, George Tenet, explained, "We continued our focus on capturing or killing Usama bin Laden."[6] Al-Qa'ida was able to keep its plan for the attacks of September 11 secret, even though these acts took years of planning in addition to ideological and physical training. This suggests that al-Qa'ida's agent handling is difficult to break through and therefore requires high-quality intelligence.[7] It was through such tactics that al-Qa'ida infiltrated many governments in the Middle East and elsewhere. Several al-Qa'ida members, especially of Egyptian and Pakistani descent, as well as Central Asians and some Europeans and U.S. citizens, have a military or police background;[8] and some of these members, in particular the Egyptians, have occupied high ranks in the Egyptian army or police forces. For example, Sayf al-'Adl was a colonel in Egypt's Special Forces before joining the Mujahidin in Afghanistan to fight the Soviet invasion. In 1998, when the Global Islamic Front against the Jews and the Crusaders was established by al-Qa'ida, Sayf al-'Adl was granted a pivotal role in military training within the organization. He then became the head of the military wing, after the Egyptian Abu Hafs al-Misri became al-Qa'ida's number three in charge, after Bin Laden and the Egyptian al-Zawahiri.[9]

These are the types of people who can plan and develop tactics and training programs along the lines of guerrilla warfare. In many of its training materials and videotapes, such as 'Cole'—a title that al-Qa'ida borrowed from the U.S. Navy guided missile destroyer USS Cole, which was attacked by al-Qa'ida on 12 October 2000[10]—al-Qa'ida's tactics are seen as new, since none of these materials or skills were seen on the battlefield in Afghanistan. Anyone with military experience can easily recognize from these materials how they train themselves militarily. One can also see that, for instance, when they attack they carry their handguns and rifles in a manner of disciplined military comportment, and do not fire their weapons in a haphazard manner.[11] Their strike forces divide themselves into groups that are small in number. The number within each group is dependent on the nature of the operation, yet each group must have an odd number of members with a leader (amir) even if there are only three. An odd number is a tactically interesting choice, since it means that a final decision may be reached by one vote alone. They may discuss matters related to their operations, but the final decision belongs to the amir, and it must be carried out without any further debate. As their ideologue, Dr. Fadl says, "each group must be in complete submission to the amir."[12] These small groups then might coordinate their security and responsibilities among themselves by using various elements of support that range from human beings to devices such as handled radios.[13]

Tactical Goals of September 11

Al-Qa'ida and similar neo-jihadist networks divide the world into Muslim and non-Muslim camps. They emphasize this division in direct opposition to what they consider the "infidel division which calls the non-Muslims (that is, the west) civilized *(mutahaddir)*, while referring to Muslims as uncivilized *(mutakhallif)*."[14] With this mentality, the jihadists consider their jihad as being to fight the 'infidels' and their Muslim supporters, 'the apostates,' rulers or ruled peoples in the Muslim world.

Focusing on the non-Muslims, al-Qa'ida paid special attention to both the U.S. and the Soviet Union as superpowers who had dictated the world order for some time. Here, the tactical thinking of al-Qa'ida focused on the question of how to deal with the military and economic strength of these superpowers. In this regard, al-Qa'ida emphasized that the strength of these superpowers was dependent mainly on three axes: the military machine; the media; and the cohesion between the institutions of the society and its various sectors, including the economy. These axes must be coordinated and work in harmony in order to maintain the strength of the superpower. Disruption to these axes could actively contribute to destroying or diminishing the strength of the superpower.

Considering these axes within the context of the world's two superpowers, al-Qa'ida distinguished between submission and control or domination. To al-Qa'ida, the control over a weaker state by a stronger one does not necessarily mean the weaker state must submit to the authority of the stronger one. In this regard, al-Qa'ida cites Afghanistan as an example to emphasize that the fall of the weaker Afghanistan to the control of the stronger USSR did not mean that Afghanistan had submitted to Soviet authority. The smaller Afghanistan resisted and fought the Soviet occupation and forced Soviet troops out. Al-Qa'ida considered the departure of the Soviet troops from Afghanistan as a defeat that contributed to the demise of the Soviet Union. This example is always portrayed by al-Qa'ida to highlight that there is no value in mere military strength in the face of 'creedal resistance' ('aqidat al-muqawama). Taking the Soviets as an example, al-Qa'ida views the strength of the other superpower, the U.S., as an illusory power. It is true that its power is "overwhelming in the estimation of humans, but in reality and after careful reflection using pure human reason," one comes to understand that this power is merely an "illusory power."[15] Therefore, these superpower states resort to using their deceptive media to portray their immeasurable powers and ability to reach anywhere in the world. On this point, al-Qa'ida says:

> The two superpowers believed, for a time, their media deception: that they were actually a power capable of controlling any place in the world. However, when a state submits to such media deception, and behaves on this basis, that is when its downfall begins. It is just as the American author Paul Kennedy says: "If America expands the use of its military power and strategically extends more than necessary, this will lead to its downfall."[16]

Al-Qa'ida emphasizes that a superpower's military strength has no value without the support of society, which, in turn, requires firm cohesion among its institutions, including those in the economic sector. Military power, al-Qa'ida says, may become a destructive factor or a 'curse' to the superpower if there is no cohesion among the society's institutions. Al-Qa'ida's point here is that the strength of the superpower lies not in its military machine but in the cohesion among the society's institutions that feed the military economically and morally. Thus, the collapse of superpowers comes not from the defeat of their armies or from the destruction of their weapons or military machines, but from within their societies. Thus, the society is the heart of the superpower and its body will remain healthy as long as its heart is healthy. In this regard, al-Qa'ida has searched its 'mind' to discover how to make this healthy body weak and sick. Al-Qa'ida's theorist, Abu Bakr Naji, found that this weakness can be facilitated by certain elements that were termed "elements of civilizational extinction." Among these elements are the following: "The corruption of religion; moral collapse; social iniquities; and excessive luxuries; selfishness; giving priority to worldly desires and pleasures; the love of the worldly pleasures over all values, and so on."[17]

The existence of these elements in any society, al-Qaʻida says, could tire out the social fabric and accelerate societal collapse, even for a superpower. A mix of these elements can coexist in an active or latent form, awaiting a catalyst to activate them and cause the downfall of the superpower. The activating factor, al-Qaʻida says, could be one or more human or natural factors, such as war, a tsunami, an earthquake, or a drought.[18] Here, al-Qaʻida reflects on the Qur'anic idea that any of these factors can be either fruitful[19] or disastrous.[20] also reflects on the following Qur'anic theme: *And when We would destroy a township, We send commandment to its folk who live at ease, but they commit abomination therein, and so the Word* [of doom] *proves true against it, so We annihilate it with complete annihilation.*[21] Thus, the activating factor can be the "decree of God." He might ordain the activating factor "in order to act on those three axes": the military, the media, and the economy. Such a factor would not only activate the latent "elements of civilizational extinction, but would also exhaust economic and military power." In this regard, al-Qaʻida considers the Soviet 'war' in Afghanistan to be an example of the consequences of a 'decree of God.' It was time for the empire of the Soviet Union to end, as had been the case for the British, French, and Roman empires. Thus, the purpose of the 'war' with the USSR was to bring the Soviet empire to a close. When the USSR put itself in this 'war' with Afghanistan and tried to take control of this small and weak country, the war worked as an activating factor and energized the 'elements of civilizational extinction.' Here, the 'decree of God' is evident to al-Qaʻida, because this war was between incomparable powers but broke the back of the superpower. The war exhausted the Soviets' military power and activated the elements that led to the downfall of the USSR.

Consequently, al-Qaʻida argued that the activating factor or the 'decree of God' led to the following: (i) the 'atheist dogma' of the USSR failed to stand up against a creed that believed in God and divorced this world and yearned for the next life; (ii) the war made it difficult for those in love with worldly desires and pleasures to stand up against those who divorced this life and therefore had nothing to lose; (iii) the war energized moral corruption, which damaged social cohesion, weakening the Soviet society's support of military power; (iv) the war exhausted the Soviet economy and brought social iniquities to the surface; (v) thus, when the war activated the 'elements of civilizational extinction,' the main axes upon which the superpower depended began to work against each other; (vi) the war worked on the media axis and removed "the respect for the Soviet army" from the hearts of the masses, whose regimes, revolving in the Soviet orbit in Europe and Asia, began to break away from the USSR; (vii) the war also worked on the Muslims and revived the "creed of jihad" in their hearts; (viii) when they saw the fruitful jihad in Afghanistan, Muslims in those countries controlled by the Soviet Union were able to stand firm in the face of Soviet power; and (ix) thus, the jihad in Afghanistan revived the jihad in the region and brought forth many Muslims from varying areas, including Chechnya and Tajikistan.[22]

After the collapse of the USSR, the world became unipolar, dominated solely by the U.S. Accordingly, al-Qaʻida shifted its tactical teachings to draw attention to the Soviet collapse as an example that might encourage al-Qaʻida's affiliates to find ways to deal with the remaining superpower. Al-Qaʻida preached the view that the U.S. was not stronger than the USSR, but that "its defeat" will not come unless the jihadists "plunge" themselves into an "active war with it," regardless of whether they have a "rational mind or theoretical research at hand." However, al-Qaʻida leaders knew very well that those who were indeed willing to go to war against the U.S. would require religious clearance. It is evident in their literature that they discussed the matter of confrontation with the U.S. Some who discussed this matter were referred to as "religious," while others were not. In either case, there was a view that the U.S. "could not be collapsed," "its power's components differed in kind from the collapsed Soviet [Union]," and "the U.S. media was much stronger than the media of the Soviet [Union]." Some others did not agree with al-Qaʻida's decision-makers, completely rejected the idea of confrontation with the U.S., and left the group.[23]

However, al-Qaʻida insisted on initiating a confrontation with the U.S. and continued to promote this idea through varying means, including theology and legal clearance as well as comparisons between the abilities of the U.S. and the USSR. Leading to the tragic events of September 11, the discussion among al-Qaʻida's affiliates went on for a long period of time. Their ideologue, Naji, called those affiliates people of "truthfulness and jihad." Some among these affiliates believed that the "U.S. is weak." This view argues that if the Americans lost "one tenth" of the number of Russians killed in Afghanistan and Chechnya, "America will flee heedlessly." They believed that the current status of the military of the U.S. and its allies was not equal to their military during the time of "colonialism," and further that the power of the U.S. rests solely with its powerful media. In terms of logistics, al-Qaʻida's decision-makers outlined that the center of the ruling power and military strength of the Soviet Union was, to a certain extent, close to the battlefields. Therefore, the supplies, the motorized units, and armed vehicles were arriving at the battlefields without much cost. Yet these matters would be quite different in the case of the U.S.

> The distance factor should help the Americans understand the difficulty that they will face to keep us in submission to them, or to keep their control over us, or to continue pillaging our wealth and resources, if we decided to not only refuse, but also enflame the confrontation to confirm our rejection. This was the picture until the momentous events of September 11 and the foretokens which appeared with the events of Kenya and Tanzania.[24]

This theme and framework underlying al-Qaʻida's tactical planning of attacks against the U.S., which began with the attacks on the U.S. embassies in Kenya and Tanzania on 7 August 1998, were also referred to by the CIA chief, George Tenet. He was not aware of al-Qaʻida's plan. Even after the attacks on the U.S. embassies in Kenya and Tanzania, Tenet was not sure and continued to say that he "had some self-doubt" about the exact perpetrators. However, he emphasized "the fact that al-Qaʻida operations are planned years in advance. We later learned that they first cased the Nairobi embassy more than four years earlier."[25] Whether or not the CIA was aware of al-Qaʻida's tactics, al-Qaʻida's discussion resulted in the decision that the jihadists must confront the U.S. Their plan began with the embassies in Africa, followed by the U.S. Navy guided missile destroyer USS Cole on 12 October 2000, and later escalated to the momentous event of 11 September 2001.[26]

Al-Qaʻida undertook some specific operations that were arranged systematically and that began with the operation of Nairobi and Dar el-Salam in order to achieve what al-Qaʻida called its "tactical goals," as outlined in the following:

1. The first was to destroy a large and important part of the respect for the U.S. and enhance the confidence in the jihadists' souls through the following means:

i.   Exposing the U.S. and the western media's deception about the strength of the U.S., to reveal that it is in fact a 'power' without real force.

ii. Forcing the U.S. to abandon its "war against Islam" through proxies of Arab and Muslim regimes and forcing it to appear and fight directly instead of through its hidden hand. This would help the decent among the Muslim masses and in the "armies of apostasy" understand that the fear of overthrowing their regimes because the U.S. protects them is misplaced. The decent among the masses will be confident that they can overthrow their corrupt regimes and oppose the U.S. if it interferes.

2. The second goal is to replace the human bases and the casualties sustained by the jihadists during the past thirty years by means of recruitment and human aid, a strategy for which al-Qaʻida predicts a degree of success for a number of reasons:

i.   The people will come to the aid of the jihadists when they hear and see that the "unbelievable" operations against the U.S. have occurred.

ii. The people will transform their accumulated anger over U.S. support for the "Zionist entity" and direct U.S. interference in the affairs of the Muslim world into actions.

iii. The accumulated and suppressed anger of the Muslim masses against their Arab and Muslim regimes of "apostasy and tyranny" will be transformed into angry action.

iv. When the Muslim masses discover the truth of the collaboration between their regimes and "the enemy of Islam," their affiliations with the jihadists will not dissipate or dry up.

v.   This requires an operation to destroy the walls of fear, the wall of silence, and to spread confidence in the hearts of the Muslim masses.

3. The third goal is that the operation must be momentous in order to expose the weakness of U.S. power in its homeland.

i.   This will force the U.S. to end its war against Islam through its agents. It will abandon its media's psychological war and wars inflicted through proxy Arab regimes and fight directly.

ii. The masses of all sects and groups, even the U.S. citizens themselves, will see that the interference of the U.S. in those distanced areas will cost America dearly.[27]

Accordingly, al-Qa'ida planned to mount substantial strikes on the U.S. homeland with a focus on the symbols of U.S. power. Al-Qa'ida has long made a point of hitting U.S. military and economic targets, starting with small and medium operations aimed at U.S. interests outside the territory of the United States itself. However, in the homeland, the World Trade Center and the Pentagon were likely targeted on September 11 because the Twin Towers were symbols of U.S. economic power, while the Pentagon symbolized U.S. military might. In a video that surfaced in December 2001, Bin Laden spoke of the September 11 attacks as a strike "in the heart" of the U.S. In August 2004, U.S. officials noted that they had uncovered what looked to be al-Qa'ida's plan to target financial sites, including the New York Stock Exchange and World Bank.[28] Al-Qa'ida leadership was keeping a close eye on the U.S. economy, and formulating a detailed strategy to bleed the U.S. bankrupt, as demonstrated in the following discussion.

Tactics after September 11
Al-Qa'ida planned September 11 in order to break what it called the "walls of fear and silence," but the swiftness and harshness of the response of the U.S. and its allies broke al-Qa'ida's back. Al-Qa'ida was hit hard and hundreds of its operatives were killed or arrested. Muslims around the world condemned the attack and supported the U.S. in the so-called War on Terror. The response and related developments were not anticipated by al-Qa'ida and did not go according to its plans.

Thereafter, al-Qa'ida began to develop its tactics and carefully plan its actions around the objective of giving the impression that it stands against the enemies of Islam. In this regard, al-Qa'ida has shifted its tactical thinking to focus first on what it perceives to be its closest enemy (that is, Arab and Muslim regimes). Instead of dividing the world into Muslim and non-Muslim camps, this time al-Qa'ida divided the world into regions consisting of a number of states. Each of these regions is labeled with a priority label, and Arabo-Muslim regions were shifted to the top of the agenda. In short, these regions are categorized into two groups: (i) the principal groups; and (ii) the remaining countries.

The aim of this division was to maximize the effectiveness of what is left of al-Qa'ida's striking power. Thus, the principal group then came to include countries such as the Gulf countries, Jordan, Nigeria, Pakistan, Arabia, Yemen, and the countries of North Africa. The second group of priority includes the rest of the Muslim world. This selection is not rigid and provides security for al-Qaʻida's operatives in each of these regions, and helps them to consider the best tactics for them based on what they see on the ground. This theme of prioritizing countries and regions, and its underlying framework, was distributed and facilitated before September 11, as admitted by al-Qaʻida in the following: "This selection was distributed three years prior to the momentous events of September. After these events and the developments that followed them, the leadership announced some modifications in which some regions were excluded from the principal group of priority to be included in the second group. They also added to the principal group two other regions, precisely, Arabia and Nigeria."[29]

Thus, the point of al-Qaʻida's flexible selection is to protect its striking power instead of dissipating its strength across regions where al-Qaʻida's work would not be as effective as hoped. The other reason is perhaps that they seek to focus on countries or pockets within countries where the central authority is relatively weak. Hence, when mentioning certain countries, al-Qaʻida does not mean the entire country but that part of it in which the central authority's control is fragile, so that al-Qaʻida's operatives can live and move around easily. The mention of Pakistan, for example, does not mean all of Pakistan, as such, but rather the tribal areas on the border between Pakistan and Afghanistan. This can also be said of Yemen, Algeria, Nigeria, and other countries. Thus, the pocket area in question can be small, or large enough to include the peripheries of the borders of one or more countries. This leads to the question of the criteria for selection; specifically on what basis al-Qaʻida selects these areas or priority regions. Al-Qaʻida focuses on regions, areas, or countries suffering from political unrest and fragile authority, which have weak links among the society's institutions, on the one hand, and between these institutions and the central government, on the other. The type of region in which al-Qaʻida prefers to work is outlined by al-Qaʻida as follows:

These regions should be in a situation similar to that of Afghanistan before the control of the Taliban. A region that is submitting to the laws of the jungle in its primitive form, whose good people and even the wise among the evildoers yearn for someone to administer this chaos. These types of regions accept any organization, regardless of whether it is made up of good or evil people. However, if the evil people administer it they will make it even worse.[30]

These words indicate how al-Qa'ida thinks of itself and its people: as good people and as the best organization to govern chaos in such regions. However, al-Qa'ida should remember that after September 11 there was no country or region whose people would accept al-Qa'ida's affiliates to live and work freely as they had done in Yemen, Somalia, or Afghanistan before September 11. Despite al-Qa'ida's awareness of this reality, it advises its followers when they come to these types of areas that they should work to win the hearts and minds of the people by spreading security; providing food; providing medical treatment; establishing shari'a; raising the level of morals; and then recruiting and training to raise the organization's combat efficiency. These are the tactics that al-Qa'ida tried to adopt in Iraq when they announced their Islamic state there; but they failed to win the hearts and the minds of the Iraqis. Al-Qa'ida also failed in Lebanon in 2007, when the al-Qa'ida network Fatah al-Islam tried to establish a foothold for an Islamic state. They also failed in Arabia and North Africa. They are always on the run with their 'caliphate' a swag hanging on their back. Their caliphate is in fact only on their websites, and it amounts merely to an electronic caliphate (EC).

The criteria that al-Qa'ida consider in selecting the countries, regions, or areas in which to conduct their work can be summarized as follows:

1. In each separate country, there should be geographical and topographical depth that permits the establishment of cantons or regions that can be managed by al-Qa'ida.
2. The central authority in these areas should be weak. The areas of weak authority are not necessarily found in the peripheries of the borders of the state, but they can sometimes be found in the internal provinces, particularly in overcrowded areas.
3. It would be much better if there were a jihadist movement in the area. If so, this movement has the potential to join al-Qa'ida's jihadists for expansion in the region.
4. In general, those who are assigned to a region should develop their awareness of the inhabitants before entering the region. They should be aware of the nature and customary behavior of the inhabitants and whether or not they carry weapons.[31]

With regard to this fourth criterion, for instance, in Yemen, Iraq, and some other Arab countries people used to be permitted to carry weapons or guns. However, this is currently outlawed in these countries and weapons were eliminated in the aftermath of September 11. In terms of the criteria, in general al-Qaʻida emphasizes that most of the priority regions are in remote areas, in the heart of the Muslim world, which are difficult for UN forces to control. Accordingly, al-Qaʻida's activity in these priority regions is aimed at al-Qaʻida's empowerment— that is, to establish its Islamic caliphate of any size, small or large, depending on the area managed to control. In the principal region, the path to empowerment is divided into three stages, each of which has tactical goals:

1. The first stage is called the "thorn of vexation and exhaustion" and is aimed primarily at the following:
   i.   Exhausting the enemy's forces with its collaborating regimes; dispersing their strength; making them unable to catch their breath by means of operations, even if the operations are small in size or effect. In either case, "a single strike on their heads will leave its effect for a long period of time."
   ii. Attracting new youth to the jihadist work by undertaking "qualitative operations" from time to time, in order to attract the attention of the people. Here, the qualitative operations refer to "medium-scale" operations like the operations in Bali (Indonesia, October 2002), in al-Muhayya (Riyadh, November 1995), in Djerba (Tunisia, April 2002), and in Turkey and Iraq.
   iii. As for operations like September 11, the advice is not to undertake some large-scale attacks without consulting the "High Command." Meanwhile, operations like those in Bali, Riyadh, and the like do not require consultation since these types of operations have already been approved in advance.
   iv. There are operatives who are trained to carry out normal or minor operations, while others are trained to undertake medium operations. If those who are undertaking small operations are able to advance and develop themselves for the undertaking of a specific medium operation, then al-Qaʻida encourages them to do so, even if the small operation has to be canceled for this purpose.

v. After an appropriate period of time in the priority region, the rate of the medium operations should increase to approach the rate of the minor operations.

vi. Either dislodging or snatching the region from the control of the central authority is chosen for special concentrated work.

vii. The tactical goal of this stage is to advance the groups through training, drilling, and operational practice. This will also prepare them psychologically and practically for the next stage.[32]

2. The second stage is called the "administration." The tactical focus of al-Qa'ida in any selected region, after dislodging that region from the central authority, is security and defense as well as some measures aimed at winning the hearts and minds of the inhabitants. This is the pattern that al-Qa'ida operatives try to implement in any area that comes under their control, as they did in Iraq for some period of time. Thus, al-Qa'ida's pattern of administration of any region under its control will focus on the following:

i. Spreading internal security and preserving it among the inhabitants.

ii. Providing food and medical treatment for the inhabitants to allay the anger they feel against their regime on the one hand and the west on the other.

iii. Securing the region from the regime's attack by establishing defensive lines and fortifications.

iv. Establishing shari'a and court rule to administer justice in the region.

v. Recruiting the youth of the region and training them both ideologically and militarily. Here, the objective is to create a militarized region with efficient fighting capabilities.

vi. Establishing an intelligence framework that is as efficient as possible.

vii. Working to win the people's hearts by any means, including offering them money.

viii. Deterring the hypocrites among the people and forcing them to hide their opinions, therefore preventing them from discouraging the public from joining al-Qa'ida or subscribing to their notion of jihad, and making them comply with al-Qa'ida's authority.

ix. Attacking the regime to repel it, plunder its wealth, and place it in a constant state of apprehension and desire for reconciliation.
x. Establishing coalitions with those groups and parties who oppose the central regime.
xi. Establishing a logistical support network for the region through regions, both near and far, which are controlled by al-Qa'ida.[33]

The Plan of Action

The general plan of action and breakdown of goals and stages are all clues to al-Qa'ida's tactical mentality. Its plan of action also begins from the premise that the world is divided according to whether one is 'with them' or 'against them.' Generally, al-Qa'ida considers all of its opponents, including those in Arab and Muslim countries, as enemies who should be fought and killed. Toward its goal to establish an Islamic caliphate, al-Qa'ida seems to have a general plan of action in its mind. Actions can be small, or medium, like those in Bali, London, and Iraq, or large like the events of September 11. Each operation has different plans and even different planners, but each operation complements the others, as all are driven by what al-Qa'ida calls the "general plan of actions." While the small and medium operations are planned by people whose experience in this work is relatively limited, the large operations like September 11 must be planned by what al-Qa'ida refers to as the High Command. Thus, the plan for September 11 was different from the plan for the operations in Iraq. Nevertheless, the tactical points listed above and the plan of action outlined here make up the theme and framework for all types of operations, big, medium, or small. This also reflects al-Qa'ida's operations in Iraqi areas such as Anbar, Basra, and others. Unlike New York or Washington, each of these Iraqi areas was considered by al-Qa'ida as a "region of priority" and dealt with accordingly, to the extent that one of these regions has come to be known, in the international media, as the Triangle of Death, which was later used as the title for a film about the region.[34] This triangle lies between Baghdad and Hillah and contains several large towns including Yusufiya, Mahmudiya, Iskandriya, and Latifiya. Al-Qa'ida's actions in what it considers "regions of priority," whether in Iraq, North Africa, or elsewhere, are not determined by a fixed plan. However, al-Qa'ida has in place a general plan of action that allows for alteration depending on the circumstances. Overall, any alteration must abide by the theme and framework of the "general plan."

For example, carrying out the plan for September 11, as emphasized by al-Qaʻida, began with sequential medium strikes against the U.S. and reached its apex with the momentous attacks of September 2001. This attack was considered by al-Qaʻida as "successful" and was intended to destroy the "prestige" of the U.S. in the minds of the masses and in the minds of the armies of the Arab and Muslim countries or "apostasy" regimes. In addition, al-Qaʻida was gambling that the strikes would mobilize the masses against the U.S. and its supporters from among the Arab and Muslim regimes. Tactically, al-Qaʻida expected from September 11 that there would be an "expansion" of the jihadist current across the Muslim world, with the response of the U.S. and the arrival of its troops and "fire" to the Muslim world. In planning for September 11, al-Qaʻida was well aware that the U.S. would respond, and this was what al-Qaʻida wanted, to satisfy its betting and gambling tendencies. The U.S. would either seek "revenge" and the "conflict will intensify" or it would launch a limited war. Both options were considered by al-Qaʻida as "traps."

Considering the 'trap' of the limited war option, al-Qaʻida's view is that a limited war would not appease the wrath of the U.S. or succeed in curbing the escalating jihadist expansion. One might argue that the U.S. caused the downfall of the Taliban, causing al-Qaʻida to lose its camps and 'Islamic state' there. However, al-Qaʻida argues that the fall of the Taliban was "planned before September 11," and that the Taliban might have "collapsed" even if September 11 had not occurred. The U.S. invasion of Afghanistan was also considered by al-Qaʻida to be a regrettable choice. To al-Qaʻida, the failure of the U.S. to achieve its goals in Afghanistan and the continuing resistance in this country, over several years, will convince the Muslim masses that opposition to the U.S. is possible. In addition, the U.S. will begin to confront the transformation of the masses into "tens of thousands" of jihadist groups like those of September 11, as these groups will turn their strikes against it. Here, the U.S. will not find a "state" in the Muslim world as an entity upon which the U.S. can exact its revenge. If the U.S. views Afghanistan as an enemy, then the remaining Muslim states are U.S. "clones." Further, the U.S. will soon realize that those regimes it supports "cannot protect it" or its interests in the region from attack. Therefore, the U.S. will have no choice but to fall into the "trap" of the first option, that is the revenge option.[35]

In the case of the "trap" that is the "revenge" option, al-Qaʿida's view is that the U.S. enacting its revenge will put its armies, which "occupy" the Middle East, in a "state of war" with the "masses" in the region. The activity of the U.S. in the region will "accelerate" the transformation that will increase the jihadist expansion and create legions among youth willing to contemplate and plan for actions against the U.S. presence in the Middle East.[36]

Thus, the U.S. "forces" that were "enjoying" their living in the region, while the people "slept right next to them and sensed no danger," engaged in war to the extent that these forces "hated their presence." Likewise, the War in Iraq made it clear to the U.S. administration that the U.S. was being "drained," and that the "ease" of entry into more than one "war" at a time was merely "hypothetical." The remoteness of the "center of power" in the U.S. mainland from the "war zones" had a profound effect on the U.S. economy and ability to bring such "wars" to an end.[37]

Ending the wars is not in al-Qaʿida's interest. Al-Qaʿida plans to expand and extend the confrontation and reshape it to include "economic targets" as well as zones other than Iraq and Afghanistan. Somalia is already not functioning, and Pakistan is on the road to chaos, while Lebanon and Yemen and Middle East peace, like the world economies, are fragile. These are simply examples of what al-Qaʿida refers to as "latent factors," which require a catalyst to accelerate their explosion. The looming war with Iran is very much in the interests of al-Qaʿida as it is one of the most effective accelerators. Indeed, al-Qaʿida would be pleased if Iran entered this game, which is described by Martin Woollacott of *The Guardian* as a "dangerous game." He writes:

If you wanted to draft a scenario for the end of the relatively orderly and prosperous world we live in, you might well begin it with an attack on Iran's nuclear facilities. After the battering that the experts say would be necessary to suppress Iran's nuclear programme, petrol at $200 a barrel would soon be a distant dream as Iran's reserves were compromised and other Middle Eastern oilfields disrupted by Iranian retaliation. Trade would shrivel, economies would cease to function, Iraq, Afghanistan, and Lebanon would slip back into chaos, Pakistan would be rocked, Iran would be broken, and extremism would flourish in the vacuum. Floundering amid the wreckage like lost boys would be the U.S. army, much of its navy, and the best military units of many other western countries. Relations between America and the world's other powers—China, Russia, Europe, India—would crash. America's own economy and political standing would be damaged irreparably, and Israel's isolation would be both complete and permanent.[38]

The underlying theme of Woollacott's words is, in fact, precisely what al-Qa'ida is looking for. It has even posted a book on its websites about how to create chaos. It is in a state of disorder that al-Qa'ida can thrive and dominate. Al-Qa'ida outlined what it calls "the plan by which we shall provoke events." It emphasizes that there is "war" in Afghanistan and "war" in Iraq and overall there is the War on Terror. In either case, "the blows that are directed toward America and its allies, in the east and the west are difficult to ignore." In this context, "the plan by which we shall provoke events from now until we have completely accomplished our goals" will be as follows: "Diversify and widen the vexation strikes against the Crusader-Zionist enemy in every place in the Islamic world and even outside it, if possible, so as to disperse the efforts of the alliance of the enemy and thus drain it to the greatest extent possible."

Al-Qa'ida outlined a few examples of past operations against selected targets. For example, if a tourist resort that the "Crusaders patronize" like that of Bali in Indonesia is hit, then all of the tourist resorts in the world will have to be secured. Doing so will require additional forces to at least double the ordinary numbers, which will in turn double the ordinary amount spent on such security, further burdening the economy. If a "usurious bank" belonging to the "Crusaders" in Turkey is struck, all of the banks of the "Crusaders" in the world will have to be better "secured" and, again, the economic drain will increase. If an "oil interest" near the Yemeni port of Aden is hit, intensive security measures will have to be put in place to protect all oil interests, and their tankers and the oil pipelines. This will also drain the economy. If two of the "apostate writers" are killed in a simultaneous operation in two different countries, they will have to secure thousands of writers. It is in this way that the "diversification" and widening of the circle of "targets and vexation strikes," which are carried out by small separate groups, occurs. Al-Qa'ida's tactic is to "repeatedly strike the same type of target two or three times to make it clear to the enemy that this type of target would continue to be vulnerable."[39]

Accordingly, economic targets, especially those concerning oil interests and everything linked to this industry, are one of the focuses of al-Qaʿidaʾs operatives. Hitting economic targets, al-Qaʿida believes, will force the enemy to push the Arab regimes into pumping in more forces for security. However, these regimes' forces are already "exhausted" from protecting the other targets. The Arab regimes have security priorities and must protect "the rulers and the ruling families, the presidential institutions and foreigners, oil interests, banks, and places of entertainment." As a result, "feebleness" will start to appear in their forces, especially since their forces are limited in number. Therefore, the peripheries and the crowded regions will be without a sufficient number of troops. Forces in these areas, for al-Qaʿida, are easy targets to be attacked in attempts to seize their weapons.

Thus, al-Qaʿidaʾs instruction to its followers, in dealing with Arab and Muslim regimes, is to focus on the region or areas selected to be a jihadist base for settlement and operations. In so doing, al-Qaʿida sends its agents to assess the area; its topography; its people, their behavior and customs, and whether they are willing to support al-Qaʿida; and the potential for establishing an al-Qaʿida group and forming a coalition between al-Qaʿida and any existing groups. If the jihadists are close to the selected "region" or there is a way to get to it and there are "spies" and "individuals" that show an interest in offering "allegiance" to the jihadists, they study the area and then move in. A number of the operative groups will "unite" in a single entity and enter the region to "manage" it and establish a link with other jihadists in the "neighboring" regions. They will balance their energies and resources between "concentrating" in one place and "spreading" out, to ensure the enemy senses the jihadists' capacity for "deterrence."

The mentality behind the tactic of deterrence focuses on the military leaders and their immediate surroundings, and aims to "frighten" them and make them feel that they are losing the trust of their "subordinates"; it should also encourage the subordinates to consider fleeing the service or joining the jihadists to die as "martyrs" rather than dying with the "tyrannical infidels." At this point, al-Qaʿida hopes that its enemy will lean toward "reconciliation," of course "without a treaty," and will be satisfied with "retreating" to the back line for the "protection" of its economy and resources, and that this is where the enemy's forces will then be "concentrated." Here, al-Qaʿida emphasizes that the enemy's return to the back line means "withdrawal" from advanced positions so that the likelihood of a "security" breakdown increases. At this point, the al-Qa'ida groups will contact other groups to "control and manage the region."

To ensure the success of this plan, al-Qa'ida instructs its members to follow these specific steps when entering a region:

1. Developing a military strategy that works to "disperse" the efforts and forces of the enemy and to exhaust and drain its monetary capabilities.
2. Developing a "media strategy" that targets two classes—the first of which comprises the "masses," and second of which is the "enemy's troops" of lower ranks. This strategy intends to encourage the common people to join the jihad, and enemy's troops in the Arabo-Muslim armies may join the jihad or "flee" their service; or at least offers logistical support such as money, food, shelter, and medicine, and adopt a negative attitude toward those who do not join.
3. "Polarising" the economy, the resources, and the media.
4. Continual training through ideological and physical programs especially designed to exploit the outcomes of the previous points.[40]

Principles of Military Action

This section focuses on al-Qa'ida's aims and objective in relation to its operatives deciding to undertake an operation. For its military operations, al-Qa'ida permits its followers to learn and use whatever means possible from the plans and military principles to the techniques and media used by "non-Muslims." Thus, borrowing from non-Muslims, in these areas, is not forbidden for al-Qa'ida. As these techniques, media, and military principles have been tested by the west and used in combat, al-Qa'ida says, there is no reason for its followers to continue to suffer from "rigidity" and "random" behavior. This is a reference to al-Qa'ida's intention to borrow whatever it can by way of technological expertise from the advanced west. To al-Qa'ida, adopting demonstrated military techniques and implementing them will not only facilitate the achievement of its goals, but will also enable the jihadists to improve the execution of their plans. Therefore, al-Qa'ida instructs its affiliates to learn and study non-Muslims' military principles and techniques in order to broaden the horizons and/or skill and capabilities of its followers. Perhaps a number of military leaders might emerge from among them. Al-Qa'ida cites several examples of principles to its members that focus the mind and help to clarify the importance of following these principles in order to improve the efficacy of the military actions of al-Qaʻidaʼs operatives. These examples have been seen in Iraq and other places in which al-Qaʻida operates. Among these examples are:

1. There is an important principle that says that "if regular armies concentrate in one place they lose control; conversely, if they spread out they lose effectiveness."[41]

   As to the first half of this principle, al-Qaʻidaʼs advice to its operatives is to reshape their operations in a way, and a location, that creates disturbance in the balance between the conglomeration of the forces of the enemy and their dispersion. This means that when the jihadists target something, it will be impossible for their 'enemy' to deploy a large number of forces in this place. If they do, they will lose control, because when the first shot is fired, the enemy's forces will strike each other. Therefore, the enemy will normally assign forces that are commensurate with the nature and size of the location. Thus, al-Qaʻida advises its operatives to study the nature and topography of the targeted locations in order to become aware of the size of the enemy's force and to prepare a force to attack it. In addition, the first half of the principle indicates the importance of learning the art of attacking the targets, identifying appropriate locations for the clash, and planning the defense in case there is a counterattack.

   Al-Qaʻida considers the second half of this military principle more important than the first. The second half argues that whenever the forces of the enemy are spread out over a larger area of land, they lose their effectiveness, and attacking them therefore becomes easier. This is the principle that al-Qaʻida and similar networks follow. Al-Qaʻida imbues this principle with great importance and says that those who ignore this portion of this principle will fail.

2. The principles of "the rate of operations." The operations may be undertaken at "(i) escalating, (ii) fixed, or (iii) undulating rates."[42] The escalating rate is sometimes adopted by al-Qaʻida in order to send a message to the masses and the enemy's low-ranking troops that the power of al-Qaʻida is on the rise. To al-Qaʻida, this tactic leaves its imprint on the enemy's mind, whether with respect to the number of al-Qaʻida fighters, or their specific characters, their capacity, or all of these elements, and gives the impression that al-Qaʻida is continually advancing, that the enemy is in retreat, and that the fate of the enemy

is defeat. This tactic is said to encourage the masses, revive their hope, and facilitate permanent support from them for al-Qa'ida. In addition, the escalation tactic is considered by al-Qa'ida to advance the knowledge and experience of its young operatives and to accustom them to confrontation. In this regard, al-Qa'ida's operatives begin with small operations, and then they may undertake medium operations, and later, larger operations. Al-Qa'ida may begin with small operations only to ignite the confrontation, and then move to medium, and then larger ones. The operation of September 11 was of course the largest of all. Thus, al-Qa'ida might begin with a number of small operations in remote places, which are located far apart, in order to give the impression that al-Qa'ida's presence encompasses a large area of land. Later, al-Qa'ida will undertake larger operations, and lessen the distances between the target locations. This tactic of escalation may be adopted at a specific stage or period of time, and then changed to a fixed or undulating rate, depending on the circumstances on the ground.

In the case of the fixed rate, the operations can be of any type, small, medium, or large, but their number is fixed. Here, the change is in the kinds of the operations or targets. The distances between the locations of the targets can be large or short. In either case, the fixed rate can also be adopted for a period of time or for a particular stage according to the developments of the circumstances on the ground.

As to operations that take the form of an undulation or "waves," al-Qa'ida considers this type suitable for those groups whose military bases and defensive positions are sufficiently strong or impregnable. It is suitable for the jihadists when they want to send a message to the enemy that they will pay a price for their actions, and that the cessation of operations for a period does not mean a permanent stoppage but rather marks a period of preparation for more waves of operations.

3. The third principle is to "strike with your maximum striking power in the weakest locations of the enemy."[43]

This principle is considered by al-Qa'ida to be important as a general strategy and also for planning small operations. Here, al-Qa'ida has admitted that its leadership was considering the youth of the "Arabian Peninsula" as al-Qa'ida's "striking force," but did not select the peninsula for regime change before September 11 because Bin Laden was wary of antagonizing the Saudi royal family and still hoped to enlist their support if needed. This decision, however, has been reversed since September 11 because the circumstances there have also changed. Now, the peninsula has become one of the regions chosen for the implementation of change and has been given top priority by al-Qaʻida's leadership. Currently, al-Qaʻida considers the Arabian Peninsula to be an ideal place for the application of this principle. As for applying this principle when planning small operations, al-Qaʻida has provided a number of examples to cover different circumstances. These examples may help to analyze the objective underlying al-Qaʻida's operations.

i. If there is a simple operation that is non-suicidal or a "non-martyrdom operation," for which only one or two individuals are needed, al-Qaʻida sends ten operatives. The purpose of this, as al-Qaʻida says, is for "massacring and terrorizing the enemy." According to al-Qaʻida, this type of tactic leaves its impact on the hearts and minds of the people, and when the people and the media discuss these events or attacks, the impression left will be that any future operations will involve an even larger number of operatives. The other objective of such tactics is to raise al-Qaʻida's profile in the media and to deter the enemy.

ii. If there is an easy target, such as a building in which the "enemy's meetings are held," and its destruction can be completed by a small explosive trap, and where there is a good cache of explosives, al-Qaʻida may use a quantity of explosives that would not only destroy the building, but would make "the earth completely swallow it up." By doing so, al-Qaʻida wants to "multiply" the enemy's fear and to achieve its goal of increased media coverage. The other objective is to force the enemy to announce its own casualties and policies. Al-Qaʻida advises its operatives to repeat this type of operation to achieve the best results.

4. The fourth principle dictates that "the most likely way to defeat the stronger enemy militarily is to drain it militarily and economically."[44]

To al-Qaʻida, this principle is one of the "pillars of war," both in the past and in the present. It believes that this principle is one of the "tactics" that will "hasten the collapse of all of its enemies." In support of its view, al-Qaʻida claims that its actions drove U.S. Secretary of Defense Donald Rumsfeld to say "to reporters in justification for his setbacks 'what more can we do? Don't forget that we are spending billions in combating an enemy that spends millions.'" Drawing on this theme, al-Qaʻida referred to certain factors that contributed to the fall of the USSR and then applied these same factors to calculate the fall of the U.S. Thus, al-Qaʻida considered Rumsfeld to be "right to a certain extent," but also that "he is lying." In al-Qaʻida's view, what caused the downfall of the former USSR was the draining of its economic and military capacities in small wars, especially the "war of Afghanistan." Likewise, al-Qaʻida claims that "the fate of America in the present wars will be approximately the same fate." Here al-Qaʻida's theorist, Naji, claims that during their discussion, there was a view that "there is no reason for the enemies of America to further drain it in order to hasten its downfall because [President] Bush is doing this job for you."[45] Thus, al-Qaʻida's tactic is to drain the U.S. economically and militarily by means of terrorist operations that may take any of the forms outlined here.

5. The fifth principle is "strictness and mighty prowess." Al-Qaʻida's mentality has been fixed on the use of violent means in the name of jihad. Justifying its use of violence is one of al-Qaʻida's most important tactics, and occupies a great deal of its literature.[46] Al-Qaʻida admitted that its jihad is but "violence," "crudeness," "terrorism," "expulsion," and "massacring." It also admitted its "violence as one thing," and "Islam as another," and that the one "should not be confused with the other." Yet al-Qaʻida also promotes its terrorism as jihad accepted by Islam and justified by the Qur'an.[47]

Drawing on the Qur'anic verses, *Ye shall be summoned (to fight) against a people given to vehement war: then shall you fight* (48:16), and *We sent over you Our servants, of mighty prowess* (17:5), al-Qaʻida stresses violence as a significant element required for victory. Seeking to justify this, al-Qaʻida turned to history and referred to an incident that took place during the Abbasid caliphate that was established in Iraq in 748. In 763 the Shiʻi Muhammad ibn ʻAbdullah, whose title was ʻal-Nafs al-Zakiya' (the Pure Soul), and his brother Ibrahim led an uprising in Iraq and briefly captured Basra and Wasit, but were soon overcome by the Abbasids. Al-Qaʻida took this episode and twisted its context in order to justify its ambition and violent actions. Thus, violence and severity became the rule, and tenderness and leniency the exception. In the battle cited above, the Abbasids were labeled violent, while the rebellious were labeled 'the Pure Soul.'

Thus, the violence of the Abbasids brought them victory, while the tenderness of the Pure Soul brought him defeat.

Accordingly, al-Qa'ida celebrates the present-day violent groups, calling them "reformist jihadist movements," and takes the Abbasids as an example that represents this trend. As for the non-violent groups, al-Qa'ida calls them "soft" and refers to the Pure Soul movement as an example that represents this trend. The 'softness' of the Pure Soul led him to ask his generals to "protect the blood" of others as much as possible.

From this story, al-Qa'ida emphasizes two points. First, those of the Pure Soul were right to a certain extent in advocating for the protection of blood, because they were "fighting Muslims" and the "rules" governing the killing of "Muslim tyrants are conflicting." The second point is that al-Qa'ida is confronting the "Crusaders" and their "supporters" among the Muslim regimes and "the apostates," and states: "Nothing is preventing us from spilling their blood; rather, we see that this is one of the most important obligations until they repent."[48]

In the previous example, al-Qa'ida compared itself to the Abbasids, but here al-Qa'ida portrays its followers as resembling the Prophet's companions, and that the Arabs today resemble the Arabs of apostasy after the Prophet's death. They call themselves the only "true Muslims" and protectors of the *umma*, while the rest are but "apostates." Thus, the situation today is similar to that at the time of apostasy, and the jihad against apostasy is the responsibility of al-Qa'ida, the true believer and protector of the faith.[49] On this account, al-Qa'ida's violence and killing are legal because they carry out jihad against infidels and the apostates. Meditating on this theme, al-Qa'ida's then second-in-command al-Zawahiri argues that the present-day Arabs have returned to their "*jahiliya* state"[50] and disassociated themselves from the obligations of the shari'a. Thus, "apostasy" took hold in many of the towns of the Arabian Peninsula.

We are now in circumstances resembling the circumstances after the death of the Prophet and the outbreak of apostasy and the like of that which the believers faced in the beginning of the jihad. Thus, we need to massacre and to take actions like those that were undertaken against Banu Qurayzah [tribes] and their like.[51]

6. The sixth principle is one of "retaliation and paying the price." It is al-Qaʻida's most important tactical policy. To al-Zawahiri, retaliation is equal in importance to the very existence of al-Qaʻida. It portrays itself as the "protector" of the *umma*; thus "the enemy will pay the price for any harm that comes to the *umma*." This theme is fundamental in al-Zawahiri's writings and his last book *al-Tabriʻa* is just one example of this. He emphasizes that when the enemy knows that any action will be faced with a reaction the enemy will think a "thousand" times before undertaking an attack.[52] Paying the price may be accomplished after a short or a long period, possibly even years. Thus, after any operation there must be a statement that claims responsibility, justifies the operation as retaliation, and reminds the enemy that it is paying the price.[53]

The method of retaliation is tactically designed and undertaken by different jihadist groups in different regions against which no hostility has yet been directed. If the enemy undertakes a hostile action against Algeria or Iraq, for instance, the retaliation might occur in Morocco, Indonesia, or Nigeria. Al-Qaʻida's policy of paying the price is directed against not only the west, but also the Arab and Muslim or 'apostate' regimes. By way of example, if the Egyptian regime undertakes an action against any of al-Qaʻida's affiliates in Egypt, al-Qaʻida's affiliates in the Arabian Peninsula or in Pakistan can direct a strike against Egyptian interests and issue a statement of "justification." They can also kidnap Egyptian diplomats and keep them as hostages until a group of jihadists is freed.

On 23 June 2004, al-Qaʻida kidnapped Egypt's diplomat Muhammad Mamduh Hilmi Qutb in Baghdad, but he was released one month later. This perhaps was al-Qaʻida's warning, but Egypt replaced him with Ihab al-Sherif, a former diplomat in Tel Aviv. In response, al-Qaʻida seized him in late June of 2005, and killed him on 7 July of that same year. Their statement posted on the al-Qaʻida website read: "We, al-Qaʻida in Iraq, announce that the judgment has been implemented against the ambassador of the infidels, the ambassador of Egypt. Oh enemy of God, Ihab al-Sherif, this is your punishment in this life."[54] Among the important tactics of al-Qaʻida's retaliation are: (i) to make the enemy feel that he has surrendered and that his interests are exposed; (ii) to humiliate the enemy, especially if the region in which the retaliation occurred is under the enemy's control; (iii) to ensure the enemy will not find a good arena in which to respond; (iv) to raise the morale of those al-Qaʻida operatives who received the initial hostility; and (v) to communicate a message to Muslims in every place that al-Qaʻida's activity "cannot be limited by borders."[55]

7. The seventh principle is that of "religious loyalty," or *al-wala' wa-l-bara'*. Al-Qaʻida considers this principle as a means to conceal its internal affairs and maintain its strength. It is thus a matter of trust at all levels for reasons of secrecy. 'Religious loyalty' means that all al-Qaʻida followers, whether individuals or groups, and at all levels, are brothers tied to one another through the bonds of faith, and common aims and objectives. Al-Qaʻida makes this religious loyalty "one of the pillars of the Islamic creed and one of the conditions of belief."[56]

These ties between the followers of al-Qaʻida are called "special loyalty" and are embodied in a covenant, the most important of which is "blood for blood and destruction for destruction," but which also includes providing shelter, giving assistance, and preserving the internal affairs of the individuals and the group. Al-Qaʻida sees itself as doing jihad on behalf of the *umma*: "We consider our jihad in this stage to be the jihad of an *umma*." Therefore, any individuals or groups who "enter the jihad and exchange loyalty with us on the basis of 'blood for blood and destruction for destruction,' are part of the jihadist movement even if they differ over the correct method in intellectual and operational matters."[57]

To justify this principle, al-Qaʻida cites Ibn Taymiya's account with regard to the Ashaʻiris. Ibn Taymiya, al-Qaʻida says, exposed the "corruption" of their thought. Despite their "heretics," the Ashaʻiris assisted the jihadists. Similarly, the rulers in Egypt and Syria were corrupt and used to favor the Ashaʻiris, but these rulers "supported" the jihadists and "engaged in the jihad against the Tartars." Therefore, Ibn Taymiya approved of their "loyalty." Likewise, he praised the Muslim ruler Salah al-Din al-Ayyubi (Saladin) for aiding the jihad against the Crusaders and for supporting the "Sunnis against the Batinites," even though the school of his state was the Ashaʻiri school.[58]

Al-Qaʻida's aim here is to highlight that it praises any individual or group that supports al-Qaʻida's affiliates, gives them shelter, or keeps their identity secret, even if this individual or that group is corrupt. Its justification for this attitude is based on its reference to history, yet it is problematic to compare al-Qaʻida to the Ashaʻiris, Salah al-Din, or the rulers in Egypt and Syria. However, this is how al-Qaʻida interweaves selected narratives in an attempt to mislead its audiences for the sake of its own survival. It takes historical events and applies them to a different time, place, and people. Those medieval organizations were not like al-Qaʻida; indeed they were states. Their wars were wars between states, which were declared by states. Al-Qaʻida is not like the state of Salah al-Din, and Bin Laden is not comparable to either Ibn Taymiya or Salah al-Din! Al-Qaʻida conflates these issues simply to serve its own purposes.

Political Games

Al-Qaʻida urges its followers in general and its leaders in particular to master the art of politics as well as that of military science. The group leaders must have a military background or be militarily trained, and have the ability to fight in the ranks. Al-Qaʻida encourages these leaders to be aware of what they call the "political game," which has a direct effect on the "conflict" between al-Qaʻida and its enemies. To al-Qaʻida, there is a strong relationship between political and military decisions and the movement's success. In support of its view, al-Qaʻida has referred to certain jihadist groups and attributed their failure to their neglect of the importance of politics. Thus, for those groups who were established through "jihad," "battles," and "military actions," but who neglected politics and considered it as a "filthy activity of Satan," or those groups who practiced politics unguided by shariʻa and finally became immersed in "infidel politics," their fate was to become a tool for the "infidel" and "apostasy" regimes to "pluck the fruits of jihad." These regimes have been labeled by al-Qaʻida as the "enemy." This is the theme upon which al-Qaʻida plans its policy and actions. Thus, the art of politics is vitally important to al-Qaʻida because "a single political mistake may lead to a result that is worse than one hundred military mistakes."

The infrastructure of al-Qaʻida is therefore constructed in a way that the political decision is always issued from the military leaders. Most of al-Qaʻida's political administrators, on any level and in any place, are made up of "warriors." These are the people who al-Qaʻida encourages to master the political dimension. This is because al-Qaʻida is of the view that the "battle is their [al-Qaʻida's] battle before it is the battle of others."

This point is clear in al-Qaʻidaʼs policy, which declares that the political decision cannot for any reason be left in the hands of those who do not engage in military actions.[59]

"Learning politics" is one of the important disciplines in al-Qaʻidaʼs ideological program aimed at ensuring that its military leaders are aware of the "political game" that motivates al-Qaʻidaʼs opponents. To al-Qaʻida, the aim that motivates its "enemies" is a "material aim," and their doctrine is a "worldly doctrine." Here, al-Qaʻida generalizes the nature of the conflict and makes it appear as though it were a religious conflict, and that al-Qaʻida itself is the protector of religion. On this account, the "conflict" is between the "doctrine of belief" and the "doctrine of unbelief." The unbelievers have nothing to believe in other than their "material interests," and this fuels the conflict. Thus, for the unbelievers all principles of "moral value," "friendship or enmity," and "peace or war" are subordinate to self-interest, and are determined accordingly. In an attempt to support this view, al-Qaʻida cites a quotation, without reference to its author, in stating that "the politicians of the west summarize the principle of self-interest in a slogan that says, 'There is no eternal enmity in politics and no eternal friendship; rather, there are eternal interests.'"[60]

Thus, the "difference" of interests between western states, al-Qaʻida says, is the cause of the "bloodshed" between them. Here, al-Qaʻida plays the card of religion and instructs its followers to remember that the "enmity toward Islam" represents a common ground of action for the regimes of "unbelief" in the west and "apostasy" in the east. Nevertheless, their ideological alliance "against Islam" is a fragile alliance, limited by a "ceiling of material interests" for each ally or state. As the interests of the allies are different, "bargaining" must occur. To al-Qaʻida, the substitute for successful "bargaining" between them is "war," which might crush all of their interests. Thus, for al-Qaʻida the allies" politics is "the art of the possible."

The allies insist on "war" only when they think that their "opponent is weak" and it is possible to "crush his will." Yet if they find "violent resistance" that makes the invasion "cost them a great deal" and of "little value," al-Qaʻida argues, the states of the allies will begin to "withdraw" one after another, preferring their own "safety" and "security." Thus, the nature of the allies' politics of bargaining, al-Qaʻida claims, lacks the quality of "stability" because it is merely a reflection of the "balance of power" at a "particular moment" and this balance is always subject to change. Consequently, there is a "breach" of agreements. Political treaties and "economic contracts" are "violated" in most cases if the benefit of the breach is greater than the benefit of honoring the pledge. Likewise, making contradictory bargains at the same time with states that have incompatible interests, al-Qa'ida says, is "commonplace in the political jungle."[61]

As to the political game of al-Qa'ida's opponents within the Islamic movements, al-Qa'ida calls these opponents "neighbors" (mujawirun). What did it mean by calling them "neighbors"? Here, al-Qa'ida refers to the Egyptian Muslim Brotherhood, al-Jama'a al-Islamiya, the Jihad group, and similar groups that have renounced the violence and terrorism that al-Qa'ida's shari'a calls jihad. These groups are living within the states that al-Qa'ida's shari'a calls "states of apostasy," but oppose those regimes. Thus, they are living within these states as "neighbors" to the apostate regimes of those states. Yet Al-Qa'ida stops short of also labeling these groups as apostates.

Nevertheless, al-Qa'ida does accuse them of not being true Muslims, of having no value, and of selling their religion only for their own survival. The politics of these movements, al-Qa'ida says, is based on a "mix of shari'a and the politics of the enemy," especially the principle of "self-interest." These groups are also seen to "distort" the text in order to trick people into believing that their "mixture" is from the shari'a. Al-Qa'ida argues that they have no value, except to strike political deals and seal bargains with the regimes of apostates while they themselves have no military power. Their capacity and influence are due to the presence of a "large number of youths" in their ranks. The regimes that al-Qa'ida calls "enemies" see these groups as representing danger only if the regimes break down. If this were to happen, their youths would "join al-Qa'ida," it is argued. Therefore, the regimes seal bargains with these groups to stay as they are and to keep the young away from al-Qa'ida. Al-Qa'ida emphasizes that the most important principle for the sake of which these groups maneuver, and the greatest interest for which they sell out their religion and shari'a, is simply survival.[62]

Al-Qa'ida urges its members to adhere to shari'a in the conflict with their "enemies" and those Islamic movements that have renounced jihad. On this, al-Qa'ida is misleading, since it does not itself adhere to the shari'a, but has its own interpretation of shari'a. In an attempt to slide away from adhering to the shari'a, al-Qa'ida has sought to find some justification within Islamic texts. Al-Qaʿida referred to Ibn al-Qayyim (d. 1350) and his magnum opus *Zad al-miʿad* (Sustenance of the Destination), from which it cites the following:

> Taking the laws, which dealt with war and Islamic interest, together with the arts of politics from the Prophet's life and history, is *more appropriate* than taking them from the opinion of the men. This is one kind and that is another kind.[63]

In this statement, al-Qaʿida finds interest in the phrase "more appropriate." It was used by Ibn al-Qayyim instead of the word "necessary." Al-Qaʿida seized on this phrase to free itself from the Prophet's rules on war and instead to depend on its members' opinions in justifying its violence and terrorism as jihad. Hence, it is not "necessary" for al-Qaʿida to adhere to the law of war as espoused in the shariʿa and in the history of the Prophet, because Ibn al-Qayyim has said so. However, when Ibn al-Qayyim said "more appropriate" rather than "necessary," he never meant to permit bloodshed or terrorism. He never permitted al-Qaʿida to devise and adhere to its own version of a shariʿa that allows violence and terrorism. Al-Qaʿida went even further and attempted to free itself completely from any questioning of its violence, suicides, and similar terrorist operations.

On this subject, al-Qaʿida again referred to Ibn al-Qayyim and quoted from his *al-Turuq al-hakima* (Governing Methods):

> Politics is an action that draws the people closer to righteousness and wellbeing and further away from rottenness and corruption, even if the Prophet did not put it in place or send it down by revelation. If by your statement you mean those things that agree with the shariʿa—meaning they do not contradict that which what the shariʿa explicitly states—then this is correct. If you mean that there is no politics save that which is explicitly endorsed by the shariʿa, then this is a mistake and puts the Companions in the wrong.[64]

Based on this passage, al-Qaʿida takes liberty to undertake whatever action it decides. Hence, no one can question al-Qaʿida about the shariʿa text that permits its suicidal, murderous, and terrorist activities, because Ibn al-Qayyim has said so. Al-Qaʿida takes from Ibn al-Qayyim's statement its defense against those who demand a shari'a text that furnishes proof for what the leadership has decided with respect to actions and matters of politics. Thus, those of al-Qa'ida's affiliates who ask al-Qa'ida's leadership to provide religious and legal justification for any operation are mistaken. Regarding Ibn al-Qayyim's statement, al-Qa'ida says:

> From this, we know the mistake of those who demand a shari'a text that proves what the Amir has decided on matters of politics, which are among his duties and regarding which he is consulting with the Shura (consultation) people [i.e., the decision-makers; those in positions of authority], who have experience in worldly affairs.[65]

Therefore, when Bin Laden decided to undertake the September 11 attack on the U.S., he consulted with his Shura people such as al-Zawahiri, Muhammad Ata, and Khalid Sheikh Muhammad. Since he did so, Bin Laden is deemed free from questioning or of the need to provide proof of the justification for these terrorist acts. Again, this is because Ibn al-Qayyim said so. Al-Qa'ida distorted the statement of Ibn al-Qayyim and took it out of context in order to free Bin Laden from questioning and justify his terrorism. Yet al-Qa'ida advises that the political leadership should be able to perform "high level political actions on the basis of shari'a." Which shari'a is this? There is no shari'a that justifies al-Qa'ida's terrorism except al-Qa'ida's shari'a, not the shari'a of Islam.

The following are some of what are called the "tactical points" that al-Qa'ida considers important for understanding the "political dimension of the battle":

1. It is not sufficient that the political leadership be able to attain a high level of political action. Rather, the jihadists must be highly qualified, have a high degree of discernment, and participate in making political decisions, especially those that have a degree of critical danger or weighty consequences.
2. As to other Islamic movements, such as the Muslim Brotherhood and those who "called themselves the Salafi reformist current," they agree on some points and differ on others. These groups are useful as examples when analyzing the positions of all like-minded groups when "we deal with them."

3. Knowledge of politics helps to define the public's and enemy's responses to any steps that the jihadists plan to undertake; so they then either proceed to take it or delay it for an appropriate time, or create circumstances in which the plan will be appropriate. From this starting point, they define who among the enemy's classes "will be targeted first." In this regard, every jihadist group has a catalogue of the targets in its region. They arrange the targets according to the importance of each and its place on the list of priorities in the confrontation. Each jihadist group also has a plan for dealing with the enemy's response to operations carried out against them. They design such plans to work in two ways: (i) to force the targeted enemy to openly admit its concealed actions; and (ii) to use the enemy's confession in justifying the jihad operations to the masses.

4. Mastering the art of politics not only concerns knowing how to deal with the enemy and those "deviant Islamic movements," but also knowing how to deal with the impressionable individuals from among the enemies who join al-Qa'ida. One must also determine how to deal with those tyrannical and apostate regimes, and those who "leave al-Qa'ida's ranks and affiliate themselves with the enemies or the United States for fame or medals. All of these kinds of defection are anticipated, especially because "our jihad is the jihad of the *Umma* and not the jihad of a movement."

5. The human "structure" of the enemy is "weak" with regard to "battle." The enemy compensates for this by using "military machines" and "deceptive media," when confronting any action of the jihadists. Therefore, learning to understand how to deal with the politics of the media is very important in winning the military and political battle.

6. "Oil is a primary and strategic interest of the enemy." Since the discovery of oil, the U.S. has viewed it as a primary and vital strategic commodity in war, a necessity in peace, and a requisite for international influence. In al-Qa'ida's view, the political and military success of targeting the enemy's economy has been historically established. Therefore, targeting the enemy's interest must be crowned by targeting petroleum sectors, because oil is the artery of life in the west.[66]

Al-Tatarrus and the Killing of Civilians

The word 'al-tatarrus' might not mean anything to millions of Muslims, but it means a great deal to al-Qa'ida and similar jihadist groups. The idea behind this word is lethal and is found within the tactical practices of all jihadist groups without exception. Most of their operations are based on this idea. It was incorporated into the jihadists' practice for decades in the Middle East and then al-Zawahiri took it with him to Afghanistan and then to al-Qa'ida. However, the concept is rarely mentioned in the western literature. This word is the rationale behind shedding the blood of innocent civilians, Muslims and non-Muslims alike. Its embodiment has killed thousands of innocent civilians and wounded an even larger number, and perhaps even wounded the world community's senses and memories.

The word al-tatarrus (reads at-tatarrus) comes from the Arabic root (t-r-s), the substantive turs (shield) and tirs (shield and disk) being the basis from which the trilateral verb tatarrasa (shielded) and the perfect yutarrisu (to shield) and other derivations have come. Thus, the word al-tatarrus is an infinitive and means to shield or provide with a shield. The individuals and groups who are used as human shields are called turs or tirs.

The concept of al-tatarrus is one of the most important concepts to have come to the fore as a result of the Middle East situation. Not unlike the concept of jihad, the concept of al-tatarrus has been brought to light, interpreted, and practiced by the jihadists in a completely different sociopolitical context from that of the early Muslims. Muntasir al-Zayyat, a former Egyptian jihadist-turned-lawyer who became the official defense lawyer of the jihadists in Egypt's military court, has pointed out that the idea of al-tatarrus was being put into practice by the jihadists during the last four decades of the twentieth century: "They have used this idea in the 1960s, in the 1970s, in the 1980s, and in the 1990s and now al-Qa'ida has expanded the idea and widened its use in Iraq in particular."[67]

This concept relates to security, but it has been altered according to al-Qa'ida's understanding. Al-Qa'ida's version has clearly flourished in the context of the Iraqi situation since the fall of Baghdad to U.S. forces in 2003. This concept legitimizes the killing of innocent civilians if they are the shield (turs) of the enemy's army or if they provide the enemy's army with a shield (turs) of any type or form, either willingly or unwillingly—that is, only if there is no other option to engage with the enemy's offensive army. Al-Qa'ida and similar jihadist groups activated this concept based on their selective reading of rulings (sing. *fatwa*) that were originally issued in a context quite different from the reality of the present.[68] Al-Qa'ida expanded this concept and thus its circle of murder expanded out of control and beyond the limits of any law or order.[69]

Al-Qa'ida turned to the idea of *al-tatarrus* when it became weak and unable to undertake operations against strong targets because of certain security arrangements. Al-Qa'ida resorted to acts based on its distorted interpretation of this idea, and attacked soft targets to influence the political and economic situations of those regimes that al-Qa'ida regards as its enemy.

Focusing on the sources used by al-Qa'ida, it is evident that the idea of *al-tatarrus* is limited to precise conditions. However, it has been expanded by al-Qa'ida under flimsy pretexts to take the lives of innocent civilians. The idea of *al-tatarrus* is an old idea about which the jurist founders of the law schools, including Abu Hanifa (d. 767), Ibn Malik (d. 795), al-Shafi'i (d. 820), and Ibn Hanbal (d. 855) have written; it was later brought to the fore by Ibn Taymiya (1263–1328), when he issued his *fatwa* in a sociopolitical context different from the present time.

Ibn Taymiya issued his *fatwa* at the time of the Mongol invasion of Muslim countries, which brought the Abbasid caliphate to its knees. In 1258, the Mongols captured and destroyed Baghdad, which was the seat of the Islamic caliphate. They burned libraries and books, and destroyed Islamic culture. The Mongols moved from town to town like a bushfire indiscriminately burning and killing everything in their path. When they took a village or a town, the Mongols seized the inhabitants and used them or their possessions and buildings as shields *(turs)* in order to deter the Islamic army from undertaking any counterattack. If they were in towns, the Mongols used the buildings and did not let the inhabitants leave for safer areas. Outside of the towns, the Mongols shielded themselves with Muslim civilians on the front lines, while shelling the neighboring areas. When they moved from one village to the desert, the Mongols took the villagers, including women and children, located them on the front lines, and forced them to travel with the Mongol army as their human shields, until they captured another town. This made it difficult for the Muslim army to undertake any counterattack against the Mongols. The Muslim army was in a defensive position and felt constrained by this Mongol tactic. It was here and under these conditions that Muslim jurists, led by Ibn Taymiya, issued a legal ruling *(fatwa)* that the Muslim army should undertake counter-offensive attacks against the Mongol army to protect the towns and the community and to free the seized civilians irrespective of the cost.

Thus, the idea of *al-tatarrus* was intended only for specific circumstances of absolute necessity. The bases and conditions of these circumstances with which Muslim jurists have justified the idea of *al-tatarrus* can be summarized as follows:

1. There must be a physically active war between two state-armies; the two armies must be in a state of engagement in head-on war. Thus, the war has been declared and it is already on. This means that if there are no warring armies, or the war is what has come to be known as a cold war, then the use of *al-tatarrus* is prohibited. In this regard, Ibn Qudama (d. 1223) and later Ibn Taymiya (d. 1328) pointed out: "If the enemy's army shielded *(tatarrasa)* itself by Muslims but the war is not *on*, then there is no necessity to kill the shield *(turs)*."[70]

2. The idea of *al-tatarrus* can be applied only if the enemy's army has taken Muslim civilians as captives and used them as a shield *(turs)* to protect itself. Here, the Muslim army should not stop attacking the enemy's army even if those Muslim captives, who are the shield *(turs)*, will be killed. If the enemy's army left Muslim civilians to live in their houses and did not use them as shields *(turs)*, then there is no necessity to kill them. With regard to such cases, Abu Hanifa (d. 767), Ibn Qudama (d. 1223), and al-Qurtubi (d. 1272) state that "killing other than the prisoners whom the enemy's army used as human shields *(turs)* is illegal. The rule of killing the *turs* cannot apply to those who live in their houses in the neighborhood of the enemy."[71]

3. The idea of *al-tatarrus* can be applied to kill those prisoners *(turs)* only if the benefit or public interest is verified and the evil will be annihilated. While this is generally accepted by the jurists, they differ among themselves with regard to the outcomes and the overall results. Al-Ghazali (d. 1111) emphasized that the Muslim army is not permitted to attack the enemy's army while it holds Muslim civilians as human shields *(turs)*, but if the decision to not attack will bring harm to the Muslim army or the community, then the Muslim army should launch its counterattack even if this attack will kill the *turs*. Likewise, the Hanbalis (the law school of Ibn Hanbal) and the Hanafis (the law

school of Abu Hanifa) were also of the view that if the no-attack decision will harm the Muslim army or the community, then the Muslim army should attack the enemy's army while the *turs* are still in the enemy's custody. However, the Malikis (the law school of Ibn Malik) generally rejected any action that might kill the *turs*.[72]

4. The *turs* cannot be killed unless there is no other option by which the Muslim army can deal with the enemy's offensives, and there is no other option to ensure the security and safety of the Muslim community. This opinion is shared also by al-Awza'i (d. 774) and Ibn Qudama (d. 1223). Likewise, al-Qurtubi (d. 1272) pointed out that the human shields *(turs)* will be killed anyway either by the enemy's army or by the Muslim army. Thus, when it is necessary the *turs* should be killed in order to secure the Muslim army as well as to improve the security and safety of the rest of the citizens (Muslims and non-Muslims) in the Muslim territory.[73]

5. If the Muslim army cannot find any other device to undertake counterattacks against the enemy's army, then the *turs* can be killed. In this regard, al-Qurtubi pointed out that "there is no difference among scholars on the rule that the *shield (turs)* should be killed if this will generally benefit the Muslim nation and protect it from the enemy's atrocity. If the Muslim army has not killed the shield *(turs)*, the enemy will do so once it has readied itself to undertake further actions to occupy what is left of the Muslim land."[74]

Thus, the idea of *al-tatarrus* is an idea of necessity and very much based on the condition that when the state finds no other option but to kill the shield, in order to stop the advance of the enemy's offensive army, the shield can be killed. Thus, (i) *al-tatarrus* is limited to situations of security, safety, and general public interest; (ii) the idea cannot be practiced in hotels and trains or in any place other than the battlefield; (iii) the decision to kill the shield *(turs)* is a state decision, not a decision of an individual such as Bin Laden; and (iv) the idea cannot be carried out by any person other than the state's army, and certainly not by terrorist individuals or groups.[75]

Muslim jurists, including Ibn Taymiya and Ibn Hanbal, did not issue their *fatwa* about *al-tatarrus* to permit those ill-minded groups to kill civilians, whether Muslims or non-Muslims. They issued their *fatwa* for a precise purpose and precise condition, for it to be applied in a specific place, by specific people, against specific people. Al-Qa'ida turned a blind eye to these limitations, thereby freeing itself from questioning with regard to shari'a approval. They used the idea of *al-tatarrus* in isolation from the guidance of any law or order.

When the jurists issued their *fatwa* about *al-tatarrus*, they defined the enemy. As it appeared in those points above, the enemy is an *army* of a state that is undertaking an offensive war against a Muslim state and occupying its land. The jurists also defined that those who can be killed under this precise condition are those who comprise the shield, and the place must be the *battlefield*, not civilians in hotels, schools, trains, marketplaces, or trade centers. Al-Qa'ida's leaders and theorists know very well that the people who are in these places are not shields and cannot be killed under Islamic law. They know that there is nothing in the shari'a that justifies the killing of civilians of any color, faith, or nationality.

The former Mufti of Egypt, Professor Nasr Farid Wasil, pointed out that the condition for which *al-tatarrus* was legislated has not existed in our present time. This legislation served a specific circumstance at a specific time. If this circumstance no longer exists, then there is no need for this legislation. He states:

> It is extremely rare for the conditions for *al-tatarrus* to arise in the modern age. Killing civilians is illegal and it is not permitted in Islam. The fundamental basis of *al-tatarrus* is that when the enemy's army undertakes an offensive war against Muslims, while also protecting itself with Muslim civilians, it is permissible for a Muslim army to launch a counterattack against the enemy's army, even if the enemy's army has shielded itself with civilians. This is permissible in order to deter the enemy's advance, and to secure and to save the rest of the community. In the defense of a country against occupation, the basic rule is to target the combatant enemy with complete belief and strong confidence that the civilians are not targeted. Therefore, killing civilians in the name of defense is not legally accepted and cannot be based on *al-tatarrus* either.[76]

Al-Qa'ida's ideologues are well aware of these conditions but have twisted them. They have distorted this concept, and permitted its operatives to use human civilians as shields and to disperse themselves among civilians.

Hence, the terrorists might undertake operations against civilians in hotels, trains, and marketplaces, and return to be dispersed among civilians. In this regard, al-Qa'ida's terrorist operations in Iraq and the operations of al-Qa'ida's affiliated group, Fath al-Islam in Lebanon, are examples that illustrate this point. Al-Qa'ida was situated among Iraqi civilians and undertook operations against civilians in Falluja and other areas to the extent that one of these areas between Baghdad and Hillah has come to be called the Triangle of Death by the international media, and a film was made with the same title.[77] Likewise, the Fath al-Islam group was led by Shaker al-Abbasi, who, after spending some time with al-Qa'ida in Iraq, traveled to Lebanon with a group that placed itself among the civilians in the Palestinian refugee camp of Nahr al-Barid. Then in 2007, the group attempted to seize the refugee camp and undertook some operations that necessitated the Lebanese Army's intervention to save the civilians and eradicate the terrorist group.[78]

Al-Zawahiri has shown his interest in the idea of *al-tatarrus* and presented to his followers selective narratives from Arabic sources to support his interpretation of the idea. Responding to his critics, among them his amir, Dr. Fadl, who led the jihad in Egypt and Afghanistan, al-Zawahiri devoted chapter eight of his latest book, *al-Tabri'a*, to justifying his use of *al-tatarrus* to kill civilian Muslims and non-Muslims alike. The entire chapter consists of selected crude material extracted from the writings of the jurists and authoritative scholars of Islam. In chapter twelve, he repeats certain sections of chapter eight. Al-Zawahiri's selected materials have been summarized to outline the opinions of the earlier jurists and the authoritative scholars of Islam in the five points presented above. The point is that al-Zawahiri selected these materials but did not elaborate on them to explain how he defends al-Qa'ida's terrorist activity of killing civilians.[79] He preferred to keep silent, perhaps because the jurists were so clear and precise on the matter, or to give the impression that he agrees with the jurists and is not against them. However, the reality confirms that he is against the jurists on this matter and many other matters related to jihad and Islam in general.

In contrast to the jurists' opinions, al-Zawahiri and his al-Qa'ida followers understood *al-tatarrus* differently. Who can justify that the people killed in the al-Qa'ida attacks on hotels, railway stations, marketplaces, trains, and trade centers were *turs*? These locations are not battlefields, and state armies were not fighting each other on the train in Madrid, or in the London underground, or in Bali, or inside the World Trade Center. Where is *al-tatarrus* here, and why have these innocent civilians, both Muslim and non-Muslim, been killed? There is no authoritative Islamic opinion that regards these attacks as instances of *tatarrus*; rather they are widely seen as terrorist acts for which the perpetrators should be brought to justice. In this regard, the Egyptian professor, Yusuf al-Qaradawi, dean of the Faculty of Islamic Law in Qatar, head of the European Council for Fatwa and Research (ECFR), and president of the International Association of Muslim Scholars (IAMS) stated:

> All Muslims ought to be united against all those who terrorize the innocents, and who permit the killing of non-combatants without a justifiable reason. Islam has declared the spilling of blood and the destruction of property as absolute prohibitions until the Day of Judgment. It is necessary to apprehend the true perpetrators of these crimes, as well as those who aid and abet them through incitement, financing, or other support. They must be brought to justice.[80]

Further, Professor 'Abd al-Mun'im Bayyoumi, of the al-Azhar Islamic Research Academy, has stated: "There is no terrorism or a threat to civilians in jihad."[81]

The chief mufti of Saudi Arabia has stated:

> First: the recent developments in the United States including the hijacking of planes, the terrorizing of innocent people, and the shedding of blood, constitute a form of injustice that cannot be tolerated by Islam, which views them as gross crimes and sinful acts. Second: Any Muslim who is aware of the teachings of his religion and who adheres to the directives of the Holy Qur'an and the Sunna will never involve himself in such acts, because they invoke the anger of God Almighty and lead to harm and corruption on Earth.[82]

Shaykh Salman bin Fahd al-'Awda is an extremist Saudi cleric who was detained in the 1990s. His incarceration by the Saudis reportedly inspired Bin Laden to action. Yet when Shaykh Salman saw al-Qa'ida killing civilians in Iraq, he appeared on Saudi television to criticize al-Qa'ida and its leadership, asking Bin Laden: "How much blood has been spilt?

How many innocent people, children, elderly, and women have been killed in the name of al Qa'ida?"[83]

Ayatollah Ali Khamene'i, the current Supreme Jurist-Ruler of Iran, says:

> Killing people, in any place and with any kind of weapons, including atomic bombs, long-range missiles, biological or chemical weapons, passenger or war planes, carried out by any organization, country or individuals is condemned. It makes no difference whether such massacres happen in Hiroshima, Nagasaki, Qana, Sabra, Shatila, Deir Yasin, Bosnia, Kosovo, Iraq, or New York and Washington.[84]

Former President Muhammad Khatami of Iran is quoted as saying: "The horrific terrorist attacks of September 11, 2001, in the United States were perpetrated by a cult of fanatics who had self-mutilated their ears and tongues, and could only communicate with perceived opponents through carnage and devastation."[85]

For a sample of all of the condemnations of al-Qa'ida by Muslims, organizations, and scholars around the world, one can refer to the Council on American Islamic Relations.[86]

Thus, al-Qa'ida hijacked the *al-tatarrus* concept, just as they hijacked other concepts, including that of jihad and Islam itself.

7
Inside al-Qaʻida:
The Ideological War

This chapter focuses on the theo-political ideas in the debate between the two main ideologues of global jihad, Dr. Fadl and Dr. Ayman al-Zawahiri. Dr. Fadl is the chief ideologue who influenced both Ayman al-Zawahiri and Bin Laden. The dispute between the three men began earlier but remained beneath the surface until late 2007. This internal war was based on theology and ideology, and caused a number of key jihadist individuals and groups to abandon al-Qaʻida and renounce violence and terrorism.

Dr. Fadl

Dr. Fadl's real name is Sayyid Imam ʻAbd al-ʻAziz al-Sharif. He was the founder of the first Egyptian Jihad organization in 1968, and was its ideologue until 1993. Throughout his life, Dr. Fadl has shied away from the press, but recently he came out to speak openly against al-Qaʻida's leadership and their theological, ideological, and political tactics. The first time he spoke to the media was in November 2007. Those outside jihad movements did not know him, nor was he known in the intellectual arena, until he published his book *Wathiqat tarshid al-jihad fi Misr wa-l-ʻalam* (Rationaliation of the Jihad in Egypt and the World) in November 2007. He has used aliases at various times, including Dr. Fadl and Dr. ʻAbd al-Qadir ʻAbd al-ʻAziz. In this book, I refer to him as Dr. Fadl, the name by which he is best known.

Islamists have always regarded Dr. Fadl as the most respected authority on jihad. He is the former amir of jihad in Egypt and Peshawar, and long-time associate of, and higher in rank than, Ayman al-Zawahiri, the leader of al-Qaʻida following the death of Bin Laden in May 2011. Unlike al-Zawahiri, Dr. Fadl preferred to keep a low profile, away from the media and cameras, but led the jihad ideologically. In terms of the violent actions known to the jihadists, Dr. Fadl was not of those carrying rifles, nor did he carry a Kalashnikov, like al-Zawahiri. He is a theoretician and author who has published several scholarly works about jihad in Egypt and the world. In Afghanistan, his books were used in the training camps to train jihadists ideologically. A number of his books, including the two-thousand-page *Risalat al-'umda fi i'dad al-'udda* (The Master Message in the Preparation for Jihad), are the fundamental sources upon which al-Qa'ida depends, and they still appear on al-Qa'ida websites under the alias of 'Abd al-Qadir 'Abd al-'Aziz. In his words, "At that time, they were calling me 'mufti al-Mujahidin' in the world, the scholar, the mufti, and mujahid Sheikh 'Abd al-Qadir ibn 'Abd al-'Aziz."[1]

Dr. Fadl met al-Zawahiri in 1968, the first year of their studies at the Faculty of Medicine, at the University of Cairo: "I got to know al-Zawahiri in 1968 in the Faculty of Medicine."[2] Thus, they began their studies together in 1968 and graduated in 1974. After their graduation, both men became involved in jihad activities in Egypt, and later found their way to Afghanistan where they continued their jihad against the USSR. Dr. Fadl was the amir of al-Zawahiri and of the Egyptian Jihad organization from 1968, while he was an undergraduate, until 1993, in both Egypt and Afghanistan. Toward the end of 1993, Dr. Fadl left Bin Laden and al-Zawahiri in Afghanistan and went to Sudan for a few months. In early 1994, Dr. Fadl left Sudan for Yemen where he lived and worked as a surgeon until 2001.

Who is Dr. Fadl? When and why did he establish the Jihad organization in Egypt? When and how did he come to know al-Zawahiri? When and why did he leave Egypt for Afghanistan? What was he doing there? What was his relationship with al-Zawahiri, 'Abdullah 'Azzam, Bin Laden, and the Global Islamic Front for the jihad (al-Qa'ida)? What has been his view about al-Qa'ida's theo-political and tactical ideas before and after September 11? What is the Islamic verdict against al-Qa'ida's ideas and its leadership? These questions and related issues will be dealt with here based on the works of these two jihadist rivals and their recent media interviews.

Fadl was born on 8 August 1950 in the city of Beni Sueif, about 113 kilometers south of Cairo. His family was ardent in their religion. He claimed that his family is one of the descendants of the Prophet

Muhammad.[3] This was reflected in Dr. Fadl's upbringing as a pious student of high achievement, later becoming one of Egypt's top students.

Fadl completed his elementary and junior education in Beni Sueif. His distinguished grades permitted his enrollment in Madrasat al-Mumtazin (the School of Excellence) in Cairo in 1965. It was the only school that sponsored distinguished students in Egypt. It provided a special curriculum of modern education and research training, in addition to accommodation and other facilities. It was from this school that he obtained his Egyptian Certificate of Education (ECE) and his grade was ranked thirteenth in all of Egypt. He then enrolled in the Faculty of Medicine at Cairo University in 1968 and graduated in 1974 with honors. He was directly appointed a resident surgeon in the Surgical Department at Cairo's al-Qasr al-Ayni, the prestigious hospital and medical college, where he confirmed his expertise and obtained his master's degree in plastic surgery in 1978, with high honors "at the hands of leading Egyptian surgeons." He then worked at Suez Canal University until he left Egypt in 1982.

In the wake of the assassination of President Sadat in 1981,[4] Dr. Fadl, al-Zawahiri, and their associates were charged in relation to this case. It was known in the Egyptian and Arab media as "the major case of the Jihad organization." Al-Zawahiri was arrested, but Dr. Fadl managed to flee Egypt for the United Arab Emirates (UAE) in 1982. He "worked" in the Emirates for a "short period" of time. In 1983, he left the Emirates for Pakistan: "I went to help the Afghan Mujahidin in the medical services." He lived in Peshawar and worked at the Kuwaiti Red Crescent Hospital as a surgeon and the hospital's director.[5] This hospital had been established in the early 1980s by the Kuwaiti government in order to help the Afghan Mujahidin. Dr. Fadl was the first Arab jihadist to arrive, in early 1983, who had surgical expertise. A year later, he learned that the Egyptian Military Tribunal had tried him in absentia in the Sadat assassination case, but dropped all charges against him in 1984, while al-Zawahiri was sentenced to three years' imprisonment.

Dr. Fadl continued to work at the Kuwaiti hospital "from 1983 until 1993—ten years." In 1993, Benazir Bhutto became prime minister of Pakistan for the second time and launched a campaign to evict the Arabs from Peshawar. In the wake of this famous campaign, Dr. Fadl left Peshawar for Sudan in late 1993. He lived in Sudan for a few months, but sensing that Islamists were not welcome there, he left for Yemen. He arrived in Yemen in 1994, where he worked as a surgeon until 2001.

In the meantime, the Egyptian Military Tribunal tried him in absentia once again in 1999, and this time sentenced him to life imprisonment in connection with what was known in Egypt as the Returnees from Albania Case, even though he had never visited Albania or returned to Egypt.[6]

In the wake of September 11, 2001, Dr. Fadl was arrested in October of that year by Yemeni authorities, interrogated in Yemen by various authorities including the CIA, and finally turned over by the Yemeni authorities to Egypt on 20 February 2004. Egypt imprisoned him for life.

Dr. Fadl is married and has four boys and three girls. His interest in reading Islamist books began in 1965. At that time, Sayyid Qutb was in jail and had been sentenced to death, and his book *Ma'alim* was published in 1964. There were also clashes between the authorities and the Muslim Brotherhood. Dr. Fadl highlighted the Egyptian regime's relations with the Brotherhood in 1965 as *the* main reason that drew his attention to reading about Islamic affairs. Yet he denied any links with the Brotherhood or any of its leaders or ideologues at the time. Of his reading, he says he went back to the literature of the early scholars and imams, "never quite trusting contemporary Islamic commentaries."

Dr. Ayman Muhammad Rabi' al-Zawahiri was Dr. Fadl's friend and fellow physician. Ayman was the eldest son in the family. Two of his brothers were also known militants. Muhammad was in charge of the Egyptian Jihad's military wing. Husayn was convicted for his role in the assassination attempt against Egypt's former interior minister, Hasan Abu Basha, in 1987. Ayman al-Zawahiri was born in Cairo on 20 July 1951. His father, Muhammad Rabi' al-Zawahiri, was a professor of medicine. His paternal grandfather al-Zawahiri was the Grand Sheikh of al-Azhar.

As for his maternal family, there is confusion in the literature among the three names 'Abdullah 'Azzam, 'Abd al-Wahhab 'Azzam, and 'Abd al-Rahman 'Azzam. However, 'Abdullah (d. 1989) was a Palestinian jihadist who became one of the jihad ideologues in Afghanistan. 'Abd al-Wahhab and 'Abd al-Rahman are Egyptians who have their family origins in Saudi Arabia. In other words, Ayman al-Zawahiri's maternal family (the 'Azzam family) had its origins in Saudi Arabia, and is not related to the 'Abdullah 'Azzam family in Palestine.

The remaining confusion about the two Egyptians of the 'Azzam family can be resolved as follows. The two 'Azzams were almost of the same age, but 'Abd al-Wahhab 'Azzam (1894–1959) was Egypt's foremost pan-Arab intellectual, dean of the Faculty of Arts at, and president of, the University of Cairo. He was appointed Egypt's ambassador to Pakistan in 1950 and to Saudi Arabia in 1954, and founded King Saud University in Riyadh, becoming its director in 1957. Among his extensive publications is *Umam ha'ira* (Wandering Nations). He died and was buried in Saudi Arabia in 1959, when Ayman al-Zawahiri was almost eight years of age. He was the nephew of 'Abd al-Rahman 'Azzam, the maternal uncle of Ayman al-Zawahiri.

'Abd al-Rahman 'Azzam (1893–1976) was the first secretary general of the Arab League in 1945. He died in 1976, when his sister's son Ayman al-Zawahiri was twenty-five.[7] Al-Zawahiri's other uncle, Salim 'Azzam (d. 2008), was the founder of the European Islamic Council in Britain, which was the first European Muslim institution in the UK.[8] His youngest uncle, Mahfuz 'Azzam, is currently vice-president of the al-'Amal Party in Egypt.[9]

Consequently, the political influences in the environment surrounding his birth must have influenced Ayman al-Zawahiri's future political and religious direction. Al-Qa'ida's linked websites such as "Minbar al-Tawhid wa-l-Jihad" (The Pulpit of Monotheism and Jihad) indicate that the young Ayman al-Zawahiri used to go to the mosque to learn the Qur'an and Hadith and meet with his friends. When he began to read, he focused on "the Salafi books, such as that of Ibn Taymiya, whose writings and, especially, his legal opinions (*fatwa*s) influenced him greatly."[10]

Al-Zawahiri completed his primary and middle-level education in Maadi, one of Cairo's wealthier suburbs. In 1968, he enrolled in Cairo University's Faculty of Medicine, from which he graduated in 1974, and obtained his master's degree in medicine in 1978.

His interest in the Islamist movement began in the mid-1960s. He said that he began to affiliate himself with "the jihad movement in 1966, when the first cell of jihad was formed, in the wake of the execution of Sayyid Qutb."[11]

Al-Zawahiri was arrested on 24 October 1981, and sentenced to three years' imprisonment for his role in the assassination of President Sadat on 6 October of that same year. After his release from jail in 1984, al-Zawahiri left Egypt to work in Saudi Arabia; then in 1986, he left Saudi Arabia for Pakistan. He lived in Peshawar and worked at its Kuwaiti Red Crescent Hospital with his amir and classmate, Dr. Fadl. Al-Zawahiri met Bin Laden for the first time in 1989, and the two men became virtually inseparable.

Later, when Dr. Fadl left Peshawar and its hospital for Sudan in 1993, and then for Yemen in 1994, al-Zawahiri left the hospital for the front lines, and later became Bin Laden's right-hand man. Together, Bin Laden and al-Zawahiri established al-Qa'ida's jihad against the world.[12]

Al-Zawahiri traveled in the mid-1990s to the U.S. and collected donations for his jihad group. He also bought sophisticated communications technology, capable of tracing satellite radio frequencies. His name appeared on U.S. terror lists with a promise of a $5 million reward to anyone who could provide information leading to his arrest. The Egyptian government had given his name to Interpol in 1996 and again in 1997, requesting his arrest and extradition. He was sentenced to death in Egypt in 1999 in a case nicknamed the "Returnees from Albania." Al-Zawahiri kept in touch with his followers in Europe and other countries, particularly after the 1998 U.S. air raid on Bin Laden's camps in Afghanistan, which he narrowly survived. Two years earlier, he had "visited several countries, including the U.S. and the UK, at one point staying with Bin Laden in a villa in Wembley, north London, owned by the latter."[13]

Due to his wealth and fame, Bin Laden was seen as al-Qa'ida's leader, and in his absence, al-Zawahiri was the only man capable of leading al-Qa'ida. However, al-Zawahiri, not Bin Laden, was the operational chief. Al-Zawahiri was the one who influenced Bin Laden and brought al-Qa'ida's jihadists and a number of the jihad groups in various countries into the so-called Global Islamic Front for the Jihad against the Jews and the Crusaders, and played a major role in formulating its thought and ideas for action. Since 1998 al-Qa'ida has become the "Global Front." At the time, al-Zawahiri was charging all Muslims and non-Muslims, and Arab and non-Arab regimes, with *kufr* (unbelief), simply because they held views different from his. He wanted to change the world with a sword that he did not have and never found in Islam. As his amir Dr. Fadl said about al-Zawahiri in Peshawar:

> None in al-Qa'ida, from Bin Laden to al-Zawahiri and others, is qualified to give legal opinion on religious matters; they are of the lay people and their view legally is not accepted. I have known al-Zawahiri since 1986; he is a phenomenal voice, *zahira sawtiya*. I previously said, there is no one who would follow al-Qa'ida, other than one ignorant of religion or an opportunist.[14]

Al-Zawahiri himself acknowledges that "Dr. Fadl was the amir of jihad. We have never taken a decision without consulting with him, and there was a complete obedience to him."[15]

In his long interview with the London-based paper *al-Hayat* in December 2007, Dr. Fadl explained how and when he came to know al-Zawahiri and how their relationship developed in Egypt and later in Peshawar, reflecting on al-Qa'ida, Bin Laden, and the establishment of global jihad. Dr. Fadl pointed out that his friendship with al-Zawahiri began in 1968, as he was a classmate, and they both discussed Islamic issues with other students.[16]

Dr. Fadl arrived in Peshawar in early 1983, but al-Zawahiri, imprisoned in Egypt for three years for his role in the assassination of President Sadat, did not arrive in Peshawar until after his release in 1986. Dr. Fadl said that in Peshawar "I was the amir of jihad for years, even after the establishment of al-Qa'ida. They were consulting me on everything." Dr. Fadl maintained that when al-Zawahiri arrived in Peshawar to work as a surgeon at the Red Crescent Hospital:

> He lacked surgical training, because he had obtained his master's degree only by a theoretical approach and through reading my books. He worked in Saudi Arabia for a short time but also as a general practitioner. During his national service he worked in the anesthetic section. When he gained employment in the Kuwaiti Crescent Hospital in Peshawar, he requested that I stand beside him to teach him operations. I kept teaching him until he began to stand on his own feet. He was very interested in the media and was attracted to the limelight. Therefore, I have written some scholarly works and I put his name on them, only to encourage him.[17]

If this was the status of the relationship between Dr. Fadl and Dr. al-Zawahiri, why did this relationship turn sour and how did the dispute between them develop? Dr. Fadl pointed out two reasons why this occurred. The first is al-Zawahiri's continual push from 1992 for the Jihad group to carry on "jihad operations in Egypt." Dr. Fadl rejected this view completely, as he says:

> I rejected and criticized this view in 1992, and repeated my criticism in 1993. However, they went on their own and carried a number of failed

operations; and in 1995 they came back to announce that they had stopped all jihad operations in Egypt. They agreed on my view after these bloody confrontations, which, in fact, were only to show off and to imitate al-Jamaʻa al-Islamiya. Al-Zawahiri stopped, only, after those large waves of brothers were driven to jails and gallows.[18]

This statement confirms the involvement of Dr. Fadl and al-Zawahiri in the jihad operations in Egypt. Among these operations were the attempts on the lives of the prime minister Atif Sidqi, the minister of interior Hasan al-Alfi, and President Mubarak.[19] They also planned an attack on the Military Tribunal and the Israeli embassy. Due to al-Zawahiri's fax to his followers, these attempts, as Dr. Fadl explained, were discovered prior to the event, and thousands were arrested. Al-Zawahiri also said the government arrested "one thousand," and "sentenced twenty-five" to death.[20] These terrorist operations in Egypt were linked to the relations between al-Zawahiri and Sudanese intelligence, as detailed by Dr. Fadl:

> In late 1993, when I heard about their operations in Egypt, I said to al-Zawahiri, have fear of God for the brothers' sake, and do not expose them to dangers that are not obligatory on them. Al-Zawahiri said to me that he was obliged to the Sudanese to carry out ten operations in Egypt and that he had received $100,000 for these operations. Among the Sudanese intelligence officials whom al-Zawahiri dealt with was Dr. Nafiʻ ʻAli Nafiʻ. There was also an intermediary between them called Muhammad ʻAbd al-ʻAziz. The general overseer of all this was Ali ʻUthman Taha, the Sudanese vice-president, and the second-in-command in the al-Turabi movement.[21]

Dr. Fadl also detailed the second reason why he ended relations with al-Zawahiri: "The second was their distortion of my book *al-Jamiʻ fi talab al-ʻilm al-sharif* [The Comprehensive Volume on Religious Studies]. The one who distorted this book was only al-Zawahiri himself. However, his entire group kept silent at what he did, therefore they are with him in sin."[22]

Dr. Fadl wrote the book in 1993, after he ended his connection with al-Zawahiri and left Peshawar for Sudan. The completed book was two thousand pages long. He recounts:

On leaving Sudan for Yemen, I left a copy for them to study and learn from and sell to help the families [of jihadists]. They announced that the book would be published in their London-based magazine, *Kitab al-'ilm* (The Book of Knowledge). At my work in the Yemeni hospital, I learned that the jihad brothers changed my book *al-Jami'*; they deleted things and changed the title to *al-Hadi ila sabil al-rashad* (The Guide to the Righteous Way). When the one who typed the book on the computer came to Yemen, he told me that al-Zawahiri is the only one who changed it. He found that the book criticized the Islamic movement. I wrote it from my experience with them. I know of no one, in the history of Islam, who distorted the books of others, before al-Zawahiri. Al-Zawahiri's act with my book is but an act of thieves.[23]

Dr. Fadl has recently published *Wathiqat tarshid al-jihad fi Misr wa-l-'alam* (A Document Rationalizing Jihad in Egypt and the World). He revised all of his previous ideas, theological and otherwise, about jihad. While writing this book, Dr. Fadl conducted a series of lectures and meetings with his fellow jihadists in detention, to discuss its theme and ideas. The Egyptian authorities facilitated these meetings and discussions. His lectures received a large number of responses from the members of the Egyptian Jihad. Based on these discussions, Dr. Fadl finalized the book and subjected it to further revision. The members of the Egyptian Jihad groups, both inside and outside Egypt, revised and approved the book, each providing consent in writing and sending it to Dr. Fadl. Their consent letters were then collected and handed over to the authorities in Egypt, for archival purposes only.

Among "the hundreds" who sent their consent from Egypt were important leaders such as al-Sheikh Nabil Na'im, Sheikh Ahmad Yusuf Hamdallah, Dr. Ahmad 'Ajiza, Sheikh Amal 'Abd al-Wahhab, and Colonel 'Abbud al-Zumur.[24]

As to the jihad leaders outside Egypt, Dr. Fadl sent his book to them through mediators, to which they responded, "We sent him back our total consent and declared full support for his efforts in favor of Islam and Muslims. No one can say a word after the imam [Sayyid Imam al-Sharif, or Dr. Fadl], not even al-Zawahiri himself. All jihad circles in the world respect this great man and consider him their final reference."[25]

Following the approval of the jihadists, the 111-page book was checked and approved by the Egyptian state's Islamic authorities, and the jihad movement's lawyer Muntasir al-Zayyat was appointed to have the book published. In November 2007, the book was serialized for about fifteen days in various Arabic newspapers such as the Kuwaiti *al-Jarida*, the Egyptian *Almasry Alyoum*, the London daily *al-Hayat* (of Kuwait), and *Asharq Alawsat* (of Saudi Arabia).

In this book Dr. Fadl provides a critical analysis of jihad, and al-Qa'ida's ideas and activities. He openly criticized al-Qa'ida and its leadership and called for a stop to jihad activities against the west and against the regimes in Muslim countries. The book generated extensive discussion and debate among Islamists and experts from Islamist movements.[26]

The Egyptian al-Jama'a al-Islamiya (EGI), one of the largest jihadist groups in Egypt, supported Dr. Fadl's book, and stressed their disagreement with al-Qa'ida and its leadership's ideas. Karam Zuhdi, the amir of EGI, together with his right-hand man Najih Ibrahim, the group's chief theorist, emphasized that al-Qa'ida's "aim is jihad, and our aim is Islam." Both Karam and Najih pointed out that al-Qa'ida's Global Front for the Jihad against the Jews and Crusaders is meant "to kill everything that belongs to the United States. The shari'a does not say so . . . . Therefore, we decided to withdraw from the Front because we found in it generalizations that distorted the shari'a."[27]

In 1997, the EGI began its own process of ideological revision. These revisions eventually led to a wide-ranging reassessment of the group's ideas, and it published a number of critical tracts against al-Qa'ida. These revisions, Najih maintains, have made it easier for the jihad group to examine and revise its position. Karam Zuhdi, the amir Najih Ibrahim, and associate leaders of the EGI have argued that the impact of Dr. Fadl's revisions on al-Qa'ida will become evident with time. As Dr. Fadl is a jihadist leader and highly respected theoretician, it was anticipated that his revisions would lead to a similar process of questioning within al-Qa'ida, or perhaps to an internal split or a weakening of support for the group. On 19 November 2007, the EGI issued a statement that advised al-Zawahiri and his associates in al-Qa'ida to reconsider their position and come to terms with Dr. Fadl's jurisprudential revisions.[28]

Al-Qa'ida's leadership strongly felt the impact of Dr. Fadl's revisions of jihad, even before his book was published. In an attempt to contain the impact, Bin Laden quickly issued a statement, in October 2007, that acknowledged and criticized the irregularities al-Qa'ida had committed in Iraq, and the killing of civilians and destruction of property in the name of jihad. Al-Zawahiri also made similar statements. In his letter to al-Qaʻida in Iraq, al-Zawahiri emphasized that tactics such as bombing mosques and killing hostages might alienate fellow Muslims. He said that "the insurgents in Iraq should avoid using tactics, such as the bombing of mosques and slaughtering of hostages, in order to prevent alienating the masses."[29] Despite his admission of the irregularities within al-Qaʻida, al-Zawahiri regarded Dr. Fadl's revisions as a deviation from jihad. Among other attempts to contain the impact of Dr. Fadl's book before the book had even been published, al-Zawahiri prepared a video called "Quwwat al-Haqq" (The Power of Truth), produced by al-Qaʻida's website "al-Sahab." In the video, al-Zawahiri tried to cast some doubt on the value of aims and objectives expressed in Dr. Fadl's book, and the relevance of its idea at this particular time (that is, while the jihadists are on the run after September 11). Al-Zawahiri argued that "Dr. Fadl's revision was simply the product of torture in the Egyptian prisons." Here, al-Zawahiri is referring to a jurisprudential point that there is "no authority for a prisoner" (la wilaya li-l-asir), such that the captive's viewpoint is not seen as valid in the context of Islamic law and has no effect in shariʻa law. This jurisprudential point is in the charter of any jihadist group, including al-Qaʻida. Dr. Fadl did little to argue the jurisprudential substance of this rule, perhaps because he was one from within, and he knew what al-Zawahiri was intending by bringing up this point. Dr. Fadl detailed his response to al-Zawahiri in the book, *Wathiqat tarshid al-jihad fi Misr wa-l-ʻalam* (Rationalization of the Jihad in Egypt and the World).

In the introduction to this new book, Dr. Fadl pointed out that he wrote the book in order to revise the ideas of jihad movements in Egypt and the world. He emphasized that there was a great deal of illegal activity and "irregularities committed by the jihadists" during their confrontations with the authorities of their countries and the authorities of the superpowers, in the name of jihad.

They altered the well-known judicial principles of *al-tatarrus* to shed blood and destroy properties, until they arrived at the point of murdering people only for their nationality, the color of their skin or hair, and their religious beliefs. They killed those who should not have been killed; Muslims and non-Muslims alike. They went too far and interpreted the concept of *al-tatarrus* on an extreme level only to extend the permissible area of killing and to destroy the property and wealth of the protected.[30]

Having referred to such proliferating irregularities as crimes against humanity and religion, Dr. Fadl provided a well-documented discussion of the basic principles that govern the activity of jihad, away from the slogan "*al-ghaya tubarrir al-wasila*" ('the aim justifies the means'). The discussion focused on the qualifications and qualities required in any individual to be legitimately able to advise others or provide legal opinions (sing. *fatwa*) about any issue in general, and about jihad in particular. Dr. Fadl stressed that there is a difference between disseminating the knowledge of shari'a and issuing a *fatwa*. As the *fatwa* is the result of the complete knowledge of shari'a, within the context of the present reality, no one other than the qualified scholars is legitimately permitted to issue a *fatwa* or to apply what is found in the books of the early scholars to the present. He also warned against the attempts at *fiqh al-tabrir* ('jurisprudence of justification'), whereby people act wrongly and then attempt to extract justification for their actions from this or that book. Piety is a duty in everything, especially in blood and wealth. He called on the young, declaring that they should not accept any *fatwa* about these sensitive issues of blood and property from any unqualified person.[31]

Focusing on the illegal activities and irregularities of al-Qa'ida's activity, Dr. Fadl responded to al-Zawahiri's argument based on the principle of "no authority for war prisoners." Al-Zawahiri claimed that Dr. Fadl's "revisions" cannot be accepted because he wrote them while in prison. However, Dr. Fadl responded to this matter from varying facets and documented his discussion in a scholarly and well-researched style summarized in the following points.

Firstly, the book is merely an opinion of one who knows. The jihadists know well the author and his capacities. Al-Zawahiri and associates in al-Qa'ida know the author very well. In al-Zawahiri's words, "Dr. Fadl was the amir of jihad. We have never taken a decision without consulting with him, and there was a complete obedience to him."[32] Thus, Dr. Fadl emphasized that the author of *Risalat al-'umda fi i'dad al-'udda li-l-jihad fi sabil Allah* (The Master Message in the Preparation for Jihad) is the same author of *Wathiqat tarshid al-jihad fi Misr wa-l-'alam*. The author has no authority to impose his view on any person, but Muslims should abide by the knowledge if the knowledge is documented and proven by shari'a.

Secondly, in terms of al-Zawahiri's claim that the captive's view has no legal effect, Dr. Fadl pointed out that this applies only with regard to matters that cannot be established by any source other than the captive's word, such as acknowledging a crime that has been committed, or acknowledging a debt. However, in matters like this, of a religious and jurisprudential nature, which can be verified by sources other than the captive's own knowledge, the captive's view of these matters can be verified by the shari'a.

Thirdly, rejecting the substance of the book *(Wathiqat tarshid al-jihad fi Misr wa-l-'alam)* on the basis only of the place where the book was written is clearly wrong. It is not true that everything that has come out of prison is invalid. The substance of the book and the evidence therein must be considered before factoring in the significance of the location. Furthermore, such unthinking rejection of ideas, Dr. Fadl argues, stands against Qur'anic teachings and Islamic history. He cites several examples, but the following are sufficient to illustrate his point. Dr. Fadl refers to the Qur'anic narration concerning the Prophet Yusuf when he was in prison, and says the "Prophet Yusuf was preaching while in prison." Dr. Fadl quoted the Prophet Yusuf's saying as mentioned in the Qur'an 39–40, *O my fellow-prisoners! Are many lords differing among themselves better, or the One God, the Irresistible? Those whom you worship beside Him are but names that you have named, you and your fathers. God has not sent down any authority for them. The decision rests with God only, Who has commanded you that you worship none but Him. This is the right religion, but most people know not.* Dr. Fadl then asks, "Was Prophet Yusuf being in prison an argument for refusing his word of truth?" With regard to the history of Islam, Dr. Fadl highlights that Ibn Taymiya wrote many of his books while in prison in Damascus, and Imam al-Sarkhasi (d. 1031) wrote his book of Jurisprudence *al-Mabsut* (The Detailed) while in prison.[33] What should be considered is "the legitimacy of the information and its evidence in the book, not where the book was written."[34]

Dr. Fadl then proceeds in his book to explain, in some detail, the jurisprudential conditions that govern jihad, with a specific focus on the illegal ideas adopted by al-Zawahiri and his associates, and the individuals and groups affiliated with al-Qa'ida. Dr. Fadl, who himself is the imam of jihad, understood the ideas of al-Zawahiri well and thus deliberately made them the main ideas of his book. Dr. Fadl emphasizes that the consequences of adopting illegal ideas, in the name of jihad, constitute crimes against religion and humanity. These ideas can be summarized by the following points:

1. Islam is a universal religion.
2. Islam is shari'a law.
3. The shari'a has the capacity and inclination to deal with the needs of human society.
4. Responsibility or Muslim duty is dependent on comprehension and the ability to perform.
5. Jihad duty is dependent on the physical ability to perform, and on financial capability.
6. Jihad is not an obligation for any Muslim who cannot provide for his dependents (that is, wife, children, parents, and so on).
7. It is not permissible for any person to obtain money through illegal means to finance jihad. Hence, kidnapping innocents for ransom, looting the wealth of people, or robbing somebody else's property, in the name of jihad, are crimes. "Which law is this? Which mind permitted this? Is this not but the consequence of the leadership of the ignorant and their advice on matters of jihad? Now we come to hear about operations to finance jihad; and operations carried out only for publicity and fund-raising for jihad. The jihad duty is dropped in the absence of money."
8. What is based on wrong is itself wrong.
9. It is not permissible for any person to conduct jihad without permission from the creditor.
10. It is not permissible for any person to conduct jihad without permission from their parents. This point addresses a major problem: nowadays parents often do not know that their son has been involved in jihad until they see his picture in the media, or he is jailed or killed.
11. The lives and property of Muslims are protected by shari'a. That is, jihadists should not throw themselves to death in the name of jihad. Jihad is not an obligation for Muslims if there is no parity between them and their enemy. Therefore, the shari'a permits negotiations, treaties, emigrations, and other facilities, depending on the circumstances.
12. Jihad against the rulers of Muslim countries, to establish the shari'a, is not permissible.
13. Jihad is not the only option for changing the world or establishing shari'a.
14. It is forbidden to harm tourists and foreigners in Muslim countries.
15. It is forbidden to harm people, either civilians or soldiers, in a non-Muslim country after entering that country with permission, such

as with a visa. Hence, killing civilians in passenger aircrafts, or in trains, towers, and hotels, is not permissible. It is not valid according to Islamic law to harm non-Muslims who have permitted your entry into their country, awarded you accommodation and political asylum, protected you and your property, and permitted you to learn and work.

16. Single individuals should not conduct jihad without permission from the ruler.

17. It is not permissible to harm Christian citizens in Muslim countries.

The book generated extensive discussion at all levels. Some observers considered Dr. Fadl's book to be a turning point in the doctrinal path of jihad. It was assumed that the book would influence jihadists, especially those trained to believe that overthrowing regimes was based on ideological doctrines. These would be existing or possible future members of Jihad organizations in Egypt and other Arab and Muslim countries, including the Armed Islamic Group in Algeria, and what is left of al-Qa'ida in Saudi Arabia, Yemen, and Indonesia. However, the dormant and semi-dormant cells of al-Qa'ida across the world, and al-Qa'ida cells in Iraq, would indeed remain unaffected. Those young jihadists who were inspired by al-Qa'ida after the dissolution of the organization would have been unable to carry out their terrorist operations if Dr. Fadl had written this book prior to the events of September 11, five years previously.[35]

As soon as the daily papers began to serialize the book, the London daily *al-Hayat* conducted a ten-hour interview with Dr. Fadl while he was in detention, in December 2007. The interview was serialized in *al-Hayat* for six days between 8 and 13 December 2007. In his interview, Dr. Fadl discussed at length the emergence of al-Qa'ida, its leadership, his relationship with al-Zawahiri, the September 11 attacks, and related issues. In his view, September 11 represents betrayal and perfidy; al-Zawahiri is a charlatan prone to betraying his friends; Bin Laden was someone who lacked a sound knowledge of religion, and whose speeches were written for him; al-Qa'ida is an organization without an expert in shari'a to guide it, and has deviated from shari'a; and its leaders should be brought to a shari'a court and tried for their crimes against Islam and humanity. Below are extracts from Dr. Fadl's interview, which illustrate these points.

On the Stages in al-Qaʿidaʾs Establishment

When I came to Peshawar in 1983, the number of Arabs there was only as many as the number of fingers on two hands. Then came Sheikh ʿAbdullah ʿAzzam, and he founded an Office for Mujahidin Services in late 1984. There were growing calls for Arab participation in the Afghan jihad, and the Arab presence gradually grew. The [Egyptian] Jihad Group was established long before al-Qaʿida, but al-Qaʿida went through four stages:

First: The stage of the camp and the front, in late 1987. Bin Laden would raise funds from Saudi Arabia and hand them over to the Afghan warlords and to Sheikh ʿAzzam. Some of the youth complained to Bin Laden about irregularities in the Office of Services; and Bin Laden decided to establish something, independent of Sheikh ʿAzzam. He started with a training camp and a combat front in the Jaji region in Afghanistan. Cadres from the Egyptian Jihad Group helped him in this and, thanks to their high level of military skills, youth started flocking to them, and as a result, the number of training camps increased.

Second: The organization stage. In 1989, when the number of youth of various nationalities increased, most of them were from Saudi Arabia and Yemen; Bin Laden started asking them to give an oath of allegiance to himself as amir of the jihad. And al-Qaʿida was transformed from a camp and a front, into an organization.

Third: The stage of shifting the organization. In 1990, some of those who have experience in the Islamic-movement work and who had pledged the oath of allegiance to Bin Laden noticed that he was rapidly changing his goals and plans, from the Afghan jihad to throwing his weight into the jihad in southern Yemen, before the end of the Afghan jihad, and from the assassination attempt against Mohammed Zahir Shah (the former king of Afghanistan) in Italy, to the preparations for participation in the Gulf War against Iraq when it occupied Kuwait. Some of his followers demanded that al-Qaʿida should have a program (a constitution) that would define the principles of its existence and the aims upon which Bin Laden would receive the oath of allegiance from the youth. Bin Laden refused to be bound by any program, in order to give himself the freedom to do what he wanted. He expelled those who had demanded a program, and from that time on, unfortunately, those who have followed Bin Laden have been one of only two types: a man ignorant in his religion or a man who seeks worldly gain. It came about that the majority of his followers were youths, from Saudi Arabia and Yemen, who were motivated more by Islamic sentiment than by the guidance of the rules of shari'a. The others were non-Arabs, from Asia and Europe, whose understanding of the religion was limited and who were motivated by religious sentiment, especially those who had recently converted to Islam and had not studied the religion.

Fourth: The stage of global confrontation. In 1993, when Bin Laden was in Sudan, he revealed his desire to enter into conflict with the international powers, America in particular. Some of his followers abandoned him, including some of his relatives and in-laws. The declaration of the Global Front for Fighting Jews and Crusaders, in 1998, was the final stage of what he had begun to prepare since 1993, by observing U.S. and European targets that he could attack in different areas of the world.[36]

On Egyptian Jihad in al-Qa'ida

Members of the Jihad Group are the ones who founded al-Qa'ida, administered it, and tried to guide Bin Laden in the right direction and to keep contradictions with shari'a to a minimum. Then I cut my ties with everyone in 1993, when I saw most of them were following their individual desires. Therefore, I say that al-Qa'ida has no program, no ideologue, and no mufti other than what Bin Laden sees as being in line with his personal opinion, and whoever opposes him is expelled. This was the path that led to the episodes of September 11, 2001. The duty of those who remained with Bin Laden was to find justification for his views and errors by using dubious views about the shari'a to deceive the ignorant.[37]

Mullah 'Umar, Bin Laden, and September 11

The events of September 2001, carried out by al-Qa'ida, constituted the betrayal of a friend and perfidy toward the enemy, and a catastrophe for Muslims. All of these are features of hypocrisy, and cardinal sins whose perpetrators are considered sinful, and whoever approves their actions shares their sin.

Betrayal: It was betrayal of a friend, because Bin Laden took the oath of allegiance to Mullah 'Umar and lived under his protection.

More than once Mullah 'Umar ordered Bin Laden not to clash with America, saying that he has no capability for this, especially since Afghanistan and its people were paying the price for Bin Laden's bombings in Nairobi and Dar al-Salam in 1998. Bin Laden and his followers lied to their amir, Mullah 'Umar, betrayed him, violated their oath to him, and carried out the events of September 11 behind his back after having planned them for more than two years in his country, Afghanistan, after Khalid Sheikh [Muhammad] suggested the idea to Bin Laden.

Perfidy: It was perfidy toward the enemy, because they entered America with a visa, which is a contract of protection. This is what the scholars agreed upon. Even if the person forged the visa and entered the country of his enemy, he is forbidden to betray the residents in anything, including their lives, their honor, their wealth and property, and there is no distinction to be made between combatants (military) and non-combatants (civilians), as long as he remains in their country. Bin Laden's followers entered America with his knowledge and by his order, and deceitfully killed people and destroyed property. They then called their treachery and their deceit a *ghazw* (raid) in order to make it similar to that of the Prophet. To tie their treachery to the Prophet is to diminish him and to mock him, and the punishment for diminishing the worth of the Prophet is well known to Muslims, as mentioned by Qadi Eyyad in *al-Shifa* (Healing), and by Ibn Taymiya in *al-Sarim al-maslul* (The Strict Sword).

Catastrophe: It was a catastrophe for the Muslims. Al-Qa'ida ignited strife that found its way into every home, and it was the cause of the imprisonment of thousands of Muslims in the prisons of various countries. They caused the death of tens of thousands of Muslims, Arabs, Afghans, Pakistanis, and others. The Taliban's Islamic Emirate was destroyed, and al-Qa'ida was destroyed. They were directly responsible for the American occupation of Afghanistan and other heavy losses, the details of which there is insufficient space to mention here. They bear the responsibility for all of this.

Bin Laden and al-Zawahiri Should Be Tried

Bin Laden, al-Zawahiri, and others fled at the start of the American bombing of Afghanistan, to the point of abandoning their wives and families to be killed along with other innocent people. In my view, a shari'a court should be established with a panel of reliable scholars, to try these people for their crimes, even in absentia, so that those who are ignorant in their religion do not repeat this futility.

American Foreign Aid

Those who admired the actions of al-Qa'ida are merely ignorant people, due to their lack of knowledge of shari'a, the conditions required for jihad, and its legal definitions. These people are ruled by emotions and they think with their ears, not with their minds; that is, they may admire what they hear without considering its true nature. What induces people to do this is their hatred for America. They have not seen any good come from it. America has always supported Israel. Al-Qa'ida plays on this chord just as Saddam Hussein, Ahmadinejad, and others have done.

Ordinary Arabs and Muslims do not even notice American foreign aid, because it consists of old weapons that America seeks to dispose of in order to provide work for its factories, old stocks of grain it wants to get rid of, or birth control pills. This is American foreign aid in the literal sense, that is, America aids itself. People hate America, and the Islamist movements feel the injustice and the impotence, and they applaud anyone who locks horns with America, be it Bin Laden, Ahmadinejad, or Saddam.

Locking horns with America has become the shortest road to fame and heroism among Arabs and Muslims. But what good is it if you destroy an enemy's building, and he destroys a country? What good is it if you kill one of his people, and he kills a thousand of your people? That, in short, is my evaluation of September 11.[38]

Al-Qa'ida's Response to Dr. Fadl

Al-Qa'ida's ideologue al-Zawahiri began to plan his defense to contain the impact of Dr. Fadl's book on al-Qa'ida's affiliates. Al-Zawahiri's defense had three facets. First, he announced the affiliation of some individuals and groups, such as the Libyan Jihad group, to al-Qa'ida. Al-Zawahiri knew that this was pure propaganda, with no truth to it. It was a tactic intended to show that Dr. Fadl's book had had no effect on al-Qa'ida. Second, in October 2007, he and Bin Laden acknowledged the irregularities committed by al-Qa'ida in the name of jihad in Iraq.[39] This level of self-criticism on al-Qa'ida's part had never taken place prior to the publication of Dr. Fadl's book. The third was al-Zawahiri's announcement that he would write a book refuting Dr. Fadl's revisions.

On 3 March 2008, al-Qa'ida's jihadist websites, including al-Sahab and al-Ikhlas media, published al-Zawahiri's new book of 188 pages under the title *al-Tabri'a: risala fi tabri'at ummat al-qalam wa-l-sayf min manqusat tuhmat al-khawr wa-l-da'f* (Exoneration: A Treatise Exonerating the Nation of the Pen and the Sword from the Blemish of the Accusation of Weakness and Feebleness). The title points the way to the contents and theme of the book, as al-Zawahiri himself notes in his book: "Because I considered [Dr. Fadl's] document to have blemished the Muslim *umma*, I preferred my response to be called 'Exoneration' to exonerate the *umma* from these charges."[40] Al-Zawahiri's response, in the form of *al-Tabri'a*, is of great importance for a number of reasons. It is the latest official document confirming al-Qa'ida's ideological position, as well as the theological and jurisprudential justifications used to justify al-Qa'ida's activities. It provides al-Qa'ida's response to the question repeatedly asked by Muslims, Arab regimes as well as by the west, which is: "Why do they hate us?"[41] It recounts al-Qa'ida's activities in the past and the present, and al-Qa'ida's plans and position in relation to the U.S. and Arab regimes in the future. It reflects the disputes between al-Qa'ida's jihadist ideologues on theological, ideological, jurisprudential, and tactical levels. It confirms the impact of Dr. Fadl's book *al-Tabri'a* on jihadist and al-Qa'ida operatives in general. In this regard, al-Zawahiri and associates carefully wrote this book with the intention of minimizing the impact of Dr. Fadl's book on al-Qa'ida's jihadists. The fact that al-Zawahiri wrote a book of this length and with this level of political, theological, and jurisprudential detail strongly suggests that the author (the Hidden Imam al-Zawahiri) has lived a life far more stable than one might think.

Al-Zawahiri divided his treatise into two parts, including nineteen chapters of varying length, an introduction, and a conclusion. From the introduction to the conclusion, al-Zawahiri undertakes a refutation of Dr. Fadl's central arguments and denounces his book based on what al-Zawahiri considers weak evidence against al-Qa'ida's version of jihad. In the introduction, al-Zawahiri points out that he and Bin Laden were the focus of Dr. Fadl's *al-Tabri'a*. This made it difficult for al-Zawahiri to choose between responding and simply remaining silent. In either case, there will be those who would think otherwise. "Therefore the *Risala* (Treatise) that I present to the readers today is the most difficult, if not the hardest I have written in my life."[42] It is difficult for him to admit the dispute between the jihad ideologues; however, al-Qa'ida was facing an unprecedented challenge from within. Al-Zawahiri rejects Dr. Fadl's book, and outlines the basis of his rejection as follows:

> It serves the interests of the Crusaders-Zionist coalitions with the Arab leaders who deviated from shari'a. It is an attempt to numb the Mujahidin and drag them away from the confrontation, on the basis that they are weak and feeble and lacking the equipment required for jihad, and that Islamic movements cannot bring about any change (p. 3). It calls for the acceptance of prejudices and a lack of concern for the affairs of Muslims. It serves a prisoner [i.e. Dr. Fadl], who saw what he provided as enough, or rather blamed himself for it, and wanted to focus on his own affairs, and this has been the position of the author [Dr. Fadl] for fourteen years. It cannot resolve the problem of a society, or people, or *umma*. I can understand why prisoners may make such decisions. I have been imprisoned twice, Praise to God, and I know imprisonment, but the Muslim *umma*, in Egypt and elsewhere, is not in need of his decision [Dr. Fadl's] at this tumultuous time in its history (p. 6).

Al-Zawahiri did not forget to link all of this to the political situations in the Middle East. He emphasizes that Dr. Fadl's book was merely a failed attempt to drag the Muslim awakening away from its goal. Here, al-Zawahiri promotes anti-American sentiment by playing the sentiment of heroism, encouraging Muslim masses to think of themselves as heroes, because of the attacks against the U.S. As Dr. Fadl previously said about the Middle East, "Locking horns with America is the shortest road to fame and heroism."[43] Playing on this chord, al-Zawahiri says:

> The Mujahidin have failed the American plan in the region. America knows well the danger of the jihadist current and al-Qa'ida to the future of America and its place in the world. Al-Qa'ida does not call only for the eviction of the occupiers, the Crusaders, and the Jews from Muslim countries, but also demands that oil be sold at its true price, whatever the effect this may have on America's authoritarian influence on the world. The only crime of the Mujahidin and al-Qa'ida is that they stand against America, the Jews, and their agents.

Al-Zawahiri devotes the first chapter to outlining seventeen general remarks on Dr. Fadl's book. The chief remark is his claim that Dr. Fadl's book was written only to entertain the Egyptian authorities in the hope that they might release him from jail. Therefore, "the book is not neutral"; rather, "its title is different from the substance of its subject." He questions the title of Dr. Fadl's book: "Rationalization of jihadist work calls for a question. Jihadist work with whom, and against whom?" (p. 10). "The book jumps directly to what he regards as errors in jihadist work, without explaining the reality from which jihadist work emerged to change it." The book "jumped to what are called errors without explaining the reasons and diagnosing the remedy; these should be dealt with first and then the author may speak of the alleged errors while speaking of the remedy" (pp. 10–11). The book "ignored what is most important and concerned itself with what he regards as important." "It ignored the crimes committed by the Crusaders and their agents, and dragged the *umma* away from fighting and standing up against them, and instead occupied itself with what are allegedly errors of the Mujahidin" (p. 11). The book "failed, not only to describe the reality and its diagnosis, but also failed to recognize treatment. It did not provide a rational alternative for healing. The seven alternatives that he provided (emigration, separation, forgiveness, sliding away, patience, concealment, and belief) do not provide a practical solution. How are those millions of Muslim youths, who want to serve Islam, supposed to migrate, and to which country should they migrate? How would they separate [themselves from the society]? How would they hide their belief?" (p. 11).

Al-Zawahiri then outlines the political circumstances in the Middle East and Muslim countries in the context of U.S. foreign policy, which he sees as "crushing the Muslim world. " Considering these circumstances, the seven alternatives that Dr. Fadl provided are "a prescription for an escape from reality" (p. 5). Dr. Fadl's book "charged the Mujahidin with alleged errors without evidence and with no reference to his sources" (p. 11). The book "does not follow the scientific method in presenting the opinions of scholars on jurisprudential matters. It did not refer to al-Shawakani's rulings on the matters of safety and protection. It did not refer to the consensus *(ijma')* on matters of *al-tatarrus*, while referring to al-Ghazali" (p. 11).

In the second chapter, al-Zawahiri responds to Dr. Fadl's reasons for writing the book. Al-Zawahiri presents thirty-five questions about the political reality of Muslim countries, with a focus on Middle Eastern countries and U.S. foreign policy therein, without forgetting to include the issue of Egypt. Through these questions he attempts to substantiate the reasons for al-Qa'ida's violence, and argues that this violence is valid by Islamic law or simply jihad.

In the third chapter, al-Zawahiri responds to Dr. Fadl's claim that al-Qa'ida's jihadists are merely ignorant and lacking in religious knowledge. Here, al-Zawahiri mentions a number of recent scholars and discusses their thoughts, particularly in relation to jihad. While these scholars are from Muslim countries, Wahhabi and Talibani scholars, as well as a number of al-Qa'ida ideologues are also among those admired by al-Zawahiri. However, no scholars from al-Azhar appear worthy of al-Zawahiri's admiration. He also refers to the Taliban's demolition of the statue of the Buddha in Afghanistan on 26 February 2001, as a point of reference on the Islam of his mullahs. Al-Zawahiri states:

> The Taliban State is the state of scholars and followers of the Dubandi school of thought, which is based on the Hanafi school of thought in Pakistan. In the Taliban State, the scholars have the final or the upper word. When the Leader of the Faithful (*amir al-mu'minin*), Mullah Muhammad 'Umar, asked the Afghan scholars about the statue, they advised that it must be demolished. Mullah 'Umar carried out their decision without question or hesitation. A delegate team consisting of [Egyptian professor, Sheikh] al-Qaradawi [living in Qatar], and the Mufti of Egypt al-Sheikh Muhammad Farid Wasil, Fahmi Huwadi [author and Islamic writer in Egypt's then-government-sponsored daily *al-Ahram*], al-Sheikh 'Ali Qurrah Daghi, and the Qatari minister for foreign affairs have come in order to convince the Afghan Emirate to keep the statue. The Qatari foreign minister also told the Taliban that he would push for their return to the Islamic Congress if they kept the statue safe. However, Mullah 'Umar sent them a team of Afghan scholars to discuss the matter of the statue, and won the argument (p. 35).

In the fourth chapter, al-Zawahiri responds to Dr. Fadl's view that jihad is not an obligation for any Muslim who cannot provide for his dependents. This means that the jihad obligation is dropped if the Muslim is incapable of carrying it out. On this subject, al-Zawahiri argues that those who are qualified to determine a Muslim's capability to carry out jihad do not include "Dr. Fadl, and certainly not the war prisoner (Dr. Fadl), who left jihad a long time ago. Those who pass judgment on jihad are the scholars who are true in themselves and true to their faith" (p. 52). After detailing the reasons as to why he considers jihad to be obligatory at the present time, al-Zawahiri argues that the Muslim world is currently in a situation of defense: "We are now in the jihad of defense" (p. 64).

From chapters five to seventeen, al-Zawahiri focuses on Dr. Fadl's ideas and conditions in relation to when jihad can be considered obligatory, the best method for changing the ruling system, obtaining permission from one's ruler or parents, the Islamic rulings concerning civil disobedience, and the change of government by force. He also focuses on the rulings concerning jihad by Muslims living in non-Muslim countries and the irregularities committed by U.S. citizens in U.S. jails and in Iraq. He does not accept Dr. Fadl's view, based on the shari'a, that Muslims are forbidden to harm people, whether civilians or soldiers, in a non-Muslim country, after entering that country with permission, such as with a visa. For al-Zawahiri, "Visas from countries that are fighting Muslims and insulting their Prophet do not protect them from punishment by Muslims" (p. 103).

Referring to Dr. Fadl's criticism of the call to "kill the Crusaders and the Jews," al-Zawahiri writes ironically, "the name of the Front was 'Jihad' not 'Kill,' but he did not explain the difference between them in al-Qa'ida's context. Instead, he emphasized that the Crusaders are those who carried and are carrying out Crusades against Muslims. But the Jews are a sect that participated in the establishment of Israel; and the difference between the Jews and Zionists is insignificant because the majority of Jews support Israel, and the rare number who are not supporters are not taken into consideration" (p. 149).

In the fifteenth chapter, al-Zawahiri focuses on Dr. Fadl's critical point that al-Zawahiri and his associates attacked the U.S. without their amir's permission (Mullah 'Umar): "He who has an amir, should not do anything without his amir's permission. He who has an amir and has given him the oath of allegiance, and then conducts jihad without telling his amir, may be responsible for the destruction of the [Taliban's] Emirate and the fall of the state. He has betrayed and deceived his amir" (pp. 149–50).

Al-Zawahiri could not deny the substance of these words but distanced himself on the basis that the decision had been Bin Laden's. Bin Laden and

Mullah 'Umar's relationship has been previously outlined (see pages 124 and 225–26). Here, however, al-Zawahiri's response admits al-Qa'ida's operations against the U.S., and reveals details of the organization's intelligence work that indicate al-Qa'ida's awareness of the U.S. attempts to arrest or kill Bin Laden. George Tenet has also remarked on many of these details.[44] Although al-Zawahiri, on his own account, kept some information close to his chest, the information he did release will continue to be of great importance as long as the file on al-Qa'ida's leadership remains open. The information's importance lies in its accuracy with respect to the intelligence and counter-intelligence work of al-Qa'ida. Al-Zawahiri's account of events begins from the summer of 1997 and ends on 10 September 2001. His references to Richard Clark,[45] George Tenet, and other senior U.S. and Pakistani officials, the attempts of the U.S. to recruit agents from among the Afghan tribes, and U.S. relations with the northern allies and Shah Massoud all point to the success of al-Qa'ida's counterintelligence work (pp. 150–59).

Al-Zawahiri's aim in releasing this bulk of intelligence information can also be seen as a justification or defense. He wanted to contain the impact of Dr. Fadl's book and to minimize the loss of recruits, since a great number of jihadists accepted Dr. Fadl's call to stop jihad. Al-Zawahiri wanted to inform his readers that even if al-Qa'ida did not attack U.S. interests, the U.S. would not leave al-Qa'ida alone. He argues that "America was preparing to arrest or kidnap Bin Laden, even before the establishment of the Global Islamic Front for the Jihad, in February 1998" (p. 150). The bombings of the U.S. embassies in East Africa came later, on 7 August 1998. Here, al-Zawahiri is appealing to the Muslims who accuse him and Bin Laden of terrorist activity in the name of jihad. Al-Zawahiri, however, does not mention the bombing of the al-Khobar towers in Saudi Arabia, on 25 June 1996, which killed twenty U.S. citizens. This and other similar terrorist actions against the U.S., which took place before the establishment of his 'Global Front for the Jihad Against the Jews and the Crusaders,' were deliberately omitted by al-Zawahiri, as part of his persuasion. In his book, al-Zawahiri also included a letter from Mullah 'Umar that calls upon Muslims to help Afghanis fight the U.S., again confirming his attempts at appeal. The letter was signed by Mullah 'Umar on AH 16/7/1422 (4 October 2001), after September 11 and before the U.S. invasion of Afghanistan on 7 October 2001. The letter emphasizes that there was no evidence to confirm the involvement of Bin Laden in the September 11 attacks. This means that Bin Laden did not discuss September 11 with Mullah 'Umar but rather left him in the dark over his plans. Mullah 'Umar also wrote that the U.S. and its allies were preparing to attack the Taliban only because they were Muslims and had established an Islamic state. The U.S.-led crusade against the Islamic Emirate of Afghanistan is thus seen as an attack on Islam. The letter asserts that jihad was obligatory, as a Muslim duty to defend Islam. Following the letter is an appeal by al-Zawahiri to Muslims to forget about Bin Laden and to help the Taliban (p. 162). This clearly indicates the impact of Dr. Fadl's book on al-Qa'ida.

Chapter eighteen, entitled "The Activities of the Jihad Organization in Egypt," is devoted to the operations of the jihad group in Egypt. It repeats what al-Zawahiri had said in previous writings. He speaks of the Egyptian regimes; the Brotherhood's aims and objectives; the relationships between Egyptian regimes and both the U.S. and the Jews; and the involvement of the U.S. and the Jews in Egyptian affairs. Al-Zawahiri did not forget to tie all of these, and other related issues, to the circumstances in the Middle East, Palestine, Iraq, Afghanistan, and the Muslim world in general. He sees these circumstances as confirmation of what he calls the "planned war against Islam." "The battle between Islam and the unbelievers (*al-kufr*) is not limited to a particular region or country, because the enemies of Islam have united themselves against Islam everywhere and in all places" (p. 171). Therefore, jihad is obligatory and the duty of every Muslim. Appealing to his audiences, al-Zawahiri asserts that this jihad is defensive, and aimed at liberating Muslim lands from Jews and Crusaders.

Also noteworthy here is al-Zawahiri's acknowledgment of the errors committed in the name of jihad. With respect to Egypt, for instance, al-Zawahiri admits the jihad errors and outlines critically how the authorities exploited these errors to influence public opinion against his movement. Among those who killed in an operation in Egypt was a girl named Shayma. She was killed during a failed attempt to assassinate Prime Minister 'Atif Sidqi in 1993. It seemed that al-Zawahiri only came to remember this girl after Dr. Fadl has published his criticisms. In 2008, al-Zawahiri declared his desire to compensate the girl's family with LE 3000 fifteen years after the event (p. 174).

In the nineteenth chapter, al-Zawahiri continues his attempts to refute Dr. Fadl's revisions, paying special attention to recent operations in the Egyptian resorts of Taba and Sharm al-Shaykh in Sinai.

In summary, al-Zawahiri's book, *al-Tabri'a*, does not offer new ideas concerning jihadist thought. In many places, he emphasizes his lack of objection to revising jihadist thought or rationalizing it, but holds that those who do so should not be motivated by U.S. intelligence or Egypt's State Security Investigations Service. However, he did not provide revisions of his own to jihadist thought or anything that might lead to a revision. Instead, he sought merely to justify his jihadist ideas, without precision, but in the known style he commonly adopts in his jihadist writings. For example, he still believes in the change of regimes by force.

In his book al-Zawahiri seeks to draw people's attention and appeal to their understanding; yet he also permits the killing of non-combatant Muslims and non-Muslims alike. He aims to defend jihadist thought, and refers to liberation, freedom, justice, equality, torture, the U.S., the Jews, Iraq, Palestine, Afghanistan, and issues related to regimes in both the Arab and Muslim worlds. He finally determines that the jihad he knows is the only true form. While he himself stays hidden, his jihadists crowd both the known and unknown prisons of the world. In Egypt itself, as Muntasir al-Zayyat, the lawyer of the jihadists, has said, "There are between two and three thousand jihadists in prison";[46] yet al-Zawahiri has done nothing to help them or their families, or improve their situation. He himself claims to have lost his wife and children during the U.S. campaign in Afghanistan in October 2001. This hidden imam is now directing the battle from in hiding, without a care for his troops or their families, for societies affected, or for the innocents who have been, or are yet to be, killed.

Conclusion

The main debate on the future of Islamic fundamentalism and its radical offshoots, such as al-Qaʻida and jihadism in general, is turning toward a consideration of ideology and doctrinal propriety, as well as issues that the jihadists perceive as matters of core belief. Recent studies agree on the fundamental importance of theology and ideology in the process of radicalization, the embracing of violence, and terrorism. While studies have confirmed that radicalism sustains terrorism at its very roots, they have also confirmed that the organizational and tactical growth of radicalism is always coupled with selective fundamental narratives and perverted interpretations. In order to counter the process of radicalization, it is necessary to understand the theological and intellectual narratives used to indoctrinate the young and attract many of them to such violent acts of terrorism. Hence, this book has investigated the theological and ideological bases of al-Qaʻida's political tactics.

Many of al-Qaʻida's radical ideas did not emerge recently, nor did they originate with al-Qaʻida, but were borrowed from earlier Islamic movements. This book therefore begins with an examination of medieval Islamic fundamentalism with a particular focus on the similarities and differences between it and modern movements such as al-Qaʻida. It then explores al-Qaʻida's theology, ideology, and tactics, and ends with an examination of the ideological war within al-Qaʻida and its self-criticism regarding the theological and ideological bases for violence and terrorism.

Hopefully, this book has shed some light on Islamist thought, and on the radicalism, violence, and terrorism, by exploring the links between medieval and modern activism, and substantiating the similarities between al-Qaʿida's motivations and justifications for its actions with those of past movements such as those of the Kharijis, Ibadis, Hanbalis, and Wahhabis. Having outlined these similarities, the book proceeds to focus on al-Qaʿida's theological and ideological narratives and assess its geographic contours, to consider the implications for global terrorism in the twenty-first century.

In terms of its attempts to maintain its growth and influence, al-Qaʿida resembles the Kharijis in many ways, and this includes its ideas and manner of self-promotion to its various audiences. As detailed in Chapter 2, al-Qaʿida usually presents itself as a movement that follows the rules of God according to the way of the Prophet Muhammad and the rightly guided ancestors (*salafis*) of the past, and whose interest is to revive the *salafi* way of life on the basis of the shariʿa. Capitalizing on social, economic, and political constraints in the Muslim world, al-Qaʿida presents itself as the only rightly guided Islamic movement defending Islam in the twenty-first century. Any individuals or groups that oppose al-Qaʿida's ideas and actions are thus labeled as infidels or, in al-Qaʿida's words, *kuffar* (non-believers). Justifying this label opens the way for al-Qaʿida to justify further rules and actions. In the context of this self-perception, al-Qaʿida considers the Muslim world's individuals or groups, whether the rulers or the ruled, who oppose al-Qaʿida, as people who have deviated from Islam. In this sense, the ideas of medieval movements have been reappropriated by al-Qaʿida as ideological tools with which to criticize their opponents, or as a point of reference. While al-Qaʿida calls its opponents Kharijis, it considers itself to be a jihadist reformist movement. Like the Kharijis, al-Qaʿida frames its use of violence in terms of jihad carried out on behalf of the Muslim *umma*: "We consider our jihad in this stage to be the jihad of an *umma*. Therefore, any individuals or groups that undertake jihad and exchange loyalty with us on the basis of 'blood for blood and destruction for destruction' are part of the jihadist movement."

Al-Qaʿida is well aware of the negative position held by the Kharijis in the minds of Muslims. Capitalizing on this awareness, al-Qaʿida labels its opponents Kharijis while adopting many Khariji ideas itself, including those of loyalty, charging others with unbelief *(kufr)*, and the condoning of regime change by force. Al-Qaʿida accuses its opponents as not being "true Wahhabis," while describing its own people as true Wahhabis. The Wahhabis even called themselves jihadists and their violence as jihad on behalf of the *umma*. This is also al-Qaʿida's claim. Wahhabism promotes itself as a reformist movement, a perception that is shared by al-Qa'ida today. As detailed in this book, the pattern of force that the Wahhabis condoned does not justify al-Qa'ida's aim of reform. The aims and objectives do not necessarily justify the means.

Al-Qa'ida often uses the Hanbali school of thought and refers to scholars and imams such as Ibn Hanbal, Ibn Taymiya, and Ibn al-Qayyim for its ideological justifications. However, many of the narratives mentioned by al-Qa'ida with reference to these and similar imams have been selectively and intentionally paraphrased or used out of context to deceive its audiences. This book has outlined numerous examples of this kind, but the following example is sufficient to illustrate the point here. The idea of *al-tatarrus* is one of the lethal ideas upon which al-Qa'ida has based almost all of its violent operations, including September 11 and other terrorist activities, that harmed civilians and destroyed buildings and property. Al-Qa'ida paraphrased this idea, took it out of context, and twisted it to suit its own purposes, specifically to justify the killing of civilians. This idea is examined in some detail in Chapter 6. These and similar narratives play a significant role not only in maintaining al-Qa'ida's organizational growth, but in generating the ties that bind its networks across borders. Not all of al-Qa'ida's followers are capable of analyzing the information fed to them or finding out the truth for themselves—a fact al-Qa'ida takes advantage of.

Focusing on the theological and ideological bases of al-Qa'ida's political tactics, one should note that the word 'ideology' is considered here to refer to a set of ideas in which individuals and groups believe and act on accordingly. In the case of al-Qa'ida, these ideas have grown considerably in number and have been sent out to reach followers, as well as enemies, across the globe, thanks to technology. In this book, many of al-Qa'ida's theological and ideological ideas have been discussed in detail. Below are only a few of the many key ideas utilized by al-Qa'ida for its own political gain.

Hakimiya (**Sovereignty**)

This concept lies at the heart of the ideology and theology of all militant organizations, including al-Qa'ida and its associated groups. The word *hakimiya* is derived from the Qur'anic word *hukm* (to govern and to rule). When the Kharijis turned against the authority of the caliphate (the state), led by 'Uthman ibn 'Affan, the third caliph, they tried to justify their violence by claiming that there is "no rule but God's rule." They besieged the caliph in his house for twelve days and finally killed him in cold blood. Later, the Kharijis used the same phrase and idea when they rebelled against 'Ali ibn Abi Talib, the fourth caliph, ultimately killing him too. Resembling the Kharijis of the past, al-Qa'ida has sought to justify its violence against the authorities of modern states. Ayman al-Zawahiri, al-Qa'ida's then second-in-command, adopted the Kharijis' rebellious ideals, and planned, along with other jihadist groups, the assassination of Egypt's President Sadat in 1981. Thus, al-Qa'ida and its associated groups are the Kharijis of our era.

As noted above, the term *hakimiya* was derived from the Qur'anic word *hukm* by the Egyptian thinker Sayyid Qutb (1906–66), who outlined and developed this concept in his writing. Militants, including al-Qa'ida, believe that *hakimiya* simply means 'God's rule.' However, this is a loose translation, as it actually means 'government by God.' They also try to shape their perception of the term along Qutb's comprehensive lines. However, not only are all the issues of politics too complex to be simplified in this manner, but the concept of 'government by God', or even 'God's rule,' has been totally misinterpreted. None of this can be seen in Qutb's concept of *hakimiya* and the state. The extremists' analyses fail to pay adequate attention to language, philosophy of law, and sociopolitical context.[1] Al-Qa'ida's understanding of government in Islam to mean 'government by God' or 'God's rule,' in Qutb's view, is but 'theocracy,' a form of governance in its entirety. Based on several Qur'anic verses (2:229; 4:59), Qutb outlined that "government in Islam is limited to regulations laid down in the Qur'an and Sunna, the primary sources of shari'a law."[2] Consequently, the government's subjection to this law does not imply theocracy or autocracy, but rather leads to democracy in its widest sense. In the view of many scholars of political theory, "limitation of governmental power in regulating the affairs of the people to the law is the central principle of constitutional rule."[3] To communicate this constitutional rule, Qutb described the limitation of governmental power in one word: *hakimiya* (sovereignty).

The concept of *hakimiya* is very important to all militants, including al-Qa'ida and its associated groups. This concept is also dangerous when misunderstood, as it may be used by the jihadists to justify their violence and terrorism. In this regard, this concept has been discussed from different perspectives in the author's previous publications. However, for further detailed consideration of this subject and related issues—for example, al-Qaʻidaʼs view on the concept of *hakimiya*, how they use this concept to intentionally deceive their followers, the difference between al-Qaʻidaʼs view and Qutbʼs view, and how Qutb observes *hakimiya* as a central principle for constitutional rule—one should consult the authorʼs recent article: "The Voice of Democratism in Sayyid Qutbʼs Response to Violence and Terrorism," *Islam and Christian–Muslim Relations* 20 (3) (2009): 315–32.

Al-Walaʼ wa-l-baraʼ (Loyalty and Disloyalty)

Both loyalty and disloyalty are closely linked to the concept of *hakimiya*. Thus, misunderstanding *hakimiya* may lead to disloyalty and violence against states and governments. Al-Qaʻida has borrowed this idea from medieval Islamic movements. The Kharijis, for instance, were the first Islamic group in the history of Islam to rebel against a legitimate Islamic government. They also were the first group to change a legitimate government by force. Viewed in relation to context of this historical example, al-Qaʻida can be seen as a Khariji movement, and its leadership, namely Bin Laden and al-Zawahiri and their affiliates, as Kharijis, who have rebelled not only against legitimate states, but also against religious authorities and communities, killing political and religious leaders, and innocent civilians, Muslims and non-Muslims alike. Promoting *al-walaʼ wa-l-baraʼ* (loyalty and disloyalty), al-Qaʻidaʼs top general and ideologue, Ayman al-Zawahiri, released a book entitled *al-Walaʼ wa-l-baraʼ* in 2002. In this book, al-Zawahiri took his understanding of *hakimiya* as a basis by which to divide the world into two camps: the true Muslims (that is, al-Qaʻida and its supporters and sympathizers); and the rest of the world (Muslims and non-Muslims who oppose al-Qaʻida). It is highly significant to note that al-Qaʻidaʼs ideologues usually employ words such as 'Muslims' and 'Islam' without providing clear definitions for them, in order to deceive their audiences. Thus, when al-Qaʻida and similar militant groups use the phrase 'true Muslims,' they are only referring to themselves. Al-Qaʻida sees the world in black and white: those who are with them and those who are against them. According to al-Qaʻida, the phrase 'true Muslims' means that all of its followers, individuals and groups, are brothers, who submit to *hakimiya* and connect to one another through the ties of faith and common aims and objectives. Al-Qaʻida considers loyalty to be "one of the pillars of the Islamic creed and one of the conditions for belief." Thus, anyone who is disloyal to al-Qaʻida is an infidel *(kafir)*, and loyalty to al-Qaʻida implies disloyalty to the all others and the imperative to undertake jihad against them. The mainstream Islamic view considers all human beings to be God's creatures and therefore deserving of respect. The differences between them should not lead to, but rather be a reason and catalyst for them to get to know each other. In Islam, there is no 'us versus them.' Indeed, Islam promotes and encourages a multicultural and multi-religious society, as outlined by the Prophet of Islam in the well-known Constitution of Medina.

Jihad

This book is not the first, nor will it be the last, to point out that 'holy war' is a mistranslation of the concept of jihad. The Arabic words for 'war' and 'fight' that do appear in the Qur'an are *harb* and *qital* respectively; however, they are never qualified by the adjective 'holy.' In mainstream Islamic thought, the word jihad means 'struggle' or 'striving,' and there are related words derived from the same trilateral root consonants *j-h-d*. It is sometimes matched with the phrase *fi sabil Allah* ('in the path of God'). It is because of this phrase that authors often refer to jihad as a 'holy war,' a view that gives credence to al-Qaʻida's interpretation of jihad. However, the phrase *fi sabil Allah* never meant 'holy' as such. In Islam, working, learning, studying, and researching all are *fi sabil Allah*. Parents' care of their offspring is *fi sabil Allah*; caring for one's aged parents, for Muslims and non-Muslims alike, is *fi sabil Allah*; caring for one's neighbors, both Muslim and non-Muslim, is also *fi sabil Allah*; and sharing, caring, and carrying out good deeds in general are all considered *fi sabil Allah*. Thus, aligning this phrase with the word 'jihad' is meant to promote the goodness of human nature, to elevate good above evil, and strengthen and encourage the human spirit to exert effort toward doing good deeds for the benefit of humanity. Etymologically, the word 'jihad' relates to the exertion of effort. This exertion of effort does not inherently refer to armed conflicts or hostilities; rather, it might include physical fighting as one of a number of different forms of exertion. This final perspective does refer to 'war,' but regardless, Islam does not participate in war without regulations and qualifications, as detailed in Chapter 5 of this book.

In opposition to the mainstream view of jihad is the militant view adopted by al-Qaʻida and its associated groups. To them, jihad means only war. They believe jihad is an obligatory act, like praying and fasting, in which all Muslims must participate. As they have divided the world into two camps—true Muslims (al-Qaʻida and its supporters) and the rest of the world—they believe in the perpetual struggle of jihad against the rest of the world. They believe in jihad as an end in itself, and that jihad will continue forever. To promote this view, they claim militarized jihad as the highest form of jihad and that it should be undertaken against all enemies of Islam. These enemies include the untrue Muslims (that is, Muslims other than al-Qaʻida and its supporters and sympathizers), the infidels, and polytheists, as well as their supporters in general. They also believe that the aim of their jihad is to achieve Muslim (meaning 'true Muslims,' that is, al-Qaʻida and similar groups) dominance over others. Since al-Qaʻida claims that permission from one's parents or other relatives to join al-Qaʻida's jihad is not required, many parents were not aware of their children's involvement with al-Qaʻida until they learned about them through the media. As detailed in this book, al-Qaʻida's view of jihad is illegitimate in the eyes of Islamic law and does not carry any religious merit.

Murji'is (Postponers)

In al-Qaʻida's view, Muslims who do not support al-Qaʻida's activity in any shape or form are "Murji'is of the Epoch" (delayers or postponers). The Murji'is were medieval groups that originally emerged from the Kharijis. Al-Qaʻida means that the Muslims of the epoch who do not support al-Qaʻida are not true Muslims; even if they do not reject shariʻa, they work to delay its application. To al-Qaʻida, all Muslim regimes are Murji'is or Rafidis that must be fought against and destroyed.

Rafidis (Rejectionists)

This is another of those labels with which al-Qaʻida charges those who they deem to be untrue Muslims. The Rafidis were one of the Khariji splinter groups. Al-Qaʻida is of the view that rejectionists are untrue Muslims because they reject al-Qaʻida's jihad and its effort to restore rule by shariʻa. Thus, al-Qaʻida considers Rafidis to be similar to Murji'is, who must be dealt with accordingly.

Declaration of War

In Islam, a declaration of war must be a state decision. Nowhere in Islamic law does it permit the declaration of war on a state by a non-state actor. Al-Qaʻida, however, seeks to justify its terrorist attacks against states. Although al-Qa'ida's theoreticians have admitted to the shari'a's ruling that the "declaration of war is not the responsibility of individuals or any organization other than the state," they argue that war can be declared only by the state that starts the war. In effect, al-Qa'ida views its terrorist acts as responses to those states that have declared war against Muslims and Islam. They argue that the U.S. had already started the war against Iraq in the early 1990s and "attacked Sudan with no declaration of war." Further, the U.S. supports Israel in Palestine, Russia in Chechnya, and India in Kashmir. On this account, the U.S. is "the aggressor" and Muslims are the "victims."[4] This is the theme and basis of their argument in attempting to justify the September 11 terrorist attacks. Focusing on Bin Laden, al-Qa'ida's theoreticians have also admitted that "even if we accept that Bin Laden had no authority to declare war against America, this declaration was already there."[5] Al-Qa'ida wrote a number of books attempting to justify its terrorist acts of September 11 against the U.S., but nothing written in these books possesses any merit or carries religious weight, as detailed in Chapter 5 of this book.

Al-Tatarrus (**Shield**)

This concept is extremely important to al-Qa'ida and its associated groups. Terrorists usually undertake their actions with the idea of *al-tatarrus* in mind. The jihadists practiced this idea for decades in the Middle East, and then al-Zawahiri took it with him to Afghanistan and then to al-Qa'ida. The concept relates to the security of the state but it has been distorted according to al-Qa'ida's understanding. The concept of *al-tatarrus* deals with the fate of innocent civilians during military engagement between two armies, although with certain conditions, and a precise framework, rules and qualifications, which are detailed in Islamic law and the literature of jurisprudence. The idea of *al-tatarrus* was brought to light by Ibn Taymiya during the time of the Mongol invasion of the Abbasid caliphate. The Mongols were using Muslim civilians as human shields while attacking the Abbasid army. The Abbasid army consequently restrained its counterattack against the Mongols in order to save the lives of those civilians who were seized and used as shields. Muslim jurists, led by Ibn Taymiya, concluded that Muslim civilians who are seized and used as human shield by the enemy's army would be killed anyway during the war, either at the hands of the enemy's army or at the hands of the Muslim army. Therefore, Ibn Taymiya issued a legal ruling that the Muslim army should not hinder its counterattack against the Mongols any longer. Instead, the Muslim army should undertake counteroffensive attacks against the Mongol army to halt its advance toward other towns and cities in order to protect the whole community and free the seized civilians, irrespective of the cost. If there is no other device (for example, negotiations or truce) to stop the enemy's advance and to save the lives of those in the shield, then the Muslim army should undertake a counterattack against the enemy's army, irrespective of whether those in the shield are killed.

In this regard, the idea of *al-tatarrus* is meant only for a specific circumstance of war between two armies. As detailed in Chapter 6, al-Qa'ida not only upturned the rules that govern the concept of *al-tatarrus*, but also expanded the concept under flimsy pretexts and claims, including the argument that Islam is under attack. In other words, the *al-tatarrus* idea, which is known to have precise rules and conditions in Islamic law and jurisprudence, became yet another concept to be reinterpreted and exploited by al-Qa'ida and its associated groups. Instead of heeding those specific conditions, al-Qa'ida has used the concept to justify its murder of civilians in hotels and trains. In Islamic law, *al-tatarrus* deals specifically with Muslim civilians seized and used as human shields by the enemy's army, but al-Qa'ida has come to kill Muslims and non-Muslims alike, without considering the attendant rules or qualifications. The only body permitted to deal with seized Muslims is the Muslim state's army, but al-Qa'ida is not a state. By all definitions, al-Qa'ida is a terrorist group and its operatives are terrorists. In addition, al-Qa'ida's operatives undertake their terrorist attacks and shield themselves among Muslim civilians. While the concept of *al-tatarrus* relates to the enemy army's use of Muslim civilians as shields, al-Qa'ida itself has come to use Muslim civilians as a shield. In so doing, al-Qa'ida has replaced the enemy in this framework with itself. Thus, al-Qa'ida upturned the well-known judicial principles underlying *al-tatarrus* and perverted its notion, rules, and qualifications. Al-Qa'ida has killed innocent civilians, Muslims and non-Muslims, destroyed the properties and wealth of the protected, and murdered people based on nationality, race, and color.

La Wilaya li-l-Asir (No Authority for the Captive)

Al-Qa'ida believes that the captive's view has no legal effect. In its writings, al-Qa'ida promotes this idea in an attempt to limit and contain the impact of the critical views of former jihadists who renounced violence and criticized al-Qa'ida's ideas and actions. Al-Qa'ida's view possesses no merit or religious weight in this regard. The principle that the captive's views are not legitimate or to be heeded is limited to matters that cannot be established by any source other than the captive's word, such as a captive's admission of his actions or crimes. If there is no other source to verify this statement, the shari'a stipulates that such a statement has no value in Islamic law, because it could be argued that the captive was pressured to give such a statement. However, if the matters can be verified by sources other than the captive, the views expressed by the captive are recognized by the shari'a. Hence, the views expressed by Dr. Fadl while in captivity against al-Qa'ida's ideology and strategy have their legal merit, because his ideas can be verified through sources other than his writings.

Al-Bay'a (Allegiance)

Allegiance is important to al-Qa'ida's ideology. Al-Qa'ida believes that allegiance or a pledge of obedience must be given to the leader (amir) of the organization. Obedience in this context is complete and blind obedience. Once the pledge is given, it cannot be broken. Anyone who breaks the pledge is guilty of a grave sin, considered a non-believer, and subjected to the leader's verdict against him. In the process of the establishment of al-Qa'ida, some members asked for a written program that would define the principles of al-Qa'ida's existence and the aims upon which Bin Laden would receive allegiance. Bin Laden refused to be bound by any such program, in order to free himself of any associated constraints on acting as he pleased.

In the mainstream Islamic view, the permissibility of the pledge is subject to the majority of those who represent a society's thinkers and intellectuals (that is, experts, scholars, jurists, rulers of the provinces in the state). In the case of al-Qa'ida, Bin Laden's leadership does not represent the majority of the Muslim community or its intellectual or scholarly leaders. Thus, he has no authority to demand allegiance (bay'a) to himself or his cause from anyone.

Takfir (Charging Others with Unbelief)

Al-Qa'ida's action of charging others with unbelief is referred to as takfir. This is a very serious decision and can lead to violence and terrorism. Al-Qa'ida, however, has regularly applied this term to Muslims, both rulers and ruled, who oppose al-Qa'ida's ideas and activity. By labeling Muslims with such a term, al-Qa'ida views them as its "nearest enemies." For al-Qa'ida, the nearest enemies are these accused Muslims, while the "further enemy" is the west. In the mainstream Islamic view, Muslims are forbidden to charge others with unbelief. If a Muslim does so, that individual is seen as casting infidelity upon him- or herself.

Al-Hijra (**Migration**)

This is another of the important principles within al-Qa'ida's ideology. In promoting this idea, al-Qa'ida is tactically attempting to maintain its growth. To promote migration, al-Qa'ida links it to jihad, as al-Qa'ida considers jihad an obligatory and religious duty that every Muslim must fulfill. Thus, migration to fulfill the jihad duty becomes obligatory also. Hence, al-Qa'ida describes migration as leaving one's home, family, country, school, and job, for the sake of God, with the intention of participating in jihad wherever the fight might be. The migrants do not require permission from their families to migrate and undertake jihad. Advocating this idea, al-Qa'ida promotes the theme that people should migrate from worldly inclinations toward heavenly goals: "migration with the intention of jihad is the road to heaven." One who dies during migration to jihad is considered a martyr. Aiming to recruit youths, al-Qa'ida declares that those who migrate in order to participate in jihad can achieve this heavenly goal and obtain beautiful virgins through suicide bombings.

Outlined above are some of the key ideas upon which al-Qa'ida bases its ideology. These and other ideas detailed in this book confirm that al-Qa'ida promotes its doctrinal propriety as a matter of core belief. In so doing, al-Qa'ida is well prepared in its use of books, pamphlets, the Internet, and other means, to promote its ideas, with the aim of maintaining its continued expansion and forging connections with followers across borders.

With regard to the growth of radicalism and jihadism, future research should focus on those jihadist ideological and doctrinal narratives that govern the relations between Muslims and non-Muslims. These issues might include the jihadists' charging Muslims and regimes with unbelief (*takfir*), their defense of certain categories of *takfir*, their defense of the doctrine and application of loyalty and disloyalty (*al-wala' wa-l-bara'*), and their defense of the doctrinal concept of *hakimiya* (sovereignty).

To maintain its growth, al-Qaʻida focuses its writings on reaching broader Muslim audiences, by addressing doctrinal issues such as those key issues outlined above. These issues are not confined to the attention of jihadists as such, but are shared by a much broader community. However, on this subject it is difficult to believe that everyone in the community has the ability to distinguish between truth and falsehood, or see through the distortions of al-Qaʻida's perverted narratives.

As this book attests, the style of al-Qaʻida's writings makes the case for its ideology within the context of the intellectual framework that has come to be known as Salafism. It is a large and growing movement that, although pietistic in focus, shares much with the rejectionist worldview of the jihadists, and much of its antipathy toward communication and contact with non-Salafists and non-Muslims.

As detailed in this book, the most effective arguments against some of jihadism's doctrinal narratives are likely to come from within the jihadist movement itself. The impact of the debate between al-Qaʻida's ideologue Ayman al-Zawahiri and his former jihad leader Dr. Fadl is merely one example. Their debate focused mainly on the contest over greater Islamic authenticity. Here, the impact of this debate led to the departure of large and important jihadist factions from the al-Qaʻida network, but the contributions from outside jihadist circles have a limited effect. Thus, it is imperative for research to focus closely on the theological and ideological starting points of jihadism, in order to formulate an effective counterargument to at least contain jihadism's sympathizers who are still growing in number throughout the Middle East, and increasing their efforts to define their identity in western countries.

Focusing on jihadist ideology and highlighting its deficiencies and illegitimacy will lead to a better understanding of the nature and complexity of the conflict. It will also provide better protection for the broader community of Muslim youth against the impact of jihadist ideological propaganda. Further, it will offer a better understanding of our position and where best we can identify our allies. The phenomenon of jihadism will be eradicated at its roots through defining the nature of the conflict, and providing solid counterarguments and the necessary support to the mainstream Islamic community in its struggle against it.

Notes

Notes to the Introduction

1   See Jason Burke, *Al-Qaeda: Casting a Shadow of Terror* (London and New York: I.B. Tauris, 2003); Rohan Gunaratna, *Inside Al Qaeda: Global Network of Terror* (New York: Berkley Books, 2002–2003); Peter Bergen, *Inside the Secret World of Osama Bin Laden* (London: Weidenfeld and Nicolson, 2001).

2   Marc Sageman, *Leaderless Jihad: Terror Networks in the Twenty-first Century* (Philadelphia: University of Pennsylvania Press, 2008).

3   Tom Quiggin, "Understanding al-Qaeda's Ideology for Counter-Narrative Work," *Perspectives on Terrorism* 3 (2) (August 2009): 18–24, esp. 20–22.

4   See Burke, *Al-Qaeda*, 24–27.

5   Montasser al-Zayyat, *The Road to al-Qaeda: The Story of Bin Laden's Right-Hand Man* (London: Pluto Press, 2004), 20–22.

6   Jonathan Paris, "A Framework for Understanding Radical Islam's Challenge to European Governments," *Transatlantic Institute*, 3 May 2007, 5–7, http://www.transatlanticinstitute.org/html/pu_articles.html?id=336.

Notes to Chapter 1: Islamic Fundamentalism

1   In the context of politics, the word 'Left' refers to those individuals or groups (that is, political organizations) that hold more socialistic views than those of the 'Right.' In this sense, the word 'Left' refers to the substance of the French Revolution and the rights of workers or laborers. During the seating of the French National Assembly in 1789, the aristocrats or the upper class (that is, nobles), who perhaps own and control most of the society's wealth and advocate government by an

aristocracy, took their seats on the president's 'Right' and left the lower class to sit on the 'Left.' It is from here that the concepts for the words 'Left' and 'Right' have originated.

2   See Qur'an 56:27–56.

3   Muhammad Umara, *al-Usuliya bayn al-gharb wa-l-Islam* (Cairo: Dar al-Shuruq, 2006), 5–6.

4   M. Lois Gurel, "Hate," *The World Book Encyclopaedia* (1990), vol. 9, 87–88.

5   James Barr, *Fundamentalism* (London: Trinity Pr Intl, 1981), 1–2.

6   Michael O. Emerson and David Hartman, "The Rise of Religious Fundamentalism," *Annual Review of Sociology* 32 (August 2006): 127–44, esp. 127–29.

7   Umara, *al-Usuliya*, 7.

8   For further details, see Stewart Grant Cole, *The History of Fundamentalism* (New York: Greenwood, 1931); Norman Furniss, *The Fundamentalist Controversy 1918–1931* (New Haven, CT: Yale University Press, 1954); Douglas Johnson, "The Word Fundamentalism," *The Christian Graduate*, March 1955, 22 and ff; Frederick M. Denny, ed., *An Introduction to Islam* (Colorado: University of Colorado Press, 1994), 345; Hasan Hanafi, *al-Harakat al-diniya al-mu'asira* (Cairo: Maktabat Madbuli, 1988), 9; Youssef Choueiri, *Islamic Fundamentalism* (London: Pinter, 1990), 9; Moojan Momen, "Fundamentalism and Liberalism," *Baha'i Studies Review* 2 (1) (1992), http://bahai-library.com/articles/momen.fundamentalism.html.

9   Robert Young, "Fundamentalism and Terrorism," *The Human Nature Review* (25 September 2001), 1–17, esp. 17.

10 Emerson and Hartman, "The Rise of Religious Fundamentalism," esp. 129–30.

11 Susan Harding, "Representing Fundamentalism," *Social Research* 58 (2) (Summer 1991): 373–74.

12 'Abd al-'Azim Ramadan, "Fundamentalist Influence in Egypt," in M. Marty and R. Scott, eds., *Fundamentalisms and the State* (Chicago: University of Chicago Press, 1993), 152–64, cf. 153.

13 Joachim Wach, *Types of Religious Experience* (Chicago: University of Chicago Press, 1951), 48–57.

14 Musa Zayd al-Kilani, *al-Harakat al-islamiya* (Beirut: al-Risala, 1995, 2nd ed.), 10.

15 Hans Wehr, *Arabic English Dictionary*, J. Milton Cowan, ed. (New York: Ithaca, 1960), 19; also see Jamal al-Din ibn Manzur, *Lisan al-'Arab* (Beirut: Dar Sadr, 1994), vol. 11, 16–17.

16   Sayyid Qutb, *Nahwa mujtama' islami* (Cairo: Dar al-Shuruq, 1993), 9, 81; Sayyid Qutb, *Fi zilal al-Qur'an* (Cairo: Dar al-Shuruq, 1992), vol. 2, 924–25; Sayyid Qutb, *al-'Adala al-ijtima'iya fi-l-Islam* (Cairo: Dar al-Shuruq, 9th ed., 1983), 76.

17   Sayed Khatab and Gary Bouma, *Democracy in Islam* (London: Routledge, 2007), 7–15.

18   Qutb, *Zilal*, vol. 2, 1083–84; *al-'Adala*, 7–8, 11, 16–18, 78.

19   Hanafi, *al-Harakat al-diniya*, 9.

20   Umara, *al-Usuliya*, 9.

21   Abu al-Hasan al-Bisri and Muhammad ibn 'Ali ibn al-Tayyib (d. 436/1057), *Sharh al-'umad* (Medina: Maktabat al-'Ulum wa-l-Hikam, 1990, 1st ed), vol. 1, 15, 18 ,19.

22   Hasan al-Banna, *Majmu'at rasa'il Hasan al-Banna* (Cairo: Dar al-Tawzi' wa-l-Nashr, 1992), 37–39.

23   Ibn Manzur, *Lisan al-'Arab*, vol. 9, 85, 91, 158.

24   *The Glorious Qur'an*, trans. Marmaduke Pickthall (Delhi: Mohindra Offset Press, 1979), 1–60, esp. 58–60 and 314–19, esp. 319.

25   al-Bisri, *Sharh al-'umad*, vol. 1,133–37; Qutb, *Zilal*, vol. 4, 2314.

26   William Shepard, *Sayyid Qutb and Islamic Activism: A Translation and Critical Analysis of Social Justice in Islam* (Leiden: E.J. Brill, 1996), xii–xiv.

27   Qutb, *al-'Adala al-ijtima'iya fi-l-Islam*, 197.

28   C.G. Weeramantry, *Islamic Jurisprudence: An International Perspective* (Baskingstoke, UK: Macmillan Press, 1988), 1. Weeramantry is professor of law, Monash University, Australia, and he is currently chief judge at the International Court in Swaziland. He was also the chief judge and vice-president of the Republic of India.

29   Imam 'Abd al-Qadir ibn Tahir ibn Muhammad al-Baghdadi (known as al-Khatib al-Baghdadi, d. 1071), *al-Kifaya fi 'ilm al-riwaya* (Hyderabad: n.p., 1357/1938), 411.

30   Sami Ahmad al-Shami, *Tahdhib hilyat al-awliya' wa tabaqat al-asfiya li Abi Na'im al-Asbahani: Ahmad ibn 'Abdullah* (Beirut: al-Maktab al-Islami li-l-Tiba'a wa-l-Nashr, 1998); Ibn Taymiya, *al-Fatawa al-kubra* (Beirut: Dar al-Kutub al-'Ilmiya, n.d.), 10:39.

31   Ibn 'Abd al-Barr al-Qurtubi, *Mukhtasar jami' bayan al-'ilm wa fadlih.* Summarized by Ahmad ibn 'Umar al-Mahamasani, edited by Muhammad al-Mar'ashli (Beirut: Dar al-Nafa'is, n.d.), 1:23 ff.

32   http://www.newworldpeace.com/Islam.html

33   Richard Nixon, *Victory without War* (New York: Simon and Schuster, 1999), 293–94

34   See C.E. Vaughan, *Studies in the History of Political Philosophy before and after Rousseau*, A.G. Little, ed. (Manchester: Manchester University Press, 1925), vol. 1.

35   Usama Salama, "al-Ikhwan al-Muslimun," *Rose el-Youssef*, no. 3418, 13 December 1993, 49–51, see 3, 8, 11, 14; Hasan Amir, "'Abd al-Nasir kan za'im sufi," *Rose el-Youssef*, no. 3427, 14 February 1994, 12–13, see 15, 26–27, 28, 40.

36   Denny, *An Introduction to Islam*, 346.

37   Charles Hutzler, "Bombing in China Kills 16 Police," *Daily Herald*, 5 August 2008.

38   Mustafa Muhammad al-Shak'a, *Islam bila madhahib* (Cairo: al-Dar al-Misriya, 1991), 491–92.

39   'Abd al-Rahman ibn Hasan ibn Muhammad ibn Abd al-Wahhab, *Qurrat 'uyun al-muwahhidin* (Lahore: Ansar al-Sunna al-Muhammadiya, n.d.), 13–16. The author is the grandson of Ibn 'Abd al-Wahhab.

40   Fazlur Rahman, *Islam and Modernity: The Transformation of an Intellectual Tradition* (Chicago: University of Chicago Press, 1980), 196–201.

41   John O. Voll, "Sudanese Mahdi," *International Journal of Middle East Studies* 10 (1979): 145–66.

42   Muhammad 'Abduh, *Risalat al-tawhid* (Cairo: Matba'at 'Ali Subayh, 1956), 6–19, 80–84; Jamal al-Din al-Afghani and Muhammad 'Abduh, *al-'Urwa al-wuthqa* (Cairo: Dar al-'Arab, 1957), 23–25, 142–52.

43   Ali Rahnema, *The Pioneers of Islamic Revival* (Kuala Lumpur: S. Abd al-Majid and Co. Publishing Division, 1995), 7.

44   Robert Lee, *Overcoming Tradition and Modernity: The Search for Islamic Authenticity* (Boulder, CO: Westview Press, 1997), 84.

45   Sayyid Qutb, *Ma'alim fi-l-tariq* (Cairo: Dar al-Shuruq, 1993), 135–48; al-Banna, *Rasa'il*, 256–60; al-Kilani, *al-Harakat*, 63, 9, 160, 168, 217; Hanafi, *al-Harakat al-diniya al-mu'asira*, 11; Richard P. Mitchell, *The Society of the Muslim Brothers* (Oxford: Oxford University Press, 1993), xv–xviii.

46   See Sayed Khatab, *The Power of Sovereignty: The Political and Ideological Philosophy of Sayyid Qutb* (London and New York: Routledge, 2006), 8–44, esp. 27–33.

47   Weeramantry, *Islamic Jurisprudence*, 1–5.

48   Qutb, *al-'Adala*, 182.

49 Peter Gran, "Political Economy as a Paradigm for the Study of Islamic History," *International Journal of Middle East Studies* 11 (1980): 522.

50 Sayyid Qutb, *al-Islam wa mushkilat al-hadara* (Cairo: Dar al-Shuruq, 1983), 21–23, 49–50, 104–106.

51 Qutb, *al-Islam wa mushkilat al-hadara*, 103–104.

52 Martin Woollacott, "The Cold War is Long Over," *The Guardian*, 21 December 2001.

53 Nixon, *Victory without War*, 293.

54 Burke, *Al-Qaeda*, 4–5.

55 Peter Lentini, "Antipodal Terrorists? Accounting for Differences in Australian and 'Global' Neo-Jihadists," in R. Devetak and C.W. Hughes, eds., *The Globalization of Political Violence: Globalization's Shadow* (London: Routledge, 2008), 181–202.

56 Burke, *Al-Qaeda*, 6.

Notes to Chapter 2: The Origins of Fundamentalism

1 Abu Bakr Naji, *Idarat al-tawahhush* (n.p.: Centre of Islamic Studies and Research, n.d.), 34.

2 Taha Hussein, *al-Fitna al-kubra* (Cairo: Dar al-Maʿarif, 1959), 47–49.

3 Abu al-Fath Muhammad al-Shahrastani, *al-Milal wa-l-nihal*, edited by Muhammad S. al-Kilani (Cairo and Beirut: Dar Saʿb, 1986), vol. 1, 114.

4 Abu Jaʿfar Muhammad ibn Jarir al-Tabari (d. 922), *Tarikh al-umam wa-l-muluk* (Beirut: Dar al-Kutub al-ʿIlmiya, 1997), vol. 3, 101–102.

5 al-Shahrastani, *al-Milal wa-l-nihal*, vol. 1, 116ff.

6 Bernard Lewis, *The Arabs in History* (Oxford: Oxford University Press, 2002), 63.

7 Ahmad ibn Muhammad ibn ʿAbd Rabbu al-Andalusi (d. 328/940), *al-ʿIqd al-farid*, edited by Ahmad Amin, Ibrahim al-Ibyari, and Abd al-Salam Harun. Introduction by ʿUmar ʿAbd al-Salam al-Tadmuri (Beirut: Dar al-Kitab al-ʿArabi, n.d.), vol. 2, 382–88.

8 ʿAbd al-Rahman ibn Khaldun (d. 808/1406), *Tarikh Ibn Khaldun* (Beirut: al-Aʿlami, 1971, 7 vols.), vol. 2, 178.

9 al-Tabari, *Tarikh al-umam wa-l-muluk*, vol. 3, 110.

10 Abu al-Fidaʾ ibn Kathir, *al-Bidaya wa-l-nihaya* (Cairo: al-Rayyan, 1st ed., 1988), vol. 4, part 1, 295.

11 al-Shahrastani, *al-Milal wa-l-nihal*, vol. 1, 118–20, esp. 120.

12 al-Tabari, *Tarikh al-umam wa-l-muluk*, vol. 3, 110, 156, 159, 169.

13   Julius Wellhausen, *The Religio-Political Factions in Early Islam*, edited by R.C. Costle, trans. R.C. Costle and S.M. Walzer (Amsterdam: North-Holland Publishing Company, 1975), vol. 3, 39.

14   Lewis, *The Arabs in History*, 76.

15   Imam 'Abd al-Qahir ibn Tahir al-Baghdadi (d. 1037), *al-Farq bayn al-firaq* (Cairo: Dar al-Kutub, 3rd ed., 2005), 49.

16   al-Shahrastani, *al-Milal wa-l-nihal*, vol. 1, 114–25.

17   Ibn 'Abd Rabbuh al-Andalusi, *al-'Iqd al-farid*, vol. 2, 382–91.

18   al-Baghdadi, *al-Farq bayn al-firaq*, 18–20.

19   Abu Muhammad 'Asim al-Maqdisi, *Imta' al-nazar fi kashf shubuhat Murji'at al-'asr* (n.p.: Minbar al-Tawhid wa-l-Jihad, 1999, 2nd ed.), 5–9, esp. 9.

20   Ibn Khaldun, *Tarikh Ibn Khaldun*, vol. 3, 18–25.

21   al-Baghdadi, *al-Farq bayn al-firaq*, 56.

22   Shawqi Dayf, *al-'Asr al-islami* (Cairo: Dar al-Ma'arif, n.d., 9th ed.), 187.

23   Wellhausen, *Religio-political Factions*, vol. 3, 20–21.

24   Ibn Kathir, *al-Bidaya wa-l-nihaya*, vol. 4, part 1, 336.

25   Wellhausen, *Religio-political Factions*, vol. 3, 69–70.

26   Ayman al-Zawahiri, *al-Tabri'a: risala fi tabri'at ummat al-qalam wa-l-sayf min manqasat tuhmat al-khawr wa-l-da'f* (n.p.: al-Sahab Foundation for Islamic Media Publications, 2008), 27–32.

27   al-Zawahiri, *al-Tabri'a*, 141–46.

28   See al-Zawahiri, *al-Tabri'a*, 27–32, 52–58, 149, 179; 'Abdullah 'Azzam, *Muqaddima fi-l-hijra wa-l-i'dad* (n.p.: Minbar al-Tawhid wa-l-Jihad, n.d.), 26–29; compare with al-Shahrastani, *al-Milal wa-l-nihal*, vol. 1, 135–36.

29   Ibn Khaldun, *Tarikh Ibn Khaldun*, vol. 2, 178.

30   J.C. Wilkinson, "The Origin of the Omani State," in Derek Hopwood, ed., *The Arabian Peninsula: Society and Politics* (London: Allen and Unwin, 1972), 67.

31   Wilkinson, "The Origin of the Omani State," 85, 87.

32   'Azzam, *Muqaddimah fi-l-hijra*, 26–29.

33   al-Zawahiri, *al-Tabri'a*, 52–58.

34   Interview by the author with Karam Zuhdi, leader of al-Jam'a al-Islamiya, Egypt, December 2006.

35   al-Shahrastani, *al-Milal wa-l-nihal*, vol. 1, 134–35.

36   'Ali Yahya Mu'ammar, *al-'Ibadiya fi mawakib al-tarikh* (Cairo: Dar al-Kitab al-'Arabi, 1964), 93–94.

37   Mu'ammar, *al-'Ibadiya*, 94.

38 Fuad Khuri, *Imams and Emirs: State, Religion and Sects in Islam* (London: Saqi Books, 1990), 120.

39 Valerie J. Hoffman, "The Articulation of Ibadi Identity in Modern Oman and Zanzibar," *The Muslim World* 94 (April 2004): 201–16, esp. 202.

40 Khuri, *Imams and Emirs*, 115.

41 Khuri, *Imams and Emirs*, 115.

42 Khuri, *Imams and Emirs*, 116.

43 'Adil Abu Talib, "al-Shaykh Ahmad bin Hamad al-Khalili, Mufti Oman: al-muqawama bi-l-Iraq Jihad, wa-l-tasamuh fi-l-Islam yantaliq min al-quwwa," *al-Ahram*, issue no. 378, 19 June 2004.

44 For details, see Christopher Melchert, *Ahmad ibn Hanbal* (Oxford: Oneworld, 2006); Abdul Hakim al-Matroudi, *The Hanbali School of Law and Ibn Taymiyyah: Conflict or Conciliation* (London: Routledge, 2006); Roy Jackson, *Fifty Key Figures in Islam* (London: Routledge, 2006), 44–47.

45 Richard C. Martin, *Islamic Studies: A History of Religion Approach* (New Jersey: Prentice Hall Inc., 1996), 113.

46 al-Shahrastani, *al-Milal wa-l-nihal*, vol. 1, 45–49.

47 Muhammad Abu Zahra, *The Four Imams: Their Lives, Works, and Their Schools of Thought* (London: Dar al-Taqwa, 2001), 385.

48 'Abd al-Rahman ibn 'Ali ibn Muhammad ibn al-Jawzi, *Manaqib al-Imam Ahmad ibn Hanbal*, edited by Muhammad Amin (Cairo: Matba'at al-Sa'ada, n.d.), 87–88.

49 al-Tabari, *Tarikh al-umam wa-l-muluk*, vol. 4, 617–20, 626, 650–56.

50 al-Tabari, *Tarikh al-umam wa-l-muluk*, vol. 5, 178.

51 'Abd al-Rahman al-Suyuti, *Husn al-muhadara fi tarikh Misr wa-l-Qahira*, 1st ed., Muhammad Abu al-Fadl Ibrahim, ed. (Cairo: Dar Ihya' al-Kutub al-'Arabiya, 1968), 328–32.

52 Jackson, *Fifty Key Figures*, 44–51.

53 Melchert, *Ahmad ibn Hanbal*, 11–15, esp. 13.

54 Melchert, *Ahmad ibn Hanbal*, 9–15.

55 Abu Zahra, *The Four Imams*, 448.

56 Abu Zahra, *The Four Imams*, 385–500, esp. 455–56.

57 Michael Cook, *Commanding Right and Forbidding Wrong in Islamic Thought* (Cambridge: Cambridge University Press, 2000), 114.

58 Cook, *Commanding Right*, 116.

59 Abu al-Hasan ibn Abi Ya'la, *Tabaqat al-Hanabila*, edited by Muhammad Hamid al-Fiqi (Cairo: al-Sunna al-Muhammadiya, 1952), vol. 2, 44.

60 Ibn Abi Ya'la, *Tabaqat al-Hanabila*, see under "al-Barbahari."

61 'Izz al-Din ibn al-Athir, *al-Kamil fi-l-tarikh* (Beirut: Dar Sadr, 1965), vol. 8, 12, 98, 156.

62 Ibn al-Athir, *al-Kamil fi-l-tarikh*, vol. 7, 114–15.

63 For more detailed information on Hanbali activism, see Ibn al-Athir, *al-Kamil fi-l-tarikh*, vol. 8, 12, 98, 156.

64 Cook, *Commanding Right*, 113.

65 Ibn Kathir, *al-Bidaya wa-l-nihaya*, vol. 7, part 1, 90–91, 94–95, 112, 127.

66 Cook, *Commanding Right*, 148.

67 See Ibn Taymiya, *al-'Ubudiya*, edited by Khalid Abd al-Latif al-'Alami (Beirut: Dar al-Kitab al-'Arabi, 1st ed., 1987), 11–12.

68 *The Holy Bible*, Revised Standard Version (Michigan: Zondervan Publishing House, 1971), Genesis 11:26, 32; 12:4; 13:14; 14:24; 17:17; 23:1; Acts 7:4; also Abu al-Fida' al-Hafiz ibn Kathir, *Qasas al-anbiya'* (Cairo: al-Maktaba al-Tawfiqiya, n.d.), 120–21, 135.

69 Ibn Kathir, *al-Bidaya wa-l-nihaya*, vol. 7, part 1, 233–34.

70 al-Matroudi, *The Hanbali School of Law*, 13–14.

71 al-Matroudi, *The Hanbali School of Law*, 14.

72 Ibn Kathir, *al-Bidaya wa-l-nihaya*, vol. 7, part 2, 141–46, esp. 142.

73 Ibn Rajab, *al-Dhayl 'ala tabaqat al-Hanabila* (Beirut: Dar al-Ma'arif, n.d.), vol. 2, 53–54.

74 Ibn Taymiya, *Public and Private Law in Islam: Public Policy in Islamic Jurisprudence*, trans. Omar A. Farrukh (Beirut: Khayat Books, 1st ed., 1966), 73–79, 99–106, 135–39.

75 Ibn Taymiya, *Public and Private Law*, 135–39.

76 Beverley Milton-Edwards, "Politics and Religion," in Youssef Choueiri, ed., A *Companion of the History of the Middle East*. Malden, MA: Blackwell Pub. Ltd., 2005), 444–46, esp. 445.

77 "Shaykh al-Imam Napoleon Bonaparte," *Rose el-Youssef*, 23 February 1998.

78 Mara'i al-Karmi, *al-Kawakib al-durriya fi manaqib Ibn Taymiya* (Beirut: Dar al-Gharb al-Islami, 1st ed., 1986), 91–99.

79 Ibn Kathir, *al-Bidaya wa-l-nihaya*, vol. 7, part 1, 251.

80 Sayed Khatab and Gary Bouma, *Democracy in Islam* (London and New York: Routledge, 2007), 176–88, 129–64.

81 Ibn Taymiya, *Public and Private Law*, 135–45.

82 Ibn Taymiya, *Public and Private Law*, 135.

83 Ibn Taymiya, *Public and Private Law*, 141.

84   Ibn Taymiya, *Public and Private Law*, 141.

85   Ibn Taymiya, *Public and Private Law*, 142.

86   Ibn Taymiya, *Public and Private Law*, 140.

87   M.J. Ghunaimi, *The Muslim Conception of International Law and the Western Approach* (The Hague: Martinus, 1968), 180–84.

88   Nagendra Singh *India and International Law* (New Delhi: S. Chand and Co., 1973), vol. 1 (part A), 90–91, fn 2; in connection with this see Muhammad ibn 'Umar al-Waqidi, *Kitab al-Maghazi*, ed. Marsden Jones (London: Oxford University Press, 3 vols., 2nd ed., 1966), vol. 3, 989–96.

89   Ibn Taymiya, *Public and Private Law*, 147.

90   Ibn Taymiya, *Public and Private Law*, 147.

91   Ibn Taymiya, *Public and Private Law*, 144.

92   M. Chamberlain, *Knowledge and Social Practice in Medieval Damascus, 1190–1350* (Cambridge: Cambridge University Press, 1994), 78.

93   Ibn Kathir, *al-Bidaya wa-l-nihaya*, vol. 7, part 2, pp. 29, 38–41, 46–47, 89, 97–98, 141–46.

94   About Ibn Muflih, Ibn al-Qayyim said, "There is no one under the dome of the sky more knowledgable about the school of Imam Ahmad than Ibn Muflih." See Muhammad ibn Nasir, *al-Radd al-wafir*, edited by al-Shawish (Beirut: al-Maktab al-Islami, 1980), 65–73. Ibn Khaldun also said that Tamerlane had asked about Ibn Muflih personally. Tamerlane's style was to seek out scholars, so his name may have been mentioned in connection with them in Damascus. See Walter Joseph Fischel (d. 1902), *Ibn Khaldun in Egypt: His Public Functions and His Historical Research, 1382–1406* (Berkeley: University of California Press, 1967), 44 and 46.

95   Ibn Rajab, *al-Dhayl 'ala tabaqat al-Hanabila*, vol. 2, 368–70.

96   BBC Arabic, "al-Jihad wa-l-pitrudular al-Sa'udi," 17 November 2007.

97   BBC Arabic, "al-Jihad wa-l-pitrudular al-Sa'udi."

98   BBC Arabic, "al-Jihad wa-l-pitrudular al-Sa'udi."

99   Albert Hourani, *Arabic Thought in the Liberal Age* (Cambridge: Cambridge University Press, 1983), 37–38.

100   Muhammad ibn 'Abd al-Wahhab, *Kitab al-tawhid* (Riyadh: Dar al-Salam, 1996), 7.

101   'Abd al-Rahman ibn Hasan ibn Muhammad ibn Abd al-Wahhab, *Qurrat'uyun al-muwahhidin* (Lahore: Ansar al-Sunna al-Muhammadiya, n.d.), 15.

102 Ibn 'Abd al-Wahhab, *Kitab al-tawhid*, 9.

103 Daniel Pipes, "The Saga of 'Hempher,' Purported British Spy, an extract from *The Hidden Hand: Middle East Fears of Conspiracy*, pp. 211–12," Daniel Pipes.org, http://www.danielpipes.org/1648/the-saga-of-hempher-purported-british-spy.

104 *Confessions of a British Spy and British Enmity against Islam* (Istanbul: Waqf Ikhlas, 1995), Section 1, Part 3, 4–5.

105 *Confessions of a British Spy*, Section 1, Part 2, 5–6.

106 *Confessions of a British Spy*, Section 1, Part 3, 7–8.

107 *Confessions of a British Spy*, Section 1, Part 1, 3–4.

108 *Confessions of a British Spy*, Section 1, Part 4, 10–11.

109 *Confessions of a British Spy*, Section 1, Part 4, 11.

110 *Confessions of a British Spy*, Section 1, Part 4, 13.

111 *Confessions of a British Spy*, Section 1, Part 4, 16–17.

112 *Confessions of a British Spy*, Section 1, Part 4, 11.

113 *Confessions of a British Spy*, Section 1, Part 4, 17.

114 *Confessions of a British Spy*, Section 1, Part 1, 4.

115 *Confessions of a British Spy*.

116 'Uthman ibn 'Abdullah Ibn Bishr, *'Unwan al-majd fi tarikh al-Najd*, edited by 'Abd al-Rahman ibn 'Abd al-Latif ibn 'Abdullah Al al-Sheikh, 2 vols. (Riyadh: Matba'at al-Malik 'Abd al-'Aziz, 1982), 65.

117 Charles Allen, *God's Terrorists: The Wahhabi Cult and the Hidden Roots of Modern Jiihad* (London: Little Brown, 2006), 48.

118 John O. Voll, "Muhammad Hayat al-Sindi and Muhammad ibn Abd al-Wahhab: An Analysis of Intellectual Groups in Eighteenth-Century Medina," *Bulletin of the School of Oriental and African Studies* 38 (1) (1975): 32–38.

119 Hourani, *Arabic Thought*, 37.

120 Hourani, *Arabic Thought*, 37.

121 Allen, *God's Terrorists*, 50.

122 Hamid Algar, *Wahhabism: A Critical Essay* (New York: Oneonta, 2002), 9–10.

123 For further information about this movement and its thought, see Khatab and Bouma, *Democracy in Islam*, 41–72.

124 Algar, *Wahhabism*, 10.

125 Ibn Kathir, *al-Bidaya wa-l-nihaya*, vol. 2, part 1, 141–42, esp. 142.

126 Isma'il al-Faruqi, trans., *Sheikh Muhammad ibn 'Abd al-Wahhab: kitab al-tawhid* (Delhi: n.p., 1988), xv.

127 George Sanavely Rentz, *The Birth of the Islamic Reform Movement in Saudi Arabia*: *Muhammad Ibn Abd al-Wahhab (1703/4–1792) and the Beginnings of the Unitarian Empire in Arabia* (Riyadh and London: Arabian Publishing, in association with the King Abdulaziz Public Library, 2004), 54–66, esp. 54–57. This is based on Rentz's PhD dissertation, University of Berkeley, California (1947).

128 George Makdisi, "Ibn Taymiya: A Sufi of the Qadiriya Order," *American Journal of Arabic Studies* 1 (1974): 118–29.

129 Ibn Bishr, *'Unwan al-majd*.

130 Abd al-Rahman, *Qurrat 'uyun*, 16.

131 Ibn Bishr, *'Unwan al-majd*, vol. 1, 28.

132 Allen, *God's Terrorists*, 51.

133 Ibn 'Abd al-Wahhab, *Kitab al-tawhid*, 11.

134 In addition to *Kitab al-tawid*, for example, see *Mu'allafat al-Sheikh al-Imam Muhammad ibn 'Abd al-Wahhab* (Riyadh: Jami'at al-Imam Muhammad bin Sa'ud al-Islamiya, 1977).

135 Algar, *Wahhabism*, 18.

136 Shaikh Abdul Aziz ibn 'Abdullah ibn Baz, "Imaam Muhammad Ibn Abdul Wahhab: His Life and Mission," Ahya.org, http://www.ahya.org/amm/modules.php?name=Sections&op=viewarticle&artid=180.

137 Ibn 'Abd al-Wahhab, "Fatawa wa masa'il al-Imam al-Sheikh Muhammad ibn 'Abd al-Wahhab," in *Mu'allafat al-Sheikh al-Imam Muhammad ibn 'Abd al-Wahhab* (Riyadh: Jami'at al-Imam Muhammad bin Saud al-Islamiya, 1977), vol, 3, 25–26.

138 Ibn 'Abd al-Wahhab, *Kitab al-tawhid*, 18.

139 Algar, *Wahhabism*, 19.

140 Allen, *God's Terrorists*, 54.

141 BBC Arabic, "New Restrictions on the Religious Police," 14 July 2007, http://newsforums.bbc.co.uk/ws/thread.jspa?threadID=7082.

142 Rentz, *The Birth of the Islamic Reform Movement in Saudi Arabia*, 51.

143 Ibn Bishr, *'Unwan al-majd*, vol. 1, 42–43.

144 Rentz, *The Birth of the Islamic Reform Movement*, 51.

145 Ahmad ibn al-Zayni Dahlan, *Khulasat al-kalam fi bayan umara' al-Balad al-Haram*. (Cairo: al-Matba'a al-Khayriya, 1888), 232.

146 'Uthman Ibn Sanad, *Tarikh Baghdad* (Bombay: n.p., 1886), 23.

147 Algar, *Wahhabism*, 19.

148 Elizabeth Monroe, *Philby of Arabia* (London: Faber and Faber, 1973), 69–70.

149 Rentz, *The Birth of the Islamic Reform Movement*, 105.

150 Allen, *God's Terrorists*, 59.

151 Ibn Bishr, *'Unwan al-majd*, vol. 1, 43.

152 Algar, *Wahhabism*, 23.

153 Allen, *God's Terrorists*, 61; Natana J. Delong-Bas, *Wahhabi Islam: From Revival and Reform to Global Jihad* (Oxford: Oxford University Press, 2004), 39.

154 Ibn Bishr, *'Unwan al-majd*, vol. 1, 46–47.

155 Rentz, *The Birth of the Islamic Reform Movement*, 116.

156 Louis Alexander Olivier de Corancez, *History of the Wahabis from Their Origin until the End of 1809*, introduced by R.M. Burrell and translated by Eric Tabet (Reading, UK: Garnet, 1995), quoted in Allen, *God's Terrorists*, 61.

157 See Algar, *Wahhabism*, 24–25.

158 Algar, *Wahhabism*, 26.

159 See Algar, *Wahhabism*, 25–26.

160 Hourani, *Arabic Thought*, 38.

161 Allen, *God's Terrorists*, 65–67.

Notes to Chapter 3: From Fundamentalism to Neo-jihadism

1 Dr. Fadl (Sayyid Imam 'Abd al-'Aziz al-Sharif), *Risalat al-'umda fi i'dad al-'udda li-l-jihad fi sabil Allah* (n.p.: n.p., 1988), vol. 2, 284.

2 See Peter Lentini, "Antipodal Terrorists? Accounting for Differences in Australian and 'Global' Neo-Jihadists," in R. Devetak and C.W. Hughes, eds., *The Globalization of Political Violence: Globalization's Shadow* (London: Routledge, 2008), 181–202, esp. 181.

3 Hasan al-Banna, *Majmu'at rasa'il Hasan al-Banna* (Cairo: Dar al-Tawzi' wa-l-Nashr, 1992), 18–30; Sayyid Qutb, *Hadha al-din* (Cairo: Dar al-Shuruq, 1995), 18–28.

4 Fazlur Rahman, *Islam and Modernity: The Transformation of an Intellectual Tradition* (Chicago: University of Chicago Press, 1980), 196–201; Ayman al-Yassini, *Religion and State* (Boulder, CO: Westview Press, 1985), 26–32.

5 John O. Voll, "Sudanese Mahdi," *International Journal of Middle East Studies* 10 (1979): 145–66; Hasan Hanafi, *al-Harakat al-diniya al-mu'asira*; 10; in addition, Fathi Yakan, *al-Islam: fikra, haraka, inqlab*, 11th ed. (Beirut: al-Risala, 1987), 48–58.

6 Ali Rahnema, *The Pioneers of Islamic Revival* (Kuala Lumpur: S. Abd al-Majid and Co. Publishing Division, 1995), 7.

7   Robert Lee, *Overcoming Tradition and Modernity: The Search for Islamic Authenticity* (Boulder, CO: Westview Press, 1997), 84; Rahnema, *Pioneers*, 7.

8   Sayyid Qutb, *Ma'alim fi-l-tariq* (Cairo: Dar al-Shuruq, 1993), 135–48; 'Abd al-Qadir 'Awda, *al-Islam bayna jahl abna'ih wa 'ajz 'ulama'ih* (Beirut: al-Risala, 1985), 38–42; al-Banna, *Rasa'il*, 256–60; Musa Zayd al-Kilani, *al-Harakat al-islamiya* (Beirut: al-Risala, 1995, 2nd ed.), 63, 69, 160, 168, 217; Hasan Hanafi, *al-Harakat al-diniya al-mu'asira*, 11; Richard P. Mitchell, *The Society of the Muslim Brothers* (Oxford: Oxford University Press, 1993), xv–xviii.

9   Muhammad Jalal Kishk, *al-Nasiriyyun qadimun* (Cairo: al-Zahra, 1989), 49, 157–59, 230, 264; *al-Ahram al-iqtisadi*, 8 February 1988, 197; Gudrun Krämer, "The Integration of the Integrists," in Ghassan Salame, ed., *Democracy without Democrats* (London: I.B. Tauris Publishers, 1994), 210; *Rose al-Youssef*, no. 3540, 15 April 1996, 5.

10   al-Banna, *Rasa'il*, 18–30; see also Qutb, *Hadha al-din*, 18–28.

11   Voll, "Sudanese Mahdi."

12   Hasan Hanafi, *al-Harakat al-diniya al-mu'asira*, 12; Fathi Yakan, *al-Islam: fikra, haraka, inqlab*.

13   Abd al-'Azim Ramadan, "Fundamentalist Influence in Egypt," in M. Marty and R. Scott Appleby, eds., *Fundamentalisms and the State* (Chicago: University of Chicago Press, 1993), 152–64.

14   For further details, see Sayed Khatab, *The Power of Sovereignty: The Political and Ideological Philosophy of Sayyid Qutb* (New York: Routledge, 2006), 175–212.

15   Nazih Ayubi, *Political Islam* (New York: Routledge, 1991), 65–66.

16   I have previously dealt with these two conceptions in some detail; see Sayed Khatab, *The Political Thought of Sayyid Qutb: The Theory of Jahiliyyah* (London and New York: Routledge, 2006), 115–71; Khatab, *The Power of Sovereignty*, 7–46.

17   Ayman al-Zawahiri, *al-Hasad al-murr: al-Ikhwan al-Muslimun fi sittina 'aman* (Amman: Dar al-Bayan, 2002), 11–12.

18   al-Zawahiri, *al-Hasad al-murr*, 11–12.

Notes to Chapter 4: Al-Qa'ida

1   Muhammad Ahmad Khalafallah, "al-Sahwa al-islamiya fi Misr," in *al-Harakat al-islamiya al-mu'asira fi-l-watan al-'arabi*, ed. Centre for the Studies of Arab Unity (n.p., August 1988), 88–90.

2 Roy, Olivier, *The Failure of Political Islam*, trans. Carol Volk, Harvard College (reprint by London: I.B. Tauris, 2007), 30, 38, 45.

3 Antoine Basbous, *L'islamisme une révolution avortée* (Paris: Hachette Littératures, 2000), 71, 28, 34.

4 Gilles Kepel, *Jihad: The Trail of Political Islam* (Cambridge, MA: Harvard University Press, 2002), 366–68.

5 Sayed Khatab and Gary Bouma, *Democracy in Islam* (New York: Routledge, 2007), 199–200.

6 Scott Thomas, *The Global Resurgence of Religion and the Transformation of International Relations: The Struggle for the Soul of the Twenty-First Century* (Cambridge: Cambridge University Press, 2005), 1–97.

7 "Riyadh Says Arrests Militants Planning Oil Attacks," *Reuters*, 24 March 2010.

8 Owen Matthews, "Home to Roost," *Newsweek*, 29 March 2010, http://www.newsweek.com/2010/03/28/home-to-roost.html.

9 Robert Michael Gates's speech at the 44th Munich Conference on Security Policy, 10 February 2008, http://www.securityconference.de/konferenzen/rede.php?menu_2008=&menu_konferenzen=&sprache=en&id=216&.

10 Daniel Byman, *The Five Front War: The Best Way to Fight Global Jihad* (New Jersey: John Wiley and Sons, 2008), 20–21.

11 See "Hacking Manual by Jailed Jihadi Appears on the Web," *Terrorism Focus*, 4 March 2008, vol. 5, no. 9; BBC Arabic, 2 July 2006.

12 Stephen Tanner, *Afghanistan: A Military History from Alexander the Great to the Fall of the Taliban* (New York: Da Capo Press, 2002), 281–82.

13 Yossef Bodansky, *Bin Laden: The Man Who Declared War on America* (London: Forum, 1999), 8.

14 Bodansky, *Bin Laden*, 9.

15 See "Invasion of Alexander," http://afghanland.com/history/alexander.html; see Tanner, *Afghanistan*, 50, 104, 226–27, 235, 245, 248.

16 Nabil Sharaf al-Din, *Bin Laden: Taliban: al-Afghan al-Arab and the Global Fundamentalism* (Cairo: Madbouli, 2002), 10–13.

17 George Tenet, *At the Center of the Storm: My Years at the CIA* (New York: Harper Collins Publishers, 2007), 14.

18 Tanner, *Afghanistan*, 273; see also 235, 245, 245, 248.

19 Tanner, *Afghanistan*, 273.

20 During the war in Afghanistan, a number of officers from the ISI's covert action division received training in the U.S., and many of the

CIA's covert action experts were "attached to the ISI" to guide it in its operations against the Soviet troops by using the Afghan Mujahidin. The U.S. provided technical and financial assistance to the Mujahidin in Afghanistan through the ISI. The immense support by Pakistan's ISI for the Taliban continued until Pakistan joined the U.S.-led global War on Terror after September 11.

21   Tanner, *Afghanistan*, 283.

22   Sharaf al-Din, *Bin Laden*, 10–14, 27–28; Bodansky, *Bin Laden*, 13–14.

23   Bin Laden, *Messages to the World: The Statements of Osama Bin Laden*, trans. and ed. Bruce Lawrence (London: Verso, 2005), title page.

24   Dean Schabner and Karen Travers, "Osama bin Laden Killed: 'Justice is Done,' President Says." *ABC World News*, 1 May 2011.

25   Bin Laden, *Messages to the World*, title page.

26   Rohan Gunaratna, *Inside Al Qaeda: Global Network of Terror* (New York: Berkley, 2002–2003), 25–45; Marc Sageman, *Leaderless Jihad: Terror Networks in the Twenty-first Century* (Philadelphia: University of Pennsylvania Press, 2008), 30–37.

27   Bodansky, *Bin Laden*, title page.

28   Roger Hardy, "Grappling with Global Terror Conundrum." *BBC News*, 15 March 2008, http://news.bbc.co.uk/go/pr/fr/-/2/hi/programmes/from_our_own_correspondent/7297139.stm.

29   Salama Yaqoob, "British Islamic Political Radicalism," in Tahir Abbas, ed., *Islamic Political Radicalism: A European Prospective* (Edinburgh: Edinburgh University Press, 2007), 279–91, esp. 279.

30   Tony Blair, Press Conference, 5 August 2005, http://www.number10.gov.uk/Page8041.

31   For al-Fawwaz's role, see Simon Reeve, *The New Jackals: Ramzi Yousef, Osama Bin Laden and the Future of Terrorism* (London: André Deutsch, 1999), 180, 192, 211–12.

32   Gunaratna, *Inside Al Qaeda*, 62–63.

33   For more on Bin Laden's disputed date of birth, see "Background on Osama Bin Laden and al-Qa'ida," CIA report, Washington, D.C. (1998), 1; Nick Fielding's interview with Bin Laden's half brother, *The Sunday Times*, 9 March 2003; Bodansky, *Bin Laden*, 2; Gunaratna, *Inside Al Qaeda*, 21; Sharaf al-Din, *Bin Laden*, 45.

34   Bin Laden statement, 10 June 1999, http://www.fas.org/irp/news/1999/06/index.html.

35   Sharaf al-Din, *Bin Laden*, 45–46.

36   Sharaf al-Din, *Bin Laden*, 46.

37   Bin Laden statement, 10 June 1999. Bin Laden's age when his father died is also in dispute. The death of his father was reported to be 1968 or 1970. If we consider Bin Laden's date of birth as 1952, 1953, 1954, or 1957, as reported, his age when his father died in 1970 would have been eighteen, seventeen, sixteen, or thirteen years, respectively. But Bin Laden himself said that he was about ten when his father died. On this assumption, his father would have died in 1968, not in 1970.

38   Bin Laden, *Messages to the World*, 31–33.

39   Bin Laden statement, 10 June 1999.

40   Sharaf al-Din, *Bin Laden*, 46.

41   For details on *hakimiya*, see Sayed Khatab, *The Power of Sovereignty: The Political and Ideological Philosophy of Sayyid Qutb* (London and New York: Routledge, 2006), 8–46.

42   Bin Laden's statement, 6 December 1996, in Brad K. Berner, ed., *The World According to al-Qaeda* (North Charleston, NC: Booksurge, LLC, 2005), 2.

43   Peter Bergen, *Inside the Secret World of Osama Bin Laden* (London: Weidenfeld, 2001), 55.

44   Robert Irwin, "Is This the Man Who Inspired Bin Laden?" *The Guardian*, 1 November 2001.

45   Gunaratna, *Inside Al Qaeda*, 23.

46   In this early period, Bin Laden was paying the Afghan Mujahidin "three million American Dollars a month." Author's interview with Muhammad Rahim, a former Mujahidin commander from Kandahar, February 2008.

47   Sharaf al-Din, *Bin Laden*, 48.

48   Interview in Cairo between Dr. Fadl and the London daily *al-Hayat*, 8 December 2007.

49   Sharaf al-Din, *Bin Laden*, 48.

50   See Brynjar Lia, *Architect of Global Jihad: The Life of Al-Qaida Strategist Abu Mus'ab al-Suri* (New York: Colombia University Press, 2008), 53, 75–78.

51   Bin Laden, *Messages to the World*, 26 and ff. 12, 31–33.

52   Sharaf al-Din, *Bin Laden*, 11.

53   Southern District of New York, "United States of America v. Bin Laden et al." (United States District Court, Southern District of New York, 14 February 2001).

54 Southern District of New York, "United States of America v. Bin Laden et al."

55 Sharaf al-Din, *Bin Laden*, 190.

56 Gunaratna, *Inside Al Qaeda*, 25.

57 Interview with Dr. Fadl in Cairo, *al-Hayat*, 8 December 2007.

58 Gunaratna, *Inside Al Qaeda*, 27.

59 Jason Burke, *Al-Qaeda: Casting a Shadow of Terror* (London and New York: I.B. Tauris, 2003), 74–75

60 Burke, *al-Qaeda*, 74.

61 'Abdullah 'Azzam, *Muqaddima fi-l-hijra wa-l-i'dad* (n.p.: Minbar al-Tawhid wa-l-Jihad, n.d.).

62 See Burke, *al-Qaeda*, 7–8; Gunaratna, *Inside Al Qaeda*, 73–74.

63 Sharaf al-Din, *Bin Laden*, 51.

64 Bin Laden's statement, 6 December 1996, in Berner, *The World According to al-Qaeda*, 175.

65 Gunaratna, *Inside Al Qaeda*, 29.

66 'Azzam, *Muqaddima fi-l-hijra*, 132–33, 140.

67 Stefano Bellucci, "Islam and Democracy: The 1999 Palace Coup," *Middle East Policy* 7 (3) (June 2000): 168. On 12 December 1999, al-Bashir put al-Turabi under house arrest.

68 Southern District of New York, "United States of America v. Bin Laden et al."

69 Sharaf al-Din, *Bin Laden*, 55.

70 "Mudhakkirat Bin Laden fi-l-Sudan: Tahqiqat wa shihadat 13," *al-Quds al-'arabi*, 24 November 2001.

71 Bin Laden's interview with CNN reporter, Peter Arnett, in March 1997, quoted from Bin Laden, *Messages to the World*, 44; Sharaf al-Din, *Bin Laden*, 56.

72 Tenet, *At the Center of the Storm*, 270–71.

73 Tenet, *At the Center of the Storm*, 100.

74 CIA, *Characteristics of Transnational Sunni Islamic Terrorism* (CIA, Washington, D.C., n.d), 2.

75 CIA, *Background on Osama Bin Laden and al-Qa'ida*, 2.

76 Tenet, *At the Center of the Storm*, 100; see also 102.

77 Bin Laden's statement, 23 August 1999, in Berner, *The World According to al-Qaeda*, 248.

78 Bin Laden's statement, 10 June 1999, in Berner, *The World According to al-Qaeda*, 196.

79   Sharaf al-Din, *Bin Laden*, 57.

80   al-Zawahiri, *al-Tabri'a*, 36.

81   Tenet, *At the Center of the Storm*, 103.

82   Bin Laden, *Messages to the World*, 23–30, esp. 27.

83   Sharaf al-Din, *Bin Laden*, 58.

84   Gunaratna, *Inside Al Qaeda*, 54.

85   Bin Laden statement on 22 December, 1998.

86   Sharaf al-Din, *Bin Laden*, 62–63.

87   Bergen, *Inside the Secret World of Osama Bin Laden*, 102.

88   Tim McGirk, "Afghanistan," *TIME* magazine, 31 August 1998.

89   Interview with an officer from Pakistani Intelligence (ISI), May (2000), see Gunaratna, *Inside Al Qaeda*, 57 ff. 71.

90   Bin Laden statement, March 1997, in his *Messages to the World*, 44–57.

91   Bin Laden statement, 22 December 1998, Al Jazeera, http://www.suhuf. net.sa/eindex.html.

92   Interview with Mullah 'Umar for the radio channel Voice of America: "Mullah Omar—In His Own Words," *The Guardian*, 26 September 2001, http://www.guardian.co.uk/world/2001/sep/26/afghanistan.features11.

93   Ayman al-Zawahiri, *al-Tabri'a*, 34–35.

94   BBC [English], "Statements from India and Pakistan," 16 June, 1998, http://news.bbc.co.uk/2/hi/events/asia_nuclear_crisis/world_media/114139.stm.

95   "Statements from India and Pakistan," *BBC News*, 16 June 1998, http://news.bbc.co.uk/2/hi/events/asia_nuclear_crisis/world_media/114139.stm.

96   CNN interview with Bin Laden in March 1997; "Transcript of Osama Bin Ladin Interview by Peter Arnett," March 1997, http://www.anusha.com/osamaint.htm.

97   Gwyn Prins, "Blood and Sand," *The Guardian*, 21 December 2001.

98   Roger Hardy, "Analysis: U.S.-Saudi 'Uneasy' Ties," *BBC News*, 29 April 2003, http://news.bbc.co.uk/2/hi/middle_east/2985131.stm.

99   Hardy, "Analysis: U.S.-Saudi 'Uneasy' Ties."

100 "Profile: Maulana Fazlur Rahman," BBC News, 6 November 2002. He was close to Bin Laden and the Taliban and is now leader of the opposition in Pakistan; see Amir Mir, "The Pakistanis Training in Al Qaeda Camps," *Cobra Post* news features, http://www.cobrapost.com/documents/TrainingAlQaeda.htm.

101 For the Arabic, see *al-Quds al-'arabi*, 23 February 1998.

102 Alan Cullison and Andrew Higgins, "A Once-Stormy Terror Alliance Was Solidified by Cruise Missiles," *Wall Street Journal*, 2 August 2002, 1.

103 David B. Ottoway and Joe Stephens, "Diplomats Met with Taliban on Bin Laden: Some Contend U.S. Missed Its Chance," *The Washington Post*, 29 October 2001.

104 Prince Turki al-Faisal, head of Saudi intelligence, interview with Dubai newspaper on 3 November 2001; see also "Taliban Agreed to Hand over Osama in 98," *Dawn Group of Newspapers*, 5 November 2001.

105 "Taliban Agreed to Hand over Osama in 98," *Dawn Group of Newspapers*, 5 November 2001.

106 Alan Cullison and Andrew Higgins, "Computer in Kabul Holds Chilling Memos," *Wall Street Journal*, 31 December 2001, 1.

107 Jason Burke interview with Saudi intelligence officer, Peshawar, August 1998, in Burke, *al-Qaeda* 167.

108 Tenet, *At the Center of the Storm*, 155.

109 http://www.globalsecurity.org/security/ops/98emb.htm.

110 Tenet, *At the Center of the Storm*, 155. The CIA's figure here included other nationals.

111 Tenet, *At the Center of the Storm*, 1, 14; also, 261.

112 Tenet, *At the Center of the Storm*, 155.

113 Author's interview with Muhammad Rahim, a former Mujahidin commander from Kandahar (February 2008).

114 The National Security Archive, "1998 Missile Strikes on Bin Laden May Have Backfired," 20 August 2008, http://www.gwu.edu/~nsarchiv/NSAEBB/NSAEBB253/index.htm.

115 Tenet, *At the Center of the Storm*, 152–55; 114–17.

116 Tenet, *At the Center of the Storm*, 112–13.

117 Interview with al-Zawahiri by Jamal Isma'il for Al Jazeera in December 1998 in the presence of Bin Laden. Isma'il reproduced this interview in his book, *Ibn Ladin wa-l-Jazeera wa ana* (Casablanca: Dar-al-Najah al-Jadida, 2001), which can be found on several websites, including, http://abu-qatada.com/r?i=3534&c=4663.

118 Tenet, *At the Center of the Storm*, 115.

119 Tenet, *At the Center of the Storm*, 115.

120 The National Security Archive, "1998 Missile Strikes on Bin Laden May Have Backfired." See also author's interview with Muhammad Rahim (February 2008).

121 Interview with al-Zawahiri by Jamal Isma'il for Al Jazeera in 1998.

122 The National Security Archive, "1998 Missile Strikes on Bin Laden May Have Backfired."

123 Tenet, *At the Center of the Storm*, 115.

124 Tenet, *At the Center of the Storm*, 115–16.

125 Tenet, *At the Center of the Storm*, 261.

126 Tenet, *At the Center of the Storm*, 114–17.

127 Tony Blair, press conference, 5 August 2005.

128 Sharaf al-Din, *Bin Laden*, 71.

129 Jason Burke, interview with Saudi intelligence officer, Peshawar, August 1998, in Burke, *al-Qaeda*, 167.

130 Sharaf al-Din, *Bin Laden*, 72.

131 Tenet, *At the Center of the Storm*, 104.

132 Burke, *al-Qaeda*, quoted on 168.

133 Department of State, "Afghanistan: Meeting with the Taliban," 11 December 1997, Confidential, 13; for further information, see The September 11th Sourcebooks, Volume VII: The Taliban File, National Security Archive. Electronic Briefing Book No. 97, ed., Sajit Gandi, 11 September 2003.

134 Ottoway and Stephens, "Diplomats Met with Taliban."

135 *Asia Political News*, 23 April 2001. Muhammad Rabbani died in 2001 after a long illness.

136 Ottoway and Stephens, "Diplomats Met with Taliban."

137 Tenet, *At the Center of the Storm*, 113–17.

138 *The Guardian*, 26 August 1998.

139 Department of State, "Afghanistan: Meeting with the Taliban," 11 December 1997, Confidential, 13; see the September 11th Sourcebooks, Volume VII: The Taliban File, National Security Archive. Electronic Briefing Book No. 97 Edited by Sajit Gandi, 11 September 2003.

140 Ottoway and Stephens, "Diplomats Met with Taliban."

141 Ottoway and Stephens, "Diplomats Met with Taliban."

142 Ottoway and Stephens, "Diplomats Met with Taliban."

143 Ottoway and Stephens, "Diplomats Met with Taliban."

144 Ottoway and Stephens, "Diplomats Met with Taliban."

145 *The Guardian*, 26 August 1998.

Notes to Chapter 5: Ideology

1   Interview with al-Zawahiri in the London daily *al-Hayat*, 1996.

2   Jamal al-Din ibn Manzur (1232–1311), *Lisan al-'Arab* (Beirut: Dar Sadr, 1994, 15 vols.), vol. 3, 134–35.

3   Sayyid Qutb, *Fi zilal al-Qur'an* (Cairo: Dar al-Shuruq, 1992), vol. 3, 1441.

4   Qutb, *Zilal*, vol. 1, 294; also see 291; vol. 3, 1431–52; 1578–83; see Sayyid Qutb, *Dirasat islamiya* (Cairo: Dar al-Shuruq, 1993), 38.

5   Qutb, *Zilal*, vol. 1, 190–91, 1446–47; vol. 2, 733 ff, n1; vol. 3, 1586–1606, 1620–38; also Abu 'Abdullah Muhammad ibn Ahmad al-Ansari al-Qurtubi (d. 671/1272), *al-Jami' li-ahkam al-Qur'an* (Beirut: Dar al-Turath al-'Arabi, 1985), vol. 2, 353.

6   Sayyid Qutb, *al-Salam al-'alami wa-l-Islam* (Cairo: Dar al-Shuruq, 1995), 28–29.

7   Qutb, *Zilal*, vol. 3, 1431–48 (esp. stages of jihad and war against unbelievers).

8   Arthur Nussbaum, *A Concise History of the Law of Nations* (New York: Macmillan, 1962), 52.

9   'Abd al-Rahman ibn Khaldun, *The Muqaddimah: An Introduction to History*, trans. Franz Rosenthal, 3 vols. (New York, Pantheon Books, 1958), vol. 1, 299–304.

10 See Nussbaum, *A Concise History of the Law of Nations*, 45–46.

11 Nussbaum, *A Concise History of the Law of Nations*, 45–47.

12 John Kelsay and James Turner Johnson, eds., *Just War and Jihad: Historical and Theoretical Perspectives on War and Peace in Western and Islamic Traditions* (New York: Greenwood, 1991), 144–50; Paul Fregosi, *Jihad in the West: Muslim Conquests from the 7th to 21st Centuries* (New York: Prometheus Books, 1998), 60–64, 78–81; Frederick Russell, *The Just War in the Middle Ages* (Cambridge: Cambridge University Press, 1975), 199–204.

13 Gilles Kepel, *Jihad: The Trail of Political Islam* (Cambridge, MA: Harvard University Press, 2002), 366–68; John Esposito, *Unholy War: Terror in the Name of Islam* (Oxford: Oxford University Press, 2002), ix, 26, 73–74, 116.

14 Majid Khadduri, *War and Peace in the Law of Islam*, 2nd ed. (Baltimore: Johns Hopkins University Press, 1955), 52–53, 155–57, 170–71.

15 Kelsay and Johnson, eds., *Just War and Jihad*, 36–37.

16 Muhammad ibn 'Umar al-Waqidi (d. 822), *Kitab al-maghazi*, ed. Marsden Jones, 2nd ed. (London: Oxford University Press, 3 vols., 1966), vol. 3, 989–96.

17 Karen Armstrong, *Holy War* (London: Macmillan, 1998), 36–37, 152–59, 306–12; al-Waqidi, *Kitab al-maghazi*, vol. 1, 38–42, 239–49; vol. 2, 694, 700; vol. 3, 1039–43.

18 Russell, *The Just War in the Middle Ages*, 12.

19 C.G. Weeramantry, *Islamic Jurisprudence: An International Perspective* (Baskingstoke, UK: Macmillan Press, 1988), 134.

20 Nussbaum, *A Concise History*, 52.

21 Weeramantry, *Islamic Jurisprudence*, 146.

22 Weeramantry, *Islamic Jurisprudence*, 146.

23 Weeramantry, *Islamic Jurisprudence*, 146.

24 Nussbaum, *A Concise History*, 53.

25 Majid Khadduri, trans., *The Islamic Law of Nations: Shaybani's Siyar* (Baltimore: Johns Hopkins University Press, 1966), 133–34 (articles 405, 406, 409).

26 Khadduri, *The Islamic Law of Nations*, 101 articles 108–109.

27 al-Waqidi, *Kitab al-maghazi*, vol. 1 (119 in connection to the Prophet's order about the prisoners; 128–29, about ransom and freedom; 130–31, names of the prisoners, and the account of Zaynab's attempt to free her husband); also see Husayn Haykal, *The Life of Muhammad*, trans. Isma'il R. al-Faruqi (Kuala Lumpur: Islamic Book Trust, 1976), 424–25.

28 al-Waqidi, *Kitab al-maghazi*, vol. 1, 119.

29 Anwar Qadri, *Islamic Jurisprudence in the Modern World* (Lahore: Karachi Bazar, 2nd ed., 1973), 280 (his references are: Imam Bukhari; Ahmad Imam ibn Hanbal, *al-Musnad li-Ahmad ibn Muhammad ibn Hanbal*, ed. Muhammad Shakir [Cairo: Dar al-Ma'arif, 1949]; al-Tabari, *Tarikh al-umam*; and more in the footnotes).

30 al-Waqidi, *Kitab al-maghazi*, vol. 1, 119.

31 al-Waqidi, *Kitab al-maghazi*, vol. 1, 106–107.

32 al-Waqidi, *Kitab al-maghazi*, vol. 1, 111, also see 106.

33 Weeramantry, *Islamic Jurisprudence*, 135.

34 al-Waqidi, *Kitab al-maghazi*, vol. 1, 119.

35 al-Waqidi, *Kitab al-maghazi*, vol. 1, 108–10.

36 Weeramantry, *Islamic Jurisprudence*, 135.

37 Weeramantry, *Islamic Jurisprudence*, 148.

38 Weeramantry, *Islamic Jurisprudence*, 148.

39 M.J. Ghunaimi, *The Muslim Conception of International Law and the Western Approach* (The Hague: Martinus, 1968), 180–84.

40 Nagendra Singh, *India and International Law* (New Delhi: S. Chand and Co., 1973), vol. 1 (part A), 90–91 ff. 2; in connection with this see al-Waqidi, *Kitab al-maghazi*, vol. 3, 989–96.

41 Khadduri, *War and Peace in the Law of Islam*, 52–53, 154–57, 170–71.

42 Nussbaum, *A Concise History*, 53.

43 Khadduri, *The Islamic Law of Nations*, 17.

44 Nussbaum, *A Concise History*, 53.

45 For example, Qur'an 2:100; 8:56; 9:7; 2:27; 3:77; 7:102.

46 Nussbaum, *A Concise History*, 54.

47 Y. Mahmud Zayid, ed., *The Qur'an: An English Translation of the Meaning of the Qur'an* (Beirut: Dar al-Shura, 1980), 64 (verse 4:94).

48 The word *harb* (war) is used in Qur'an, 2:279; 5:33, 64; 8: 57; 47:4. As for the word '*qital*' (to fight) used in the Qur'an, see 2:192, 246; 3:13; 4:75, 90; 9:83; 48:16.

49 See for example Qur'an 4:79, 100.

50 al-Qurtubi, *al-Jami*', vol. 5, 336.

51 Weeramantry, *Islamic Jurisprudence*, 135.

52 Dr. Fadl, *Risalat al-'umda fi i'dad al-'udda li-l-jihad fi sabil Allah* (N.p.: n.p., 1988), vol. 2, 284.

53 Peter Lentini, "Antipodal Terrorists: Accounting for Differences in Australian and Global Neo-Jihadists," in Richard Devetak and Christopher W. Hughes, eds., *The Globalization of Political Violence* (London: Routledge, 2008), 181–202, esp. 181–82.

54 Ayman al-Zawahiri, *al-Tabri'a: risala fi tabri'at ummat al-qalam wa-l-sayf min manqasat tuhmat al-khawr wa-l-da'f* (n.p.: al-Sahab Foundation for Islamic Media Publications, 2008), 149.

55 Ayman al-Zawahiri, interview by Kamil al-Tawil, *al-Hayat*, 1996. Published by *al-Wasat* and republished online by "Minbar al-Tawhid wa-l-Jihad," http://www.tawhed.ws/.

56 Ayman al-Zawahiri, interview by Kamil al-Tawil, *al-Hayat*.

57 Dr. Fadl, *Risalat al-'umda*, vol. 2, 260–68.

58 Muhammad ibn 'Abdullah al-Mas'ari, *Markaz al-tijara al-'alami* (London: Lajnat al-Difa 'an al-Huquq al-Shar'iya, 2002), 5–7.

59 Abu Muhammad Asim al-Maqdisi, *Imta' al-nazar fi kashf shubuhat murji'at al-'asr* (n.p.: Minbar al-Tawhid, 1999), 52–47, 85–88, 115–24.

60 For more details see Imam 'Abd al-Qahir ibn Tahir al-Baghdadi (d. 1037), *al-Farq bayn al-firaq*, 3rd ed. (Beirut: Dar al-Kutub, 2005), 18–20.

61   Dr. Fadl, *Risalat al-'umda*, vol. 2, 284–86.

62   Dr. Fadl, *Risalat al-'umda*, vol. 2, 289–90.

63   Dr. Fadl, *Risalat al-'umda*, vol. 2, 293–94.

64   Ayman al-Zawahiri, *al-Hasad al-murr: al-Ikhwan al-Muslimun fi sittina 'aman* (Amman: Dar al-Bayan, 2002), section one, 2–5 and section two, 1–5.

65   Dr. Fadl, *Risalat al-'umda*, vol. 2, 295.

66   'Abdullah 'Azzam, *Muqaddima fi-l-hijra wa-l-i'dad* (N.p.: Minbar al-Tawhid wa-l-Jihad, n.d.) 26–29, esp. 53.

67   'Azzam, *Muqaddima fi-l-hijra*, 26, see 29, 31, 34, 35, 37, 41.

68   'Azzam, *Muqaddima fi-l-hijra*, 43, 45.

69   'Azzam, *Muqaddima fi-l-hijra*, 88, see 53.

70   'Ali bin Nufay' al-'Alyani, *Ahamiyyat al-jihad* (Riyadh: Dar Tibah, 1985), 124–33.

71   Dr. Fadl, *Risalat al-'umda*, vol. 2, 296–300, esp. 298.

72   Dr. Fadl, *Risalat al-'umda*, vol. 2, 300–301.

73   Muhammad ibn Abdullah al-Mas'ari, *Qital al-tawa'if al-mumtani'a* (London: Muntada al-Tajdid al-Islami, 2003), 2–5.

74   al-Mas'ari, *Qital al-tawa'if al-mumtani'a*, 5.

75   al-Mas'ari, *Qital al-tawa'if al-mumtani'a*, 10; see also by al-Mas'ari, *Markaz al-tijara al-'alami* (n.p.: n.p., 2003), 3–10.

76   al-Mas'ari, *Qital al-tawa'if al-mumtani'a*, 10.

77   al-Mas'ari, *Qital al-tawa'if al-mumtani'a*, 10–11.

78   al-Mas'ari, *Qital al-tawa'if al-mumtani'a*, 11.

79   al-Mas'ari, *Qital al-tawa'if al-mumtani'a*, 11.

80   al-Mas'ari, *Qital al-tawa'if al-mumtani'a*, 11.

81   al-Mas'ari, *Qital al-tawa'if al-mumtani'a*, 12.

82   al-Mas'ari, *Qital al-tawa'if al-mumtani'a*, 18.

83   al-Mas'ari, *Qital al-tawa'if al-mumtani'a*, 19.

84   al-Mas'ari, *Qital al-tawa'if al-mumtani'a*, 19.

85   Muhammad ibn 'Abdullah al-Mas'ari, *Qissat Abu Basir: ta'sil shar'i mufassal li-hudud mashru'iyyat i'lan al-afrad li-l-harb* (London: Lajnat al-Difa' 'an al-Huquq al-Shar'iya, 2002), 8.

86   W. Montgomery Watt, *Muhammad: Prophet and Statesman* (London: Oxford University Press, 1961), 198–200; Maxime Rodinson, *Muhammad*, trans. Anne Carter (London: Allen Lane, 1971), 256–57.

87   al-Mas'ari, *Qissat Abi Bashir*, 4–14.

88   Watt, *Muhammad*, 199.

89   Rodinson, *Muhammad*, 257.

90   al-Zawahiri, *al-Tabri'a*, 5–6, 26, 43.

91   Imam Abu 'Abdullah Muhammad ibn Idris al-Shafi'i (d. 204/819), *Kitab al-umm* (Beirut: Dar al-Fikr, 1990), vol. 2, part 2, 176–77.

92   'Azzam, *Muqaddima fi-l-hijra*, 122.

93   'Azzam, *Muqaddima fi-l-hijra*, 79.

94   'Azzam, *Muqaddima fi-l-hijra*, 26.

95   Dr. Fadl, *Risalat al-'umda*, vol. 2, 306.

96   Dr. Fadl, *Risalat al-'umda*, vol. 2, 307.

97   Salim bin Hammud al-Khalidi, *Mu'aradat al-awghad fi da'wahum jawaz al-jihad* (n.p.: Ansar al-Mahdi, n.d.), 6–7.

98   Dr. Fadl, *Risalat al-'umda*, vol. 2, 307.

99   Dr. Fadl, *Risalat al-'umda*, vol. 2, 307.

Notes to Chapter 6: Al-Qa'ida's Tactics

1   Abu Bakr Naji, *Idarat al-tawahhush* (n.p.: Centre of Islamic Studies and Research, n.d.), 10.

2   Muhammd ibn 'Abdullah al-Mas'ari, *Qital al-tawa'if al-mumtani'a* (London: Muntada al-Tajdid al-Islami, n.d.), 2–5.

3   Ayman al-Zawahiri, *al-Tabri'a: risala fi tabri'at ummat al-qalam wa-l-sayf min manqasat tuhmat al-khawr wa-l-da'f* (n.p.: al-Sahab Foundation for Islamic Media Publications, 2008), 32–57.

4   al-Zawahiri, *al-Tabri'a*, 107–13.

5   al-Zawahri, *al-Tabri'a*, 7–10.

6   George Tenet, *At the Center of the Storm: My Years at the CIA* (New York: Harper Collins Publishers, 2007), 225.

7   Sayf al-'Adl, "al-Amn wa-l-istikhbarat," in fortnightly periodical *Mu'askar al-Battar*, issue no. 20 (Sha'ban 1425/September 2004), 28.

8   Rohan Gunaratna, *Inside Al Qaeda: Global Network of Terror* (New York: Berkley Books, 2002–2003), 101–102.

9   Stephen Ulph, "Al-Qaeda's Strategy until 2020," *Terrorism Focus* 2 (6) (17 March 2005).

10   Bandar bin Abdurhman al-Dikhayl, "Wa sayfun yanhar," in *Mu'askar al-Battar*, issue no. 20 (Sha'ban 1425/September 2004), 14

11   See al-Dikhayl, "Wa sayfun yanhar," 7–17

12   Dr. Fadl, *Risalat al-'umda fi i'dad al-'udda li-l-jihad fi sabil Allah* (n.p.: n.p., 1988), vol. 1, 135

13   Sayf al-'Adl, "al-Amn wa-l-istikhbarat."

14 Muhammad al-Amin Ahmad, "al-Khalq 'ind Allah sinfan: muslim wa kafir," Minbar al-Tawhid wa-l-Jihad, http://almaqdese.net/r?i=i0mngcsq.

15 Naji, *Idarat al-tawahhush*, 7.

16 Naji, *Idarat al-tawahhush*, 7.

17 Naji, *Idarat al-tawahhush*, 7.

18 *The Guardian* newspaper published a series of articles in July 2006 in which it concluded that the Tripartite (British, French, and Israeli) invasion of Egypt in 1956 was one of the significant factors that contributed to the downfall of the British Empire. See *al-Ahram*, 14 July 2006, 1.

19 Qur'an 16:10–14, 65; 22:5, 63.

20 Qur'an 11:40–45.

21 Qur'an 17:16; see also 22:49.

22 Naji, *Idarat al-tawahhush*, 8–9.

23 'Abduh Zayna, "Dr. Najih Ibrahim yatahaddath ila *Asharq Alawsat*," *Asharq Alawsat*, 14 August 2006.

24 Naji, *Idarat al-tawahhush*, 9.

25 Tenet, *At the Center of the Storm*, 114–16, 270, esp. 115.

26 Tenet, *At the Center of the Storm*, 175–80, 197–99.

27 Naji, *Idarat al-tawahhush*, 9–10.

28 CBS News, "Bin Laden's Target: U.S. Wallet," 11 February 2009.

29 Naji, *Idarat al-tawahhush*, 15–16, esp. 15.

30 Naji, *Idarat al-tawahhush*, 11.

31 Naji, *Idarat al-tawahhush*, 16.

32 Naji, *Idarat al-tawahhush*, 16–17.

33 Naji, *Idarat al-tawahhush*, 16–18.

34 Wolfdogfilms: www.wolfdogfilms.com

35 Naji, *Idarat al-tawahhush*, 17.

36 Naji, *Idarat al-tawahhus*, 18.

37 Naji, *Idarat al-tawahhush*, 18–19.

38 Martin Woollacott, "Cyanide on the Table," *The Guardian*, 10 July 2008.

39 Naji, *Idarat al-tawahhush*, 19.

40 Naji, *Idarat al-tawahhush*, 20–21.

41 Naji, *Idarat al-tawahhush*, 28.

42 Naji, *Idarat al-tawahhush*, 28–29.

43 Naji, *Idarat al-tawahhush*, 29.

44 Naji, *Idarat al-tawahhush*, 30.

45 Naji, *Idarat al-tawahhush*, 30.

46 See Ayman al-Zawahiri, *al-Hasad al-murr: al-Ikhwan al-Muslimun fi sittina 'aman* (Amman: Dar al-Bayan, 2002), 123–50, 182–90; al-Zawahiri, *al-Tabri'a*, 32–57; Bin Laden, *Messages to the World: The Statements of Osama Bin Laden*, edited and introduced by Bruce Lawrence (London: Verso, 2005), 45–52, 62–67; 'Abdullah 'Azzam, *Muqaddima fi-l-hijra wa-l-i'dad*, (n.p.: Minbar al-Tawhid wa-l-Jihad, n.d.), 132–238, 140–49; Dr. Fadl, *Risalat al-'umda*; Dr. Fadl, *al-Jami' fi talab al-'ilm* (N.p.: n.p., 1993); Dr. Fadl, *al-Murshid ila tariq Allah* (n.p.: n.p., 2006); Dr. Fadl, *Wathiqat tarshid al-jihad fi Misr wa-l-'alam* (London: al-Hayat, 2007); Muhammad ibn 'Abdullah al-Mas'ari, *Markaz al-tijara al-'lami* (London: Lajnat al-Difa' 'an al-Huquq al-Shar'iya, 2002), 5–11.

47 al-Zawahiri, *al-Tabri'a*, 137–39.

48 Naji, *Idarat al-tawahhush*, 31.

49 al-Zawahiri, *al-Tabri'a*, 25.

50 al-Zawahiri, *al-Tabri'a*, 32.

51 Naji, *Idarat al-tawahhush*, 32.

52 al-Zawahiri, *al-Tabri'a*, 43–46, see 1–62.

53 al-Zawahiri, *al-Tabri'a*, 17.

54 Goliath, "Kidnapped Egyptian Diplomat Killed in Iraq," http://goliath. ecnext.com/coms2/gi_0199-4505908/IRAQ-July-7-Kidnapped-Egyptian.html; *Herald Tribune*, "Egypt's Top Envoy Kidnapped in Baghdad," 3 July 2005.

55 al-Zawahiri, *al-Tabri'a*, 53–55.

56 Abdulmalik al-Qasim, "al-Wala' wa-l-bara,'" http://www.murajaat. com/alwala_walbra.php.

57 Naji, *Idarat al-tawahhush*, 34.

58 Naji, *Idarat al-tawahhush*, 34.

59 Naji, *Idarat al-tawahhush*, 34.

60 Naji, *Idarat al-tawahhush*, 38.

61 Naji, *Idarat al-tawahhush*, 38.

62 Naji, *Idarat al-tawahhush*, 39.

63 Naji, *Idarat al-tawahhush*, 39.

64 Naji, *Idarat al-tawahhush*, 39.

65 Naji, *Idarat al-tawahhush*, 39.

66 Naji, *Idarat al-tawahhush*, 40–41.

67 Muntasir al-Zayyat, interview with Al Arabiya, 11 November 2007.

68 al-Zawahiri, *al-Tabri'a*, 11, 20 n.3, 107–13, 137.

69   Dr. Fadl, "Wathiqat tarshid al-jihad fi Misr wa-l-'alam" (2007), series, no. 1, 5.

70   Muhammad Karam Zuhdi, Najih Ibrahim 'Abd Allah et al., *Tafjirat al-Riyad: al-ahkam wa-l-athar* (Cairo: al-Turath, 2003), 97.

71   Zuhdi, *Tafjirat al-Riyad*, 97.

72   al-Zawahiri, *al-Tabri'a*, 107–13.

73   al-Zawahiri, *al-Tabri'a*, 107–13.

74   al-Zawahiri, *al-Tabri'a*, 107–13.

75   For more details on public interest, see Sayed Khatab and Gary Bouma, *Democracy in Islam* (London: Routledge, 2007), 48–50.

76   Wasil Nasr Farid, Islamonline, http://www.islamonline.net/servlet/Satellite?pagename=IslamOnline-Arabic-Ask_Scholar/FatwaA/FatwaA&cid=112252862368.

77   David Kozin, "The Triangle of Death," *The NEIU Independent*, 12 March 2007.

78   Independent Media Review Analyst (IMRA), 26 May 2007.

79   al-Zawahiri, *al-Tabri'a*, 11, 20 n. 3, 107–13, 137.

80   *The Washington Post*, 11 October 2001.

81   *Al-Ahram Weekly*, 22 September 2001, http://weekly.ahram.org.eg/index.htm.

82   Press release, http://www.cair.com/americanmuslims/antiterrorism/islamicstatementsagainstterrorism.aspx

83   Peter Bergen and Paul Cruickshank, "The Unravelling: The Jihadist Revolt against Bin Laden," *The New Republic*, 11 June 2008.

84   Ayatollah Ali Khamene'I, Islamic Republic News Agency, 16 September 2001, http://www.iranmehr.com/directory/moreinfo/1126.html.

85   Muhammad Khatami's address to the United Nations General Assembly, 9 November 2001, reported in "Iran Chief Rejects Bin Laden Message," *The New York Times*, 10 November 2001, http://query.nytimes.com/gst/fullpage.html?res=990CE7DF1538F933A25752C1A9679C8B63&scp=1&sq=Khatami%20in%20the%20UN%20(2001)&st=cse.

86   Council on American-Islamic Relations (CAIR), "Response to September 11, 2001 Attacks" (Washington: CAIR, 2007), 23, 24, http://www.cair.com/Portals/0/pdf/September_11_statements.pdf.

Notes to Chapter 7: Inside al-Qa'ida

1   Interview with Dr. Fadl, *al-Hayat*, 9 December 2007.

2   Interview with Dr. Fadl, *al-Hayat*, 9 December 2007.

3   Interview with Dr. Fadl, *al-Hayat*, 10 December 2007.

4   For further details see Sayed Khatab, *The Power of Sovereignty: The Political and Ideological Philosophy of Sayyid Qutb* (New York: Routledge, 2006), 194–212.

5   *Asharq Alawsat*, 8 May 2007.

6   *Asharq Alawsat*, 9 March 1999.

7   See Mahir Hasan, "Wafat 'Abd al-Rahman Basha Azzam awwal amin li-l-Jami'a al-'Arabiya," *Almasry Alyoum*, 2 June 2009, 2.

8   *Muslim Weekly*, 8–14 February 2008, http://www.themuslimweekly. com/NewsPaper.aspx.

9   See Mahfuz Azzam, in his party's newspaper *al-Sha'b*, http://alarab-news.com/alshaab/06-05-2005.htm.

10   Minbar al-Tawhid wa-l-Jihad, http://www.tawhed.ws/a?a=3i806qpo.

11   Minbar al-Tawhid wa-l-Jihad, http://www.tawhed.ws/a?a=3i806qpo.

12   Minbar al-Tawhid wa-l-Jihad, http://www.tawhed.ws/a?a=3i806qpo.

13   Ahmed Moussa, "Egypt's Most Wanted," *Al-Ahram Weekly*, 18–24 October 2001.

14   Interview with Dr. Fadl, *al-Hayat*, December 2007.

15   Ibrahim Rami, "Rad al-Zawahiri 'ala Dr. Fadl," *al-Jarida*, 20 November 2007.

16   Interview with Dr. Fadl, *al-Hayat*, December 2007.

17   Interview with Dr. Fadl, *al-Hayat*, December 2007.

18   Interview with Dr. Fadl, *al-Hayat*, December 2007.

19   President Mubarak survived several attempts on his life: in 1993 his visit to the U.S. was canceled for security reasons; in June 1995 in Ethiopia; in 1999 in Port Said; and on the road via Salah Salim Street in Cairo in the 1990s.

20   al-Zawahiri's interview with Kamil al-Tawil for *al-Hayat* in 1996, published in *al-Wasat* and republished in "Minbar al-Tawhid wa-l-Jihad," www.tawhed.ws/r?i=2832&c=2449.

21   Interview with Dr. Fadl, *al-Hayat*, December 2007.

22   Interview with Dr. Fadl, *al-Hayat*, December 2007.

23   Interview with Dr. Fadl, *al-Hayat*, December 2007.

24   See *Almasry Alyoum*, 17 April 2007 and 13 November 2007.

25   See *Almasry Alyoum*, 15 November 2007.

26   See *al-Jarida*, issue no. 152, 26 November 2007, http://www.aljarida. com/aljarida/Default.aspx?date=26112007.

27   Interview with Dr. Najih, *Asharq Alawsat*, 14 August 2006.

28 See *Almasry Alyoum*, 19 November 2007.

29 "Ally's Tactics Give al-Qaeda Pause, U.S. Says," *Los Angeles Times*, 7 October 2005.

30 Dr. Fadl, "Wathiqat tarshid al-jihad fi Misr wa-l-'alam," *al-Hayat* (2007), series no. 1.

31 Dr. Fadl, "Wathiqat tarshid al-jihad fi Misr wa-l-'alam," *al-Hayat* (2007), series no. 2.

32 Ibrahim Rami, "al-Zawahiri's Response to Dr. Fadl,' *al-Jarida*, 20 November 2007.

33 Zahir ibn Ahmad al-Sarkhasi is a prominent imam of Islamic jurisprudence.

34 Dr. Fadl, "Wathiqat tarshid al-jihad fi Misr wa-l-'alam," *al-Hayat* (2007), series no. 2.

35 Salah Eissa, "Muraja'at al-jihad wa haqiqat al-ihtikar," *Almasry Alyoum*, 24 November 2007.

36 Dr. Fadl, interview, *al-Hayat*.

37 Dr. Fadl, interview, *al-Hayat*.

38 Dr. Fadl, interview, *al-Hayat*.

39 See *Almasry Alyoum*, 19 November 2007.

40 Ayman al-Zawahiri, *al-Tabri'a: risala fi tabri'at ummat al-qalam wa-l-sayf min manqusat tuhmat al-khawr wa-l-da'f* (n.p.: al-Sahab Foundation for Islamic Media Publications, 2008), 179.

41 See Chris Toensing, "Muslims Ask: Why Do They Hate Us?" *Global Issues*, 25 September 2001, http://www.globalissues.org/article/256/muslims-ask-why-do-they-hate-us; also see Ontario Consultants "Aftermath of the September 11 Terrorist Attack," *Religious Tolerance*, 12 September 2001.

42 al-Zawahiri, *al-Tabri'a*, 3.

43 Dr. Fadl, interview, *al-Hayat*.

44 See Tenet, *At the Center of the Storm*, 100–17, esp. 114–16.

45 Richard Clark was the counter-terrorism coordinator for the National Security Council during Bill Clinton's presidency and the first year of George W. Bush's time in office, and the special advisor to the president on cybersecurity and cyberterrorism until his resignation in 2003.

46 Al Arabiyya website, 19 November 2007.

Notes to the Conclusion

1   Ayman al-Zawahiri, *Knights under the Prophet's Banner*, translation of *Firsan taht rayat al-rasul* by Foreign Broadcast Information Service (London: *Asharq Alawsat*, 2002), 66, 98.

2   Sayyid Qutb, *Nahwa mujtama' islami* (Cairo: Dar al-Shuruq, 1993), 151, 152.

3   Rizq al-Zalabani, "al-Siyasa al-dusturiya al-shar'iya: shakl al-hukuma wa 'alaqatiha f-l-Islam," *al-Azhar* 18 (7) (1947): 130–36, cf. 130.

4   Ayman al-Zawahiri, *al-Tabri'a: risala fi tabri'at ummat al-qalam wa-l-sayf min manqusat tuhmat al-khawr wa-l-da'f* (n.p.: al-Sahab Foundation for Islamic Media Publications, 2008), 55.

5   Muhammad ibn 'Abdullah al-Mas'ari, *Markaz al-tijara al-'alami* (London: Lajnat al-Difa' 'an al-Huquq al-Shar'iya, 2002), 18.

Bibliography

'Abduh, Muhammad. *Risalat al-tawhid*. Cairo: Matba'at 'Ali Subayh, 1956.

Abu Zahra, Muhammad. *The Four Imams: Their Lives, Works, and Their Schools of Thought*. London: Dar al-Taqwa, 2001.

———. *Ibn Taymiya*. Cairo: Dar al-Fikr al-'Arabi, 1974.

al-Afghani, Jamal al-Din, and Muhammad 'Abduh. *al-'Urwa al-wuthqa wa-l-thawra al-taharruriya al-kubra*. 1st ed. Cairo: Dar al-'Arab, 1957.

Ahmad, Muhammad al-Amin. "al-Khalq 'ind Allah sinfan: muslim wa kafir," Minbar al-Tawhid wa-l-Jihad, http://almaqdese.net/r?i=i0mngcsq.

Al Arabiya. 11 November 2007. Interview with Muntasir al-Zayyat.

Al Arabiya. 19 November 2007, http://www.flickr.com/photos/27708668@N00/1524738824/

Al Jazirah Internet Services, http://www.suhuf.net.sa/eindex.html.

Algar, Hamid. *Wahhabism: A Critical Essay*. New York: Oneonta, 2002.

Aljarida, no. 152, 26 November 2007, http://www.aljarida.com/aljarida/Default.aspx?date=26112007

Allen, Charles. *God's Terrorists: The Wahhabi Cult and the Hidden Roots of Modern Jihad*. London: Little Brown, 2006.

al-Alyani, 'Ali bin Nufay'. *Ahamiyyat al-jihad*. Riyadh: Dar Tibah, 1985.

Amir, Hasan. "'Abd al-Nasir kan za'im sufi." *Rose el-Youssef*, no. 3427, 14 February 1994.

al-Andalusi, Ahmad ibn Muhammad Ibn 'Abd Rabbu (d. 328/940). *al-'Iqd al-farid*. Edited by Ahmad Amin, Ibrahim al-Ibyari, and 'Abd al-Salam Harun. Introduction by 'Umar 'Abd al-Salam al-Tadmuri. All volumes. Beirut: Dar al-Kitab al-'Arabi, n.d.

al-Ansari, Nasir. *Mawsu'at hukkam Misr min al-fara'ina wa hatta al-yawm*. 2nd ed. Cairo: Dar al-Shuruq, 1987.

Armstrong, Karen. *Holy War*. London: Macmillan, 1988.

Awda, 'Abd al-Qadir. *al-Islam bayna jahl abna'ih wa 'ajz 'ulama'ih*. Beirut: al-Risala, 1985.

Ayatollah Ali Khamene'i. Islamic Republic News Agency, 16 September, 2001, http://www.iranmehr.com/directory/moreinfo/1126.html.

Ayubi, Nazih. *Political Islam: Religion and Politics in the Arab World*. London and New York: Routledge, 1991.

'Azzam, 'Abd al-Wahhab. "The Shi'ites." *al-Risala* 2 (1934): 1398–91.

'Azzam, 'Abdullah. *Muqaddima fi-l-hijra wa-l-i'dad*. N.p.: Minbar al-Tawhid wa-l-Jihad, n.d.

al-Baghdadi, Imam 'Abd al-Qahir ibn Tahir ibn Muhammad (known as al-Khatib al-Baghdadi, d. 1037). *al-Farq bayn al-firaq*, 3rd ed. Cairo: Dar al-Kutub, 2005.

———. *al-Kifaya fi 'ilm al-riwaya*. Hyderabad: n.p., 1938.

al-Banna, Hasan. *Majmu'at rasa'il Hasan al-Banna*. Cairo: Dar al-Tawzi' wa-l-Nashr, 1992.

al-Bardisi, Muhammad Zakariya. *Usul al-fiqh*. Cairo: Dar al-Thaqafa li-l-Nashr, 1985.

Barr, James. *Fundamentalism*. London: Trinity Pr Intl., 1981.

Basbous, Antoine. *L'islamisme une révolution avortée*. Paris: Hachette Littératures, 2000.

BBC Arabic. al-Jihad wa-l-pitrudular al-Sa'udi." BBC Arabic, 17 November 2007, http://news.bbc.co.uk/hi/arabic/news/.

BBC Arabic. "New Restrictions on the Religious Police." BBC Arabic, 14 July 2007, http://newsforums.bbc.co.uk/ws/thread.jspa?threadID=7082.

Bellucci, Stefano. "Islam and Democracy: The 1999 Palace Coup." *Middle East Policy* 7 (3) (June 2000).

Bergen, Peter. *Inside the Secret World of Osama Bin Laden*. London: Weidenfeld and Nicolson, 2001.

Bergen, Peter, and Paul Cruickshank. "The Unravelling: The Jihadist Revolt against Bin Laden." *The New Republic*, 11 June 2008, http://www.tnr.com/article/the-unraveling.

Berner, Brad K., ed. *The World According to al-Qaeda*. North Charleston, NC: Booksurge, LLC, 2005.

Bin Laden, Usama. *Messages to the World: The Statements of Osama bin Laden*. Edited and introduced by Bruce Lawrence. London: Verso, 2005.

———. "Statement." 10 June 1999, http://www.fas.org/irp/news/1999/06/index.html

al-Bisri, Abu al-Hasan, and Muhammad ibn 'Ali ibn al-Tayyib (d. 436/1057). *Sharh al-'umad*. 1st ed. Medina: Maktabat al-'Ulum wa-l-Hikam, 1990.

Bodansky, Yossef. *Bin Laden: The Man who Declared War on America*. London: Forum, 1999.

Bouma, Gary. "The Emerging Role of Religion in Public Policy in the Asia Pacific." In Marika Vicziani, David Write-Neville, and Pete Lentini, eds., *Regional Security in the Asia Pacific: 9/11 and After*, 67–79. Cheltenham, UK, and Northhampton, MA: Edward Elgar, 2004.

British Government. "Al-Mujtahid: A Biography of the Freedom Fighter Osama Bin Laden." British Government's translation, n.d.

Burke, Jason. *Al-Qaeda: Casting a Shadow of Terror*. London and New York: I.B. Tauris, 2003.

Byman, Daniel. *The Five Front War: The Best Way to Fight Global Jihad*. New Jersey: John Wiley and Sons, 2008.

CBS News. "Bin Laden's Target: U.S. Wallet," 11 February 2009, http://www.cbsnews.com/stories/2004/10/29/terror/main652373.shtml.

Central Intelligence Agency (CIA). "Background on Osama bin Laden and al-Qa'ida." CIA report, Washington, D.C., 1998.

———. "Characteristics of Transnational Sunni Islamic Terrorism." CIA report, Washington, D.C., n.d.

Chamberlain, M. *Knowledge and Social Practice in Medieval Damascus, 1190–1350*. Cambridge: Cambridge University Press, 1994.

Choueiri, Youssef. *Islamic Fundamentalism*. London: Pinter, 1990.

Cole, Stewart Grant. *The History of Fundamentalism*. New York: Greenwood, 1931.

Confessions of a British Spy and British Enmity against Islam. Istanbul: Waqf Ikhlas Publications, 1995, http://www.hakikatkitabevi.com/download/english/14-ConfessionsOf%20ABritishSpy.pdf.

Cook, Michael. *Commanding Right and Forbidding Wrong in Islamic Thought*. Cambridge: Cambridge University Press, 2000.

Council on American-Islamic Relations (CAIR). "Response to September 11, 2001 Attacks." Washington D.C., 2007, http://www.cair.com/Portals/0/pdf/September_11_statements.pdf.

Coury, Ralph M. *The Making of an Egyptian Arab Nationalist: Early Years of Azzam Pasha, 1893–1936*. London: Ithaca Press, 1998.

Crawford, M.J. "Civil War, Foreign Intervention, and the Question of Political Legitimacy: A Nineteenth-Century Saudi Qadi's Dilemma." *International Journal of Middle East Studies* 14 (2) (1982): 227–48.

Dahlan, Ahmad ibn al-Zayni. *Khulasat al-kalam fi bayan umara' al-balad al-haram*. Cairo: al-Matba'a al-Khayriya, 1888.

Dayf, Shawqi. *al-'Asr al-islami*. 9th ed. Cairo: Dar al-Ma'arif, n.d.

"Deadly Iraqi Sect Attacks Kill 200." *BBC News*, 15 August 2007, http://news.bbc.co.uk/2/hi/6946028.stm.

De Corancez, Louis Alexander Olivier. *History of the Wahabis from Their Origin until the End of 1809*. Introduced by R.M. Burrell, translated by Eric Tabet. Reading: Garnet, 1995.

Delong-Bas, Natana J. *Wahhabi Islam: From Revival and Reform to Global Jihad*. Oxford: Oxford University Press, 2004.

Denny, Frederick M., ed. *An Introduction to Islam*. Colorado: University of Colorado Press, 1994.

al-Dikhayl, Bandar Bin Abdurhman. "Wa sayfun yanhar." *Mu'askar al-Battar*, no. 20, (September 2004).

Dr. Fadl (Sayyid Imam 'Abd al-'Aziz al-Sharif). *al-Jami' fi talab al-'ilm al-sharif*. N.p.: n.p., 1993.

———. *al-Murshid ila tariq Allah*. N.p.: n.p., 2006.

———. *Risalat al-'umda fi i'dad al-'udda li-l- jihad fi sabil Allah*. N.p.: n.p., 1988.

———. Wathiqat tarshid al-jihad fi Misr wa-l-'alam. London: al-Hayat, 2007.

Emerson, Michael, and David Hartman. "The Rise of Religious Fundamentalism." *Annual Review of Sociology* 32 (August 2006): 127–44.

Esposito, John. *Unholy War: Terror in the Name of Islam*. Oxford: Oxford University Press, 2002.

al-Faruqi, Isma'il. *Sheikh Muhammad ibn 'Abd al-Wahhab: kitab al-tawhid*. Translated by Isma'il al-Faruqi. Delhi: n.p., 1988.

Fischel, Walter Joseph. *Ibn Khaldun in Egypt: His Public Functions and His Historical Research, 1382–1406*. Berkeley: University of California Press, 1967.

Fregosi, Paul. *Jihad in the West: Muslim Conquests from the 7th to 21st Centuries*. New York: Prometheus Books, 1998.

Furniss, Norman. *The Fundamentalist Controversy, 1918–1931*. New Haven, CT: Yale University Press, 1954.

Gates, Robert Michael. "Speech at the 44th Munich Conference on Security Policy." 10 February 2008, http://www.securityconference.de/konferenzen/rede.php?menu_2008=&menu_konferenzen=&sprache=en&id=216&.

Ghunaimi, M.J. *The Muslim Conception of International Law and the Western Approach.* The Hague: Martinus, 1968.

Goldziher, Ignaz. *Muslim Studies.* Abany, NY: University of New York Press, 1966.

Goliath. "Iraq—July 7—Kidnapped Egyptian Diplomat Killed in Iraq," 9 July 2005, http://goliath.ecnext.com/coms2/gi_0199-4505908/IRAQ-July-7-Kidnapped-Egyptian.html.

Gran, Peter. "Political Economy as a Paradigm for the Study of Islamic History." *International Journal of Middle East Studies*, no. 11 (1980): 511–26.

Gunaratna, Rohan. *Inside Al Qaeda: Global Network of Terror.* New York: Berkley Books, 2003.

Gurel, M. Lois. "Hate." *The World Book Encyclopaedia*, vol. 9, 87–88. Chicago and London: A Scott Fetzer Company, 1990.

Haass, N. Richard. "The Age of Nonpolarity: What Will Follow U.S. Dominance." *Foreign Affairs.* May/June 2008.

Hanafi, Hasan. *al-Harakat al-diniya al-mu'asira.* Cairo: Maktabat Madbuli, 1988.

Harding, Susan. "Representing Fundamentalism." *Social Research* 58 (2) (Summer 1991): 373–74.

Hardy, Roger. "Analysis: US-Saudi 'uneasy' ties." BBC News, 29 April 2003, http://news.bbc.co.uk/2/hi/middle_east/2985131.stm.

———. "Grappling with Global Terror Conundrum." BBC News, 15 March 2008, http://news.bbc.co.uk/2/hi/programmes/from_our_own_correspondent/7297139.stm.

Haykal, Husayn. *The Life of Muhammad.* Translated by Isma'il R. al-Faruqi. Kuala Lumpur: Islamic Book Trust, 1976.

Hoffman, Valerie J. "The Articulation of Ibadi Identity in Modern Oman and Zanzibar." *The Muslim World* 94 (April 2004): 201–16.

Holt P.M. "The Mamluk Institution." In Youssef Choueiri, ed., *A Companion to the History of the Middle East*, 154–86. Malden, MA: Blackwell, 2005.

The Holy Bible. Revised Standard Version. Michigan: Zondervan Publishing House, 1971.

Hourani, Albert. *Arabic Thought in the Liberal Age.* Cambridge: Cambridge University Press, 1983.

Hussein, Taha. *al-Fitna al-kubra.* Cairo: Dar al-Ma'arif, 1959.

Ibn 'Abd al-Hadi, Muhammad (d. 1343). *al-'Uqud al-durriya.* Riyadh: Matba'at al-Mu'ayyad, n.d.

Ibn 'Abd al-Wahhab, 'Abd al-Rahman ibn Hasan ibn Muhammad (Al al-Shaykh). *Qurrat 'uyun al-muwahhidin.* Edited by Sa'id ibn 'Abd al-Rahman ibn Hasan ibn Muhammad ibn 'Abd al-Wahhab (Al al-Shaykh). Lahore: Ansar al-Sunna al-Muhammadiya, n.d.

Ibn 'Abd al-Wahhab, Muhammad. "Fatawa wa masa'il al-Imam al-Sheikh Muhammad Ibn 'Abd al-Wahhab." In *Mu'allafat al-Sheikh al-Imam Muhammad ibn 'Abd al-Wahhab.* Riyadh: Jami'at al-Imam Muhammad bin Sa'ud al-Islamiya, 1977.

——. *Kitab al-tawhid.* Riyadh: Dar al-Salam, 1996.

——. *Mu'allafat al-Sheikh al-Imam Muhammad ibn 'Abd al-Wahhab.* Riyadh: Jami'at al-Imam Muhammad bin Sa'ud al-Islamiya, 1977.

Ibn Abi Ya'la, Abu al-Hasan. *Tabaqat al-Hanabila.* Edited by Muhammad Hamid al-Fiqi. All volumes. Cairo: al-Sunna al-Muhammadiya, 1952.

Ibn al-Athir, 'Izz al-Din Abi al-Hasan 'Ali ibn Muhammad. *al-Kamil fi-l-tarikh.* 10 vols. Beirut: Dar Sadr, 1965.

Ibn Baz, Shaikh Abdul Aziz ibn 'Abdullah. "Imaam Muhammad Ibn Abdul Wahhab: His Life and Mission," Ahya.org, http://www.ahya.org/amm/modules.php?name=Sections&op=viewarticle&artid=180.

Ibn Bishr, 'Uthman ibn 'Abdullah. *'Unwan al-majd fi tarikh al-Najd.* Edited by 'Abd al-Rahman ibn 'Abd al-Latif ibn 'Abdullah Al al-Sheikh. 2 vols. Riyadh: Matba'at al-Malik 'Abd al-Aziz, 1982.

Ibn Hanbal, Ahmad. *al-Musnad li-Ahmad ibn Muhammad ibn Hanbal.* Edited by Muhammad Shakir. Cairo: Dar al-Ma'arif, 1949.

Ibn al-Jawzi, 'Abd al-Rahman ibn 'Ali ibn Muhammad. *Manaqib al-Imam Ahmad ibn Hanbal.* Edited by Muhammad Amin. Cairo: Matba'at al-Sa'ada, n.d.

Ibn Kathir, Abu al-Fida' al-Hafiz. *al-Bidaya wa-l-nihaya.* 1st ed., 7 vols. Cairo: Dar al-Rayyan, 1988.

——. *Qasas al-anbiya'.* Cairo: al-Maktaba al-Tawfiqiya, n.d.

Ibn Khaldun, 'Abd al-Rahman (d. 808/1406). *The Muqaddimah: An Introduction to History.* 3 vols. Translated by Franz Rosenthal. New York: Pantheon Books, 1958.

——. *Tarikh Ibn Khaldun.* 7 vols. Beirut: al-A'lami, 1971.

Ibn Manzur, Jamal al-Din (1232–1311). *Lisan al-'Arab.* 15 vols. Beirut: Dar Sadr, 1994.

Ibn Nasir, Muhammad. *al-Radd al-wafir.* Edited by al-Shawish. Beirut: al-Maktab al-Islami, 1980.

Ibn Rajab. *al-Dhayl 'ala tabaqat al-Hanabila.* Beirut: Dar al-Ma'arif, n.d.

Ibn Sanad, 'Uthman. *Tarikh Baghdad*. Bombay: n.p., 1886.

Ibn Taymiya. *al-Fatawa al-kubra*. Beirut: Dar al-Kutub al-'Ilmiya, n.d.

———. *Public and Private Law in Islam: Public Policy in Islamic Jurisprudence*. Translated by Omar A. Farrukh. 1st ed. Beirut: Khayat Books, 1966.

———. *al-'Ubudiya*. Edited by Khalid 'Abd al-Latif al-'Alami. 1st ed. Beirut: Dar al-Kitab al-'Arabi, 1987.

Independent Media Review Analyst (IMRA), 26 May 2007 http://www.imra. org.il/.

Irwin, Robert. *The Middle East in the Middle Ages*. Carbondale: Southern Illinois University Press, 1986.

Isma'il, Jamal. Interview with al-Zawahiri. Al Jazeera, December 1998, aired 10 June 1999 by Al Jazeera television, Qatar.

Jackson, Roy. *Fifty Key Figures in Islam*. London: Routledge, 2006.

Jamestown Foundation. "Hacking Manual by Jailed Jihadi Appears on the Web." *Terrorism Focus* 5 (9) (March 2008).

Jira, 'Abd al-'Aziz Ahmad. "al-Duktur 'Abd al-Wahhab 'Azzam, al-Azhari wa-l-safir." *Majallat al-Azhar*, no. 55 (March 1983): 5–6.

Johnson, Douglas. "The Word Fundamentalism." *The Christian Graduate*, March 1955, 22–25.

al-Karmi, Mara'i. *al-Kawakib al-durriya fi manaqib Ibn Taymiya*. 1st ed. Beirut: Dar al-Gharb al-Islami, 1986.

Kelsay, John, and James Turner Johnson, eds. *Just War and Jihad: Historical and Theoretical Perspectives on War and Peace in Western and Islamic Traditions*. New York: Greenwood, 1991.

Kepel, Gilles. *Jihad: The Trail of Political Islam*. Cambridge, MA: Harvard University Press, 2002.

Khadduri, Majid. *War and Peace in the Law of Islam*. 2nd ed. Baltimore: Johns Hopkins University Press, 1955.

Khadduri, Majid, trans. *The Islamic Law of Nations: Shaybani's Siyar*. Baltimore: Johns Hopkins University Press, 1966.

Khalafallah, Muhammad Ahmad. "al-Sahwa al-islamiya fi Misr." In *al-Harakat al-islamiya al-mu'asira fi-l-watan al-'arabi*. Edited by the Centre for the Studies of Arab Unity. N.p.: n.p., 1988.

al-Khalidi, Salim bin Hammud. *Mu'aradat al-awghad fi da'wahum jawaz al-jihad*. N.p., Ansar al-Mahdi Print, n.d.

Khatab, Sayed. *The Political Thought of Sayyid Qutb: The Theory of Jahiliyyah*. London and New York: Routledge, 2006.

————. *The Power of Sovereignty: The Political and Ideological Philosophy of Sayyid Qutb*. London and New York: Routledge, 2006.

Khatab, Sayed, and Gary Bouma. *Democracy in Islam*. London and New York: Routledge, 2007.

Khuri, Fuad. *Imams and Emirs: State, Religion and Sects in Islam*. London: Saqi Books, 1990.

al-Kilani, Musa Zayd. *al-Harakat al-islamiya fi-l-Urdun wa Filistin*. 2nd ed. Beirut: al-Risala, 1995.

Kishk, Muhammad Jalal. *al-Nasiriyyun qadimun*. Cairo: al-Zahra, 1989.

Kozin. David. "The Triangle of Death." *The NEIU Independent*, 12 March 2007, http://www.neiuindependent.com/2.12879/the-triangle-of-death-1.1684807.

Krämer, Gudrun "The Integration of the Integrists." In Ghassan Salame, ed., *Democracy without Democrats: The Renewal of Politics in the Muslim World*. London: I.B. Tauris Publishers, 1994.

Lawrence, Bruce. *Messages to the World: The Statements of Osama Bin Laden*. Translated and edited by Bruce Lawrence. London: Verso, 2005.

Lee, Robert D. *Overcoming Tradition and Modernity: The Search for Islamic Authenticity*. Boulder, CO: Westview Press, 1997.

Lentini, Peter. "Antipodal Terrorists? Accounting for Differences in Australian and 'Global' Neojihadists." In R. Devetak and C.W. Hughes, eds., *The Globalization of Political Violence: Globalization's Shadow*, 181–202. London: Routledge, 2008.

Lewis, Bernard. *The Arabs in History*. Oxford: Oxford University Press, 2002.

Lia, Brynjar. *Architect of Global Jihad: The Life of al-Qaida Strategist Abu Mus'ab al-Suri*. New York: Columbia University Press, 2008.

Makdisi, George. "Ibn Taymiya: A Sufi of the Qadiriya Order." *American Journal of Arabic Studies* 1 (1974): 118–29.

al-Maqdisi, Abu Muhammad Asim. *Imta' al-nazar fi kashf shubuhat Murji'at al-'asr*, 2nd ed. N.p.: Minbar al-Tawhid wa-l-Jihad, 1999.

al-Mardawi, 'Ali. *al-Insaf*. Edited by al-Faruqi, 2nd ed. Beirut: Mu'assat al-Tarikh al-'Arabi, n.d., vol. 10.

Martin, Richard C. *Islamic Studies: A History of Religion Approach*. New Jersey: Prentice Hall Inc., 1996.

al-Mas'ari, Muhammad ibn 'Abdullah. *Markaz al-tijara al-'alami*. London: Lajnat al-Difa' 'an al-Huquq al-Shar'iya, 2002.

————. *Qissat Abu Basir: ta'sil shar'i mufassal li-hudud mashru'iyyat i'lan al-afrad li-l-harb*. London: Lajnat al-Difa' 'an al-Huquq al-Shar'iya, 2002.

———. *Qital al-tawa'if al-mumtani'a*. London: Muntada al-Tajdid al-Islami, 2003.

Matthews, Owens. "Home to Roost," *Newsweek*, 29 March 2010, http://www.newsweek.com/2010/03/28/home-to-roost.html.

Al-Matroudi, Abdul Hakim. *The Hanbali School of Law and Ibn Taymiyyah: Conflict or Conciliation*. London: Routledge, 2006.

McGirk, Tim. "Afghanistan." *TIME*, 31 August 1998.

"The Meeting of the Brother Leader with the Heads of Churches Present throughout the Great Jamahiriya, the Ambassadors of Friendly Countries, and Political, Religious and Cultural Figures in Libyan Society." Al-Gathafi Speaks, http://www.algathafi.org/html-english/cat_01_02.htm.

Melchert, Christopher. *Ahmad ibn Hanbal*. Oxford: OneWorld, 2006.

Milton-Edwards, Beverley. "Politics and Religion." In Youssef Choueiri, ed., *A Companion of the History of the Middle East*, 444–46. Malden, MA: Blackwell Pub. Ltd., 2005.

Mir, Amir. "The Pakistanis Training in Al Qaeda Camps." *CobraPost*. http://www.cobrapost.com/documents/TrainingAlQaeda.htm.

Mitchell, Richard. *The Society of the Muslim Brothers*. Oxford: Oxford University Press, 1993.

Momen, Moojan. "Fundamentalism and Liberalism: Towards an Understanding of the Dichotomy." *Baha'i Studies Review* 2 (1) (1992), http://bahai-library.com/articles/momen.fundamentalism.html.

Monroe, Elizabeth. *Philby of Arabia*. London: Faber and Faber, 1973.

Mottahedeh, Roy P. "The Shu'ubiyya: Controversy and the Social History of Early Islamic Iran." *International Journal of Middle East Studies*, no. 7 (1979): 161–82, esp. 161.

Mu'ammar, 'Ali Yahya. *al-'Ibadiya fi mawakib al-tarikh*. Cairo: Dar al-Kitab al-'Arabi, 1964.

al-Munufi, Ahmad Muhammad. "Bayn al-Islam wa ghayrihi min al-adyan." *Majallat al-Azhar* 10 (April 1992): 1201–209.

Naji, Abu Bakr. *Idarat al-tawahhush*. N.p.: Centre of Islamic Studies and Research, n.d.

The National Security Archive. "1998 Missile Strikes on Bin Laden May Have Backfired." 20 August 2008, http://www.gwu.edu/~nsarchiv/NSAEBB/NSAEBB253/index.htm

———. "Document 24. Department of State, Cable, 'Afghanistan: Meeting with the Taliban.'" 11 December 1997. Confidential, http://www.gwu.edu/~nsarchiv/NSAEBB/NSAEBB97/index.htm.

————. The September 11th Sourcebooks—Volume VII: The Taliban File. National Security Archive *Electronic Briefing Book No. 97*. Edited by Sajit Gandi. 11 September 2003, http://www.gwu.edu/~nsarchiv/NSAEBB/ NSAEBB97/index.htm.

Nixon, Richard. *Victory without War*. New York: Simon and Schuster, 1999.

Nussbaum, Arthur. *A Concise History of the Law of Nations*. New York: Macmillan, 1962.

Paris, Jonathan. "A Framework for Understanding Radical Islam's Challenge to European Governments." *Transatlantic Institute*, 3 May 2007.

Pickthall, Marmaduke. *The Glorious Qur'an*. Delhi: Mohindra Offset Press, 1979.

Pipes, Daniel. "The Saga of 'Hempher,' Purported British Spy, an extract from *The Hidden Hand: Middle East Fears of Conspiracy*, pp. 211–12," Daniel Pipes.org, http://www.danielpipes.org/1648/the-saga-of-hempher-purported-british-spy.

Qadri, Anwar. *Islamic Jurisprudence in the Modern World*. 2nd ed. Lahore: Karachi Bazar, 1973.

al-Qasim, 'Abd al-Malik. "al-Wala' wa-l-bara'," http://www.murajaat.com/ alwala_walbra.php.

Quiggin, Tom. "Understanding al-Qaeda's Ideology for Counter-Narrative Work." *Perspectives on Terrorism* 3 (2) (August 2009): 18–24.

al-Qurtubi, Abu 'Abdullah Muhammad ibn Ahmad al-Ansari (d. 671/1272). *al-Jami' li-ahkam al-Qur'an*. Beirut: Dar al-Turath al-'Arabi, 1985.

al-Qurtubi, Ibn 'Abd al-Barr. *Mukhtasar jami' bayan al-'ilm wa fadlih*. Summarized by Ahmad ibn 'Umar al-Mahamasani, edited by Muhammad al-Mar'ashli. Beirut: Dar al-Nafa'is, n.d., 1:23 ff.

Qutb, Sayyid. *al-'Adala al-ijtima'iya fi-l-Islam*. 9th ed. Cairo: Dar al-Shuruq, 1983.

————. *Dirasat Islamiya*. Cairo: Dar al-Shuruq, 1993.

————. *Fi zilal al-Qur'an*. Cairo: Dar al-Shuruq, 1992.

————. *Hadha al-din*. Cairo: Dar al-Shuruq, 1995.

————. *In the Shade of the Qur'an. Fi zilal al-Qur'an* translated by Adil Salahi and Ashur Shamis. Markfield, UK: The Islamic Foundation, 1999.

————. *al-Islam wa mushkilat al-hadara*. Cairo: Dar al-Shuruq, 1983.

————. *Ma'alim fi-l-tariq*. Cairo: Dar al-Shuruq, 1993.

————. *Nahwa mujtama' islami*. Cairo: Dar al-Shuruq, 1993.

————. *al-Salam al-'alami wa-l-Islam*. Cairo: Dar al-Shuruq, 1995.

Rahman, Fazlur. *Islam and Modernity: The Transformation of an Intellectual Tradition*. Chicago: University of Chicago Press, 1980.

Rahnema, Ali. *The Pioneers of Islamic Revival*. Kuala Lumpur: S. Abd al-Majid and Co. Publishing Division, 1995.

Ramadan, 'Abd al-'Azim. "Fundamentalist Influence in Egypt: The Strategies of the Muslim Brotherhood and the Takfir Groups." In Martin E. Marty and R. Scott Appleby, eds. *Fundamentalism and the State*, 152–83. Chicago: University of Chicago Press, 1993.

Reeve, Simon. *The New Jackals: Ramzi Yousef, Osama Bin Laden and the Future of Terrorism*. London: Andre Deutsch, 1999.

Religious Tolerance.org. "Aftermath of the 9/11 Terrorist Attack." 12 September 2001, http://www.religioustolerance.org/reac_ter1.htm.

Rentz, George Sanavely. *The Birth of the Islamic Reform Movement in Saudi Arabia: Muhammad Ibn Abd al-Wahhab (1703/4–1792) and the Beginnings of the Unitarian Empire in Arabia*. Riyadh and London: Arabian Publishing, in association with the King 'Abd al-'Aziz Public Library, 2004.

Rodinson, Maxime. *Muhammad*. Translated by Anne Carter. London: Allen Lane, 1971.

Roy, Olivier. *The Failure of Political Islam*. Translated by Carol Volk. London: I.B. Tauris and Co. Ltd., 2007 (reprint).

Russell, Frederick. *The Just War in the Middle Ages*. Cambridge: Cambridge University Press, 1975.

Sageman, Marc. *Leaderless Jihad: Terror Networks in the Twenty-first Century*. Philadelphia: University of Pennsylvania Press, 2008.

Salama, Usama. "al-Ikhwan al-Muslimun yumawwiluna al-tatarruf." *Rose el-Youssef*, no. 3418, 13 December 1993.

Salha, Rima. "Sina'at al-mawt." Interview aired by Al Arabiya, 4 January 2008.

———. "Sina'at al-mawt." Interview aired by Al Arabiya, 2 May 2008.

Sayf al-'Adl. "al-Amn wa-l-istikhbarat." *Mu'askar al-Battar*, no. 20, September 2004.

al-Shafi'i, Imam Abu 'Abdullah Muhammad ibn Idris (d. 204/819). *Kitab al-umm*. Beirut: Dar al-Fikr, 1990.

al-Shahrastani, Abul Fath Muhammad (1086–1153). *al-Milal wa-l-nihal*. Edited by Muhammad S. al-Kilani. Cairo and Beirut: Dar Sa'b, 1986. All volumes.

al-Shak'a, Mustafa Muhammad. *Islam bila madhahib*. Cairo: al-Dar al-Misriya, 1991.

al-Shami, Sami Ahmad. *Tahdhib hilyat al-awliya' wa tabaqat al-asfiya li Abi Na'im al-Asbahani: Ahmad ibn 'Abdullah*. Beirut: al-Maktab al-Islami li-l-Tiba'a wa-l-Nashr, 1998.

Sharaf al-Din, Nabil. *Bin Laden: Taliban: al-Afghan al-Arab and the Global Fundamentalism*. Cairo: Madbouli, 2002.

"Shaykh al-Imam Napoleon Bonaparte." *Rose el-Youssef*, 23 February 1998.

Shephard, William. "'Fundamentalism' Christian and Islamic." *Religion* 17 (1987): 355–78.

———. "Islam and Ideology: Towards a Typology," *International Journal of Middle East Studies* 19 (1987): 307–36.

———. *Sayyid Qutb and Islamic Activism: A Translation and Critical Analysis of Social Justice in Islam*. Leiden: E.J. Brill, 1996.

Singh, Nagendra. *India and International Law*. New Delhi: S. Chand and Co., 1973.

"Statements from India and Pakistan." BBC News, 16 June 1998, http://news.bbc.co.uk/2/hi/events/asia_nuclear_crisis/world_media/114139.stm.

al-Suyuti, 'Abd al-Rahman. *Husn al-muhadara fi tarikh Misr wa-l-Qahira*. Edited by Muhammad Abu al-Fadl Ibrahim. 1st ed. Cairo: Dar Ihya' al-Kutub al-'Arabiya, 1968.

al-Tabari, Abu Ja'far Muhammad ibn Jarir (d. 922). *Tarikh al-umam wa-l-muluk*. 6 vols. Beirut: Dar al-Kutub al-'Ilmiya, 1997.

Tanner, Stephen. *Afghanistan: A Military History from Alexander the Great to the Fall of the Taliban*. New York: Da Capo Press, 2002.

Tenet, George. *At the Center of the Storm: My Years at the CIA*. New York: Harper Collins Publishers, 2007.

Thomas, Scott. *The Global Resurgence of Religion and the Transformation of International Relations: the Struggle for the Soul of the Twenty-First Century*. Cambridge: Cambridge University Press, 2005.

Toensing, Chris. AlterNet. "Muslims Ask: Why Do They Hate Us?" *Global Issues*, 25 September 2001, http://www.globalissues.org/article/256/muslims-ask-why-do-they-hate-us.

"Transcript of Osama Bin Ladin Interview by Peter Arnett." CNN interview with Bin Laden in March 1997, http://www.anusha.com/osamaint.htm.

Ulph, Stephen. "Al-Qaeda's Strategy until 2020." *Terrorism Focus* 2 (6) (17 March 2005).

Umara, Muhammad. *al-Usuliya bayn al-gharb wa-l-Islam*. Cairo: Dar al-Shuruq, 2006.

Vaughan, C.E. *Studies in the History of Political Philosophy before and after Rousseau*. 2 vols. Edited by A.G. Little. Manchester: Manchester University Press, 1925.

Voll, John O. "Muhammad Hayat al-Sindi and Muhammad ibn 'Abd al-Wahhab: An Analysis of Intellectual Groups in Eighteenth-Century Medina." *Bulletin of the School of Oriental and African Studies* 38 (1) (1975): 32–38.

———. "Sudanese Mahdi." *International Journal of Middle East Studies* 10 (1979): 145–66.

Wach, Joachim. *Types of Religious Experience: Christian and non-Christian*. Chicago: University of Chicago Press, 1951.

al-Waqidi, Muhammad ibn 'Umar (d. 822). *Kitab al-Maghazi*. Edited by Marsden Jones. 3 vols. London: Oxford University Press, 1966.

Wasil, Nasr Farid. Islamonline, http://www.islamonline.net/servlet/Satellite? pagename=IslamOnline-Arabic-Ask_Scholar/FatwaA/FatwaA&cid= 1122528623684

Watt, W. Montgomery. *Islamic Political Thought*. London: Edinburgh University Press, 1986.

———. *Muhammad: Prophet and Statesman*. London: Oxford University Press, 1961.

Weber, Max. *The Protestant Ethic and the Spirit of Capitalism*. Translated by Talcott Parsons. Foreword by R.H. Tawney. 5th ed. New York: Charles Scribner's Sons, 1956.

Weeramantry, C.G. *Islamic Jurisprudence: An International Perspective*. Basingstoke, UK: Macmillan Press, 1988.

Wehr, Hans. *Arabic English Dictionary*. J. Milton Cowan, ed. 3rd ed. New York: Ithaca, 1960.

Wellhausen, Julius. *The Religio-Political Factions in Early Islam*. Edited by R.C. Costle. Translated R.C. Costle and S.M. Walzer. Amsterdam: North-Holland Publishing Company, 1975.

Wilkinson, J.C. "The Origin of the Omani State." In Derek Hopwood, ed., *The Arabian Peninsula: Society and Politics*. London: Allen and Unwin, 1972.

"World Islamic Front for Jihad Against Jews and Crusaders: Initial Fatwa Statement." *al-Quds al-'arabi*, 23 February 1998, http://www.library.cornell.edu/colldev/mideast/fatw2.htm.

Yakan, Fathi. *al-Islam: fikra, haraka, inqlab*. 11th ed. Beirut: al-Risala, 1987.

Yaqoob, Salama. "British Islamic Political Radicalism." In Tahir Abbas, ed., *Islamic Political Radicalism: A European Prospective*. Edinburgh: Edinburgh University Press, 2007.

al-Yassini, Ayman. *Religion and State in the Kingdom of Saudi Arabia*. Boulder, CO: Westview Press, 1985.

Young, Robert. "Fundamentalism and Terrorism." *The Human Nature Review*, 25 September 2001, 1–17.

al-Zalabani, Rizq. "al-Siyasa al-dusturiya al-shar'iya: shakl al-hukuma wa 'alaqatiha fi-l-Islam." *al-Azhar* 18 (7) (1947): 130–36.

al-Zawahiri, Ayman. *al-Hasad al-murr: al-Ikhwan al-Muslimun fi sittina 'aman*. Amman: Dar al-Bayan, 2002.

———. Interview by Jamal Isma'il for Al Jazeera Channel in December 1998. See the interview in Jamal Isma'il's book *Ibn Ladin wa-l-Jazira wa ana*. Casablanca: Dar-al-Najah al-Jadida, 2001.

———. Interview with Kamil al-Tawil for *al-Hayat* in 1996, published in *al-Wasat* and republished by Minbar al-Tawhid wa-l-Jihad, www.tawhed. ws/r?i=2832&c=2449.

———. *Knights under the Prophet's Banner*. Translation of *Firsan taht rayat al-Rasul* by Foreign Broadcast Information Service (FBIS). London: Asharq Alawsat, 2002.

———. *al-Tabri'a: risala fi tabri'at ummat al-qalam wa-l-sayf min manqasat tuhmat al-khawr wa-l-da'f*. N.p.: al-Sahab Foundation for Islamic Media Publications, 2008.

Zayid, Y. Mahmud, ed. *The Qur'an: An English Translation of the Meaning of the Qur'an*. Beirut: Dar al-Shura, 1980.

Zayna, 'Abduh. "Dr. Najih Ibrahim yatahaddath ila *Asharq Alawsat*." *Asharq Alawsat*, 14 August 2006.

al-Zayyat, Montasser. *The Road to al-Qaeda: The Story of Bin Laden's Right-Hand Man*. London: Pluto Press, 2004.

Zuhdi, Muhammad Karam, Najih Ibrahim 'Abd Allah et al. *Tafjirat al-Riyad: al-ahkam wa-l-athar*. Cairo: al-Turath, 2003.

Index

expansionism, 132
exoneration, 147

Fadl (Dr.), 7, 56, 77, 83, 95, 97, 145,
    170, 205, 241
    biographical sketch of, 209–12, 213
    criticism/revisions of
        al-Qa'ida, 218
    interview in *al-Hayat, 223*
        extracts from, 224–27
    on jihad, 221–23
    writings of, 216–18
    and al-Zawahiri, 214, 216, 219,
        220, 248
Fahd (king), 100
Faisal (king), 92
faith, reality of, 43
Falluga, Iraq, 205
fanaticism, 36
Fansa, Henry, 59
fatwa, 220
    on jihad, 102
fear tactic, 189
fiqh al-tabrir (jurisprudence of
    justification), 220
fight *(al-qital)*, 129
fighters, Arab, 98
fitna (the great upheaval), 28
Fitna (film), 18
foreign rule, 38, 39
foreigner protection *(musta'man)*, 137
Fouda, Farag, 4
free will, 42
freedom(s), 18, 46
fundamentalism *(usuliya)*/fundamen-
    talists, 12, 17, 21, 80, 81
    Christian, 11–12
    Islamic, 1–4, 6, 9–26, 78–81, 103,
        119, 237
fundamentals *(usul)*, 12–14

Gates, Robert, 86
Geneva Conventions, 145

al-Ghazali, 202
global conflict, 23–24
'Global Islamic Front for the Jihad
    Against the Jews and Crusaders,'
    146, 167, 169, 214, 218
globalization, 24, 168
God's will, 43
Gorbachev, Mikhail, 22–23
government, Islamic, 33, 158
governments, Middle Eastern, 169
Great Britain, and Ottoman
    Empire, 62
        guerrilla unit (055 Brigade), 111
the great upheaval *(fitna)*, 28
Guantánamo, 158
guerrilla warfare, 169
Guidance and Reform (media
    organization), 91
Gulf War (1991), 102

Hadith (sayings of the Prophet), 32,
    41, 55
Hadramant, 36
hakimiya (power of sovereignty), 21,
    83, 93, 239–41
Hanbalis/Hanbalism, 4, 5–6, 27,
    41–48, 49, 55–56, 58, 202,
    238, 239
Hafisis (al-Hafisiya), 36
Hanafi/Hanafis, 80, 202–203
Hani al-Sa'igh, 109
al-Haram Mosque (Mecca), 117
Haran (Syria), 48–49, 50
al-harb (war), 129
Harithis (al-Harithiya), 36
Hardy, Roger, 90–91, 115
Haroris, 26
Harun al-Rashid, 43
Hasan Abu Basha, 212
Hasan al-Alfi, 216
al-Hayat (newspaper), 218, 223
Hekmatyar, Gulbuddin, 97, 111
heroism, 36

prisoner(s), 219, 220
    of war, 135–36, 138–41
Prophet's Companions, 44
psychological warfare, 52, 141
'the Pure Soul' (al-Nafs al-Zakiya),
    190–91

Qaboos bin Sa'id (sultan), 39–40
Qadirya order, 65
al-Qa'ida, 7, 24, 25, 27, 36, 37, 57, 83,
    85–128, 178
    activities illegal/irregular, 220
    Arabic writings of, 7–8, 36
    Attacks against the U.S., 174
    Bin Laden and, 214
    condemnations by Muslims, 207
    focus on Arab and Muslim
      regimes, 176, 177
    followers of, 193, 239
    fundamental sources for, 210
    foundation of, 98–109
    group leaders of, 194
    ideologues of, 209
    ideology of, 3–5, 7, 25, 33, 34,
      36, 44, 46, 77, 129–66, 209–35,
      237, 239
    in Iraq, 181, 183, 205, 218
    jihad concept of, 52 , 53, 54, 116,
      163–66, 199
    and Kharijism, 27–35
    military leaders of, 194–95
    Muslim opponents of, 26, 35,
      47, 156
    narratives, perverted, 248
    neo-jihadism, 145–51
    operatives, 186, 214
    opposition to, 218, 238
    organizational infrastructure
      of, 95
    "pillars of war," 189
    "political game(s)," 194–99
    political tactics of, 7, 25, 44, 167,
      181, 192, 237

profile in the media, 189
    rate of operations, 187–88
    research on, 2, 24–25
    response (written) to Dr. Fadl,
      227–33
    selection of areas in which to
      work, 178
    self-criticism by, 227–28, 237
    and the shari'a, 196
    specific operations, 174
    strike forces of, 169
    in Sudan, 103–108
    tactics of, 129, 167–207, 237
    "targets and vexation strikes," 184
    al-tatarrus, interpretation of,
      205–206
    terrorist activities of, 129
    theology of/theological issues, 37,
      45, 168, 209, 237
    theo-political ideas, 209
    war focus of, 36–37, 129–67, 218
    websites, 86, 213, 219, 228
al-Qaradawi, Yusuf, 206
al-qital (fight), 129
al-Quds al-'arabi (newspaper), 112, 116
Qur'an, 28, 32, 35, 41, 42, 44
Qur'ans, stuck on ends of lances,
    29–30
Quraysh tribe, 54, 141, 159
Qutb, Sayyid, 15, 20, 79, 80, 82, 83,
    93, 94, 130, 212, 213
Quwwat al-Haqq (The Power of
    Truth) (video), 219

al-rabat (stand-by), 151
racial conflict, 18
radicalism, 2–3, 25, 28, 32, 34, 41,
    56, 85, 91
radicalization, 237
Rafidis (al-Rafida), 47, 147, 24–33
    jihad against, 152–53
Rahman, Fazlur, 116
Ramzi Ahmad Youssef, 105

Rashid Rida, 20
Reagan, Ronald, 22
rebel(s), 53
recruitment centers, 95
reformist movement, 64, 168
regime change, 35, 45, 238
regimes, deviant, 153
religion, role of, 36, 50, 81, 85, 171
religious movements, 49
renewer or restorer *(mujaddid)*, 58
retaliation, 192
Returnees from Albania Case, 212
revenge option, 182–83
al-Ridi, Essam, 96
"right," contrasting meanings of, 9
    "religious right," American, 11
rise *(zuhur)*, 37
Riyadh, 72–73
Roman Empire, 132
Rose al-Youssef (magazine), 50
rule and judgment *(hukm)*, 30
rulers, corrupt, 82, 154
Russia. *See* Soviet Union
Rustaq (Oman), 39

Sabil Allah, 144
Sadat, Anwar, 4, 10, 81, 88, 97
    assassination of, 211, 213
Saddam Hussein, 62, 100–101
Sadiq al-Mahdi, 103
Safar al-Hawli (sheikh), 103, 104
safe conduct covenant/*'ahd al-aman*, 137
al-salaf al-salih (the Pious Predeces-
    sors/Forerunners), 14, 44, 64, 238
Salafism, 14, 15, 146, 155, 198, 238, 248
Salah al-Din al-Ayyibo. 193, 194
Salim 'Azzam, 213
Salman al-'Awda (sheikh), 103, 104,
    206
al-Sanusi, Muhammad, 20, 82
al-Sarkhasi (imam), 221
Saud (king), 92

Saudi Arabia, 66, 70, 71, 85, 87, 101,
    146, 176
    and jihad, 72
    royal family of, 188
    U.S. military forces in, 101, 112,
        115, 116, 117
Sayyaf, 97
scholars and theologians, Islamic, 4,
    14, 15, 44, 55–56, 63
schools of thought *(madhhabs)*, 61
seclusion and emigration, 148, 149
secularism/secularization, 10, 24, 85
security breakdown, 186
security priorities, 185
selfishness, 171
separatist movements, 3, 87
September 11 (2001) attacks, 1, 4, 26,
    59, 82, 84, 85, 157, 158, 167, 169,
    174, 178, 182, 227, 239
    Muslim response to, 176
    tactical goals of, 170–76
al-Shafi'i, 201
Shah Massoud, 97
Shah Waliyyuallah al-Delhawi, 63
Shaker al-Abbasi, 205
Sharaf al-Din 'Abdullah, 65
shari'a, 4, 15, 16, 27, 89, 196
al-Shawkini, 81
Shawqi al-Istambulli, 97
al-Shaybani, 133
shield *(turs* of enemy's army)*, 200,
    201, 202, 204
shield, to *(al-tatarrus)*, 4–5, 6, 7, 168,
    200–207, 219, 239, 244–45
Shi'is, 87
    view on concealment, 38, 74
shirk (associating partners with God),
    64, 66, 72, 149
Shu'ubis, 42
Sidqi, Atif, 216
Siffan (town), 29
Six Day War, 81
social inequities, 121

vetos on Palestine issue in
Security Council, 122
Ur (city), 48
U.S.S Cole, 169, 174
usul (fundamentals), 12–14
usuliya (fundamentalism), 12
'Uthman ibn 'Affan (caliph), 28, 29
'Uthman ibn Mu'ammar, 68

victory, 51
violence, 190, 196
violent groups, 191

Wahhabis/Wahhabism, 4, 5, 6, 26, 27,
56–74, 147, 238
Wa'idis (al-Wa'idiya), 33
al-wala' wa-l-bara' (loyalty and disloyalty), 193, 241–42, 247
war(s)/warfare, 36, 37, 54, 129–30,
131, 136, 141, 158–59
declaration of, 243–44
laws/rules of, 135, 156, 197
prisoners of, 135–36, 138–41
private wars, 132
prophibited acts in, 144–45
War on Terror, 24–25, 85, 90, 122,
176, 184
warlords, Afghani, 107–108
war *(al-harb)*, 129
wars, 183
al-Wathiq (caliph), 44, 45
*Wathiqat tarshid al-jihad fi Misr wa-l-
'alam* (book), 217–18, 220–21
weapons, 135, 178–79

websites, 86, 213, 219, 228
Weeramantry (judge), 16
westernization, 9, 24
Wilders, Geert, 18
women's liberty movement, 40, 41
Woollacott, Martin, 183–84
words, war of, 141
World Trade Center (New York),
1993 attack on, 105, 107
worldly pleasures, 171

Yasa/al-Yasiq, 50
Yazidis (al-Yazidiya), 36
Yemen, 10, 176, 183, 210
Yusuf (prophet), 221

zakat (tax), 70, 137, 153
Zanzibar, 36, 39
al-Zawahiri, Ayman, 7, 29, 35, 37, 44,
46, 56, 82, 83–84, 86, 88, 97, 108,
116, 146, 149, 168, 191, 192, 198,
200, 205, 209–10, 211, 226
authors book refuting Dr. Fadl's
revisions, 223, 228–35
biographical sketch of, 212–15
jihad, ideas on, 221–23
on al-Qa'ida in Iraq, 218–19
role in Sadat assassination, 213
relationship with Dr. Fadl, 215,
219, 220
and Sudanese intelligence, 216
Zuhdi, Karam, 218
zindiq (non-believers), 156
zuhur (rise), 37